Historical Edition

Historical Edition

THE THEATRE:

An Introduction

OSCAR G. BROCKETT

HOLT, RINEHART AND WINSTON
New York   Chicago   San Francisco   Atlanta   Dallas
Montreal   Toronto

Libarary of Congress Cataloging in Publication Data
Brockett, Oscar Gross
    Historical edition. The theatre: an introduction

    Chapters 4-16 of the author's The theatre.
    Includes index.
    1. Theatre — History.   2. Drama — History and criticism.
3. Theatre — United States.   I. Title.
PN2101.B719   1979   78-10000
ISBN 0-03-043116-6

Printed in the United States of America
    7 8 9 016 9 8 7

To
MARK

Preface

This book is one part of a longer work, *The Theatre: An Introduction*, published simultaneously in its fourth edition. The *Historical Edition* reprints those sections of *The Theatre* dealing with the development of theatre and drama from the beginnings to the present. It treats representative dramatists, forms, and styles, and gives an overview of theatrical practice through the ages. It is being printed separately from the main work for the first time at the suggestion of instructors who have found the historical sections of *The Theatre* suitable to their courses but who do not wish to use the other sections. In content, *The Historical Edition* is identical with Part 2 of *The Theatre*. It provides a survey of theatre history and dramatic literature at a beginner's level and is intended especially for courses restricted to one semester in length.

Each chapter of the *Historical Edition* includes detailed discussions of one or more plays. Thirteen of these—*Oedipus the King, The Menaechmi, The Second Shepherds' Play, King Lear, Tartuffe, The School for Scandal, The Wild Duck, From Morn till Midnight, The Good Woman of Setzuan, Death of a Salesman, The New Tenant, Raisin in the Sun,* and *Streamers*—are included in their entirety in an anthology, *Plays for the Theatre*, 3rd edition, edited by Oscar G. and Lenyth Brockett and published by Holt, Rinehart and Winston in 1979.

My indebtedness to others is deep. It would be impossible to enumerate all those scholars whose work is reflected here. Some measure of my debt can be gained from the Bibliography. The sources of the illustrations are acknowledged in the captions that accompany them.

A few persons deserve special mention. I am deeply indebted to Deborah Lazar for assistance in locating illustrations, and to James Stacy and John Berseth for editorial work. I also wish to acknowledge my gratitude to those teachers and students who through their response to earlier editions of *The Theatre, an Introduction* have made this separate printing of the historical section seem desirable. Most of all, I would like to express my gratitude to Mark Pape for his thoughtful reading and helpful suggestions for improving the manuscript.

Oscar G. Brockett
University of Texas at Austin
November 1978

Contents

1

Theatre and Drama in Ancient Greece

The Origins of Theatre and Drama

No one really knows how the theatre began, but there are many theories about it. The one most widely accepted today is based upon the assumption that theatre evolved from ritual. The argument for this view goes as follows. In the beginning, human beings viewed the natural forces of the world, even the seasonal changes, as unpredictable, and they sought, through various means, to control these unknown and feared powers. Those measures which appeared to bring the desired results were then retained and repeated until they hardened into fixed rituals. Eventually stories arose which explained or veiled the mysteries of the rites. As humans progressed in knowledge, some rituals, such as those involving human sacrifice, were abandoned, but the stories, later called myths, persisted and provided material for art and drama.

Those who believe that drama evolved out of ritual also argue that primitive rites contained the seeds of theatre because music, dance, masks, and costumes were almost always used. Furthermore, a suitable site had to

1

be provided for performances, and when the entire tribe did not participate, a clear division was usually made between the "acting area" and the
"auditorium." In addition, there were performers, for, since considerable
importance was attached to avoiding mistakes in the enactment of rites,
priests usually assumed the task for the tribe. Wearing masks and costumes, they often impersonated men, animals, or supernatural beings, and
mimed the desired effect—success in hunt or battle, the coming of rain,
the revival of the sun—as an actor might. From such dramatic rituals,
theatre is said to have emerged as man became sufficiently sophisticated to
separate dramatic from religious activities.

The theory that drama and theatre originated in ritual has much to
recommend it, since it is probably true that unsophisticated peoples do
not distinguish among the various aspects of their lives (work, religion,
play) as clearly as more advanced societies do. The weakness of the
theory lies in the fact that all of man's attempts to deal with his
world (science, philosophy, art) were in the beginning just as much a part
of ritual as theatre was. In seeking to ensure a bountiful harvest, primitive peoples performed rituals (rather than, for example, spreading fer-
tilizer); in these rites they summed up their conception of themselves and
their universe. In most ceremonies, theatrical and dramatic elements were
present. But the theory of ritual origin does not explain why theatre and
drama continued to be valued and to grow in importance after they were
divorced from religious rite and thus lost their former status as effective
means of influencing man's welfare.

Another theory traces the theatre's origin from the human interest in
storytelling. According to this view, tales (about the hunt, war, or other
feats) are gradually elaborated, at first through the use of impersonation,
action, and dialogue by a narrator and then through the assumption of
each of the roles by a different person. A closely related theory traces theatre to those dances that are primarily rhythmical and gymnastic or from
imitations of animal movements and sounds.

Still another theory relates drama and theatre to the human "play" instinct, both in the sense of recreational activity and of playing at being
someone else in a particular activity or situation. This instinct may be
what Aristotle had in mind when he wrote in the *Poetics* that human
beings are instinctively imitative—that they both enjoy imitating others
and seeing imitations, for they desire to know how it would feel to be
another person or why others act as they do. Furthermore, he adds, imitation is one of their chief methods of learning about their world, as when
children learn speech and behavior by imitating adults.

In the twentieth century, a number of psychologists have suggested that
human beings have a gift for fantasy through which they seek to reshape
reality into more satisfying forms than those of daily life. Thus, through
fiction (of which drama is one form) they objectify their anxieties and
fears so that they may confront them or so that they may imaginatively
fulfill their hopes and dreams. Consequently, theatre is one tool whereby

Shrine priest dancing at Bonkwae Brong festival (a traditional religious festival of Ghana). (Photo made in 1970; courtesy Michael Warren.)

humans define and understand their world or one whereby they escape from unpleasant realities.

But while most groups have produced rituals and tales and while man may be an imitator and maker of fantasies, not all societies have produced theatre and drama divorced from ritual. At least two other conditions also seem to be required: a society that can recognize the artistic value of theatre and drama, and individuals capable of organizing theatrical elements into an experience of a high order. For these reasons, the Greeks are usually considered to be the primary originators of drama, for it was they who first developed the form as it was to be known in the Western world.

Egypt and the Near East

Nevertheless, some prior activities deserve brief notice. Ritual probably dates back to the dawn of human history, but our knowledge of it first begins to take definite shape about 4000 B.C., when the civilizations of Egypt and the Near East entered an advanced stage.

Much of our information about the Egyptians is derived from hieroglyphics and artifacts preserved in the pyramids built as tombs for the pharaohs and in the temples of the numerous Egyptian gods. Many of these remains relate to Egyptian myths concerning the recurrent cycle of life and the seasons. In turn, these myths seem to have been utilized in various rituals, about which there has been much controversy concerning the extent to which they were dramatic. Some scholars argue, for example, that the more than fifty surviving "Pyramid Texts" (composed of hieroglyphics and scenes depicting the trials through which the spirit must pass before achieving an honorable place in afterlife) are dramas that were enacted by priests. But, since there is no definitive evidence to support this view, other scholars have denied that the texts are dramatic or that they were ever acted. Other contested rituals relate to the coronation of pharaohs and to the return of spring.

But, in terms of the theatre, the most important of the Egyptian rituals is the so-called Abydos Passion Play, which is concerned with the death and resurrection of the god Osiris. Although it was performed annually from about 2500 to about 550 B.C., no part of the ritual's text remains; all we know of it is deduced from an account left by Ikhernofret, a participant in the ritual some time between 1887 and 1849 B.C. Again, however, scholars differ markedly in their interpretations of Ikhernofret's account. According to some, the ritual was one of the most elaborate spectacles ever staged, including, among other things, battles, processions, and burial ceremonies. Others deny that the life and death of Osiris were reenacted and describe the ritual as a commemoration of all the dead pharaohs and as based on the form of a royal funeral. Considering these opposing views, it is difficult to decide how dramatic or theatrical Egyptian rituals actually were.

In addition to Egyptian rituals, records of others (dating from c. 2500 B.C. onward) in the Near East have been discovered. For the most part, they are concerned with the seasonal pattern of birth, growth, maturity, death, and rebirth. Although some historians have suggested that the rituals of Egypt and the Near East influenced the development of drama in Greece, no direct connection has yet been found. Even if direct influence could be verified, an important difference would still set Greece off from its neighbors. The Egyptians maintained an advanced civilization for about three thousand years (a period longer than that which separates us from the beginnings of Greek drama) and never progressed dramatically beyond ritual. The Greeks, on the other hand, took the steps that established theatre as an autonomous activity. Therefore, it is to Greece that one must look to find the beginnings of the Western tradition in theatre and drama.

The Beginnings of Drama in Greece

For several centuries, Greek drama was presented exclusively at festivals honoring Dionysus, the god of wine and fertility. Supposedly the son of Zeus (the greatest of Greek gods) and Semele (a mortal), Dionysus was killed, dismembered, and then resurrected. Thus, myths about him relate to the life cycle and to seasonal changes: birth, growth, decay, death, and rebirth; spring, summer, fall, and winter. His worship was designed in part to ensure the return of spring and fertility As the god of wine, he also represented many of the world's irrational forces, and his worship was a recognition of man's elemental passions. In the early centuries of Dionysian worship, sexual orgies and drunkenness were accepted parts of the religious impulse, but as time went by these were gradually sublimated, although the basic purpose of Dionysian worship—the inducement of fertility—remained unchanged.

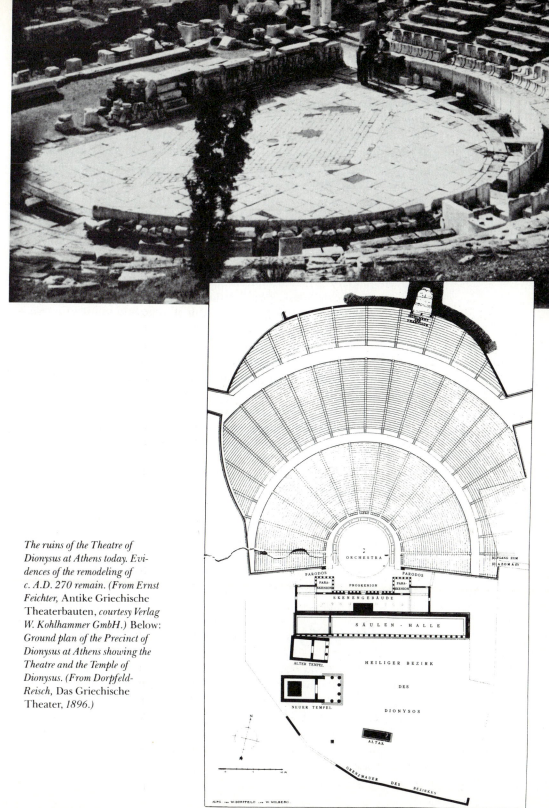

The ruins of the Theatre of Dionysus at Athens today. Evidences of the remodeling of c. A.D. 270 remain. (From Ernst Feichter, Antike Griechische Theaterbauten, *courtesy Verlag W. Kohlhammer GmbH.) Below: Ground plan of the Precinct of Dionysus at Athens showing the Theatre and the Temple of Dionysus. (From Dorpfeld-Reisch,* Das Griechische Theater, *1896.)*

THEATER UND BEZIRK DES DIONYSOS IN ATHEN. IV. JAHRHUNDERT v. CHR. ERGÄNZUNG.

The inclusion of such irrational forces within the sphere of religion illustrates well the Greek belief that the failure to give due honor to any part of nature can lead to destruction. The Greeks constantly sought to achieve harmony among all conflicting forces, both within and without.

The worship of Dionysus was introduced into Greece from Asia Minor around the thirteenth century B.C., and by the seventh or eighth century B.C., contests of choral dancers were being held at festivals given in his honor. These dances were accompanied by dithyrambs (ecstatic hymns) honoring the god. Aristotle says that it was out of improvisation by the leaders of these hymns and dances that drama developed.

The Greeks did not observe a holy day comparable to our sabbath. Rather, they honored their many gods through religious festivals scattered through the year. By the sixth century B.C., there were four festivals each year in honor of Dionysus alone: the Rural Dionysia (in December); the Lenaia (in January); the Anthesteria (around the end of Feburary); and the City (or Great) Dionysia (around the end of March). Plays were performed at all of these, with the exception of the Anthesteria. Drama was not a part of the festivals held in honor of any other god.

The first definite record of drama in Greece is found in 534 B.C., when the City Dionysia was reorganized and a contest for the best tragedy instituted. Drama probably existed prior to that time, for otherwise a contest would be difficult to explain. The only dramatist of this period whose name has survived is Thespis, who won the first contest. (Since he is also the first known actor, performers are still often called *thespians*.)

The drama of Thespis was relatively simple, since it involved only one actor and a chorus. This does not mean that there was only one speaking character in each play, but rather that all characters were played by the same actor. This single actor used masks in shifting his identity; when he left the stage to change roles, the chorus filled the intervals with singing and dancing. The chorus, therefore, was the principal unifying force in this early drama. Face-to-face conflict between opposing characters, which most later periods have considered a basic feature of drama, was impossible so long as one actor took all roles (unless, of course, the chorus assumed the role of antagonist).

Tragedy in the Fifth Century

Although drama was written and performed in Greece for many centuries, plays by only five writers—Aeschylus, Sophocles, Euripides, Aristophanes, and Menander—now exist. Out of the vast number of plays written, only forty-five survive—thirty-two tragedies, twelve comedies, and one satyr play. All but four of these plays were written during the fifth century.

Aeschylus (525–456) is the earliest dramatist whose plays have survived. He began competing in the contests for tragedy around 499 B.C., but did not win a victory until 484; after that time he won thirteen contests. The titles of seventy-nine of his plays have come down to us but only seven works remain: *The Persians* (472), *Seven against Thebes* (467), the *Oresteia*—a trilogy of plays made up of *Agamemnon, Libation Bearers,* and *Eumenides* (458), *The Suppliants,* and *Prometheus Bound* (exact dates unknown). *The Persians* is unique among surviving Greek dramas in having been based on an historical event (the Persian war) rather than on mythology, although other now-lost plays on historical subjects were written.

Aeschylus' major innovation was the introduction of the second actor, which encouraged face-to-face conflict. The subsequent increase in emphasis on the actor reduced the importance of the chorus, though it remained a dominant force.

The power of Aeschylus' drama can best be appreciated through the only surviving Greek trilogy, the *Oresteia,* one of the great monuments of dramatic literature. As in most of his plays, Aeschylus is concerned here with man's relationship to the gods and the universe and with moral principle. The *Oresteia* dramatizes a development in the concept of justice. In the first two plays the characters conceived of justice as personal revenge, but in the final play, private justice is replaced by the impersonal power of the state. This evolutionary process is demonstrated through a powerful story of murder, reprisal, and remorse, in which the gods participate both directly and indirectly.

Sophocles (496–406) is frequently called the greatest of the Greek dramatists. He is credited with over a hundred plays, of which only seven now exist: *Ajax* (dated variously from 450 to 440), *Antigone* (around 440), *Oedipus the King* (approximately 430 to 425), *Philoctetes* (409), *Electra and Trachiniae* (dates unknown, though considered to be late plays), and *Oedipus at Colonus* (written shortly before Sophocles' death). In addition, a substantial part of *The Trackers,* a satyr play, is extant. He won twenty-four contests, the first in 468 when he defeated Aeschylus. Sophocles introduced a third actor and thus allowed for still greater dramatic complexity than had been possible with two actors. He was much more directly concerned with human relationships than with the religious and philosophical issues which had interested Aeschylus. Furthermore, his dramas place more emphasis upon building skillful climaxes and well-developed episodes than those of Aeschylus, which are sometimes crude in structure. (The qualities of Sophocles' drama will be explored at greater length in the detailed examination of *Oedipus the King*).

Euripides (480–406) was the last of the great Greek tragedians. He is said to have written ninety-two plays, of which seventeen tragedies have survived. Among these the most famous are: *Alcestis* (438), *Medea* (431), *Hippolytus* (428), *Ion,* and *Electra* (dates unknown), *The Trojan Women* (415), and *The Bacchae* (produced after his death). In addition, *The Cyclops* is the only complete satyr play that now exists. Although Euripides achieved great popularity in later times, he was not widely appreciated in his own day, winning only five victories in the tragic contests.

Euripides reduced the role of the chorus in his works until its connection with the rest of the play was often vague. His interests were principally philosophical and psychological. He was a skeptic who questioned many Athenian ideals; even the gods did not escape examination, and in his plays they were frequently made to appear petty and ineffectual; he probed the motives of his characters and found little to admire. He also turned toward melodrama and frequently resorted to contrived endings. Thus he has been admired for his ideas and his psychological realism, but has been criticized for faulty dramatic structure. With his death, the great era of Greek tragedy came to an end.

The Satyr Play

During the fifth century B.C., each writer of tragedy was also required to present a satyr play, along with three tragedies, whenever he competed in the festivals. A satyr play was comic in tone (usually burlesquing a Greek myth) and used a chorus of satyrs. Following the three tragedies, it formed a kind of afterpiece, for it was short and sent the audience home in a happy frame of mind. Since the actors and choruses were the same for both tragedies and satyr play, the conventions of acting, costuming, and scenery were probably similar for both forms, although they were given a marked satirical turn in the satyr plays.

Actors of a satyr play. From a vase of the late fifth century, B.C. Note the masks and the various kinds of costume (From Baumeister, Denkmaler des Klassichens Altertums, *1888.)*

Only one complete satyr play—the *Cyclops* by Euripides—still exists. Like all satyr plays, it is divided into five sections by four choral odes after the manner of tragedy and is a parody of a serious story—in this instance, Odysseus' encounter with the Cyclops. A substantial part of one

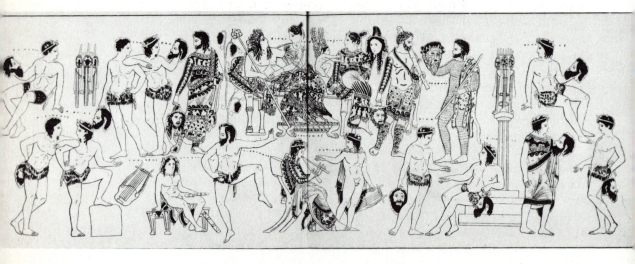

other satyr play—*The Trackers* by Sophocles—is also extant. It deals with Apollo's attempts to recover a herd of cattle stolen from him by Hermes and has the same structural features as the *Cyclops*. Although the satyr play was a regular feature of the Athenian theatre of the fifth century, it has had little subsequent influence and ceased to exist as a form when Greek drama declined.

Play Production

Greek drama can best be appreciated through a detailed examination of a representative play. For this purpose *Oedipus the King* has been chosen. But, since information about the theatrical conventions for which it was written will contribute much to our understanding of the play, it will be helpful first to explore the practices that prevailed around 430 B.C., the approximate time when Sophocles' play was first performed.

It was at the City Dionysia, one of the great religious and civic occasions of the year, that *Oedipus the King* was first presented. If a tragic dramatist wished to enter plays at the City Dionysia, he applied to the principal civic magistrate (the *archon eponymous*) for a chorus. We do not know how this official decided among the applicants, but three tragic writers were granted choruses at each City Dionysia.

The magistrate also appointed the *choregoi*, or wealthy citizens who bore the expense of the choruses. One *choregus* was appointed for each dramatist, and the *choregoi* and playwrights were then matched by lot. *Choregoi* for the next City Dionysia were appointed approximately one month after the conclusion of the preceding City Dionysia. This would have allowed almost a year for planning and rehearsal, although not all of this time may have been used.

The *choregus* paid for the training of the chorus, their costumes, the musicians, the supernumerary actors and their costumes, and perhaps for the scenery. In other words, he was responsible for everything except the theatre and the speaking actors. Since he might be either generous or miserly, the *choregus* could seriously affect the playwright's chances of mounting his play satisfactorily. Usually, however, the *choregus* looked upon the proper outfitting of his plays as a civic duty and as a matter of personal pride.

If a playwright were granted a chorus, he was required to present three tragedies and a satyr play. With rare exceptions, the playwright also directed his own works and was in charge of the production as a whole. Until the time of Sophocles the playwright acted in his own plays as well. For his efforts, the playwright was no doubt given some financial remuneration by the state and there was a prize for the winner of the contest, but the amount of money a playwright might receive for his work is unknown. It is extremely doubtful, however, that any of the Greek dramatists of the fifth century earned a living from work as a writer. (Most were from well-to-do families and most probably did not consider play-writing their primary profession.)

The state paid the actors and supplied their costumes; it also furnished the theatre in which the plays were performed. Dramatic production in the fifth century, thus, was financed either by wealthy citizens or by the state, and was looked upon as a religious and civic function of major importance.

The City Dionysia, at which the plays were produced, was considered so important that during it no legal proceedings were allowed and prisoners were released. It opened with a procession in which the statue of the god Dionysus was taken from his temple at the foot of the Acropolis and carried outside the city. His original entry into Athens was then reenacted in a procession that included much revelry. The ceremony concluded with a sacrifice to the god.

The next principal feature of the festival was the performance of *dithyramb*s (hymns to Dionysus sung and danced by choruses of fifty). There were ten choruses each year, five with men and five with boys. Next came the contest for comedies, five probably given on a single day; this was followed by three days devoted to tragedies. On each of these days, three tragedies and a satyr play were performed. After the festival ended, there was a day devoted to evaluating the festival and receiving complaints about its conduct or the misbehavior of citizens during the festival.

To this civic and religious celebration everyone was welcome. Admission was probably free originally, but was later set at the small sum of two *obols,* and even then a public fund was established to provide tickets for those who could not afford the price of admission. The theatre was considered to be the right of everyone rather than a function for the few. Audiences took a keen interest in the contests. In the fifth century, prizes were awarded at each City Dionysia for the best plays (there was a prize for the best comedy and for the best group of tragedies, the honor being shared by the playwright and the choregus), to the best tragic actor, and to the best dithyrambic choruses. The state supervised the judging, and elaborate precautions were taken to insure the secrecy of voting.

The Theatre of Dionysus

At Athens plays were presented in the Theatre of Dionysus situated on the slope of the Acropolis above the Temple of Dionysus. This theatre underwent many changes. In the sixth century it consisted of the hillside on which the spectators stood or sat, and a flat terrace at the foot of the hill for the performers. In the middle of this terrace or *orchestra* (the "dancing place") was an altar (or *thymele*). There probably was no scenic background. Seats, forming an auditorium or *theatron* (the "seeing place"), were gradually added for spectators.

Drawings by Ernst Fiechter of varying conceptions of the stage house for the theatre of Dionysus in the fifth century B.C. (From Fiechter, Antike Griechische Theaterbauten, courtesy Verlag W. Kohlhammer GmbH, Stuttgart.)

A conjectural reconstruction of the stage of the Theatre of Dionysus remodeled to conform to the Hellenistic ideal about 150 B.C. (From Fiechter.)

During the fifth and fourth centuries this basic structure was elaborated: a scene house was added and the whole theatre was reconstructed in stone, although this process was not completed until well into the fourth century. The auditorium was the first part of the theatre to assume permanent form when stadiumlike seating was provided by setting stones into the hillside. The semicircular auditorium, which seated about 14,000 persons, curved around the circular orchestra, which measured about sixty-five feet in diameter.

The stage house (or *skene*) was late in developing as a part of the theatre. It was the last part to be constructed in stone, and was remodeled many times after that. For all of these reasons, it is difficult to get a clear impression of the scenic background of plays in the fifth century. The *skene* was originally a place where actors might dress and retire to change roles. Gradually this house came to be used as a background for the action of the play, and its usefulness for scenic purposes was exploited. At the time when *Oedipus the King* was first performed the *skene* was probably a long building which, with its projecting side wings (called *paraskenia*), formed a rectangular background for the orchestra on the side away from the spectators. It was not joined to the auditorium, and the space on each side between the *paraskenia* and the auditorium provided entrances into the orchestra. These entrances were called *parodoi*. (For a

The appearance of the skene is much debated. Most of the plays are set before temples or palaces, but some take place outside of caves or tents or in wooded landscapes. Consequently, there is much disagreement over the extent to which the background may have been altered to meet these differing demands.

Most scholars believe that the same formalized background was used for all plays. Others, however, argue that, since it was not entirely permanent, the appearance of the skene could have been changed from year to year or from play to play. They point to a series of holes that have been discovered forward of the *skene* foundations and suggest that these could have been used to support upright timbers to which scenery was attached, and that such an arrangement would have facilitated rapid changes in the scenic background. It is impossible to know the truth, but, considering the lack of realistic detail in the plays, it seems unlikely that the Greek ever attempted to create the illusion of a real place in their theatre. Some indication of a play's setting, however, may have been attempted at times through scenic devices.

It is unclear whether there was a raised stage in the theatre of the fifth century, for there is not enough evidence to settle the question definitely. Since the plays seem to require that the actors and the chorus mingle freely, if a platform were used it was probably low enough to allow free access between stage and orchestra. If there were no stage, both the chorus and actors would have used the acting area composed of the orchestra and the rectangular space formed by the scene house. The roof of the stage house also could be used as an acting area.

Since the number of stage entrances varies from play to play, some difference of opinion has arisen about how many doors there were in the stage house. It has become customary to state that there were three in the *skene* and one in each of the *paraskenia,* but in actuality the number is far from certain. Most frequently the actors entered from the stage house, while the chorus used the *parodoi.* There are examples, however, of the chorus entering from the stage house, and of actors using the *parodoi.*

When the available information about the Greek theatre is assembled, a fairly clear picture of its basic structure emerges, but the details of the scenic background remain unclear.

While most of the action of Greek plays takes place out of doors, occasionally interiors are indicated. For example, most deaths occur offstage, but the bodies are frequently displayed afterward. For this purpose the large central doorway seems to have been opened and a wheeled platform moved forward. This device is called an *eccyclema* or *exaustra.*

Another effect frequently demanded in Greek plays is the appearance of gods. These characters may descend to the orchestra level or be lifted up from the orchestra to the roof of the stage house. For this purpose, a cranelike device called the *machina* was used. The overuse of gods to resolve difficult dramatic situations led to the expression *deus ex machina* to describe any contrived ending. The eccyclema and the machina are the only two machines that can definitely be ascribed to the fifth century, and these were not used extensively.

It is possible, however, that *periaktoi* were also in use, although these probably belong to a later period. *Periaktoi* are constructed of three flats put together to form a triangle; the triangle is then mounted on a central pivot. Since each surface can be exposed or concealed as desired, it may be used for sudden revelations or for changes in the background.

The Actor

From the time of Sophocles onward, the number of speaking actors in Greek tragedy seems to have been restricted to three, although there might be *extras* who were not considered to be actors. In the second half of the fifth century the state supplied three speaking actors for each tragic playwright competing in the contests. A principal actor was assigned to each playwright by lot. The playwright and his leading actor probably chose the other two actors. All were male and all acted in each of the four plays presented by the same dramatist. Since there were only three actors, each might be asked to play a number of roles.

The style of acting cannot be determined. The plays themselves call for simple realistic actions (such as weeping, running, and falling to the ground). On the other hand, many elements argue against any marked realism. The fact that the same actor played many roles and that men assumed women's parts suggests that realism was not a primary concern. Furthermore, some plays could be performed by three actors only if the same role were played by a different actor in different scenes of the play.

Terracotta figure of an actor found in an Athenian grave; probably fourth century B.C. (Courtesy of the Metropolitan Museum of Art, Rogers Fund, 1913.)

The Greek comic actor and his costume. Terracotta statuette from an Athenian grave c. fourth century B.C. (Courtesy of the Metropolitan Museum of Art, Rogers Fund, 1913.)

The large musical element, the use of dance, and the rather abstract treatment of the story also argue against a realistic style of acting. Nevertheless, the performances should not be thought of as devoid of clearly identifiable human actions. The details of daily life were stripped away but the action did not become so abstract that the audience could not sympathize with the characters. The style suggested by the scripts may be characterized as simple, expressive, and idealized.

Costume

A precautionary note seems necessary at this point. Many theatre historians have failed to distinguish between the practices of the fifth century and those of later Greek times. Nowhere is the failure more misleading than in the treatment of costumes. Frequently the tragic actor is depicted as wearing a high headdress, a mask with distorted features, thick-soled boots, and padded clothing. This costume may have been typical of later periods, but has little to do with the practices of the fifth century, the more typical features of which are outlined below and shown in the accompanying illustrations.

All the actors in Greek tragedy wore masks constructed of lightweight linen, cork, or wood. There were several reasons for this practice: Each actor played a number of roles; all the actors were male though many of the characters were female; the range of age and character types played by a single actor was great. (There is little evidence to support the argument sometimes advanced that the mask acted as a megaphone for the voice.) Although the mouths were open, the features were not exagger-

Greek Bird costumes probably similar to those used in Old Comedy. (From Dieterich, Pulcinella, *1897.)*

ated to any marked degree. Headdresses seem to have followed relatively closely those normally worn during the period.

A variety of clothing was used for stage purposes. A long-sleeved, ankle-length, heavily embroidered tunic, or *chiton*, was worn by certain characters, and some historians have argued that it was used for all the principal roles of tragedy. Since some plays contain references to mourning dress, to ragged garments, and to distinctions in clothing between Greeks and foreigners, however, it seems likely that costumes varied considerably. It may be that the sleeved, embroidered tunic (which was not worn in Greek daily life), was reserved for supernatural and non-Greek characters, while native dress was used for others. An ankle-length or knee-length chiton was the usual daily dress in Greece. The selection of the costume was probably determined at least in part by its appropriateness to the role. The tragic actor usually wore a soft, flexible, high-topped boot in common use at that time.

While the actor's appearance was somewhat changed by his costume from what would have been considered normal in that period, he remained relatively undistorted in terms of size and shape. His costume allowed for freedom of movement and speech and facilitated the rapid change of roles.

The Chorus, Music, and Dance Music

Although tradition has it that the tragic chorus originally consisted of fifty members, was later reduced to twelve, and then raised to fifteen, there is little evidence to substantiate any of these figures. Nevertheless, it is generally assumed that during Sophocles' lifetime the chorus was composed of fifteen persons. Usually the chorus performed in unison, but at times it was divided into two semichoruses of seven members; these semichoruses might perform in turn or might exchange or divide speeches. The chorus leader sometimes had solo lines, but the chorus probably spoke and sang as a group (though some modern editions of the plays divide the speeches and assign them to individual chorus members). The chorus usually makes its entrance after the prologue (or opening scene) and except in rare cases remains until the end of the play.

The chorus serves many functions. First, it is an actor in the drama. It expresses opinions, gives advice, and sometimes threatens to interfere in the events of the play. As a rule, it is sympathetically allied with the protagonist. Second, the chorus often establishes the ethical framework of the play. It may express the author's views and set up a standard against which the actions of the characters can be judged. Third, the chorus is frequently the ideal spectator, reacting to the events and characters as the author would like his audience to respond. Fourth, the chorus helps to set the mood of the play and to heighten its dramatic effects. For example, a

The theatre at Epidaurus during a recent production. Note the modern stage house erected over the ruins of the ancient skene.

mood of foreboding may be created through the chorus' expression of doubts about what is to come; or the chorus may help to achieve more powerful reversals, as when its expression of elation is followed immediately by disastrous events. Fifth, the chorus adds color, movement, and spectacle. In the fifth century, all the choral interludes were accompanied by music and were both sung and danced. Thus, if offered powerful auditory and visual appeals. Sixth, the chorus serves an important rhythmical function. This may best be explained through an analogy. A typical **Greek** temple has columns all around the exterior, without which there would be an uninteresting continuous blank wall. The columns serve to make the eye pause but do not prevent it from moving on. Greek drama without its choral passages would have a similar effect, for the action would move too fast. These retardations—these pauses in which to look backward and forward—contribute enormously to the over-all emotional effect; they are part of the design without which the whole would be incomplete or unsatisfying.

The exact nature of Greek music and dance is unknown. Only a few fragments of Great music have survived, but we do know that the Greeks believed that both music and dance had ethical content—that some types were moral and that others were immoral. Since tragedy displays a strong ethical bias, it is reasonable to assume that in most tragedies the music and dance displayed those qualities the Greeks associated with stateliness and moral uprightness.

Theatre and Drama
in Ancient Greece

17

Oedipus the King

With this background in mind, let us now look at Sophocles' *Oedipus the King* as an example of Greek tragedy.

Themes and Ideas. Like all great plays, *Oedipus the King* develops a number of important themes. One is stated in the final lines:

> let none
> Presume on his good fortune until he find
> Life, at his death, a memory without pain.

The play shows the fall of Oedipus from the place of highest honor to that of an outcast, and demonstrates the uncertainty of human destiny.

A second motif is man's inability to control his own fate. Oedipus is a man who attempts to do his best at all times; he wants to help his people. He has taken what he considers the necessary steps to avoid the terrible fate predicted by the oracle (that he will kill his father and marry his mother). But humans are limited in their vision, no matter how they may attempt to avoid mistakes. The contrast, then, between humans seeking to control their destiny and other forces determining destiny is clearly depicted. But while fate (or the will of the gods) is always the superior force in the play, it works through human beings. It is Jocasta's attempt to destroy the infant Oedipus, Oedipus' desire to avoid his parents, and Oedipus' search for the murderer that lead inevitably to the outcome. At the end, while Oedipus accepts his fate as he must, he still does not see himself entirely under the control of the gods:

> Dear
> Children, the god was Apollo.
> He brought my sick, sick fate upon me.
> But the blinding hand was my own!

It is significant that no attempt is made to explain why destruction comes to Oedipus. It is implied that man must submit to fate and that in struggling to avoid it he only becomes more entangled. There is then an irrational, or at least an unknowable, force at work. This idea is emphasized through the various attempts to communicate with the gods (through oracles) and to propitiate them. The plague is viewed as a punishment from the gods, the exiling of Oedipus is an attempt to placate them, but no one asks why the gods have decreed Oedipus' fate. The truth of the oracles is established, but the purpose is unclear. The Greek concept of the gods, however, did not demand that all the gods be benevolent, since all forces were deified whether good or evil. Therefore, a god might visit evil upon human beings, and they had to be constantly on guard not to offend any of the many gods.

It is also possible to interpret this play as suggesting that the gods, rather than having decreed events, have merely foreseen and foretold what the characters will do when confronted with certain problems. Such

an interpretation, while it shifts the emphasis somewhat, does not contradict the picture of humans as victims of forces beyond their control, no matter by what name we call those forces.

Another implication, which may not have been a conscious one with Sophocles, is that Oedipus is a scapegoat. The city of Thebes will be saved if the **one guilty** man can be found and punished. Oedipus, in a sense then, takes the sins of the city upon himself, and in his punishment lies the salvation of others. Thus, Oedipus becomes a sacrificial offering to the gods. There is a parallel here with the crucifixion of Christ, the sacrificial lamb offered up for the sins of all those who believe in Him. This parallel cannot be extended very far, however, since there are more points of difference than of similarity in the two figures.

Another motif—blindness versus sight—is emphasized in poetic images and in various overt comparisons. A contrast is repeatedly drawn between the physical power of sight and the inner sight of understanding. For example, Tiresias, though blind, can see the truth which escapes Oedipus, while Oedipus, who has penetrated the riddle of the Sphinx, cannot solve the puzzle of his own life. When it is revealed to him, he blinds himself in an act of retribution.

These themes indicate that *Oedipus the King* is a comment in part on humankind's relationship to the gods and on humans' attempt to control their own destiny. While the Greek views of these problems may not be ours, the problems and many of the implications are still vital and meaningful.

Plot and Structure. The skill with which *Oedipus the King* is constructed can be appreciated if we compare the complex story (which actually begins with a prophecy prior to the birth of Oedipus) with Sophocles' ordering of the events. In the play there is a simultaneous movement backward and forward in time as the revelation of the past moves Oedipus ever nearer to his doom in the present.

The division of the play into a prologue and five espisodes separated by choral passages is typical of Greek tragedy. The prologue is devoted principally to exposition: a plague is destroying the city of Thebes; Oedipus promises to help and explains the action already taken; Creon returns from Delphi with a command from the Oracle to find and punish the murderer of Laius; Oedipus promises to obey the command. Thus, all of the necessary information is given in a very brief scene, and the first important question (Who is the murderer of Laius?) is raised. The prologue is followed by the *parados*, or entry of the chorus and the first choral slong, in which the plight of Thebes is restated and prayers for deliverance are offered to the gods.

The first episode begins with Oedipus' proclamation and his curse upon the murderer. This proclamation has great dramatic power because Oedipus is unknowingly pronouncing a curse upon himself. Then Tiresias, the seer, enters. It is important to remember that Oedipus has sent for Tiresias on the advice of Creon, since otherwise Oedipus' suspicion of conspiracy between Creon and Tiresias is not understandable. Tiresias' refusal to answer questions provokes Oedipus' anger, the first display of a response which is developed forcefully throughout the first four episodes. It is his quick temper, we later discover, that caused Oedipus to kill Laius. By the time Tiresias has been driven to answer, Oedipus suspects some trickery. This complication is necessary, for had Oedipus summoned Tiresias, heard his story, and believed him, the play would be over. Sophocles has boldly brought out the truth but has cast doubt upon it, for, as Oedipus points out, if Tiresias knew the truth why did he not speak out at the time of Laius' murder? The scene ends in a stalemate of accusations.

It is interesting to note that while all of the first four episodes move forward in the present, they go successively further backward in time. This first episode reveals only that part of the past immediately preceding Oedipus' arrival at Thebes.

The choral passage which follows the first episode reflects upon the previous scene, stating the confusion which Sophocles wishes the audience to feel. The chorus ends by declaring that since Oedipus has saved the city in the past it will continue to have faith in him until he is proven wrong.

The second episode builds logically on the first. Creon comes to defend himself from the accusation that he has conspired with Tiresias. Oedipus, however, is not open to reason. Jocasta is drawn to the scene by the quarrel and she and the chorus persuade Oedipus to abate his anger. This quarrel illustrates Oedipus' complete faith in his own righteousness, since despite Tiresias' accusation, no suspicion of his own guilt has entered his mind. Ironically, it is Jocasta's attempt to placate Oedipus that leads to his first suspicion about himself. She tells him that oracles are not to be believed and as evidence points to Laius' death, which did not come in the manner prophesied. But her description recalls to Oedipus the circumstances under which he has killed a man. He insists that Jocasta send for the one survivor of Laius' party. Thus, a considerable change occurs within this scene—Oedipus' self-righteousness is shaken, and the possibility of his involvement creates additional suspense. The scene also continues the backward exploration of the past, for Oedipus tells of his life in Corinth, his visit to the Oracle of Delphi, and the murder of the man who is later discovered to have been Laius.

The choral song which follows is concerned with the questions Jocasta has raised about oracles. The chorus concludes that if oracles are proven untrue, then the gods themselves are to be doubted. The song, while reflecting upon the scene immediately past, looks forward to a solution of the question.

Oedipus the King directed by *Tyrone Guthrie, 1955. Center: Douglas Campbell as Oedipus. Rear: Eleanor Stuart as Jocasta, Robert Goodier as Creon. (Production photo by Donald McKague, courtesy of the Stratford Shakespearean Festival Foundation of Canada.)*

Though Jocasta has called oracles into question, she obviously does not disbelieve in the gods themselves, for at the beginning of the third episode she makes offerings to them. She is interrupted, however, by the entrance of the Messenger from Corinth, who brings news of the death of Oedipus' supposed father, Polybus. But this news, rather than arousing grief, as one would expect, is greeted with rejoicing, for it seems to disprove the oracle which had predicted that Oedipus would kill his father. This seeming reversal only serves to heighten the effect of the following events. Oedipus still fears returning to Corinth because the oracle also has prophesied that he will marry his own mother. Thinking that he will set Oedipus' mind at ease, the Messenger reveals that he himself brought Oedipus as an infant to Polybus. The circumstances under which the Messenger acquired the child bring home the truth to Jocasta. This discovery leads to a complete reversal for Jocasta, for the oracles she has cast doubt upon in the preceding scene have suddenly been vindicated. She strives to stop Oedipus from making further inquiries, but he interprets her entreaties as fear that he may be of humble birth. Jocasta goes into the palace; it is the last we see of her, although her actions are later revealed. This scene has not only revealed the truth to Jocasta, it has also diverted attention from the murder of Laius to the birth of Oedipus. It goes backward in time to the infancy of Oedipus. Only one step remains.

The choral song which follows is filled with fanciful hopes, as the chorus speculates on Oedipus' parentage and suggests such possibilities as Apollo and the nymphs. The truth is deliberately kept at a distance here in order to make the following scene more powerful. These speculations, however, do serve to concentrate attention on the question while diverting it from the right solution.

This extremely brief choral song is followed by the entry of the Herdsman (the sole survivor of Laius' party at the time of the murder and the person from whom the Corinthian Messenger had acquired the infant Oedipus). The Herdsman does not wish to speak, but he is tortured by Oedipus' servants into doing so. In this very rapid scene everything that has gone before is brought to a climax. We are taken back to the beginning of the story (Oedipus' birth), we learn the secret of his parentage, we see the truth of the oracle, we find out who murdered Laius, we discover that Oedipus is married to his own mother. The climax is reached in Oedipus' cry of despair and disgust as he rushes into the palace. The brief choral song which follows comments upon the unpredictability of fate and points to Oedipus' life as an example.

The final episode is divided into two parts. A Messenger enters and describes what has happened offstage. The "messenger scene" is a standard part of Greek drama, since Greek sensibilities dictate that scenes of extreme violence take place offstage, although the results of the violence (the bodies of the dead, or in this case Oedipus' blindness) might be shown. It is doubtful, however, that spectators of any age could witness without revulsion the sight of Oedipus jabbing pins into his eyes. Following the messenger scene, Oedipus returns to the stage and seeks to prepare himself for the future.

Oedipus the King is structurally unusual, for the resolution scene is the longest in the play. Obviously, Sophocles was not primarily concerned with discovering the murderer of Laius, for the interest in this lengthy final scene is shifted to the question: What will Oedipus do now that he knows the truth?

Up to this scene the play has concentrated upon Oedipus as the ruler of Thebes, but in the resolution Oedipus as a man and a father becomes the center of interest. By this point he has ceased to be the ruler of Thebes and has become the lowest of its citizens, and much of the intense pathos is due to this change. An audience may feel for Oedipus the outcast as it never could feel for the self-righteous ruler shown in the prologue.

Oedipus' act of blinding himself grows believably out of his character, for it is his very uprightness and deep sense of moral outrage that causes him to punish himself so terribly. Although he is innocent of intentional sin, he considers the deeds themselves (murder of a blood relative and incest) to be so horrible that ignorance cannot wipe away the moral stigma. Part of the play's power resides in the revulsion with which people in all ages have viewed patricide and incest. That they are commited by an essentially good man only make them more terrible.

Oedipus the King maintains completely the unities of action, time, and place. There is nothing in the play that is not immediately relevant to the story being told. There are no subplots, and even the main plot it treated as simply as its events will allow. The time that elapses in the play coincides with the amount of time it would take in performance, and all of the events occur in the same place. The play, thus, has a late point of attack and shows only the final stages of the story. Out of very simple means, the playwright created a drama of concentrated and powerful effect.

Characters and Acting. Sophocles pays little attention to the physiological level of characterization. The principal characters—Oedipus, Creon, and Jocasta—are mature persons, but Sophocles indicates almost nothing about their ages or appearances. One factor which is apt to distract modern readers—the relative ages of Jocasta and Oedipus—is not even mentioned by Sophocles, for it is basically unimportant. According to legend, Jocasta was queen of Thebes when Oedipus answered the riddle of the Sphinx. His reward, being made king, carried with it the stipulation that he marry Jocasta. Sophocles, it should be noted, never questions the suitability of the marriage on the grounds of disparity in age.

Although Sophocles does not dwell on the physical attributes of his major characters, he does give brief indications of age for other roles. The Priest of the Prologue is spoken of as being old; the Chorus is made up of Theban Elders; Tiresias is old and blind; the Herdsman is an old man. In almost every case, age is associated with wisdom and experience. On the other hand, there are a number of young characters, none of whom

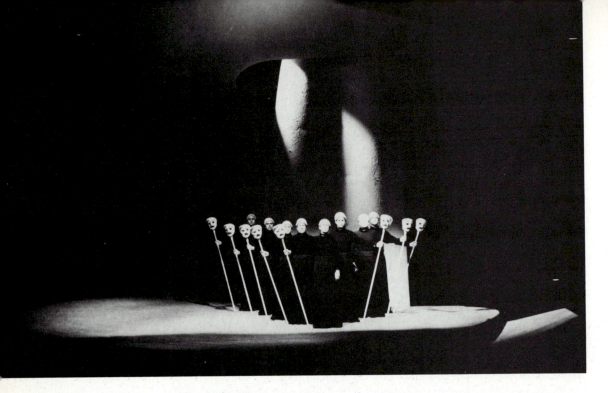

Scene from Oedipus the King *as performed at the Landestheater, Darmstadt, in 1952. Directed by G. R. Sellner, designed by Fritz Mertz. (Photo by Pit Ludwig. Courtesy of the exhibition,* The New Theatre in Germany, *circulated by the Smithsonian Institution.)*

speaks: the band of suppliants in the Prologue includes children, the Antigone and Ismene are very young. Here, the innocence of childhood is used to arouse pity.

On the second level of characterization (social position or class), Sophocles again indicates little. Oedipus, Creon, and Jocasta hold joint authority in Thebes, although the power has been delegated to Oedipus. Vocational designations—a priest, a seer, a herdsman, servants—are used for some of the characters.

Sophocles is principally concerned with psychological and ethical characteristics. For example, we never know how old Oedipus is, but we learn about his moral uprightness, his reputation for wisdom, his quick temper, his insistence on discovering truth, his suspicion, his love for his children, his strength in the face of disaster. It is through these qualities that we come to understand Oedipus. But even here, a very limited number of traits, only those necessary to the story, are shown.

Creon is given even fewer characteristics. He has been Oedipus' trusted friend and brother-in-law, and is one of the rulers of Thebes. Quick to defend his honor, he is a man of common sense and uprightness who acts as honorably and compassionately as he can when the truth is discovered. Jocasta is similarly restricted. She strives to make life run smoothly for Oedipus, she tries to comfort him, to mediate between him and Creon, to stop Oedipus in his quest; she commits suicide when the truth becomes clear. We know nothing of her as a mother, and the very existence of the children is not mentioned until after her death.

This treatment of character—the use of few but essential traits—is another sign of Sophocles' economy in writing. His methods are quite unlike those of modern realistic playwrights who tend to build character out of a large number of small details.

In the first production of *Oedipus the King,* all of the speaking roles would have been taken by three actors. The most likely casting would be as follows: The first actor would play Oedipus throughout, since he is present in every scene; the second actor would play Creon and the Messenger from Corinth; the third actor would play the Priest, Tiresias, Jocasta, the Herdsman, and the second Messenger. The greatest range is required of the third actor, while the greatest individual power is required of the first. The demands made on the third actor raises questions about the degree to which he differentiated between characters and the importance masks and costumes played in keeping characters separated for the audience. One should remember, however, that no two of the roles played by the third actor closely resemble each other and that the separation in terms of type might make his task simpler than it at first appears.

In addition to the three speaking actors, a large number of supernumeraries is required, many of whom no doubt appeared in more than one scene. For example, the band of suppliants in the Prologue includes children, two of whom could later appear as Antigone and Ismene. Some who portrayed suppliants probably also appeared later as servants and attendants. To the actors must be added the chorus of fifteen members. Therefore, the total number in the cast was probably not less than thirty-five.

Just as the details of characterization are few, so too the kinds of actions required of the actors are restricted. The physical movement specifically demanded by the script is slight: entering, exiting, kneeling, pouring of sacrificial offerings, torturing the Herdsman, and displays of anger. The use of masks, the doubling of roles, the fact that Jocasta was played by a man, the relatively small range of action—all these factors suggest that, while the aim was to create moving representations of human actions, the overall effect would be considerably more abstract than the acting normally seen in the modern theatre.

Setting, Spectacle, Music, and Dance. The reader used to all the stage directions given in modern scripts may find a Greek tragedy lacking in spectacle upon first reading. If he tries to envision the action as it unfolds moment by moment, however, quite a different impression results.

First of all, the Greek theatre had no curtain. The play begins, therefore, with the procession of the suppliants through one of the *parodoi.* Oedipus arrives to hear their pleas; then Creon enters. Later the suppliants leave, and immediately the Chorus enters with a song which is accompanied by music and dance. This simple outline of the prologue and *parodos* is indicative of the complexity and variety found throughout the play.

The setting of *Oedipus the King* is simple. The stage house represents a palace; no changes are made and no machinery is needed. Relatively few of the characters enter from the palace: Oedipus, Jocasta, the second Messenger, Antigone, Ismene, and sometimes Creon. Most of the characters, however, enter either through the *parodoi* or from the *paraskenia*. The Chorus and the suppliants would also enter through the *parodoi* and would perform in the orchestra.

There would be an altar in the middle of the orchestra, but there would also be altars near the stage house upon which Jocasta could place her offerings. Since the play was performed out of doors in daylight, no artificial illumination was necessary.

Costumes also would add to both setting and spectacle. Since most of the characters, including the Chorus, are dignified Greek citizens, they probably would wear long *chitons*. But there would also be many distinctions among the characters. Suppliants would carry branches as symbols; the Priest, Tiresias, and the Herdsman would wear garments indicative of their occupations. The rich costumes of Oedipus, Jocasta, and Creon would contrast effectively with the simpler garments of the servants. Each actor would wear a mask indicative of his age and character.

Choral dancing is an important element of the spectacle. Since dance had ethical connotations for the Greeks, that used in *Oedipus the King* would have been in keeping with the moral position represented by the chorus of the play. Since the Chorus is made up of elderly, wise men, whatever dance they performed must have been dignified and stately, and

A nineteenth-century reconstruction of a Greek Comedy. (Culver Pictures.)

probably appealed as much through shifting patterns as through dance steps.

The aural appeals were several: instrumental music, singing, and the speech of actors. The Greeks placed great emphasis on effective oral delivery. The actors' voices, therefore, must have been well trained, and no doubt they created considerable aural beauty. Plays were performed with musical accompaniment. Occasionally, music was used during the episodes, but normally it was reserved for choral passages, all of which were sung and danced to flute music. Not only does music offer an appeal in its own right, it is also helpful in staging choral interludes, for it makes singing and dancing in unison much easier. Furthermore, music, through volume and tempo, aids in building choral passages to a climax. Movement, music, and song were combined to make the choral interludes among the most striking and effective features of Greek tragedy.

When the dramatic, visual, and musical appeals of Greek drama are considered, it becomes easier to understand why these plays, even after the passage of 2500 years, are still powerful and meaningful works of art.

Comedy

Greek comedy developed later than tragedy did. It was not officially recognized as a part of the festivals—that is, it was not granted a chorus—until about 487 B.C., when it became a regular feature of the City Dionysia. After 487, one day of each festival was devoted to the presentation of five comedies. At the City Dionysia, however, comedy was always considered inferior to tragedy; it was to find its true home at the Lenaia—the January Dionysian festival—at which it was given official state support beginning around 442 B.C. At the same time, contests for both comic poets and comic actors were inaugurated there. The festival arrangement and the production procedures were similar to those for the City Dionysia, though the Lenaia festival was less elaborate. Five comic poets competed at the Lenaia, as at the City Dionysia. After 432, two tragic dramatists provided two tragedies each year as well. Satyr plays and dithyrambs were never presented at the Lenaia.

Comedy used a chorus of twenty-four members, which like the tragic chorus might be divided into two semichoruses. The chorus also sang and danced and served the same functions as the tragic chorus, but its music and dance were directed, as a rule, toward creating comic effects, although Aristophanes frequently inserted beautiful lyrical choruses into his comedies.

The most typical costumes seems to have been a very tight, too-short *chiton* worn over flesh-colored tights, which created a ludicrous effect of partial nakedness. This effect was further emphasized by the *phallus* (male sexual organ), which was attached to the costumes of most male characters. The phallus was both a source of ribald humor and a constant reminder of the Dionysian purpose of the festival. Masks also were used to emphasize the ridiculous appearance of the characters. (See the illustrations).

Occasionally comic masks were used to depict actual persons. For example, when *The Clouds* was first produced Socrates is said to have stood up in the theatre so the audience might compare the actor's mask with his own facial features. Other masks and costumes created appropriate (though not necessarily realistic) likenesses for the nonhuman choruses —of birds, frogs, clouds, wasps, and so on—that abound in Old Comedy.

Principally, however, comedy differed from tragedy in its subject matter. Most typically it was concerned with contemporary matters of politics or art, with questions of peace or war, with persons or practices disliked by the comic writer. Occasionally the playwright used mythological material as a framework for his satire, but usually he invented his own plots, and often referred to contemporary persons or situations. The allusions were no doubt a source of considerable pleasure to the audiences of the day, but they are often obscure to a modern reader.

Numerous authors wrote Old Comedy, as the plays prior to 400 B.C. are called, but works by only one—Aristophanes (c. 448–380)—have survived. Aristophanes wrote about forty plays, of which eleven are extant: *The Acharnians* (425), *The Knights* (424), *The Clouds* (423), *The Wasps* (422), *Peace* (421), *The Birds* (414), *Lysistrata* (411), *Thesmophoriazusae* (411), *The Frogs* (405), *Ecclesiazusae* (392 or 391), and *Plutus* (388). Aristophanes began competing in the contests in 427, and though he may have acted in a few of his plays, he usually depended on others to produce his works.

His comedies mingle farce, personal abuse, fantasy, beautiful lyric

A redrawing from a vase painting of a type of costume probably used for tragedy in the fifth century B.C.

poetry, literary and musical parody, and serious commentary on contemporary affairs. Here *The Clouds* will be examined in some detail as an example of Aristophanes' work. It was produced at the City Dionysia in 423 B.C. and was awarded the third prize. Aristophanes later revised the script, but it is unclear how the present version differs from the original.

The Clouds

Themes and Ideas. The dominant idea of *The Clouds* is the corrupting influence of the Sophists, in whose teachings Aristophanes saw a danger to Athenian values. The Sophists were interested in rhetoric and argumentation, but, because they were skeptical of absolute values, to Aristophanes they appeared more anxious to win contests than to defend valid positions.

While Socrates was not a Sophist, he was probably the most colorful figure among the teachers of that time. Aristophanes did not pretend to present Socrates' ideas accurately, but used him to epitomize the Sophistic teacher. Nor are the ideas of the Sophists truthfully represented; they too are altered for comic purposes.

The satire is directed at two aspects of Sophism: its methods and its effects. The scenes in the school are concerned with the first of these, while the evasion of obligations and Phidippides' treatment of his father are designed to show the latter.

Plot and Structure. The plot of an Old Comedy usually revolves around a "happy idea" and the results of putting it into practice. In *The Clouds*, the idea is conceived that paying debts can be avoided by using the "wrong logic" of Sophistic learning. After much ridicule of its methods, the new learning is put into practice with the anticipated results. But while it is effective in ridding Strepsiades of his debtors, it has also taught his son, Phidippides, to beat and abuse him.

Structurally, Old Comedy follows a typical pattern composed of these elements: a *prologue*, during which the happy idea is conceived; the *parodos*, or entry of the chorus; the *agon*, or debate over the merits of the idea, ending with a decision to adopt it; the *parabasis*, a choral passage addressed to the audience and most frequently filled with advice on civic or other contemporary problems; a *series of episodes* showing the happy idea put into practice; and the *komos*, or exit to feasting and general revelry. Although all of the usual structural features are present in *The Clouds*, they have been rearranged. The deviations will be noted in the discussion which follows.

In the prologue to *The Clouds*, Strepsiades sets forth his predicament in a straightforward expository monologue. He is heavily in debt because of the extravagances of his son, Phidippides. He concludes that the only solution is to send his son to Socrates' school to learn how to avoid paying the debts. When Phidippides refuses to attend school, Strepsiades decides to go himself. The scene shifts instantly from Strepsiades' house to Socra-

Production photograph of The Clouds *as presented in 1951 by the Greek National Theatre. (Reproduced by permission.)*

tes' school. A number of satirical and farcical jokes about the school and its students concludes the prologue.

The parodos follows. Like many Greek comedies, *The Clouds* takes its title from the chorus, which frequently, as it does here, points up the element of fantasy. The clouds represent the spirit of the new learning which leads men on and then punishes them. The opening song also illustrates the element of lyrical poetry for which Aristophanes is noted.

Usually the agon follows the parodos, but in *The Clouds* an episode is introduced to ridicule additional aspects of the new learning. This episode is followed by the parabasis, which denounces the audience for not properly appreciating Aristophanes' merits. He unashamedly praises himself and ridicules his opponents.

The parabasis is followed by still another episode showing Strepsiades' inability to absorb the new learning. This episode implies that a man brought up in the old straight-laced ways of Athens cannot really understand the subtleties of the new way. After a choral ode, Strepsiades finally forces Phidippides to attend Socrates' school.

At this point, the long-delayed agon, or debate, occurs. The participants are personifications of Right Logic and Wrong Logic, another example of the fantasy that is typical of Old Comedy. As is usual, at the end of the agon all of the characters agree upon a line of action; here it is decided that Phidippides will be educated in the tradition of Wrong Logic.

This decision is followed by a short second parabasis, directed to the judges of the contest, suggesting that Aristophanes should win the prize.

Time passes very rapidly in the next thirty-five lines, for at that point Phidippides reenters having already completed his training.

A series of episodes showing the results of Strepsiades' plan follows: The creditors appear one by one and are effectively silenced. Strepsiades is overjoyed with his success and leads Phidippides away for feasting and revelry. This exist constitutes the komos and would normally conclude the play.

The joy is short-lived, however, for after a brief choral ode Strepsiades reappears, having been beaten by Phidippides, who then proves by the lesson learned from Wrong Logic that it is his duty to punish his father. The play ends as Strepsiades, in a fit of rage and frustration, attempts to burn Socrates' school. Such an ending is atypical of Old Comedy, for as a rule joy and harmony prevail.

The unity of Old Comedy is to be found in its ruling idea rather than in a sequence of causally related events. Consequently, its structure often seems haphazard. The episodes which show the idea being put into practice are especially apt to appear disconnected. The order could be rearranged and the number of episodes could be increased or reduced without seriously altering the story. They do build in comic intensity, however, and they carry out the author's purpose effectively.

The treatment of time and place in *The Clouds* is dictated by dramatic needs without any attempt at creating an illusion of reality. Sometimes hours or days are assumed to have passed during one or two speeches, and the place changes at will. Stage illusion is broken frequently: the characters make comments about the audience, and the chorus addresses the spectators directly in the parabasis.

The element of fantasy can be seen in both the personification of the clouds and in the exaggeration of ideas and situations. Thus, while the incidents are related to contemporary affairs, they are treated through the techniques of the "tall story."

Characters and Acting. Aristophanes' plays seem to indicate that all men are governed by materialistic and biological instincts and are in part corrupt and selfish. That Aristophanes held this opinion of his audience as well is suggested by his frequent practice of implying that the adoption of his point of view will bring monetary and sexual rewards.

Old Comedy puts much more emphasis on the physical aspects of characterization than tragedy does. Aristophanes' major characters are usually drawn from the well-to-do landowners (comparable to the middle class today), while the minor characters are either members of the same class or slaves. Occasionally heroes or gods appear, but they are always brought down to the level of ordinary human beings by emphasizing their materialistic and selfish instincts.

Typically, the main character in a play by Aristophanes is the common man, but one who is worse than the average audience member considers himself to be. Although any comedy may arouse a feeling of superiority,

Aristophanes puts this response to special use. Because he wants reform, he makes it seem possible by letting the members of the audience feel that they are wiser than the characters in the play.

Aristophanes' characters are never villainous, merely ridiculous. Rather than focusing attention upon the moral nature of the "idea," he emphasizes the ludicrous or happy results of adopting it. Thus, the characters are usually concerned with expediency—how well a plan can serve their own purposes—rather than with moral implications. Strepsiades, for example, never considers the moral implications of cheating his creditors, only the means by which it can be done. But, although the moral issues are never allowed to become the center of his plays, Aristophanes never lets the audience forget that the situations have wider and more important applications. Again, he achieves his purpose in part by allowing his audience to feel morally superior to the characters.

The acting style emphasized the physical, ridiculous, and ordinary details of everyday life. For example, at the opening of *The Clouds*, Strepsiades and Phidippides, wraped in blankets, are snoring; Strepsiades awakens and sends for a lamp and his account books. Later the characters catch bedbugs, beat each other, and climb onto the roof.

Old Comedy is as far removed from tragedy as possible; it ridicules man for giving into his materialistic and petty instincts, whereas tragedy empathizes with man's attempt to rise above those instincts. Thus, comic acting was probably no more realistic than that in tragedy; its deviation

Scene from Greek New Comedy. Drawing of a bas relief. (From Pougin, Dictionnaire, 1885.)

from normal behavior was in a different direction, for it ridicules some aspects of human behavior just as tragic acting dignified others.

Setting, Spectacle, Dance, and Music. *The Clouds* demands a more complex setting and shows more clearly the facilities of the Greek theatre than *Oedipus the King* does. One interior and two exterior scenes are indicated. The interior was probably suggested by the *eccyclema*, while the two exteriors could be distinguished by the widely separated doors of the *skene*. The *machina* and the roof of the scene house were also used.

Many of the jokes in *The Clouds* are "sight gags." For example, Socrates is suspended in the machine (usually reserved for the gods) to indicate the pretentiousness and essential impracticality of the new learning. Other elements of note include the cloud costumes of the chorus, the grotesque and ludicrously obscene appearance of other characters, and the lively music and dance.

Thus, Old Comedy is a theatrical form of varied appeal. It is a strange mixture of fantasy, farce, and poetry which celebrates man's instincts while implicitly demanding that he act rationally. It is the reverse side of the coin of which tragedy is the face. Together comedy and tragedy indicate the range of the Greek view of man.

Late Greek Drama

Aristophanes was the last important exponent of Old Comedy. Furthermore, since all the great tragic dramatists were gone by the time he died in 380 B.C., Greek drama declined markedly in quality, if not in quantity, during the fourth century. Nevertheless, the theatre continued to expand, both in geographical distribution and in popularity.

In the fourth century, the Macedonians overran Greece. Their leader, Alexander the Great, then went on to conquer Asia Minor and northern Africa. Since the Greeks had already established colonies in southern Italy and Sicily, by the end of the fourth century almost all of the Mediterranean area had been "Hellenized." Pergamum (in Asia Minor) and Alexandria (in Egypt) soon rivaled Athens as centers of learning. Wherever the Greek influence was felt, theatres were built.

Although the taste for tragedy continued, comedy was the preferred form. But the comedy which satisfied this taste was not that of Aristophanes, for citizens were no longer free to ridicule their rulers or to demand reforms. Athens and other Greek territories were now ruled by despots. The New Comedy (as it is usually called) which amused these people is most intimately associated with Menander (c. 342–292 B.C.), a native of Athens. He is said to have written over one hundred comedies of which only one, *The Grouch* (rediscovered in 1957) remains in its entirety. Substantial portions of several other plays (*The Woman of Samos, The Shield, The Arbitration,* and *She Who Was Shorn*) also have been recovered.

A reconstruction of the Hellenistic theatre at Oropos. Painted panels could be set between the columns below, while some scenic representation may have been used in the alcoves at the rear of the raised stage. (From Ernst Fiechter, Antike Griechische Theaterbauten, *courtesy Verlag W. Kohlhammer GmbH.)*

New Comedy was divided into five parts by four choral interludes. By this time, however, the chorus was of little importance and served merely to break the play into scenes. But the major change was in subject matter, which was now drawn from the everyday life of middle-class Athenians. The plays were light in tone and perhaps most typically showed a son's attempt to marry in spite of his father's opposition. The son was usually aided by a clever slave, who was the major source of humor. Eventually the father was reconciled to the son's choice, frequently because the girl was discovered to be the long-lost child of a friend.

New Comedy used costumes which were reasonsly close copies of everyday garments, and masks which depicted basic character types of the period. Altogether, it marked a movement toward realism in staging, and toward conventionalization in depicting human behavior.

At the same time, the staging of tragedy moved further away from realism. It is to the period after 336 (usually called the Hellenistic age) that the distorted masks, high headdresses, thick-soled boots, and padded bodies of tragic actors belong. New theatres were built with stages raised from eight to thirteen feet above the level of the orchestra. The actor became increasingly the center of interest as he performed on this new stage high above the orchestra. Plays now ceased to be produced exclusively at the Dionysian festivals and were given on many other civic or religious occasions.

As the fondness for theatrical performances grew, the demand for trained personnel became so great that performers organized the Artists of Dionysus, which supplied towns with the actors, trainers for choruses, musicians, and other personnel needed for the production of plays. It set fees for services, and its rights were recognized by international agreement. Many of its members were exempt from military service, had freedom of travel, and sometimes served as ambassadors between states.

In the third century B.C. Rome began to expand as a power and came into contact with the theatre for the first time. As it absorbed the Hellenic world, it took over the theatre and transformed it in accordance with its own needs. The distinctively Greek theatre had almost disappeared by the second century B.C., and from then until the sixth century A.D. the theatre was to be principally a Roman institution.

2
Roman Theatre and Drama

Tradition has it that Rome was founded in the eighth century B.C. At first a small town of little consequence, it did not begin to assume prominence until the third century B.C. But by the beginning of the Christian era it had extended its power over most of the then known world. The Romans were remarkable for their ability to assimilate whatever attracted them elsewhere. Thus, when they found drama in the Greek colonies in Sicily and southern Italy, they imported it to Rome.

Long before regular drama was introduced, however, other types of theatrical entertainment were well established in Rome. Around 364 B.C., in an attempt to appease the gods when a plague was ravishing the city, musical and dancing performances were imported from neighboring Etruria and thereafter flourished. From the Etruscans the Romans also borrowed chariot racing, boxing, and gladiatorial contests, all of which were to be presented alongside drama, creating the circuslike atmosphere that surrounded theatre in Rome.

The first regular comedy and tragedy, by Livius Andronicus, a Greek from southern Italy, were presented in 240 B.C. Soon native-born authors

36

were writing plays, and the Greek form of drama had been naturalized in Rome.

Although a vast number of plays were written in Rome, works by only three dramatists survive: twenty-one comedies by Plautus, six comedies by Terence, and nine tragedies by Seneca. The comedies of Plautus and Terence date from about 205 to 160 B.C., the tragedies of Seneca from the first century A.D.

Roman Festivals

The *ludi,* or festivals, at which plays were performed in Rome, were not associated with the worship of Dionysus, but were of various types. Most were official religious celebrations, but some were financed by wealthy citizens for special occasions, such as the funeral of a distinguished figure or the triumphal entry of a victorious army. At first drama was given only at the *ludi Romani,* or Roman Games, and was probably restricted to a single day. But the popularity of dramatic entertainments insured their gradual expansion, and as the number of Roman festivals was increased so were the occasions for presenting plays. By 78 B.C., 48 days each year were devoted to dramatic entertainments at religious festivals. By A.D. 354, there were 175 public festival days of which 101 were devoted to theatrical spectacles.

Scene from a Roman comedy. After a wall painting in Pompeii. (From Navarre, Dionysos, *1895.)*

In the time of Plautus and Terence (the second century B.C.), plays were given principally at four festivals: the *ludi Romani*, held in September, with at least four days devoted to drama; the *ludi Plebeii*, established in 220 B.C. held in November, with at least three days given over to plays; the *ludi Apollinares*, begun in 212 B.C. and held in July, with approximately two days devoted to drama; and the *ludi Megalenses*, initiated in 204 B.C. and held in April, with six days of theatrical entertainments.

All state-financed festivals were religious celebrations in honor of the gods, but the Romans were more concerned with the letter than the spirit of the celebration. They believed that each festival, to be effective, must be carried through according to prescribed rules and that any mistake necessitated the repetition of the entire festival, including the plays. Since such repetitions were frequent, many more days were devoted to drama than might be supposed.

As in Greece, production expenses were undertaken by the state or by wealthy citizens. The Senate made an appropriation for each festival as a whole, and frequently the officials in charge contributed additional funds. These officials normally contracted for productions with the managers of theatrical companies, who then were responsible for all details of production: finding scripts, providing actors, musicians, costumes, and so on. Although each manager was assured of a certain sum of money, special incentives were provided in the form of prizes for the most successful troupes. The manager probably bought the play script outright from the author; it then remained the manager's property and might be played as often as he wished or as audiences demanded.

Admission was free to everyone, seats were not reserved, audiences were unruly, and no refreshments were available in the auditorium. Composed of a series of plays, the programs were lengthy; and, since the plays often had to compete with rival attractions, the troupes were forced to provide a kind of entertainment that would satisfy a mass audience.

The Theatre and Stage
in the Time of Plautus and Terence

Besides paying basic production expenses, the state supplied the theatre in which plays were presented. In the time of Plautus and Terence, it was a temporary one, for no permanent theatre was built in Rome until 55 B.C. Since plays were given in connection with religious festivals, each of which honored a specific god, and because each god had his own precinct and temple, it is likely that at each festival a theatre was set up near the temple of the god being honored.

Current ideas of the features of the early theatre are derived largely from the extant stone structures. Most of the surviving theatres, however, date from the first century A.D. or later, and do not necessarily provide an accurate picture of the temporary structures.

The theatre of Plautus and Terence probably included temporary scaffolds (outlining a semicircular orchestra) which provided seating for the spectators, and a long narrow stage rising about five feet above the orchestra level (the existing stages are over one hundred feet long), which was bounded by the stage house at the back and ends.

The appearance of the stage background, called the *scaenae frons*, is disputed. Some think that it was a flat wall upon which columns, statues, or other details were painted. Others believe that there were three-dimensional niches and porticoes and, for evidence, point to the many scenes in Roman comedy which require one character to remain unseen by others, even though all are on stage at the same time. This is not a wholly convincing argument, however, because stage convention in almost every period has permitted characters to see each other or not as the dramatic situation demands and has not depended on the use of places that would be considered adequate for concealment in real life. The back wall of the stage probably contained three openings, each of which might be treated, in comedy, as the entrance to a house. The stage then became a street, and the entrances at either end of the stage were assumed to be continuations of that street. Since windows and a second story are also required by some comedies, the background must have provided these as well.

Costumes and Masks for Comedy

Costumes in the Roman theatre varied with the type of play. The works of Plautus and Terence were adapted from Greek New Comedy and retained the Greek setting and garments. Other playwrights, however, wrote of Roman characters, and the costumes varied accordingly. In either case, the costumes were similar to those of daily life, although those of the more ludicrous comic characters were perhaps exaggerated.

Since most of the characters in Roman comedy were "types," the costumes also became standardized. There is evidence to suggest that certain colors were associated with particular occupations, such as yellow with courtesans and red with slaves. This conventional use of color extended to wigs as well. All of the actors wore masks, which made the doubling of parts much easier and simplified the casting of such roles as the identical twins in *The Menaechmi*. Each actor in comedy also wore a thin sandal or slipper, called a *soccus*.

Comic Playwrights

Although there were numerous comic writers in Rome, works by only two—Plautus and Terence—have survived. Titus Maccius Plautus (c. 224–

184 B.C.) is the earliest Roman playwright whose works still exist. Innumerable plays have been attributed to him, but the titles of only twenty-one have been agreed upon, all of which survive. The oldest dates from about 205 and the last from about the time of Plautus' death. Some of his most famous works are: *Amphitryon, The Pot of Gold, The Captives, The Braggart Warrior,* and *The Twin Menaechmi.*

Publius Terentius Afer, commonly called Terence, was born in 195 (some accounts say 185) and died in 159 B.C. A native of North Africa, he was brought to Rome as a slave, was later freed, and became the friend of many of the great men of his day. He wrote only six plays, all of which still exist: *The Woman of Andros, The Self-Tormenter, The Eunuch, Phormio, The Mother-in-Law,* and *The Brothers.*

The Conventions of Roman Comedy

The existing Roman comedies are adapted from Greek New Comedy. In this process of adaptation, the following changes seem to have been made (although so few New Comedies have survived that conclusions must be tentative). First, the chorus has been abandoned, doing away with the division of the texts into acts or scenes. (The divisions found in most modern editions were made in later times.) Second, the musical elements formerly associated with the chorus have been scattered throughout the plays: In some respects a Roman comedy resembled a modern musical, since certain scenes were spoken, others were recited to musical accompaniment, and a number of songs might be included. In Plautus' plays about two-thirds of the lines were accompanied by music, and the average number of songs was three. Although Terence did not use songs, music accompanied approximately half of his dialogue.

Roman comedy, like Greek New Comedy, is concerned not with political and social problems but with everyday domestic affairs. Almost invariably the plots turn on misunderstandings of one sort or another: mistaken identity (frequently involving long lost children), misunderstood motives, or deliberate deception. Sometimes the misunderstanding leads to farce, as in most of Plautus' plays, but it may also be used for sentimental effects, as when Terence emphasizes the problems of lovers or parent-child relationships.

Plautus typically employs a single plot and a complicated intrigue. In an expository prologue he explains the dramatic situation, and then he develops the farcical possibilities of the situation in the episodes that follow. Terence, on the other hand, uses a double plot, dispenses with the expository prologue, and treats his characters with sympathy and delicacy. His plays may be classified as romantic comedies, whereas those of Plautus are usually comedies of situation or farces.

Roman comedy deals with the affairs of the well-to-do middle class, and

Terra cotta of a Roman comic figure, The Thief (British Museum, Castellam Collection; print from Culver Pictures.)

the characters fall into clearly defined types: the older man who is concerned about his wealth or children, the young man who rebels against authority, the clever slave, the parasite, the courtesan, the slave dealer, and the cowardly soldier. A number of other types appear with less frequency. Of all the characters, the most famous is perhaps the slave, who, to help his master, devises all sorts of schemes, most of which go awry and lead to further complications. Very few respectable women appear in Roman comedy, and while love affairs may be the source of a play's misunderstandings, the women involved are often kept off stage. The number of characters varies from seven to fourteen, although the average is from ten to twelve.

All action takes place in the street. This often leads to the necessity of staging scenes out of doors that would more logically occur inside, and characters must frequently explain what has happened indoors. Occasionally the conventions of Roman comedy strain the modern reader's belief, but they were apparently accepted without question by Roman audiences.

The Menaechmi, probably the most popular of Plautus' plays, will be examined as an example of Roman comedy. In it, the comic possibilities of mistaken identity involving identical twins are handled with great effectiveness.

The Menaechmi

Plot and Structure. As in most of Plautus' plays, *The Menaechmi* begins with a prologue which clarifies the backgrounds of the dramatic action. All important information is repeated more than once. At the same time, Plautus works in several jokes about the theatre and tries to put the audience in a comic frame of mind.

Following the prologue, the introductory scenes of the play establish the present conditions out of which the comedy will grow: the dispute between Menaechmus I and his wife; the visit of Menaechmus I to the courtesan, Erotium, his gift to her of a dress stolen from his wife, their plans for a banquet later in the day, and the departure of Menaechmus I to the Forum; the entrance of Menaechmus II and his slave, Messenio. The remainder of the play presents a series of scenes in which the two Menaechmi are in turn mistaken for each other and accused of acts about which they know nothing. Eventually they meet, and the complications are resolved.

Menaechmus II's failure to guess the cause of his difficulties, inasmuch as he has come to Epidamnus to look for his identical twin, is sometimes said to be a weakness in the play. Indeed, even when he is brought face to face with his brother, he is unable to recognize the truth until it is pointed out by his slave. Plautus has overcome this objection in part, however, by having Messenio warn Menaechmus II that Epidamnus is

Production photograph of Plautus' The Menaechmi. Directed by Harrold Shiffler; scenery by Richard Baschky.

famous for its swindlers. Messenio even suggests that Erotium, who greets Menaechmus by name, has sent a servant to the docks to seek out information about new arrivals.

Plautus has been less successful in making Menaechmus II's search for his brother believable. Both twins are depicted as completely selfish men, and consequently it seems unlikely that Menaechmus II would devote years to seeking a brother he has not seen since early childhood. But such objections are quibbles in the light of Plautus' main intention—to entertain his audience. In performance the inconsistencies go unnoticed, and it is only on reflection that they become obvious.

Plautus subordinates everything to his main purpose. He brings characters on stage when he needs them and sends them away when the need is gone. Although this is not unusual in drama, Plautus does not always try to hide his contrivances. For example, the wife of Menaechmus I sends for her father, and he appears four lines later though he lives some distance away; in other cases, Plautus allows characters to see each other only when it suits his dramatic purposes. He also uses eavesdropping as a motivation for a number of complications.

Nevertheless, Plautus has developed his material with great economy. Not only has he eliminated everything that does not contribute to his principal aim, but he has made effective use of such devices as the stolen dress, which becomes a source of unity since it passes through the hands of practically all the characters and is used as evidence to support almost all the charges brought against the two Menaechmi.

Although Plautus' comic sense is everywhere evident, it may be seen at work especially in the reunion, which might have concluded the play on a sentimental note. Instead, the final lines give the story a twist in keeping with the sophisticated tone of earlier scenes: Menaechmus I offers all of his goods for sale—including his wife, if anyone is foolish enough to buy her.

Characters and Acting. The characters of *The Menaechmi* bear a certain resemblance to those found in the plays of Aristophanes, for they too are motivated principally by selfish and materialistic interests. With the possible exceptions of Messenio and the father, none of the characters may be considered admirable. Unlike Aristophanes, however, Plautus has little interest in social satire. He concentrates on the ridiculous situation without exploring its significance. Consequently, when his characters indulge in adultery, stealing, or deception, they merely contribute to the overall tone of good-humored cynicism.

As in most Roman comedy, the characters in *The Menaechmi* are types rather than individuals. Some roles are summed up in their names: Peniculus (or "Brush") suggests the parasite's ability to sweep the table clean; the cook is called Cylindrus (or "Roller"), and the courtesan is named Erotium (or "Lovey"). Each character has a restricted number of motivations: The twins wish to satisfy their physical desires; the wife wants to reform her husband; the father desires to keep peace in the family; and the quack doctor is seeking a patient upon whom he can practice a lengthy and costly treatment. In spite of the restricted number of traits, however, each character is sufficiently delineated for its function in the play.

The ten speaking roles of *The Menaechmi* could easily be performed by a company of six actors. In the Roman theatre, all parts were played by men. Extras (used in nonspeaking roles) were employed as needed. The play does not require actors who are skilled in the subtle portrayal of a wide range of emotions. Rather, they must have that highly developed comic technique that produces precision in the timing of business and dialogue. The scenes of quarreling, drunkenness, and madness indicate that physical nimbleness is essential.

Scenery and Music. Since *The Menaechmi* is set in a street before two houses, the stage and its architectural background would be sufficient to meet the scenic demands. The frequent eavesdropping and the failure of characters to see each other suggest that there may have been alcoves or projections in which the actors could conceal themselves, but these would by no means have been essential.

The costumes were based on those of everyday Greek life, but were conventionalized according to social class, occupation, age, and sex. Each of the characters also wore a mask and wig. Since the performances took place in unroofed theatres and during the day, no artificial illumination was required.

Because the music is now lost, it is sometimes difficult for the modern reader to remember that music played an important role in the original productions of all Roman comedies. It was performed on a "flute" with two pipes, each about twenty inches long, which was bound to the performer's head so as to leave his hands free to work the stops. The flute player was on stage throughout the performance and supposedly moved about to accompany first one character and then another. Well over half of the dialogue in *The Menaechmi* was accompanied by music, and a number of the characters probably had "entering" songs on their first appearance. The total effect must have been comparable to that of present-day musical comedy.

Thus, *The Menaechmi* is a farcical comedy designed primarily to divert an audience. It is very successful in fulfilling this aim, and the play's worth is clearly demonstrated by the fact that it has continued to entertain readers and audiences throughout the more than two thousand years that have passed since its first presentation.

Other Roman Drama

The surviving Roman comedy is of the type called *fabula palliata* (*fabula* means play, and *palliata* designates a Greek garment worn by the characters). There were, however, several other kinds of Roman drama. The *fabula togata,* or comedy on Roman themes, while taking its form and techniques from Greek New Comedy, drew its material from native life.

Tragedy also played an important role in the Roman theatre. As with comedy, Greece provided the models upon which the Roman playwrights built. Also like comedy, tragedy is usually divided into two types according to whether it used Greek or Roman themes. The former is called *fabula crepidata,* and the latter *fabula praetexta.* Both types featured horrifying plots, characters almost totally good or totally depraved, and bombastic speeches.

The only Roman tragedies that now exist are based on Greek themes and are the work of Lucius Annaeus Seneca (4 B.C.–65 A.D.), a philosopher and satirist, and one of Nero's principal advisers. Nine of his tragedies are

An ivory statuette of a tragic actor, probably Roman, although the Greek tragic actor of the Hellenistic period probably wore similar costumes and masks. Note the high headdress, distorted features of the mask, and thick-soled boots, concealed beneath the robe. The statuette stands on two pegs, by means of which it was attached to a base, now missing. (Reprinted from Monumenti Inediti, *Vol. XI, 1879.)*

extant, of which five are adapted from plays by Eurpidies. A tenth play is sometimes attributed to Seneca, but is undoubtedly the work of a later author.

Seneca was not a professional dramatist and his plays probably were not staged. Nevertheless, because they were to be a major influence on Renaissance tragedy, the characteristics of his work are important.

First, Seneca's plays are divided into five acts by choral interludes. These interludes, however, are largely irrelevant and can be eliminated without serious loss. Although Renaissance dramatists seldom used a chorus, they did adopt Seneca's five-act structure.

Second, Seneca wrote elaborately constructed speeches which often resemble forensic addresses, and his work as a whole tends to emphasize rhetorical display. The presence of similar qualities in Elizabethan drama may be attributed in part to his influence.

Third, Seneca, a moral philosopher, filled his plays with *sententiae* (brief moral conclusions, resembling proverbs, about human behavior) and sensational deeds which illustrate the terrible effects of unrestrained emotion. The characters often lack self-control and set out to perform evil acts from which they cannot be dissuaded. Thus, moral lessons are taught through horrifying examples and sententiae, a practice followed by many Renaissance dramatists.

Fourth, Seneca's plays show many violent actions. In *Oedipus*, Jocasta kills herself on stage by ripping open her abdomen; in another play a dismembered body is reassembled; and in *Thyestes* the flesh of children is served at a banquet. Such deeds of horror are found also in many plays of the Renaissance.

Fifth, Seneca is preoccupied with magic and death, as may be seen from his frequent use of ghosts and magical rites. This emphasis on the close connection between the human and supernatural world may be found in Renaissance drama as well.

Sixth, each of Seneca's main characters is dominated by a single motive which drives him to his doom. Most frequently the motivations, such as revenge, are either evil or obsessive. This practice was to be taken up by writers in the Renaissance.

Seventh, many of Seneca's technical devices, such as the soliloquy, aside, and *confidant* (a character whose main function is to listen to and advise the protagonist), were to influence later dramatists.

Today Seneca's plays are usually treated condescendingly. But they cannot be ignored, for when Renaissance writers turned to the past, they were attracted to him rather than the Greek tragedians.

In addition to comedy and tragedy, a number of minor dramatic types were performed in the Roman theatre. After the first century B.C. there is no record of an author making a living from regular comedy or tragedy. Rather, the stage was taken over by minor dramatic forms, especially the *fabula Atellana*, mime, and pantomime.

The *fabula Atellana*, a short farce, was one of the oldest of Roman the-

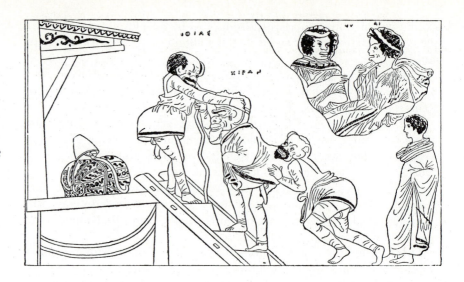

The fabula Atellana *and mime were probably influenced by the* phlyax *of Sicily and southern Italy.* Phlyax *(a form of mime) dealt primarily with mythological travesty and farcical situations; it flourished c. 400-200 B.C. As this vase painting shows, the costumes were similar to those of Greek Old Comedy. Note also the stage with steps leading up to it. (From Baumeister,* Denkmaler des Klassischen Altertums, *1889.)*

atrical forms, having been imported from Atella, an area near Naples. It appears to have employed a set of stock characters: Maccus, a fool or stupid clown; Bucco, a glutton or braggart; Pappus, a foolish old man who was easily deceived; and Dossenus, a cunning swindler and glutton, who was probably hunchbacked. Originally, apparently, the dialogue was improvised. The plots revolved around various forms of trickery, cheating, and general buffoonery in a rural setting. Music and dance also played an important part. After the *fabula Atellana* was converted into a literary form in the first century B.C., the short farce became the most popular of all dramatic types.

The mime may be traced back to the sixth century B.C. in Greece, but the earliest record of its appearance in Rome is found in 211 B.C. Many mime troupes traveled widely and performed on makeshift stages. Their plays were short, topical, farcical, and, in the beginning, improvised. While the mime had certain features in common with the *fabula Atellana*, there were also important differences: The female roles were played by women (thus the mime was the first form to make use of actresses), the actors did not wear masks, and its subjects were primarily drawn from urban life.

Like the Atellan farce, the mime became a literary form in the first century B.C. The subjects of the later mime were often adultery and unnatural vices, and the language was frequently indecent. These characteristics set the rising Christian religion against the mime troupes, who retaliated by ridiculing the sacraments and beliefs of the church. Thus, the mime was more responsible than any other form for the opposition of Christians to the theatre.

One other dramatic type, the pantomime, was also popular in late Rome. This silent interpretive dance was performed by a single actor who played many roles, each of which was indicated by a mask with a closed mouth. A chorus narrated the story, which was usually serious and drawn from mythology, while the action was accompanied by music, played by an orchestra composed of flutes, pipes, cymbals and other percussion instruments. In late Rome, pantomime largely replaced tragedy and was especially popular with the ruling classes.

The degeneration of the theatre under the Roman Empire—which superseded the Republic in 27 B.C.—is further illustrated by the fact that gladiatorial contests were sometimes held in the orchestras and on the stages of theatres. Furthermore, in many theatres the orchestras could be flooded for water ballets or sea battles (called *naumachia*). More frequently, however, such spectacles as animal baiting, animal–human fights, chariot racing, acrobatic shows, gladiatorial contests, and sea battles were held elsewhere—especially in amphitheatres and circuses. Nevertheless, the theatre increasingly had to compete with these often bloodthirsty and indecent entertainments, especially from the first century A.D. onward. Although plays such as those by Plautus and Terence may have been staged occasionally, the usual theatrical fare during the Empire was mime, pantomime, and nondramatic spectacle.

A somewhat fanciful reconstruction of a naumachia. *(From Laumann,* La Machinerie au Théâtre, *1897.)*

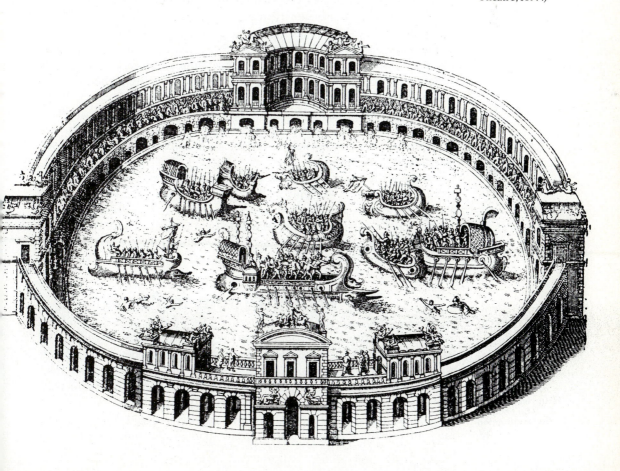

The Theatre Building
of the Roman Empire

The permanent theatres of both Greece and Rome were constructed after their great dramas had been written. The first permanent theatre on the Roman plan was built at Pompeii about 75 B.C.; Rome itself did not have a permanent theatre until 55 B.C. After this time new theatres were built wherever Rome's dominance extended, and most of the existing Greek theatres were remodeled along Roman lines. The latter structures are often called Greco-Roman theatres, since they display characteristics of both types.

The typical Roman theatre was constructed on level ground—unlike the Greek, which used a hillside to support its seats. The stage house and the auditorium were of the same height and formed a single architectural unit. (In a Greek theatre, the scene building and the auditorium were not joined and were, in effect, two separate structures.) The orchestra of a Roman theatre was a half-circle with the front of the stage set on its diameter and the seats of the auditorium following the lines of its circumference. The auditorium typically seated between 10,000 and 15,000 spectators, although some are said to have accommodated many more.

The stage itself was raised about five feet above the level of the orchestra, and measured one hundred to three hundred feet in length and twenty to forty feet in depth. It had a permanent architectural background called the *scaenae frons*) with a minimum of three doors in the rear wall (though frequently there were more), and at least one at either end of the stage. The *scaenae frons* was two or three stories high, was decorated with columns, niches, statues, and porticoes, and, in some cases, was gilded or painted.

Two other features distinguish the Roman from the Greek stage. First, some time between 133 and 56 B.C., a curtain was introduced in the Roman theatre. It was dropped into a slot at the front of the stage at the beginning of a performance and was raised at the end. Second, the Roman stage had a roof, which served at least two functions: it protected the elaborate *scaenae frons* from the weather, and it improved the acoustics.

The End of Drama in Rome

The immorality and decadence of the Roman theatre alienated the early Christians. At first Christianity was of little importance, but after it was recognized as the semiofficial religion of Rome by the Emperor Constantine, who ruled from A.D. 312 to 337, the theatre encountered increasing difficulties. Despite restrictions, however, performances continued to be popular and their eventual abandonment seems to have been a result more of invasions from northern tribes than of the moral scruples of

Romans. By 467, Rome itself had twice been sacked. Although festivals were revived for a time, the last recorded performance is found in A.D. 533.

The accomplishment of the Roman theatre is not great when compared with the Greek, but it did produce three playwrights of importance—Plautus, Terence, and Seneca. Furthermore, its drama and theatre were to be major influences on Renaissance writers and theatre artists, and consequently they helped to shape the European theatre of later times.

A reconstruction of the theatre at Ostia. It is one of the oldest permanent Roman theatres, having been built between 30 and 12 B.C. (From D'Espouy, Fragments d'Architecture Antique. *Vol. I, 1901.)*

Roman Theatre
and Drama

3

The Middle Ages

Although it is sometimes stated that theatrical activities were completely suppressed during the centuries that followed the fall of Rome, numerous contemporary documents attest to the continued presence of *mimes, histriones,* and *ioculatores* (Latin terms for actors). Little is known about these performers, however, for the opposition of the church made it difficult for them to entertain openly. Actors were forbidden the sacraments of the church, and, between the sixth and tenth centuries, religious authorities issued frequent injunctions against both presenting and attending any type of theatrical entertainment. In addition to surreptitious theatrical activities, many pagan rites and festivals containing dramatic elements also persisted despite Christian opposition. Spring fertility rites were performed throughout Europe, and midwinter ceremonies designed to revive the waning sun also were common. Some historians have argued that the church introduced its own dramatic ceremonies in order to combat the appeal of these pagan rites.

Regardless of the type and extent of these activities, the theatre did not develop openly or extensively until the church began to make use of dramatic interludes in its own services. This innovation, begun in the tenth century, was the first step in restoring the theatre to a respected place in society, although this was not the church's intention.

Drama in the Church

It is not clear why the church began to use dramatized episodes, but the most likely answer is that it wished to make its lessons more graphic. Furthermore, since the majority of persons could not understand Latin (the language of the church), spectacle had long been an important means of vivifying church doctrine, and dramatic interludes were merely a further development of this tendency.

The organization of the church year around the principal events of the Old and New Testaments also encouraged the development of drama. The calendar begins in November with Advent, a period of preparation for the birth and second coming of Christ; next there is Christmas and Epiphany (the revelation of Christ to the Gentiles); then, after the forty days of Lent, which symbolize the wanderings of both the Israelites and Christ in the wilderness, come the commemorations connected with the

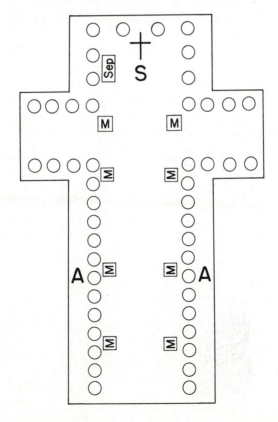

A ground plan of a medieval cathedral. A —aisles. M —mansions. S —sanctuary. Sep— sepulchre.

death and resurrection of Christ, culminating in Easter; Easter is followed by Ascension and Pentecost, or Whitsunday, the traditional time for baptisms. Thus, the church calendar itself suggested the dramatization of incidents appropriate to each season. Easter was the first to be given dramatic treatment in church services, while other events were dramatized later. The majority of church plays, however, always centered around Christmas and Easter.

The oldest existing Easter trope is the *Quem Quaeritis* (c. 92 A.D.), reproduced here in its entirety. (A trope is any interpolation into an existing test.)

ANGELS: Whom seek ye in the tomb, O Christians?
THE THREE MARYS: Jesus of Nazareth, the crucified,
O Heavenly Beings.
ANGELS: He is not here, he is risen as he foretold.
Go and announce that he is risen from the tomb.

This passage, found in the introductory portion of the Easter Mass, was probably merely antiphonal (that is, sung responsively by two groups) rather than acted out. But the step into drama was soon taken. The earliest extant playlet, complete with directions for its performance, is found in the *Regularis Concordia* (or *Monastic Agreement*) compiled between 965 and 975 by Ethelwold, Bishop of Winchester (England). By the end of the tenth century, such plays were common in many parts of Europe.

For two hundred years drama was to remain within the church, for not until about 1200 were religious plays performed out of doors. Liturgical drama spread as far east as Russia and from Scandinavia in the north to Italy and Spain in the south. The length and complexity of the plays differed considerably, some being only a single episode a few lines in length, others much longer and including a number of related events. Next in number to the plays dealing with the Easter season are those associated with Christmas and Epiphany, but numerous other biblical subjects were also dramatized.

Drama was not produced in all churches but was confined as a rule to cathedrals and monasteries—in other words, to those churches that had enough clergy to present plays, since the actors, and sometimes the audiences, were members of the monastic community.

In the church a number of staging conventions evolved that were to remain in use throughout the Middle Ages. The acting space was divided into two parts: the *mansions* and the *platea*. The mansions (also called stations, seats, or *sedes*) were simple scenic devices for indicating the location of incidents. For example, a throne might be used to suggest the residence of Pilate. Each place was represented by a different mansion, and all remained in view throughout the play. Since the action could not be performed in the limited space provided by the typical mansion, the actors used as much of the adjacent floor area as they needed. Often the same space was used in many different scenes. This generalized acting

area was called the *platea* (or sometimes the place or playne). Thus, a series of mansions was arranged around a neutral playing space, and the performers moved from one mansion to another as the action demanded.

A page from the manuscript of the Valenciennes Passion Play, with the simultaneous depiction of several scenes. (Courtesy of the Bibliothèque Nationale.)

Drama Outside the Church

It is unclear why performances began to be given out of doors. It has been suggested that the plays had begun to interfere with the liturgy and that drama had developed as far as it could within the restricted confines of church services. Regardless of the motives, around 1200, plays began to be performed outside as well as inside churches. Although plays continued to be presented in churches for another three hundred years, their subsequent history is of little interest since they did not significantly affect future developments.

We know little about outdoor performances between 1200 and 1350, perhaps because the productions were no longer integral parts of church

The Middle Ages

services but had not yet been taken over by secular organizations. During the fourteenth century, when lengthy vernacular religious plays appeared, information becomes much more plentiful. The usual view has been that the vernacular drama came into existence through a gradual process in which individual, short, liturgical plays, having first been moved out of doors, were brought together to form long plays that were then translated into the vernacular languages and performed by laymen. Recently, this view has been challenged by those who suggest that the cycles developed quite independently of the liturgical drama and that the similarity between the two forms is attributable not to direct descent but to common sources—the Bible and other religious and devotional literature.

Regardless of the reasons, a number of significant changes had occurred in religious drama by 1400. Outdoor plays had come to be staged primarily during the spring and summer months, in large part because of favorable weather. The most usual time was Corpus Christi (the date of which may vary from May 23 to June 24), but other popular times were Easter, Whitsunday, or the feast day of a city's patron saint. Another important change was the abandonment of Latin in favor of the vernacular tongues. This change not only led to the substitution of spoken for chanted dialogue, but also made the use of laymen as actors possible.

With the vernacular drama came secular control over most aspects of production. In some areas, trade guilds became the principal producers of plays; in others, municipal authorities assumed control; in still others, special societies were formed to present religious dramas.

Many scholars have argued that the church abandoned the drama when it was moved outdoors. But this older view seems to be incorrect for while the church participated less and less in the actual process of production, its approval continued to be necessary. Plays dealt with religious matters, and the church could not afford to ignore such powerful teaching instruments. Furthermore, each trade guild had its own priest, patron saint, and chapel, and was not entirely a secular organization. Thus, it is likely that the production of plays continued to be a cooperative venture, in which the church supplied approval and encouragement while secular groups provided the money and personnel.

Under this arrangement, the medieval theatre flourished. From about 1350 to 1550 it steadily grew in complexity and technical proficiency.

Staging Techniques

The stages on which the vernacular plays were performed might be either fixed or movable. The placement of the fixed stages varied considerably, but most typically they were set against buildings on one side of a town square. They might also extend down the middle of a square (and

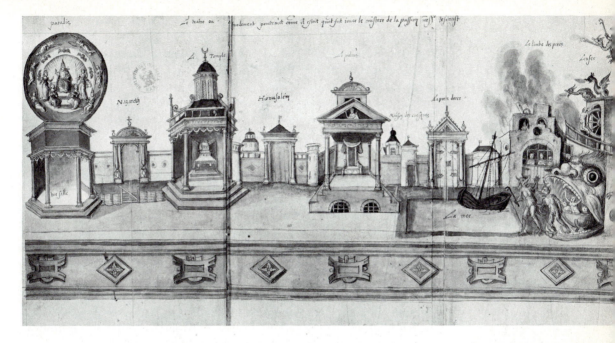

The stage for the Passion Play produced at Valenciennes, France, in 1547. From the left the various mansions represent: Paradise, Nazareth, the Temple, Jerusalem, a palace, the Golden door, the sea, and Hell's mouth. (From a manuscript in the Bibliothèque Nationale; reproduced through their courtesy.)

be viewed from three sides), or they might be set up in an ancient Roman amphitheatre or other circular place (and be viewed in the round). The movable stage was usually a wagon on which mansions were mounted and moved from one location to another. The movable stage was exploited most fully in England and Spain, but either type of stage might be found throughout Europe.

Regardless of the type of stage, the basic approach to production was the same everywhere. First, the scenic conventions were those inherited from the church—a series of mansions abutting onto a generalized acting area (the *platea*). Second, the script was composed of a series of playlets, each more or less complete in itself and connected with the others only because all were taken from the Bible or some other religious source; the order in which the playlets were performed was determined by the original source rather than by any causal relationship among them. Third, every production involved three planes of being—Heaven, Earth and Hell—and all were represented scenically. Spatially, the different realms might be arranged either horizontally or vertically. The typical platform stage used a horizontal placement, with Heaven always on the right and Hell on the left (as one faced the audience). The earthly scenes were staged between these two points. On the wagons Heaven, Earth and Hell were often arranged vertically, although a single wagon seldom depicted all three levels. Fourth, the greatest attention was devoted to special

The Middle Ages

55

effects, which were made convincingly realistic. Although such efforts may be explained in part by a love of spectacle, an equally important factor was the desire to embody (without raising doubts about) the miraculous events described in the Bible. Regardless of their motives, medieval producers welcomed the challenge posed by such episodes as Christ walking on the water and being lifted up to the top of a temple. Special pains were also taken in the depiction of Hell and its horrors. The entrance to Hell was often represented as the mouth of a fire-breathing monster (hence the name *hell mouth*), out of which fire, smoke, and the cries of the damned issued.

To achieve these special effects, a considerable amount of stage machinery (called *secrets*) was invented. Much of it was operated from beneath the stage, and numerous trap doors also permitted the appearance and disappearance of persons and objects. For the scenes which required "flying," pulleys and ropes were attached to adjoining buildings. The overhead machinery was sometimes hidden by cloths painted to represent clouds or the sky.

Such machinery was not the work of inexperienced amateurs. As effects became more and more elaborate, machinists and stage managers became increasingly skilled. For a play staged at Mons in 1501, two technicians were hired to construct the secrets; seventeen people were needed to operate the Hell machinery alone; five men were paid to paint the scenery; and four actor-prompters were employed both to act and to help with the staging. Thus, while the majority of persons connected with a production were amateurs, other theatre workers eventually achieved at least semi-professional status as productions grew in complexity.

Obviously special effects could be more extensive on a fixed than on a movable stage. It is not surprising, therefore, that the stationary stages had more elaborate stage machinery than the pageant wagons did.

It was not, however, the sole aim of the medieval stage to produce convincing special effects, for these realistic features were used in conjunction with fragmentary scenery and symbolic devices. No place was depicted in its entirety: a small building might represent Jerusalem, a chair under a portico might become the palace of Herod. Moreover, all of the places needed for the play were present simultaneously, thus further preventing the illusion of a real place. Typically, even the wagon stages carried more than one mansion.

Just as the stage usually included mansions representing Heaven, Earth and Hell, so too the costumes had to distinguish between the inhabitants of the three realms. God, the angels, the saints, and certain biblical characters wore church garments, often with added accessories. (For example, angels wore church robes with wings attached, while God was dressed as a high church official.) Each of the saints and important biblical personages was also associated with a specific symbol. (For example, St. Peter was identified by his keys to the Kingdom of Heaven.) Since the audience was familiar with such visual symbolism, the mere display of an emblem served to identify the character. Secular, earthly characters wore the contemporary medieval garments appropriate to their ranks, for there was no attempt to achieve historical accuracy. The greatest imagination went into costuming the devils, who were usually fancifully conceived with wings, claws, beaks, horns, or tails. While Heaven and its representatives were intended to inspire awe and reverence, Hell and its inhabitants were expected to arouse fear and scorn. The human beings who dwelt between were representative of the common man caught between the forces of good and evil.

Conventions of Thought Affecting Medieval Drama

The Fool and the Devil. From a woodcut in Sebastian Brant's Ship of Fools, *published in 1497.*

Since we no longer think in medieval terms, some attempt to recapture the outlook of that time is essential, for otherwise its drama is apt to seem childish or naïve. In that period, man was said to participate in two kinds of time: eternal and temporal. God, the Devil, and man's immortal soul exist in eternity—which, unlike man's physical existence, has neither beginning nor end. If man considers only his earthly life, therefore, time may appear to be limited, but if he contemplates God, he sees that life is merely a preparation for eternity, in which his immortal soul participates. When he leaves his earthly existence, he enters into either eternal salvation or damnation. Thus temporal existence is a short interlude, a preface to the ultimate reality, which is eternal. The central part of the stage then—the earthly and temporal realm—was framed by Heaven and Hell, the eternal realms, one of which man must choose.

For the medieval mind, earthly time and place were relatively unimportant. The historical period or geographical location of an event were insignificant when set against the framework of eternity. Consequently, little sense of history is evident in medieval plays. Audiences did not consider it anachronistic when ancient Israelites or Roman soldiers were dressed in medieval garments, or when Old Testament characters referred to Christian saints.

The fluidity of time is also reflected in the structure of medieval cycles, in which a series of short plays often dramatized biblical material beginning with Creation and concluding with the Last Judgment. Although not all cycles were so ambitious, most of them encompassed lengthy segments of time and a variety of events. Seldom was any causal relationship established among plays or even among the incidents of a single play. Again, however, such techniques are not necessarily signs of poor playwriting. For the medieval mind, Providence played a large part in human affairs, and events were thought to happen simply because God willed them. Since an audience brought this frame of reference to performances, it did not expect or need to see it overtly dramatized in the plays.

An episode from "The Creation of Noah's Ark," The Wakefield Mystery Plays. *(Production photo courtesy of the Mermaid Theatre at Puddle Dock, London.)*

Another factor which sometimes puzzles the modern reader is the presence of comic elements in religious plays. Our austere view of religion, however, dates primarily from the sixteenth century. Prior to that time, the church permitted many satirical elements in its festivals. The Feast of Fools, for example, was a kind of New Year's rite during which the minor clergy were allowed to ridicule the mass and church officials. It is not surprising, then, that comic elements were included in plays. Usually, however, the comic was restricted to devils, evil persons, or nonbiblical, lower-class characters.

The Mystery Play

The mystery play, which drew its subjects from scripture, was the major form of medieval drama, being produced throughout western Europe. Its name was probably derived from *mystère*, the French word used in the Middle Ages to designate any trade or craft. Thus, "mystery" came to mean those plays produced by the trade guilds. Other names were used elsewhere. In Italy *sacre rappresentazione* and in Spain *auto sacramentale* were the common designations.

The dramas most readily available for study are those written in English. Although cycles of mystery plays were produced in over one hundred English towns during the Middle Ages, most of the existing plays are from four cycles: the York, containing forty-eight plays; the Chester, containing twenty-four; the Townley manuscript plays, or Wakefield cycle, containing thirty-two plays; and the *Ludus Coventriae,* or N Town cycle, containing forty-two plays (The blank was filled in with the name of the town where the cycle was to be performed, although some scholars now think the plays originated in Lincoln.)

Staging of Cycle Plays in England During the Fifteenth Century

English plays were usually staged as a part of the Corpus Christi festival, the essential feature of which was a procession through a town with the consecrated bread and wine (or host). This custom may explain why several towns in northern England adopted the processional form of staging—that is, the mounting of plays on wagons, and the movement of these wagons to a series of places throughout the town.

Although plays were not given each year, they were presented at reasonably regular intervals, and on those occasions the Corpus Christi festival was extended, since an average of four or five days was needed to perform the cycles. The town council decided whether the plays were to be in-

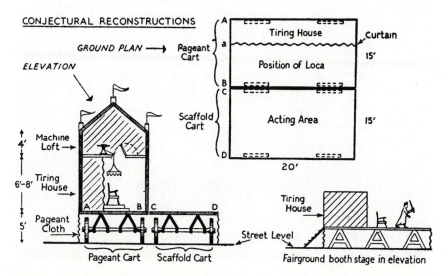

A conjectural reconstruction of an English pageant wagon and stage. From Glynne Wickham's Early English Stages, *Volume I, 1959. (Courtesy of Columbia University Press and Mr. Wickham.)*

cluded, and the guilds assumed primary responsibility for producing them.

Each trade guild was assigned one play, or, in the case of small guilds, two or more might produce a play together. The master copy of the cycle, which had the approval of the church, was retained by the town council, and each guild was cautioned to stage its play with care and to remain faithful to the text. A fine was imposed if a guild was proven negligent.

No adequate description of the pageant wagons has been preserved. They were probably as large as the narrow city streets would permit and were designed to meet the requirements of specific plays (each guild always presented the same play). A wagon almost always had to carry two or more mansions, and might include machinery for special effects as well.

Reconstruction of a medieval pageant wagon (From Sharp's A Dissertation on the Pageants or Dramatic Mysteries, *1825.)*

In some plays, places or characters were suddenly revealed during the action; in others, persons or objects ascended or descended either from above or beneath the stage. The account books of the guilds show sizable expenditures for painted drops, curtains, properties, special effects, and for the pageant wagon itself.

Scholars disagree about where the acting took place. Some argued that it occurred only on the wagon; others believe that the actors used both the wagon and the street; and still others state that the wagons were pulled up alongside a platform, which served as the acting area, or *platea,* while the wagon provided the mansions. The final argument is a persuasive one, since the action of many plays is too complex to be staged on a wagon that also carried scenery. It appears unlikely that very many scenes were played in the street itself, for the standing spectators would have obstructed the view of much of the audience. On the other hand, the actors did make occasional use of the street, and it is possible that the wagon, a platform, and the street were all used as acting areas.

The actors were primarily amateurs, although they may have received some pay for their services. Account books indicate that they were provided with considerable quantities of food and drink during the rehearsal period. A few actors were paid large sums, however, and it is likely that these were skilled performers who played the leading roles, helped with the staging, and coached the other actors.

Most characters could be costumed from either the ecclesiastical, military, or civil garments of the day, but occasionally special costumes were required for devils and other exotic figures. Music figured prominently in some dramas and was often used to fill the interval between plays. For the latter purpose, professional musicians were often hired.

Each guild presented its play at several places, the first of which was usually the church or monastery. The other locations were chosen by the town council. Thus, audiences gathered at a number of points and the plays were brought to them in a manner that combined a parade and dramatic entertainment.

The Second Shepherd's Play

The Second Shepherds' Play is probably the best known of the English cycle plays. It is the thirteenth part of the Wakefield cycle, from which thirty-two plays—ranging from Creation to the Last Judgment—have survived. It is called the "Second" Shepherds' Play because the surviving manuscript includes two plays (of which this is the later) on the same subject.

Plot and Structure. Most of *The Second Shepherds' Play* is an elaboration of a single sentence from the *New Testament* (Luke 2:8): "And there were in the same country shepherds abiding in the field, keeping watch over their flock by night." This hint has been transformed into a medieval story rich in contemporary details and farcical humor. The number of shepherds is not specified in the Bible, but three are used in the play, probably to suggest a parallel with the three wise men.

Like most medieval dramas, *The Second Shepherds' Play* has an early point of attack. It introduces in leisurely fashion the characters and situation as each shepherd in turn complains about a different problem: general social conditions, marriage, insufficient food and drink. The opening is made even more casual by the inclusion of a song.

Yet this simple beginning serves several purposes that may not be readily apparent. First, through the various complaints, it depicts a world that needs some correction—one that stands in need of Christ's coming. Second, it relates the biblical story to the contemporary scene and thereby to the audience. Thus, the coming of Christ is placed in the atmosphere of the Middle Ages. Third, the introduction prepares for an unusual occurrence through the third Shepherd's recital of abnormal conditions, concluding with:

> We that walk in the nights our cattle to keep,
> We see sudden sights when other men sleep.

There is little forward movement in the story, however, until Mak appears.

Mak's reputation as a trickster is established immediately by the Shepherds' concern for their sheep. Soon, however, they all lie down for the night. When the Shepherds are safely asleep, Mak steals a sheep and carries it home to his wife, Gill. As a precaution against discovery, she suggests that they place the sheep in a cradle and pretend that it is a newborn baby. Mak then goes back to the fields and lies down as before.

The Shepherds awake and, with difficulty, arouse Mak, who has been feigning sleep. After Mak takes his leave, the Shepherds discover that a sheep is missing. They immediately suspect Mak and search the house while Mak protests his innocence and Gill counterfeits postchildbirth pains. As they are leaving, one of the Shepherds remembers the child and insists upon presenting it a gift; the sheep is discovered and Mak is tossed in a blanket as punishment. This portion of the play is closely related to the medieval farce (to be discussed later) in its characterizations of Mak and Gill, in the comic inventiveness of its plot, and in its resolution. It also shows much greater skill in writing than other parts of the play.

After recovering their sheep, the Shepherds return to the field. A marked change now takes place as the tone of the play becomes serious and devotional. An Angel appears and announces the birth of Christ; the Shepherds go to Bethlehem, worship the child, and present their gifts. Christ has appeared within a familiar scene; his promise is not to some forgotten past but to the immediate present.

Themes and Ideas. *The Second Shepherds' Play* has frequently been viewed as a work composed of two unrelated stories of sharply contrasting tone. A close examination of the work, however, reveals that it is unified through its themes and ideas. The most important of these are man's

depravity and the promise of salvation, placed side by side in the form of a demonstration.

The Shepherds represent the common man; they are involved first with Mak (the godless man) and then with the Christ child (God incarnate). The many parallels between the two stories suggest that this juxtaposition is intentional. In both there is a father, mother, and child. The child is in a cradle; one "child" is a lamb, and the other is Christ, the "Lamb of God." The Shepherds present gifts to both. The difference between the two stories is to be found in the significance of the events: one shows a world in need of Christ, and the other portrays his arrival. Succeeding plays in the cycle dramatized both the life and the teachings of Christ.

Characterization and Acting. There are seven roles—not counting the infant—in *The Second Shepherds' Play*. All parts were played by men, and the same actor could have played both Gill and Mary.

Little is indicated about the physical appearance of the characters. All are adults of unspecified age except the third Shepherd—a boy—and the Christ child—probably represented by a doll. The sociological traits are also limited. The Shepherds, Mak, and Gill are peasants; it is implied that Mak lives by stealing.

Psychological characterization is slight but effectively drawn. The three

Details from Denis von Alsloot's "The Triumph of Isabella," 1615. Although these wagons were not used for play production, they may be similar to those employed in staging the English cycle plays. (Courtesy of the Victoria and Albert Museum. Crown copyright.)

The Middle Ages
63

Shepherds are differentiated primarily through their opening monologues, in which each is concerned with a different problem. All are generous, as may be seen from their reactions to the supposed child of Gill and to the Christ child, and from their decision not to prosecute Mak. (In medieval times, stealing was a capital offense.) A good impulse, the desire to give the "child" a gift, leads to the discovery of Mak's guilt.

Mak is a clever knave, who is somewhat henpecked and cowardly. Gill is shrewish and clever; it is her idea to put the lamb in the cradle and pass it off as a child. The role of Mak requires more acting skill than any other. The comic plot progresses principally through him, and he must convey a rather wide range of responses, many of which are supposed to communicate one impression to the Shepherds and another to the audience. Since the sheep-stealing scenes are meant to be comic, both Mak and Gill must be able to convey the ludicrous aspects of the situation.

The Shepherds' roles, while longer than those of Mak and Gill, are more nearly serious and demand little exaggeration. They must project the humorous points in the opening speeches and be able to pass from the bantering tone of the first part to the devout tone of the final scene. There is considerable physical action in the play and, with the exception of the Angel's appearance, all of it is reasonably realistic. Transitional action, however, is indicated only sketchily. For example, the Shepherds lie down and appear to fall asleep instantly. The actors, therefore, must supply many details or the action will seem abrupt. Because they each have only one speech, Mary and the Angel are characterized least and seem especially stiff and stereotyped when compared with the other characters.

Most of the actors must sing. The Shepherds have a song in the introductory scene and another at the end of the play. Mak sings a lullaby to his stolen sheep, and the Angel sings *Gloria in excelsis*.

Spectacle and Music. *The Second Shepherds' Play* calls for three locales: the fields, Mak's house, and the stable at Bethlehem. One mansion might be sufficient, however, since the fields really require no background, and the other two are so similar in scenic demands that the same mansion could be used in both.

No doubt the mansion used for Mak's house and the stable was equipped with a curtain which could be drawn to reveal the interior. Neither Gill nor Mary is visible throughout the play; rather each is "revealed" at the right moment. Mak's house must have a door (at which he knocks), a cradle, and a bed. All of these would be appropriate items for the stable (the bed for Mak's house need only be made of straw).

It is difficult to imagine this play being performed on a wagon which would, at the very least, have to be divided into two parts. It is more logical to suppose that the wagon carried only the necessary scenic background and could be pulled up alongside another platform which would serve as the platea, or generalized acting area. Such an arrangement would effectively solve most of the difficulties of staging.

The costume demands for the play are simple: for the Shepherds, Mak, and Gill, the everyday contemporary dress of the lower classes; for the Angel, an ecclesiastical garment with wings added; for Mary, an upper-class medieval garment (the traditional way of representing her in art by this time) and the symbols associated with her.

The musical requirements are also relatively simple. The Shepherds' first song and Mak's lullaby would have been contemporary popular songs. The *Gloria,* sung by the Angel, and the Shepherds' final song would have been taken from contemporary church music.

Although the staging demands are simple, *The Second Shepherds' Play* has a considerable range of visual and aural appeals. Its variety makes it an excellent example of that combination of teaching and entertainment which was typical of medieval drama.

Production on Fixed Stages

The staging of *The Second Shepherds' Play* is relatively simple in comparison with most productions given on fixed stages, where all the parts of a cycle were performed on a single platform. The latter arrangement made the whole process far more complex than in the former, where responsibility for each part of a cycle was assumed by a different guild, each of whom worked more or less independently to mount its play on its own pageant wagon. When wagons were used, the actual performance required virtually no coordination beyond arranging the wagons in proper sequence. But for productions on fixed stages, coordination at every step was crucial. Not only did coordination include financial arrangements but also extended as well to casting, rehearsals, the acquisition of scenery, and the perfection of special effects. Furthermore, a place capable of holding the entire audience at once had to be found. (The plays mounted on pageant wagons were performed at several locations scattered throughout the town.) Because of all these problems, the responsibility for an entire production was usually assumed by a committee, although it often delegated the actual work of staging to a small group or even to one person.

But if the managerial problems of the fixed stage were great, so were its potentials for scope and spectacle, and these were increasingly exploited. *The Acts of the Apostles,* presented at Bourges in 1536, for example, had a cast of three hundred and required forty days to perform; the passion play staged at Valenciennes in 1547 required twenty-five days. Fixed stages were sometimes as much as two hundred feet long and sixty feet deep. On them all of the mansions (sometimes as many as twenty) needed for a full day of playing were erected and were visible simultaneously throughout the day. Furthermore, more spectacular special effects could be arranged on fixed than on movable stages. At Valenciennes, for example, such scenes as Christ being lifted up some forty feet to the top of a temple and the storm at sea with Christ walking on the water were shown; in 1501 at Mons, Noah's flood was represented by a rain that continued for five minutes; in another play, St. Paul's decapitated head bounced three times and at each spot a spring flowed, one of milk, one of blood, and one of water. Unified control over production also facilitated double casting and the liberal use of crowd scenes. Considering all of these factors, it seems certain that the productions given on fixed stages were far more impressive visually than those mounted on wagons.

A few detailed promptbooks of productions done on these fixed stages have survived. The most readily available are those from Mons (1501) and Lucerne (1583). In them, nothing is left to chance; every detail has been worked out and recorded. They are the work of men who were stage directors in the modern sense.

Other Religious Dramatic Forms

Thus far, only church drama (often called *liturgical* drama) and cycle (or *mystery*) plays have been discussed. But there are many other kinds of medieval drama.

Miracle plays dramatize incidents from the lives and works of saints or martyrs. Although many of the deeds shown in the plays are fictional, all demonstrate miraculous powers at work or divine intercession in human affairs. This type of play was usually performed on the feast day of the saint honored by the play and, typically, was staged by some group especially associated with him. Although it was less extensively developed than the mystery, the miracle play was an important part of medieval theatre.

Morality plays flourished between 1400 and 1550. They are historically significant, since they dramatize the spiritual trials of the average man, whereas mystery and miracle plays treat biblical or saintly characters. Thus, they form a bridge between religious and secular drama. Examples of the morality play include: *Pride of Life* (about 1410), *The Castle of Perseverance* (about 1425), *Mankind* (about 1475), and *Everyman* (about 1500).

The plays are allegories about the moral temptations that beset all men. The protagonist (usually called Mankind or Everyman) is advised and cajoled by personifications of good and evil (such as good and bad angels, the seven virtues, and the seven deadly sins), and is surrounded by such characters as Mercy, Good Deeds, Knowledge, Mischief, and Death.

The purpose of the morality play is clarified if the place of the action is considered to be man's soul, for it is the struggle to possess this battlefield that constitutes the drama. In the conflict, man seems to play little active part, because so many of the personifications are human drives and motivations. When these psychological forces are externalized, the protagonist is left with few traits. The other characters are usually one-dimensional, since each personification represents only the essence of a quality such as

pride or wealth. The exception is Vice, a misguided, mischievous, and frequently humorous character, sometimes used to satirize contemporary manners.

The most famous morality play is *Everyman*. It is somewhat atypical, however, because of its restricted scope. Whereas many morality plays cover man's entire life. *Everyman* deals only with his preparation for death. Everyman searches to find one among his former companions (Kindred, Goods, Beauty, Strength, Discretion, Five Wits) who will

The Middle Ages

accompany him to the grave; eventually only Good Deeds goes with him. In his search, Everyman comes to understand his past life and its relation to his salvation. *Everyman* is a moving drama with universal appeal, since all men must face death and must do so alone.

During the sixteenth century the morality play was gradually secularized, and its former subjects were replaced by such new ones as the proper training of rulers and the appropriate content of education. Then, at the time of the religious reformation in England, it became a vehicle for controversy. For example, John Bale (1495–1563) mixed abstract figures with historical personages in *King John* to denounce the papacy. Such changes moved the morality play increasingly toward a drama with completely secular subject matter and human characters.

Since morality plays came to be performed by small professional troupes, they are more closely connected with the development of professionalism than are cycle plays. Thus, both in content and presentation, the morality play pointed toward the establishment of a secular and professional stage.

Everyman. *Frontispiece to the edition published by John Sklot, c. 1530.*

Secular Dramatic Forms

In addition to religious and didactic plays, there were a number of secular dramatic forms in the Middle Ages. The first, and probably least important, is the *folk play*, which depicts the adventures of such popular heroes as Robin Hood or St. George. The folk play is noteworthy principally, however, for such elements as sword fights, dances, deaths, and resurrections derived from pagan fertility rites. Folk plays were performed by amateurs, who went from house to house, usually at the Christmas season.

The *farce* is probably the most interesting and important of medieval secular forms. It was especially well developed in France, although it also had important exponents in England, the best known of whom is John Heywood (c. 1497–1580). The farce is lacking in religious or *didactic* elements, but shows, rather, the ridiculous depravity of man.

Probably the best example of medieval farce is *Pierre Patelin,* an anonymous French play of the fifteenth century. Patelin, a lawyer, is near financial ruin. He nevertheless persuades a merchant to let him have a fine piece of cloth. The merchant agrees to come to Patelin's house to collect his money and to have dinner. When the merchant arrives, Patelin is in bed, and his wife swears that he has not been out of the house. Patelin pretends madness, beats the merchant and drives him away. This part of the plot is rather loosely joined to a second one. Patelin meets a shepherd and agrees to defend him in court against a charge of sheep stealing. He cautions the shepherd to answer only "baa" no matter what anyone says

Scene from Pierre Patelin. *After a woodcut illustration in the first edition of the play printed in 1490. (From* L'Ancienne France: Le Théâtre… et La Musique…*1887.)*

Folk play performed in the banqueting hall of Haddon Hall, Derbyshire. (From Joseph Nash, The Mansion of England in Olden Times, *Vol. I, 1869.)*

to him. In court, the accuser turns out to be the cloth merchant, who creates such bewilderment with his alternating charges against Patelin and the shepherd that the judge (in view of the confusion and the shepherd's seeming feeblemindedness) dismisses the case. When Patelin tries to collect his fee, however, the shepherd runs away, calling "baa." The story shows a series of clever knaves outwitting each other. The final comic twist comes when the master knave is outwitted by an apparent simpleton. *Pierre Patelin* is filled with high spirits and cynicism; it has remained popular with audiences to this day.

Another dramatic form is the *secular interlude*, a nonreligious serious or comic play. It began to appear near the end of the fifteenth century, and was performed by traveling players or by troupes employed by noblemen. Such plays were probably called interludes because they were performed between the parts of a celebration (for example, the courses of a banquet). In the sixteenth century, the secular interlude was not always distinguishable from the morality play or the farce. All eventually merged into Renaissance drama.

Nineteenth-century reconstruction of a banquet with interlude entertainment. (From Pougin's Dictionnaire Historique et Pittoresque du Théâtre ... *1885.)*

Decline and Transition

Many factors account for the decline of medieval drama. First, the increasing interest in classical learning (to be discussed in Chapter 7) introduced many new concepts which affected the writing and staging of plays. Second, changes in the social structure gradually destroyed the feudal and corporate life which had encouraged such community projects as the presentation of cycle plays. Third, and perhaps most decisive, dissension within the church led to the prohibition of religious plays. After the Church of England was officially established in 1536, cycle plays were altered to delete any reminders of Rome. Continuing strife, however, caused Elizabeth I to forbid religious plays when she came to the throne in 1558. Although some of the English cycles were performed after this date, they were gradually suppressed.

On the continent, a parallel movement was under way. The secessionist movements led to a demand for reformation in the Roman Catholic Church. Therefore, the Council of Trent, held intermittently between 1545 and 1563, attempted to purify the church of all objectional practices. One result was the abandonment of dramatic entertainments as a means of religious teaching, except in the case of the Jesuits, who were permitted to have theatres in their schools. In 1548 religious plays were forbidden in Paris, and they were prohibited or gradually abandoned elsewhere. It was only in Spain, where they were not outlawed until 1765, that plays continued to be an important part of religious festivals. For the most part, however, the drama of the Middle Ages had by the late sixteenth century ceased to be a vital force.

In the long run, perhaps the most significant change is to be seen in the relationship between the theatre and society. In Greece, Rome, and medieval Europe the theatre enjoyed the active support of governmental and religious groups. Essentially it had been a community offering used to celebrate special events considered significant to all. Beginning in the sixteenth century, however, the theatre ceased to have a religious and civic function, and henceforth it had to justify itself on commercial or artistic grounds. At first it was sustained by noblemen and rulers, who continued the system of private patronage inherited from the Middle Ages. With this help, the professional theatre was gradually able to establish itself throughout Europe. Thus, at the end of the medieval period, the theatre began a new phase in its existence.

4
The Italian Renaissance

Even before the medieval dramatists had ceased to be productive, Italy, under the impact of the Renaissance, had begun to transform its stage. Atlhough its playwrights were to be of little lasting importance individually, as a group they exerted marked influence on dramatists elsewhere and did much to shape the drama of subsequent periods. Equally or more important, Italian innovations during the Renaissance introduced those conventions of theatre architecture and stage spectacle that were to dominate European practice until the twentieth century.

Background

Many forces helped to create the Renaissance. Probably the most important of these was the increased secularization of thought as men ceased to be preoccupied with the theological questions and devoted greater attention to the worth of humanity and earthly life. Since medieval learning was deficient in such humanistic speculation, the classical

72

world served as a major source of the inspiration. Rome exerted far greater influence than Greece because Latin was the language of the educated classes whereas Greek was not widely known until the sixteenth century.

The interest in classical learning soon extended to plays. Although the study of Latin drama had never been completely out of favor, Seneca's tragedies had been read principally as illustrations of moral lessons or rhetorical devices and the comedies of Terence and Plautus as models of oral style. The rediscovery in 1429 of twelve of Plautus' lost plays greatly increased his reputation. Greek plays also gradually became known, and when Constantinople fell to the Turks in 1453, scholars fleeing to the West brought with them many valuable manuscripts, including those of the Greek dramas. These Greek plays were not widely disseminated, however, until the sixteenth century.

The spread of classical learning was aided by the invention of the printing press, which made it possible for the first time in history to reproduce an unlimited number of copies of the same work. It also reduced the price of books and thus made them available to a much wider public. The classical dramas were printed shortly after the printing press was imported to Italy in 1465: Plautus' plays in 1472, Terence's in 1473, Seneca's between 1474 and 1484, Aristophanes' in 1498, Sophocles' in 1502, Euripides' in 1503, and Aeschylus' in 1518.

This new interest in classical drama was accompanied by an inquiry into literary principles. What is the purpose of drama? Are there rules for writing plays? What distinguishes comedy from tragedy? For answers to these and many other questions, Renaissance critics turned to the works

Many court spectacles were staged in gardens, courtyards, or streets. Here is a scene designed by Buontalenti for a wedding celebration in 1589 and staged in the courtyard of the Pitti Palace in Florence. (From a print in the University of Iowa Library.)

of Horace and Aristotle. Horace's *Art of Poetry* (written in the first century B.C.) was published in 1470, and Aristotle's *Poetics* (written in the fourth century B.C.) was published in 1498. The theorizing based on these two works eventually crystallized into those neoclassical precepts that dominated dramatic writing for almost two hundred years.

The theatre of Greece and Rome also attracted attention. The chief source of information was *De Architectura* by Vitruvius, a Roman architect of the first century B.C. This treatise, rediscovered in 1414, was first printed in 1486 and had had twenty-three editions by 1600.

Interest in plays of the past soon led to a desire to see them staged, and the courts and academies vied for preeminence in theatrical production. Italy at this time was a collection of independent states many of them quite small, each ruled by a duke or prince. The maintenance of a sumptuous court at which the arts were patronized became a common means of demonstrating the supposed cultural superiority of one ruler over another. It was in court theatres, supported by state funds, that those scenic conventions that were to dominate the European stage until the modern era were first developed.

Although less wealthy than the courts, the academies also contributed significantly to the development of the theatre in the Renaissance. An academy was a clublike organization formed for the purpose of studying a specific subject. Those devoted to classical architecture did much to popularize Vitruvius' work; others studied classical drama or literary theory. Some constructed theatres and staged plays. Their greatest influence, however, was exerted through the formulation, dissemination and popularization of theories about the physical theatre and drama.

The personnel of theatres both at court and in the academies were essentially amateurs, for the actors were usually courtiers or students, the plays were normally written by authors under royal patronage, and the scenery was most often designed by court architects or members of academies. Furthermore, performances were open only to select audiences and were given only on special occasions—such as royal betrothals or weddings, the birthdays of rulers, or visits of important foreigners.

Italian Drama of the Renaissance

Since medieval drama was scorned as formless and old-fashioned, the works staged by courts and academies were either Roman plays or close imitations of them. The first comedy written in Italian was Lodovico Ariosto's (1474–1533) *La Cassaria* (*The Casket*), staged at the court of Ferrara in 1508. In this comedy, a favorite Roman plot (in which lovers are united following the discovery that the girl is the long-lost child of a rich father) is placed in a contemporary Italian setting. The play with the greatest appeal today is *Mandragola* (c. 1513–1520) by Niccolò

Machiavelli (1469–1527). It shows how a jealous old man is tricked into approving of an adulterous relation between his wife and a young man. It is an amusing comedy which combines classical form with the cynicism and subject matter of medieval farce. By 1540 a native comedy was well-established in Italy. Although few of the writers are now remembered, they were the first in Europe to master the techniques of Latin comedy and to adapt them to contemporary tastes. After 1575, their plays were read with increasing frequency in England and France, where they exerted considerable influence on the emerging drama in those countries.

Another court spectacle, Das Rossballet, *at the court of Vienna in 1667. (From Alexander von Weilen's* Geschichte des Wiener Theaterwesens. *Vol. 1, Vienna, 1899.)*

The first important tragedy written in Italian was *Sofonisba* (1515) by Giangiorgio Trissino (1478–1550), who sought to follow Greek rather than Senecan practices. His influence was greatly diminished, however, by the popularity of Giambattista Giraldi Cinthio's (1504–1573) plays. Cinthio's *Orbecche* (1541), a tale of revenge in the Senecan manner, was the first vernacular tragedy to be produced on the Italian stage. Although none of Cinthio's successors achieved his popularity, many were admired both at home and abroad and did much to reestablish the tragic mode which had lain fallow since Roman times.

A third form, the *pastoral,* also came into prominence in the sixteenth

The Italian Renaissance

century. Although like the Greek satyr play in its use of rural settings and of characters such as nymphs, satyrs, and shepherds, it deviated markedly from the Greek form since its emphasis was on fine sentiments, delicate emotions, and romantic love stories. The most popular of the pastoral plays were *Aminta* (1573) by Torquato Tasso (1544–1595) and *The Faithful Shepherd* (c. 1590) by Giambattista Guarini (1538–1612), both of which were imitated throughout Europe.

Intermezzi and Opera

Since the love for spectacle could not always be satisfied by this classically inspired drama, most of which required only a single setting, the taste for allegorical devices, processions, and miraculous occurrences, a heritage from the Middle Ages, had to be met in other ways. From the late fifteenth century until about 1600, the principal spectacular pieces were *intermezzi*, presented between the acts of regular dramas. Typically, the subjects for intermezzi were drawn from Greek and Roman mythology, especially those stories that allowed the use of elaborate special effects, such as Hercules descending into Hades, or Perseus on his flying horse fighting a sea monster. Each character and event was given an allegorical interpretation that related it to the royal patron, his enemies, or friends. Music and dance also were emphasized. Originally the several intermezzi performed on a single occasion might have no connection with each other or the main piece, but eventually they came to be related both to each other and to the play they accompanied. By the 1580s intermezzi were more popular than the regular drama.

The appeal of intermezzi was undermined by the rise of opera, since most of the characteristics of intermezzi were absorbed into the newer form. Opera received its first impetus from the Camerata Academy in Florence, a group especially interested in Greek music and its relation to drama. The members of the Camerata knew that Greek tragedy had had a chorus, that it had included music and dance, that at least part of the dialogue had been sung or chanted, and that the plots had been drawn from Greek mythology. Out of their efforts to write plays of this kind, opera took shape.

The first opera was *Dafne* (1594), with text by Ottavio Rinuccini and Giulio Caccini and music by Jacopo Peri. The dialogue and choral passages were recited or chanted to a musical accompaniment that served merely to enhance the dramatic effectiveness of the dialogue. The first great operatic composer was Claudio Monteverde (1567–1643), whose *Orfeo* (1607) enlarged the role of instrumental music and began the shift in interest from dramatic to musical excellence. Other composers continued these trends. By 1650 the new form was popular throughout Italy and was rapidly spreading to all of Europe. After 1600 opera became the favorite form with Italians and it was increasingly important in stimulating experiments with scenery and special effects. It was also along with opera that Italian theatrical practices were first imported into most European countries.

Development of the Italian Stage

Although there were a number of theatrical centers in Italy, those at Florence, Ferrara, Urbino, Mantua, Rome, and Milan were of primary importance. A stage was built in the Vatican as early as 1452, and there are scattered references to temporary theatres during the remainder of the fifteenth century. The major developments, however, had to wait until the sixteenth century.

From the very beginning, two influences were at work: one that stemmed from the architectural treatise of Vitruvius, and another derived from the contemporary interest in perspective. Attempts to combine these two forces eventually led to the picture-frame stage.

It is possible that the earliest Renaissance productions utilized a stage similar to that shown in the late-fifteenth-century editions of Terence's

The "Terence stage" as depicted in the edition of Terence's plays published in Lyon in 1493. Here is shown a scene from Adelphi. *Note the several doors, each with a name above to identify it as the house of a character.*

plays. In these, a continuous façade, either straight or angled, is divided into a series of curtained openings, each of which represents the house of a different character. This stage was first depicted in an edition printed in Lyons in 1493 and was copied or elaborated upon in many later editions. Some scholars have argued that this "Terence stage" was used throughout Europe for productions of school dramas written under classical influence.

But if the Terence stage was used at first, it was soon modified by the addition of perspective painting. Credit for systematizing the principles of perspective is usually given to the painter Masaccio (1401–1428) and the architect Filippo Brunelleschi (1377–1446), who, although not the originators, synthesized earlier discoveries in a manner that could be taught. Consequently, most Italian artists had mastered it by 1450. It is difficult today to appreciate the reaction of the Renaissance mind to perspective, which was sometimes viewed as a form of magic, since through its use the artist created the illusion of space and distance where they did not actually exist. Perspective gave the artist a power he had not previously possessed, and he applied it in all possible ways. It is not surprising, then, that he recognized its possibilities for stage scenery. Although perspective settings may have been used as early as the 1480s, the first certain example is that for Ariosto's *La Cassaria* at Ferrara in 1508 designed by Pellegrino da San Daniele.

The joint influence of Vitruvius' work and of perspective are evident in the first treatise on staging in the Renaissance: a portion of *Architettura* (1545) by Sebastiano Serlio (1475–1554). In his book Serlio shows how a theatre is to be laid out, how the stage is to be erected, how scenery is to be arranged; he outlines the rules of perspective and discusses a number of additional topics. Since, like most of his contemporaries, Serlio assumed that theatres would be set up in already existing halls, his plan is an adaptation of Vitruvius' description of the Roman theatre to an indoor, rectangular space. Stadium seating is set up at one end of the hall, and a platform is constructed at the other. The space between the stage and the seats is left free in imitation of the Roman orchestra. (See the illustrations).

The stage floor is divided into two parts from front to back. The front, which is reserved for the performers, is flat, while the rear, used for scenery, is sloped upward toward the back. The floor is painted in squares, the lines of which diminish in size and converge toward the center back. The upward slope and the diminishing squares help to create a sense of distance in a very limited space.

Houses constructed of canvas stretched over wooden frames are set up on both sides of the stage. The first three houses on either side are painted on angled wings (composed of two parts, one parallel to the front of the stage and the other extending upstage), while the fourth is painted on a two-dimensional flat wing set parallel to the front of the stage. The plan is completed by a back-cloth hung at the rear of the stage. All of the scenery is constructed and painted to give the illusion of dimin-

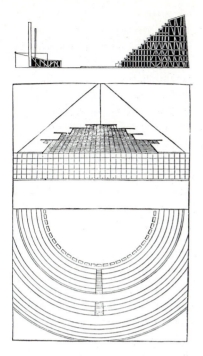

Top: *Left, a cross section of Serlio's theatre above his ground plan for a theatre. Right, Serlio's design for the comic scene. (From Sebastiano Serlio's* Architettura, *1545.)*
Below: *Left, Serlio's tragic scene; right, his pastoral scene. (From Serlio's* Architettura, *Book 2, 1569 ed.)*

ishing size and distance as it nears the back wall of the stage. To help in this illusion the flats are placed progressively nearer the center of the stage and their tops are shaped to slope downward just as the floor slopes upward toward the back.

Serlio envisioned the need for only three settings—one for tragedy, one for comedy, and one for pastoral. His engravings illustrating these settings were imitated by other designers all over Europe. Serlio's scenes for comedy and tragedy are essentially the street scenes of the Roman theatre translated into perspective settings. He does not mention any framing device (or proscenium arch) to cut off the spectator's view at the sides or top. Presumably, the side houses continued until they met the walls of the hall in which the stage was set up. A valance (or drapery hung from the ceiling) probably cut off the view at the top.

Serlio and most of his contemporaries who designed stage scenery were court architects who constructed stages and scenery as needed. This may explain why so many of the architectural details of scenery in the sixteenth century were three-dimensional rather than merely painted on flats. It also helps to explain why scene shifting was not widely practiced until the seventeenth century, when flats became entirely two-dimensional.

As the theatre gained a more solid foothold, the need for permanent theatres was felt. Although a few permanent structures may have been built earlier, the oldest surviving Renaissance theatre is the Teatro Olimpico, built between 1580 and 1584 by the Olympic Academy of Vicenza. Founded in 1555 to study Greek drama, the Academy at first used temporary stages but eventually commissioned Andrea Palladio (1518–1580), one of the most influential architects of the century, to construct a classical theatre. Palladio died before the theatre was completed, however, and it was finished by his pupil, Vincenzo Scamozzi (1552–1616). First used in 1585, the Teatro Olimpico still stands and occasional performances are staged there.

The stage, the stage background, and the auditorium of the Teatro Olimpico more nearly follow Vitruvius' plan of a Roman theatre than any other edifice of the period. But even here the influence of perspective scenery is felt, for Scamozzi raked the floor upward behind the façade doors and constructed a street in perspective behind each. (See photograph on page 00 and plan on page 00.) The result is somewhat like a city square into which a number of streets emerge. The street scenes were entirely fixed and could not be shifted. The Teatro Olimpico, therefore, was not in line with the growing demand for more spectacle.

The form which the theatre was ultimately to take can be seen clearly for the first time in the Teatro Farnese, built in the ducal palace at Parma in 1618. Its importance lies in the fact that it is the first theatre known to have been constructed with a permanent proscenium arch.

The origin of the proscenium arch is a much-debated question. Some scholars argue that it comes from the enlargement of the central doorway of the Roman stage façade. Others claim that it is derived from the trium-

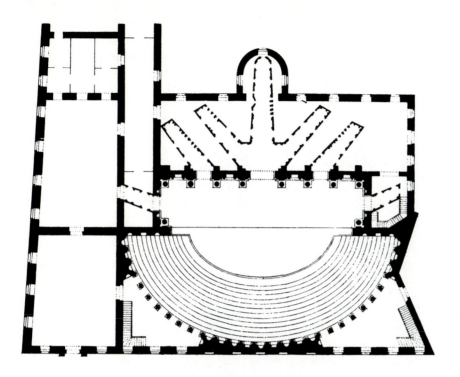

TOP: *A ground plan of the Teatro Olimpico at Vicenza. (From A. Streit's* Das Theater, *Vienna, 1903.)* BELOW: *Teatro Olimpico, Vicenza. Built between 1580 and 1584 by Italian architect Vincenzo Scamozzi from the basic design by Andrea Palladio. (Inigo Jones later imported Palladio's classical style into England where Palladian motifs became popular.)*

phal arches used in street pageants staged for the entries of rulers into cities and for processions of various kinds. Still others argue that it is indebted to paintings in which buildings and other objects are used to frame the perspective picture. Any or all of these may be true, since the proscenium arch filled a need felt clearly for the first time in the Renaissance, and it may have been suggested by a number of different sources.

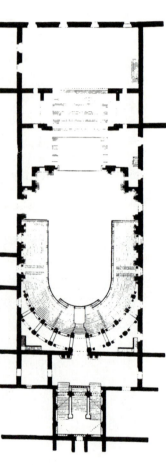

The Teatro Farnese in Parma. The ground plan. Above, left. *The stage.* Below, left. *The auditorium. (From A. Streit's* Das Theater, Vienna. 1903.)

Regardless of its origin, however, the proscenium arch serves two basic functions. First, if perspective is to be effective, there must be some means of restricting the view of the audience. For example, if the audience can see the back wall of the stage above the painted cloth, the illusion of place and of distance is destroyed. The proscenium frames the picture and focuses attention upon it. Second, if scenery is to be shifted (and by the seventeenth century there was a growing demand for more spectacle), some framework to hide the machinery and the offstage spaces is desirable. The proscenium helps to maintain the magic of the theatre by concealing the mechanics by which that magic is created.

Some kind of framing device had been used prior to the construction of the Teatro Farnese, but it had been temporary and designed to fit the needs of each play. The Farnese put into permanent form a device which had been evolving over a number of years, and thereby became the prototype of theatres up to modern times.

The new picture-frame stage was unlike any which had preceded it, for it attempted to create the illusion of a single place in its entirety. The medieval stage had suggested symbolically a great number of places all present simultaneously, while the classical theatre had made use of a permanent architectural façade which might serve as any number of places—a street, a temple, or a palace. The desire to create the illusion of more and more complex places in the Renaissance manner was largely responsible for succeeding developments in the proscenium-arch theatre.

Major Features of the Italian Theatre

Although the stage of the Teatro Farnese was the prototype of those that followed, its auditorium was still that of a conventional court theatre. To discover the prototype of future auditoriums, therefore, one must turn to the public opera houses, the first of which was opened in Venice in 1637. Although its features were never completely standardized, public theatres characteristically were to have auditoriums arranged in the following manner. Overall, the auditorium was usually shaped like an elongated U. Around the walls, boxes were set in tiers one above the other. The number of tiers varied from one theatre to another, but there were usually two or more. The boxes contained the most expensive seats, although the view of the stage was not always good except from those at the rear of the house, and these were not always well situated for hearing. Boxes were valued, however, for their relative privacy and were especially popular with well-to-do and socially respectable persons.

Above the top row of boxes there was often an undivided gallery, normally occupied by servants or members of the lower classes. The central floor space (the orchestra or pit) was not popular with the elite until the late nineteenth century. In many cases, there were no seats in the pit until near the end of the eighteenth century, and consequently the spectators stood and moved about freely. This area was usually occupied by fashionable young gentlemen and would-be critics. The price of admission to this part of the house was less than that charged for boxes, but more than that charged for the gallery.

The stage was divided from the auditorium by the proscenium arch. The stage floor was raked upward toward the back. Usually there was considerable space below the stage floor for machinery and trap doors, and space above for painted drops, curtains, and additional mechanical devices, although by modern standards this space was limited. There was only a small amount of space at either side of the stage.

Since these were indoor theatres, they required artificial lighting. Candles and oil lamps were the standard illuminants until around 1825, when gas was introduced. Chandeliers often hung in the auditorium and sometimes over the stage itself. Lights were mounted behind the proscenium arch (both at the sides and above), footlights were used at the front edge of the stage, and lights might be mounted on vertical poles behind each set of wings. Ordinarily, stage lights were concealed both for greater illusion and to avoid too much strain on the eyes of spectators. Although the stage was sometimes darkened by the use of stovepipelike devices lowered around the lights or by some similar means, for the most part there was little effective control over intensity, color, or distribution.

Another important feature of this theatre was its scene-shifting devices. Because the Serlian settings, with their three-dimensional details, were difficult to shift, the intermezzi were staged at first by drawing pageant wagons into the space forward of the stage or by carrying portable set

In his Recreational Architecture, *1640, Furttenbach shows the use of* periaktoi. *Note the curved borders above the stage,* right, *and the pit for special effects at the rear of the raked stage. (From von Weilen. Vol. I, 1899.)*

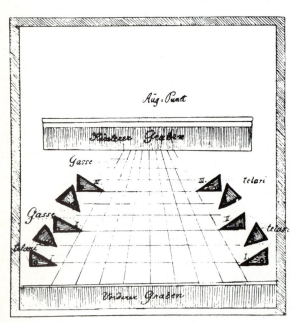

pieces onto the platform. But around 1550, periaktoi began to be used for changing the wings, and by 1638 Nicola Sabbattini (1574–1654), in his *Manual for Constructing Theatrical Scenes and Machines* (a major source of information about seventeenth-century practices), could list four methods of shifting scenery. One required periaktoi, while two others were rather clumsy means of changing the angled wings by maneuvering new frames around those already there or by pulling painted canvas over the visible surfaces. The fourth applied only to the flat wings at the rear of the stage.

It was this fourth method which eventually triumphed, as angled wings were replaced by flat wings. The first clear record of a setting composed entirely of flat wings is found in 1606, but by 1650 this arrangement, probably because of its greater mobility, had virtually replaced all others. Using this method, flats (or wings) were set up parallel to the front of the stage in a series from front to back. At each wing position as many different flats were put up (one immediately back of another) as there were scenes to be depicted during the performance. To change from one scene to the next, the visible wings were pulled offstage, thereby revealing others on which the new scene was painted. The set was enclosed at the back by shutters, that is, painted flats which met at the center of the stage. Several back-scenes could be set up, one behind the other, and shifted in the same way as the side wings.

Borders (two-dimensional framed cloths) hung above each set of wings and continued the scene overhead. The borders might be painted to represent the sky or clouds in an outdoor setting, or the beams, ceiling, or vaulting of an interior scene. Not only did they block the audience's view of the overhead area, but space between them permitted lighting and special effects to operate from above.

Borders, side wings, and back-scenes were the three basic elements of every set. To shift them simultaneously and instantaneously was the ideal. At first many stagehands were used to make quick changes, but the results were not always entirely satisfactory since it was difficult to synchronize their movements. The final solution, eventually adopted throughout Europe with the exception of England, was the *chariot-and-pole* system. At each wing and back-scene position, slots were cut in the stage floor parallel to the front of the stage. At corresponding positions under the stage, tracks were set up. Frames on casters (*carriages*) were placed in these tracks, and to each carriage were attached poles which extended upward through the slots in the floor. In turn, the wings and back-scenes were attached to these poles. Moving the carriages toward the center of the stage thrust a set onstage, while the reverse process moved it offstage.

This basic arrangement was further mechanized by a system of ropes and windlasses. Any carriage or border could be attached by rope to a windlass. When the wings, borders, and the back-scene of a single setting were attached to the same windlass, one man could change the entire set

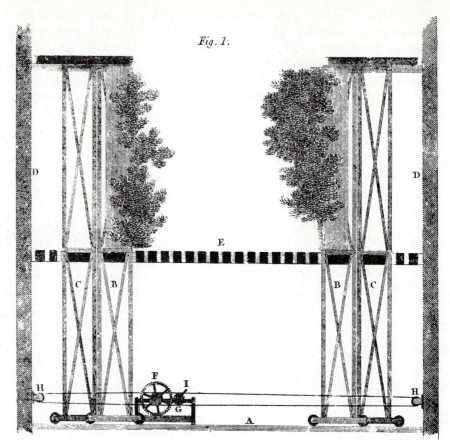

Fig. 1.

A diagram showing the operation of the chariot and pole or "continental" system of shifting scenery. A —the tracks in which the chariot rides; B and C —the chariots; D —stage walls; E — stage floor; F, G, H, and I —the lines, pulleys, and levers which operate the system. (From Rees' Cyclopedia, XX, 1803.)

by turning a single crank. The change could be accomplished instantly and all of the pieces of the set moved in unison.

The groove system, first used in England around 1640, was less complicated. Strips of wood overhead and on the stage floor created grooves in which the flats could slide on and off stage. The scenic elements might be rigged so they could be changed by windlass, but the English normally depended on a number of stagehands for making scene changes. Both systems fulfill the same function and were utilized as long as the *wing and drop* setting dominated the stage.

The *chariot-and-pole* system was perfected by Giacomo Torelli (1608–1678) between 1641 and 1645 in the public opera houses of Venice, where he created such seemingly magical feats that he won the nickname, "the Great Wizard." In 1645 he went to Paris, where he was largely responsible for transforming the French stage.

By Torelli's time, scenery on the Italian stage had become relatively standardized. Behind a proscenium arch a series of side wings and overhead borders terminated in a back-scene. On the flat surfaces of these elements was painted a perspective vista, the vanishing point of which was

A design by Giacomo Torelli for Act II of Andromède *by Pierre Corneille, 1650. Note the "glories." (From a contemporary engraving, courtesy of Alois Nagler.)*

in the center of the back-scene. If the actors moved too far upstage, the perspective effect was ruined by the disparity between the size of the actor and the objects painted on the backdrop. As a result, actors performed principally at the front of the stage. The scenery thus became a background rather than an integral part of the characters' environment. This uneasy relationship between actor and stage setting continued until the eighteenth century when angle perspective was perfected.

Machinery for special effects was also important in the Italian theatre, which merely exploited what had already been extensively developed during the Middle Ages. The stage floor had a number of trap doors through which could be manipulated such special effects as flames and smoke; the appearance or disappearance of buildings, trees, mountains, or persons; and earthquakes or seemingly magical occurrences. Other devices were operated from overhead. A favorite effect was the appearance of supernatural beings in clouds, astride mythical animals, or in chariots. These machines, sometimes called *glories,* were usually merely wooden platforms concealed by painted clouds and suspended by ropes, pulleys, and cranes. Flying animals or chariots, made of wooden frames covered

The Italian Renaissance

87

with painted canvas, were also popular. Some of these flying machines were so elaborate that they occupied almost all of the available space.

The front curtain was used only to keep the setting hidden until the performance was ready to begin and thereby to heighten surprise when the stage was revealed. Thereafter the scenery was changed in full view and was considered in itself to be a special effect (because of the seemingly magical way in which one place was transformed into another).

By the mid-seventeenth century all elements of the picture-frame stage had developed: the wing–drop–border perspective setting, the proscenium arch, scene-shifting devices, and machinery for elaborate special effects. The auditorium also had relatively standardized features: the elongated semicircle with pit, boxes, and gallery. This theatre evolved in Italy, spread to all of Europe before 1700, and remained relatively unchanged until the late nineteenth century. Many of its elements still dominate theatre architecture and staging practices.

Commedia dell'arte

Alongside the drama of the court and academy there grew up another quite different form, *commedia dell'arte.* (*Arte* signified that the actors were artists or professionals in contrast to the amateurs who performed the *erudita* or learned drama.) It was actor-centered, improvised, and adaptable to almost any playing condition.

The actor was the heart of commedia dell'arte and almost the only essential element. The script was a scenario which merely outlined the principal action and its outcome. The actors improvised the dialogue and developed the complications as the situation seemed to demand.

The same set of stock characters appeared in all the plays performed by a single troupe, and the same actor always played the same role. The typical characters may be divided into three categories: lovers, masters, and servants.

The performers of the lovers' roles did not wear masks and were expected to be handsome and sympathetic. There were always one male and one female lover, and often there was an additional pair. Although the plot often centered around some obstacle to their marriage, the lovers were not usually the center of interest. They provided an excuse for the plot and served as the norm against which other characters could be judged; they were dressed fashionably and frequently spoke elegantly and poetically.

Three masters appeared most frequently: Pantalone, an old merchant, miser, and often the father or suitor of a young woman; Dottore, a pedantic lawyer, and frequently the father of a young man or a suitor to a young woman; the Capitano, a soldier who boasted of his prowess in love and war but invariably proved to be a coward. Each of these characters had his own distinctive mask and costume which he wore in all plays.

Pantalone. Illustration by Maurice Sand for his work on actors and types of Italian comedy, Masques et Bouffons, *1859.*

The principal comic roles were those of the servants, or *zanni*, employed by members of the first two groups. They resorted to all sorts of machinations in helping or thwarting the lovers or masters. They varied from the stupid to the clever, and might have marked physical characteristics, such as a large nose or a humped back. Each had his own mask, costume, and fixed characterization. The most famous of the zanni were Harlequin, Coviello, Pulcinello, Brighella, Scaramouche, and Tartaglia. There were also one or two female servants who attended the female lovers and engaged in intrigues. Frequently they carried on love affairs with the male servants. All female roles were played by women.

These were the basic types. While each play was improvised, the actors, after a time, developed a set of speeches, well-polished comic routines, and other dependable aids in holding attention. Each troupe had a number of proven *lazzi*, or extended bits of comic business which could be utilized when appropriate or when audience attention wandered.

There are many theories about the origin of commedia dell'arte. Some scholars argue that it was descended directly from the Atellan farce of Rome, and that after the fall of Rome actors preserved traditions which sprang back into prominence when times became more favorable. There are similarities in physical appearance and basic traits among some of the commedia stock figures and those of Atellan farce, but there is no positive evidence to prove any direct connection between them. A variation on this theory traces the commedia from troupes of Byzantine mimes who supposedly fled to the west when Constantinople fell in 1453. Other historians argue that commedia grew out of improvisations by actors on the plays of Plautus and Terence. Still another theory sees the commedia as entirely native to Renaissance Italy without any necessary antecedents.

Harlequin. An illustration by Maurice Sand from his Masques et Bouffons. *1859.*

Scaramucia.   Fricasso.

Two commedia *figures. From Jacques Callot's* Balli di Sfessania, *a series of 24 etchings made c. 1621-22.*

Any of these theories may be right, for the beginnings of commedia remain obscure.

Regardless of origin, the troupes came into prominence after 1550. The first clear reference to improvisation is found in 1568; soon afterwards commedia dell'arte troupes were popular throughout Italy, and before the end of the century were playing in France and elsewhere. In the seventeenth century the commedia spread to all of Europe. It declined after 1750 and was vitrually dead by 1800.

Probably the most important troupes were the Gelosi and the Accesi. The Gelosi was probably the most prominent of all the troupes because of the popularity of its leader, Francesco Andreini (1548–1624) and his wife, Isabella (1562–1604). The latter was a favorite with many of the literary figures of the day and was herself a poet. The Gelosi existed from about 1570 to 1604, during which time it played throughout Italy and France. The Accesi troupe flourished between 1590 and 1635. Its leaders were Pier Maria Cecchini (1575–1645), Tristano Martinelli (c. 1557–1630), and Flaminio Scala (active 1600–1621), the last an important composer of scenarios. The Accesi paid at least two visits to France. Other notable troupes were the Confidenti, the Desiosi, the Fedeli, and the Uniti.

The commedia actors played for all types of audiences and produced a genuinely popular theatrical form. Many troupes were invited to play at the courts, but they were equally at home in the market place or at fairs; they at times performed regular drama, but were more famous for their improvised scripts.

After public theatres began to be built in Italy in the seventeenth century, the troupes made use of them, and scenarios were written to take advantage of perspective scenery, machinery, and special effects.

Almost eight hundred commedia dell'arte scenarios still exist. Since they only outline the action, however, it is difficult to get a clear picture of the actual quality of a commedia performance, although all accounts testify to the great skill of the actors. The popularity of the troupes for a period of over two hundred years also attests to their genuine appeal. The commedia exerted considerable influence on a number of later writers, perhaps most notably Molière in France.

The renewed interest in classical drama, the development of the picture-frame stage, perspective scenery, elaborate machinery for special effects and scene shifting, opera, and commedia dell'arte—all of these products of the Italian Renaissance were to be important influences on the theatre of later times.

5

Elizabethan England and Spain

Two European countries—England and Spain—produced strong popular theatres and major playwrights before the end of the sixteenth century. They were affected by the revival of interest in Greek and Roman culture, then well underway in Italy, but were probably influenced even more by their medieval heritage. Since the English theatre was to be of greater significance than the Spanish, it will be considered first and in more detail.

Emergence of the Professional Acting Company

Although there were wandering players in England by the fifteenth century, actors (if they had no other profession) were, according to the laws of the time, vagrants and rogues. Those performers attached to the households of nobles were exempted from this category, however, because they were classified as servants rather than actors. To avoid legal difficulties, then, performers needed patrons, and their ties with the gentry strengthened as the popularity of acting grew. By 1500 the royal family and many English nobles were maintaining their own companies.

Acting was first recognized as a lawful profession in 1572 in a royal decree that required each company to obtain a license from a nobleman or from two justices of the peace and forbade all others to perform. While this law reduced the number of English troupes, it accorded those able to obtain licenses clear legal status as actors (rather than as servants) for the first time.

The ruling of 1572 had allowed local officials (justices of the peace) to license companies, but in 1574 a new decree assigned to the Master of Revels (a court official) the duties of examining all plays and licensing all acting companies, a change that placed the English theatre under the direct control of the central government. To receive a license under the new arrangement, a troupe had to be under the patronage of a nobleman, who would allow it to use his name. Equipped with this protection and a license from the Master of Revels, a company had a clear legal right to perform. Usually the nobleman contributed nothing to the financial support of the troupe that bore his name, except on those occasions when the company gave private performances at his request. In 1574 the first of these groups, the Earl of Leicester's Men, received a license from the central government. By 1600 there were always at least two companies, and frequently more, playing in London.

Without the sanction of Queen Elizabeth and her nobles, the growth of the theatre in England would have been seriously hampered. For, unlike

A nineteenth-century engraving of a performance at the court of Elizabeth I of England, c. 1563. (Culver Pictures.)

the aristocracy who encouraged it, the merchant class viewed the theatre with distrust. Many believed that it took people away from their jobs and thereby interfered with productive pursuits, that plays encouraged immorality, and that the theatre was only a camouflage for even more undesirable activities. The powerful town councils, largely composed of middle-class tradesmen, were for the most part opposed to professional theatrical activities of any kind.

The royal licensing of acting troupes did not quiet objections to the theatre. Matters were complicated by the fact that the central government had neither a standing army nor a police force of any size, and had to depend on local authorities to enforce its laws. Therefore, there was often an uneasy truce between the crown and local officials. Licensed acting troupes were sometimes tolerated by town councils, but they also were sometimes paid by them not to perform.

Since the theatre was centered in London, it was there that local officials raised the most strenuous objections to it. Consequently, when theatres came to be built (the first in 1576), their owners chose to locate them just outside the city limits in order to escape the jurisdiction of the London council. Overall, then, it was largely owing to the protection of the central government that the theatre was able to persist and grow in England, and by the 1580s it was on the threshold of one of the most productive eras the theatre has ever known.

Influences on the Development of Elizabethan Drama

The drama that emerged in the late 1580s owed much to many earlier influences, the most important of which were the schools and universities, the Inns of Court, and the popular theatre.

The revival of interest in classical learning that had begun in Italy reached England in the late fifteenth century but did not become a major force there until the sixteenth century. As a result of this new concern, plays came to be studied and produced in schools and universities.

The development of school drama may be divided into three phases: First, the plays of Plautus, Terence, and Seneca were read, studied, and performed in Latin. Second, Englishmen began to write plays in both Latin and English in direct imitation of the Romans. Third, English dramatists fused classical techniques with English subjects and backgrounds. In this final phase, the imitation of classical models was largely unconscious, and the plays, although most frequently written and produced at universities, could easily be transferred to the public stage.

Some of the best early plays of the English Renaissance were written and produced in the schools. *Ralph Roister Doister* by Nicholas Udall (1505–1556) was probably performed at Eton while Udall was headmas-

Goodluck returned, characters from Ralph Roister Doister. *(From a sketch by Holbein in Erasmus's* Encomium morias, *print from Culver Pictures.)*

ter there between 1534 and 1541. Heavily indebted to Plautus' *The Brag-gart Warrior*, it shows the foolish posturings of a boastful coward and his discomfiture in his courtship of a widow. *Gammer Gurton's Needle* (by "Mr. S") was acted at Cambridge University sometime between 1552 and 1563. Fusing subject matter and characters similar to those of medieval farce with techniques borrowed from Roman comedy, it develops a series of misunderstandings (most of them initiated by Diccon, the bedlam or fool) between two neighboring households over the loss of a needle. Both of these plays belong to the second phase of development, for they show clearly the influence of Roman comedy.

Thus, schools and universities held a significant position in the develop-ment of Elizabethan playwriting, for they acquainted students with classi-cal ideas of dramatic form and structure. Furthermore, English drama blossomed only after such school-trained dramatists as John Lyly, Thomas Kyd, and Christopher Marlowe began to write for the professional stage.

The Inns of Court—combined residences and training centers for law-yers—were a second influence on the development of Elizabethan drama. Lawyers in this period came primarily from the upper classes, and many were interested in current trends in literature and the new classical learn-ing. Like the schools, the Inns of Court produced plays for themselves and for important guests. The first regular English tragedy, *Gorboduc* by Thomas Sackville and Thomas Norton, was produced at one of these Inns in 1561 with Queen Elizabeth in attendance. The subject was chosen from the legendary history of England, but its treatment was pseudo-Sene-can. If *Gorboduc* now seems weak as a play, at the time it made such a deep impression that it had been reprinted five times by 1590.

Although Elizabethan drama owes much to classical influence, to the schools, and to the Inns of Court, an equal or possibly greater debt is due the medieval drama and the plays produced by the professional troupes in the sixteenth century. The latter plays were a bizarre mixture of ele-ments from all the preceding native drama, as well as smatterings of the

An English inn yard, a possible forerunner of playhouses. (From the Folger Shakespeare Library Prints.)

new classical learning. Perhaps the most famous of these plays is one written by Thomas Preston in the 1560s. Its full title indicates both its episodic structure and its contents: *A Lamentable Tragedie Mixed Full of Pleasant Mirth, Containing the Life of Cambises, King of Persia, from the Beginning of his Kingdom, Unto his Death, His one Good Deed of Execution, after that Many Wicked Deeds and Tyrannous Murders, Committed by and through Him, and Last of All, his Odious Death by God's Justice Appointed.* Set in Persia, it mixes local characters with abstractions typical of the morality play (such as Shame, Diligence, Trial and Proof), classical mythological figures (such as Cupid and Venus), and English low-comedy farcical types called Hob, Lob, and Marian-May-Be-Good. Probably no play demonstrates better the chaotic condition of popular drama between 1550 and 1585. It was out of these various influences that a new drama emerged between 1585 and 1642, when England produced many of the world's greatest plays.

The Elizabethan Theatre Structure

Before considering how the dramatists of Shakespeare's age built upon the work of their predecessors, it will be helpful to examine the physical theatre and staging conventions in use between 1585 and 1642. Evidence

England and Spain

from this period is not always sufficient to permit definitive conclusions, but we can describe the probable practices and conventions.

Two kinds of theatre buildings—open-air structures and indoor halls —were in use during Shakespeare's career. The former are often referred to as "public" and the latter as "'private." In actuality, both were public in the sense that they were open to anyone willing to pay admission, but "private" theatres were smaller, charged higher admission fees, and played to a more select audience. Beginning about 1610, the same troupes played in public theatres in summer and in private theatres in winter. Since it was for the public theatres that Shakespeare wrote most of his plays, the following discussion will treat them first.

At least nine public playhouses, not counting remodelings and reconstructions, were built before 1615: The Theatre (1576), The Curtain (1577), Newington Butts (c. 1579), The Rose (1587), The Swan (c. 1595), The Globe (1599, reconstructed 1614), The Fortune (1600, reconstructed 1621), The Red Bull (1605), and The Hope (1613). All were built outside the city limits, either in the northern suburbs or on the

Johannes de Witt of the Netherlands visited London in 1596 and made a sketch of The Swan Theatre. De Witt's friend, Arend van Buchell, made a copy of the sketch, which is reproduced here. De Witt's own drawing has not survived. Since this sketch is the only contemporary pictorial evidence, it influences attempts to reconstruct the Elizabethan theatre. (From Bapst's Essai sur l'Histoire du Théâtre. *Paris, 1893.*

south bank of the Thames River. It is logical to assume that the buildings differed considerably in their details, just as theatres in any period do.

The theatres varied in size, but the most elaborate seated about two thousand spectators. They were of differing shapes: round, square, five-sided, eight-sided. Typically, they were laid out in this manner: a large central unroofed space, called the *pit* or *yard*, was enclosed by three tiers of roofed galleries which formed the outside of the building. At the door to the theatre each person paid the same admission price. This entitled him to stand in the yard; if he wished to sit, he paid an additional fee and was admitted to the galleries. At least one gallery had some private boxes, or "Lords' rooms," the use of which required still another fee.

A raised stage (from four to six feet high) extended to the center of the yard. This large platform, sometimes called the forestage or main stage, was the principal acting area. Spectators could stand around three sides, and the galleries also commanded a view from at least three sides. At the rear of the stage, there was a multileveled façade. On the stage level, at least two large doors served as entrances and exits for actors and as passageways through which heavy properties and set pieces could be moved.

The greatest disagreement about the Elizabethan theatre concerns the *discovery space* (variously called the "inner below," the "'study," and the "'pavilion") at the rear of the forestage. In many plays of the period characters, objects, or places must be revealed or concealed. Scholars generally agree, therefore, that there was an area at the rear of the main stage for this purpose. They do not agree, however, about its size and location. The two major answers have been: (1) that this area was recessed into the back wall with a curtain across the front; and (2) that this area jutted onto the forestage like a pavilion and thus had curtains around three sides. Recently it has been suggested that there was no separate discovery space and that the area immediately behind the doors was used for this purpose.

About the main stage it is probably sufficient here to know that there was a large acting area which jutted into the middle of the yard, that there were two or more doors opening onto this platform, and that there was a space (or spaces) of some sort which could be used for revelations and concealments. A discovery space may have been sufficiently large that entire scenes could be played inside it, or it may have resembled a medieval mansion, in that it may have been used merely to indicate the locale. In that case, the acting would have taken place on the forestage, which served as a platea.

The second level of the façade also had an acting area. Conclusions about this upper stage tend to be based on those about the discovery space. Those scholars who believe that there was an "inner below" state that there was a similar recessed space on the second level called the "inner above"; those who prefer the "pavilion" argue that there was an acting area on top of this forward projection; and those who question

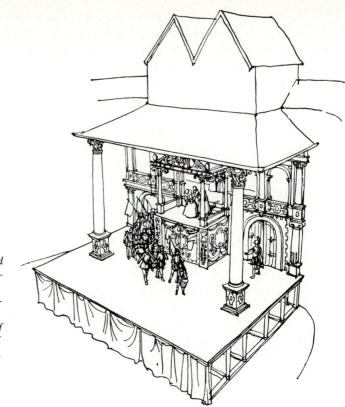

Right: *The inner stage conceived of as a pavilion.* Below: *A reconstruction of the Fortune Theatre built in London in 1600. The contract still exists for this building, and is another principal source of information about the features of the Elizabethan theatre. (From C. Walter Hodges,* The Globe Restored. *London: Ernest Benn, Ltd.)*

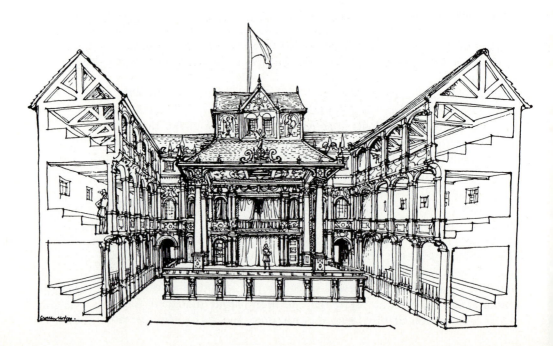

both inner stage and pavilion concede the use on the second level of nothing more elaborate than openings resembling windows or doors. In any case, this second level was probably used to represent balconies, battlements, upper-story windows, and other high places. The façade may also have had a third level. Those who believe that it did usually refer to it as the "musicians' gallery" because of its supposed primary use. If it existed, it may have been used occasionally by actors in scenes representing very high places.

The basic outlines of the stage, then, are simple: (1) a large platform (at the Fortune Theatre it was approximately forty-three feet wide by twenty-seven-and-a-half feet deep) jutting to the middle of the theatre structure; (2) two or more doors at the rear of this stage; (3) at least one discovery space; (4) an acting area on the second level; and (5) possibly a third level.

This stage seems to have been designed for a continuous flow of dramatic action. As the actors left the forestage by one door at the end of a scene, another group might enter at another door to begin the next scene; or a discovery space might be opened and the stage would become a new place; or a scene on the forestage might be followed by one on the upper level; or more than one level might be used at the same time. One scene flowed into the next without pause. (Most of the plays were not divided into acts; for the most part such divisions are additions by later editors.)

It is usual today to assume that no scenery was used in the Elizabethan theatre, but the records kept by Philip Henslowe (a businessman asso-

Interior of the second Blackfriars Theatre as reconstructed by J. H. Farrar. (Courtesy the Architect of the Greater London Council.)

ciated with the Admiral's Men) list such items as rocks, trees, beds, a hell mouth, and a cloth representing the "city of Rome." It is possible that there were a number of set-pieces, or that mansions may have been put up occasionally as on the medieval stage. It is also possible that mansions were used in the early years and later were discarded. It seems unlikely, however, that very much scenery requiring shifting was used, as it would have seriously interrupted the flow of scenes.

Machinery was housed both below and above the stage. Trapdoors in the floor allowed for grave scenes, for the appearances of ghosts and devils, for fire and smoke, and for other special effects. Typically, a roof (supported by posts at the front of the stage) extended over the stage. Cranes, ropes, and pulleys for raising and lowering objects were housed there. Sound effects (such as thunder, alarm bells, cannons, and fireworks) were also created in this area.

The first private theatre was opened in 1576 in Blackfriars, a fashionable residential area which had formerly been a monastery and which was still under the direct authority of the crown. Remodeled from a large room in one of the monastic buildings, it was used by boys' companies until closed in 1584. The second Blackfriars Theatre was built by James Burbage in 1596, perhaps in anticipation of moving there when his lease on The Theatre's site expired in 1597. The opposition of local residents put an end to his plans, however, and in 1600 the theatre was leased to the manager of another boys' company, which was extremely successful until 1608 when it was silenced for violations of censorship.

When the boys' company was forbidden, the Burbages resumed possession of the Blackfriars Theatre, which became the winter home of the King's Men after 1610. The success of this innovation led other adult troupes to open private theatres, of which there had been at least six in London by 1642. In 1629–1630 a cockfighting ring was converted into a private theatre (the Cockpit at Court) to provide a suitable space for performances by professional companies at the court of Charles I. Between 1610 and 1642 private theatres surpassed public theatres in prestige, and the open-air structures came to be used only during the five warm-weather months.

In basic features, the private theatres differed little from the public ones. Roofed and restricted in size, their seating capacities were only about one-fourth to one-half of that of the outdoor theatres. All spectators were seated—in the pit, galleries (of which there were from one to three), or in private boxes. The stage (raised about three–four feet and without a proscenium arch or front curtain) and the background were similar to those in the public theatres and are subject to the same scholarly debates. Since companies moved freely from public to private theatres, staging conventions must have been similar at both.

The Elizabethan theatre, with all its originality, included many features similar to those of past structures. For example, it depended primarily on a permanent stage façade for its scenic background, as had the

Roman theatre, and the acting area was surrounded by spectators, as in the Greek theatre. Other features were clearly related to those of the medieval stage: the generalized acting area, the practice of having specta-tors stand in the yard, the special effects, and the possible use of mansions —all of these recall the medieval theatre. But, the Elizabethan theatre combined all these features to create a unique structure that was both derivative and original.

Lighting and Costumes

In the public theatres no artificial illumination was required, since the performances occurred out of doors and in the afternoon. The private theatres probably used candlelight, but little is known of stagelighting practices. In both kinds of theatres, night scenes were indicated by bring-ing on candles, lanterns, or torches.

While little scenery was used, the Elizabethan stage was certainly not devoid of color and pageantry. Banners and other devices were employed to distinguish between armies or factions; there were many battles, pro-cessions, and dances. Most important, costumes were an ever-present source of visual pleasure.

The costumes for the Elizabethan stage were of two basic kinds: con-temporary clothing and conventional dress. By far the majority of roles

Costumes by Inigo Jones for antimasque characters in Jonson's Chloridia *(1631.) (Devonshire Collection, Chatsworth. Reproduced by permission of the Trustees of the Chatsworth Settlement.)*

Design by Inigo Jones. (From Peter Cunningham's Inigo Jones*...1848.*

were costumed in Elizabethan garments appropriate to the rank or profession of each character. Like the medieval, the Elizabethan mind had little sense of history, and characters from almost any place or time could be dressed in Elizabethan garments.

On the other hand, however, certain stereotypes of the period made it necessary to use conventionalized dress for some characters. These conventionalized costumes were used principally for: (1) special foreign groups, such as Romans, Turks, or Spaniards, (2) supernatural beings, such as fairies, classical gods, ghosts, and witches, (3) certain professional types, such as clerics, senators, and clowns, and (4) animals, such as lions, boars, and bears.

In spite of this apparent complexity, however, the majority of costumes were basically Elizabethan garments, and most of the conventionalized costumes were created by superimposing a few simple elements onto contemporary dress. For example, Roman characters were identified by the addition of drapery to Elizabethan clothing. Nevertheless, a large wardrobe was necessary, since each company changed its program almost daily and had many plays in its repertory. An actor might wear his own clothing in some roles, but the company assumed primary responsibility for costumes. Consequently, its wardrobe was one of a company's primary expenses.

The Acting Troupes

Adult acting companies included from ten to twenty members, of whom approximately ten were shareholders (that is, partners in the management) and the rest hired men. The latter (who included extras, doorkeepers, musicians, and stagehands) were paid a set wage comparable to that received by skilled laborers in other trades. The shareholders divided the money left after all expenses were paid. Thus, shareholders had an interest in the financial success of the company, and the largest shares were usually allotted to the members most essential to the well-being of the troupe. Typically, upon the formation of a company, the shareholders agreed to stay together for a stated period of time; the conditions under which a member might leave or under which new shareholders might be taken in were also specified. The hired men were usually engaged for a period of two years.

In addition to being a shareholder, an actor might also be a "householder," or part owner of the theatre building in which the company performed. If the company did not have the capital needed to build a theatre or to buy costumes and equipment, it had to enter into agreements with others, who then usually became householders. For their investment, the householders received half of the gallery receipts, while the acting company retained the other half and all of the general admission fees.

Besides the adult actors, each company included apprentices (from three to five boys) who performed child and female roles. A boy began his apprenticeship when he was between ten and fourteen and continued until he reached the age of eighteen to twenty-one. At the end of his training, he might be taken into a troupe as a regular member, or he might enter another trade. Each boy was apprenticed to an individual actor who trained him and gave him room and board. The company paid the master for the boy's services.

Each actor probably specialized in a limited range of roles. The playwright, as a rule, wrote for a specific company and thus he could write for the special capabilities of the actors. At times this may have been a limitation, but it could also be advantageous since he knew what could be expected from each actor. The range of Richard Burbage (c. 1567–1619), who played most of Shakespeare's leading roles, suggests that he was one of the great actors of the English stage, and it may have been his potential that inspired Shakespeare to write some of his most complex characterizations.

The adult acting companies performed a large repertory, changing the bill amost daily. A play was repeated several times during a season if there was sufficient demand; when no longer popular it was dropped and a new work was added. Each actor had to perform a great number of roles each season and was kept busy rehearsing and playing both new and old pieces.

The children's companies were composed primarily of choir boys from court chapels or cathedrals. Under the guise of training, the choir masters exploited their students' talents by staging plays for which they charged admission. In the children's companies, the masters were completely in charge and reaped the profits, which were considerable, especially from 1576 to 1584 and from 1600 to 1608, when the children rivaled the adults in popularity. The finest dramatists of the day, with the exception of Shakespeare, wrote for them and they were patronized by an elite audience.

Some companies paid dramatists a weekly salary to furnish a number of plays each season, while others bought plays outright. The playwright was expected to assist at the rehearsals of his works. Before a play could be performed, it had to be approved by the Master of Revels. Each actor's part (with cues) was then copied and given to him (he never received a copy of the entire play). A summary of exits, entrances, and the play's story was posted backstage so that actors might consult it during performances. The bookholder (who served as prompter or stage manager) kept the master (or prompt) copy of the play, in which were indicated exits and entrances, properties required for specific scenes, and cues for stagehands and musicians.

On days when plays were to be presented, a flag was raised above the theatre. Performances were given regularly except during plagues, certain religious seasons, or upon the death or severe illness of a ruler or important public official. The audience was composed of all sorts of persons: noblemen, merchants, workmen, and women. No doubt the level of appreciation varied considerably among the spectators. Some playwrights wrote disparagingly of them, especially the "groundlings" who stood in the yard, while others praised their perceptivity.

Principal Dramatists Prior to Shakespeare

By the time Shakespeare began to write for the stage around 1590, several competent and successful dramatists had appeared. Among these, the most influential were Kyd, Marlowe, and Lyly.

Thomas Kyd (1558–1594), who had studied Roman drama as a student at the Merchant Taylors School, won unprecedented fame with *The*

Spanish Tragedy (c. 1587), the most popular English play of the age. Kyd's drama shows the influence of Seneca to a marked degree in its sensational subject matter (including several murders), the motive of revenge, and the use of ghosts and a chorus (here a single character). It is an outstanding representative of the "revenge" play (of which *Hamlet* is also an example), one of the most popular dramatic types of the period. Perhaps more important, Kyd showed his successors how to construct striking situations, startling reversals, and suspenseful plots. Compared to Shakespeare's plays, *The Spanish Tragedy* seems crude, but it represents a remarkable advance in dramatic technique over the English plays that preceded it.

Christopher Marlowe (1564–1593), educated at Cambridge University, began writing for the theatre at about the same time as Kyd. His plays include *Doctor Faustus, Edward II, Tamburlaine,* and *The Jew of Malta.* Marlowe is usually said to be the finest English writer of tragedy prior to Shakespeare. His principal contributions to Elizabethan playwriting are the perfection of blank verse as a medium for drama, and the organization of plays around one strong character whose motives are explored thoroughly. In addition, with the possible exception of Shakespeare, Marlowe developed the history play to its highest point.

John Lyly (c. 1554–1606) is noted principally for his prose comedies, written in an elegant and sophisticated style on themes taken from

England
and Spain

105

mythology. The plays have pastoral settings—a kind of "never-never land" where everything is delicate and graceful. Widely admired, they were considered important advances over the rather crude farces of the preceding era. The influence of Lyly can best be seen in Shakespeare's *A Midsummer Night's Dream, As You Like It,* and *Twelfth Night.*

Shakespeare

William Shakespeare (1564–1616) is generally conceded to be the greatest of Elizabethan dramatists. Little is known of his early life, but by 1590 he seems to have been established in London, and by 1595 was a shareholder and actor in the Lord Chamberlain's company (later the King's Men). After 1599, he was a householder in the Globe Theatre as well. As householder, actor, director, and playwright, he was the most versatile theatrical figure of his age.

Shakespeare began writing plays around 1590 and completed about thirty-eight. Like most of his contemporaries, Shakespeare borrowed much from novels, older plays, history, mythology, and other sources. His plays have been divided into three groups: histories, comedies, and tragedies. In the first he dealt with the English past, especially the period of the War of the Roses. The histories (*Richard II, Henry IV,* Parts I and II, *Henry V, Henry VI,* Parts I, II, and III, *Richard III,* and *Henry VIII*) show his skill at reducing large masses of material to the demands of the stage. His comedies represent a wide range of types. *The Comedy of Errors* (based on Plautus' *Menaechmi*), *The Taming of the Shrew,* and *The Merry Wives of Windsor* emphasize farce; *A Midsummer Night's Dream, As You Like it,* and *Twelfth Night* are romantic comedies; *All's*

Engraving of the banquet scene in a nineteenth-century production of Macbeth. *(New York Public Library Picture Collection.)*

Well That Ends Well, Measure for Measure, and *Troilus and Cressida* are plays so nearly serious that they are frequently termed *dark* comedies.

But it was in tragedy that Shakespeare displayed his greatest genius, although here too he used a wide range of subject matter and treatment. *Romeo and Juliet, Hamlet, Julius Caesar, Macbeth, Othello, King Lear,* and *Antony and Cleopatra* must be ranked among the greatest tragedies ever written. More problematical are *Titus Andronicus,* with its Senecan horrors, and the tragicomedies *Cymbeline, The Winter's Tale,* and *Pericles.* Since it is impossible to discuss all of Shakespeare's plays, a single work, *King Lear,* will be examined in detail.

King Lear

Themes and Ideas. One motif in *King Lear* is the relationship of parents and children; it appears in the main plot, concerning Lear and his daughters, and in the subplot, dealing with Gloucester and his sons. Since the parent–child relationship is a fundamental human experience, *King Lear* treats issues that are universal.

A second motif is appearance versus reality. Both Lear and Gloucester are deceived (on very little evidence) by an appearance of perfidy and lack of gratitude in children who are actually loyal and true, and both accept as truth the lies told by children who deliberately deceive them. As in *Oedipus the King,* a contrast is drawn between physical sight and spiritual blindness. Gloucester says, after his eyes have been put out, "I stumbled when I saw." In Lear's case, madness is substituted for blindness. The perfidy of his daughters causes Lear to lose his reason, but in this state he grasps truth more firmly than when he was sane. As Edgar points out, Lear has found "Reason in madness!" Near the end of the play, Lear and Gloucester explore the meaning of their experiences.

LEAR.   . . . yet you see how this world goes.
GLOU.   I see it feelingly.
LEAR.   What! Art mad? A man may see how this world goes with no eyes.
       Through tattered clothes great vices do appear;
       Robes and furred gowns hide all. Plate sin with gold,
       And the strong lance of justice hurtless breaks:
       Arm it in rags, a pigmy's straw does pierce it.
       . . . .
                 Get thee glass eyes
     And, like a scurvy politician, seem
     To see things thou dost not.

Both Lear and Gloucester learn the difference between appearance and reality—the difference between those like Cordelia and Edgar and those like Goneril, Regan, and Edmund. In one sense, then, the play dramatizes the results of choices made on the basis of appearance. Through suffering comes wisdom, though in Lear's case it comes too late.

King Lear *at the Old Vic, London, 1958. Scene showing Goneril, Regan, the Fool, and Lear. Directed by Douglas Seale; setting and costumes by Leslie Hurry. (Photo by Angus McBean. Courtesy the Old Vic Company and Angus McBean.)*

A third theme concerns the degree to which an individual's fate is determined by forces outside himself. For instance, Gloucester, early in the play, suggests that strange happenings in human affairs are caused by a dislocation in the planets; later he says: "As flies to wanton boys are we to th' gods;/ They kill us for their sport." Fortune also is referred to as a governor of man's fate.

In the Elizabethan period, Fortune was frequently pictured as a goddess with a wheel, who might raise a person to the pinnacle of fame for no demonstrable reason and just as inexplicably dash him down again. It is in this context that Kent says: "Fortune, good night; smile once more; turn thy wheel." On the other hand, there are numerous suggestions in the play that man's fate is determined by his own decisions. It is Lear's first choice that makes all of the later events possible; similarly, it is Gloucester's hasty belief in Edmund's lies that leads to his downfall. Thus, in the final scene, Edgar states: "The gods are just, and of our pleasant vices/Make instruments to plague us."

These opposing views of human destiny are partially explained by the Renaissance conception of the universe. Humanity, as the final creation of God, was thought to be the center of God's concern, since God had created the earth and all its nonhuman inhabitants for human use. Furthermore, at this time it was still believed that the entire universe revolved around the immobile earth. The planets were said to move in concentric spheres, one inside the other. Because all parts of the universe were connected like the cogs of a machine, the well-being of the whole was affected by each part. Harmony among all created a "music of the spheres," but chaotic conditions in any part reverberated unpleasantly throughout the universe. This belief explains why physical manifestations of disorder play such a large part in Shakespeare's tragedies. The storm in *King Lear,* for example, is a metaphorical indication of the disruption of order.

Although his characters state contrary views of fate and responsibility, Shakespeare seems to suggest that man is not a mere puppet but an intelligent being free to choose his own path. Consequently, he depicts human beings as frequently violating the divine order and suffering accordingly.

No doubt there are other themes in *King Lear,* since the implications of such a great play cannot be easily exhausted. These three—parent-—child relationships, appearance versus reality, and the degree to which man is free to choose his own path—are themes, however, that have interested human beings in all ages.

Plot and Structure. Shakespeare's skill in play construction may be seen by examining the overall movement of the main plot of *King Lear.* The opening scene establishes Lear's position as an absolute monarch. He disposes of the kingdom as though it were his own private property and passes sentence on his daughters and subjects without consulting anyone. He is accustomed to having every whim satisfied: he expects his daughters to express publicly their love for him, and he disowns Cordelia when she will not flatter him; he banishes Kent for presuming to offer advice. In this way Lear's dominant traits are established. Furthermore, without this scene it would be impossible to appreciate the extent of Lear's fall. The opening also prepares for later events by revealing the true motives of Goneril, Regan, Cordelia, and Kent.

Between this beginning and Lear's reunion with Cordelia near the play's close comes a series of humiliations for Lear which, though mild at first, lead to his abandonment in a raging storm and culminate in his madness. Although Lear's downfall is not undeserved, the undisguised evil of Goneril and Regan arouse our indignation at his treatment and create constantly increasing sympathy for him. Compassion is aroused as Lear's growing recognition of his mistakes is accompanied by a loss of power to rectify them. In the storm scene he is completely stripped of authority and is forced to face himself as a man, powerless and at the mercy of his inward torment just as he is at the mercy of the outward torment of the elements.

The scenes that follow the storm show Lear's attempts to reorient himself. In his powerless state he comes to know the difference between freely offered devotion and what is pretended for the sake of reward. But the evil forces Lear has unleashed through Goneril and Regan prevent him from rebuilding a life based on his new-found wisdom.

Much the same progression is found in the subplot. There are significant differences, however, for while Lear himself sets his destruction in motion when he divides his kingdom, Edmund is the moving force behind Gloucester's downfall. Gloucester's blindness (which parallels

Lear's madness) is caused by his loyalty to Lear, and is not inflicted by his own children. Like Lear, however, Gloucester is forced to reexamine himself and he too experiences a spiritual rebirth.

Perhaps Shakespeare's structural skill can be seen most clearly in the intertwining of the two plots in a number of ways: by having Gloucester and Edmund present at Lear's abdication; by having Gloucester serve as host to Regan and the Duke of Cornwall; through Gloucester's attempts to aid Lear; and through the relationships among Edmund, Goneril, and Regan. Furthermore, the resolutions of the two stories are essentially one: Goneril and Regan kill each other over love of Edmund; Edmund orders the deaths of Lear and Cordelia; the revelation of Goneril's love for Edmund leads to a duel between Edgar and Edmund and to Edmund's death. Thus, while the subplot has its own intrinsic interest, it simultaneously serves to point up the themes found in the main plot and motivates much that happens to Lear. Gloucester's story, therefore, is essential to the main plot and not a distraction.

The unity of action found in *King Lear* differs, however, from that in *Oedipus the King,* in which all attention is focused upon Oedipus and his search. Shakespeare uses a much broader canvas than Sophocles does, and he includes in his play more facets of the story, more characters, and a wide range in time and place. Nevertheless, he has not sacrificed unity, for the various elements have been carefully integrated.

Characterization and Acting. The role of Lear is far more complex than any other in the play. It is sometimes difficult to distinguish between Goneril and Regan because of the few traits assigned each; both have the same motives, and the overall impression is that each is completely depraved. Cordelia, on the other hand, has as little trace of evil as her sisters have of good.

Shakespeare gives scant information about the physical and social attributes of his characters and emphasizes psychological motives instead. Each of the secondary personages has one dominant drive that is placed in opposition to that of another character. Thus, Cordelia is contrasted with her sisters, Edgar with Edmund, Cornwall with Albany, Kent with Oswald, and France with Burgundy.

Although the secondary characters are not as complex as Lear, they are effectively conceived, for they fulfill well their functions in the dramatic action. Furthermore, each role offers the imaginative actor a challenge to create a characterization of considerable depth. For example, Edgar must assume a series of disguises (madman, peasant, unknown knight), change his speech from poetry to prose and from standard English to peasant dialect, and convey a sense of deep emotional involvement even when his disguise will not permit the open expression of his true feelings. Thus, a basic character type (the good son) is individualized by involving him in a series of unusual events. Nevertheless, the dominant impression created by Edgar is one of simplicity rather than of complexity, and actors who have played the role have sometimes experienced difficulty in making

Edgar interesting to audiences. The same is true of Cordelia, but less so of Goneril, Regan, and Edmund, since evil characters always seem more fascinating than good ones.

Gloucester comes near to being an echo of Lear. Both are old men, easily deceived, and they undergo many of the same experiences. Lear's role, however, is developed at much greater length and in more depth than is Gloucester's. In the opening scene, both Gloucester and Lear seem vigorous, but by the end of the play both are decrepit and broken. The decline from vigor to debility is dramatically effective. Furthermore, visible physical change seems essential to the play's development.

Lear is a difficult role for an actor because the part encompasses a wide range of action, emotion, and psychological change. In the opening scene, Lear is in complete command; he is easily angered and insists upon having his every wish satisfied. This habitual, and somewhat childish, behavior defeats him when he no longer has the power to enforce his desires. Impotence commences during his first clash with Goneril, and his sense of frustration grows until it leads to madness. Lear's insanity is portrayed with variety. At first he shouts imprecations; then he becomes quiet and withdrawn; his dialogue shifts to prose, and he becomes preoccupied with sex, devils, and tortures. From this low point, Lear gradually begins a spiritual ascent, though he never regains his physical vigor. His psychological regeneration develops slowly, for he feels undeserving of Cordelia's love, and only with difficulty can he comprehend her forgiveness. When he at last understands the extent of her devotion, he determines to make recompense for the past. Their reunion, which reaches heights of happiness, followed by death and despair, requires consummate acting skill on the part of the actor portraying Lear.

England
and Spain

111

Throughout the play, Shakespeare includes details that humanize Lear. Perhaps the most obvious of these comes in one of the final speeches, into which Lear injects, "Pray you, undo this button." Here, a figure fighting with overwhelming emotions is suddenly reduced to the level of common humanity. It is a simple touch, but one that arouses pathos more effectively than any description of Lear's feelings could.

The part of the Fool is used as a foil for Lear. His privileged state allows him to speak openly what others must leave unsaid, and it is significant that he is present only in those scenes that can profit from such outspokenness. When Lear himself is turned into a simpleton by insanity, he speaks in the same blunt fashion as the Fool. After the storm scene the Fool does not reappear, for he is no longer needed.

Lear, thus, is the center of concern for Shakespeare. The other characters are well-drawn, but none approaches the complexity of the title role.

Language. Shakespeare's dramatic poetry is generally conceded to be the finest in any language. The basic medium is blank verse, which allows much of the flexibility of ordinary speech while elevating and formalizing it. The final lines in a scene, usually written in rhymed couplets, serve to round off and brake the forward movement of the verse, like a *coda* in music.

This pattern (blank verse ending in a rhymed couplet) is varied frequently, however, by the injection of passages written in prose, which, typically, are spoken by lower-class characters and are often used for comic purposes. In *King Lear,* however, both Edgar and Lear turn to prose in the mad scenes, for though they do not change rank in actuality, they look at life from the standpoint of the simple mind and speak as though they were members of the lower class.

Probably the most important element in Shakespeare's dialogue is figurative language. The principal purpose of a figure of speech in dramatic poetry is to set up either direct or indirect comparisons. Shakespeare's superiority over other writers of dramatic poetry is due in large part to his use of comparisons which enlarge the significance without distracting the attention from the dramatic situation. For example, in the following passage he associates the storm with Lear's daughters and at the same time suggests that the storm is a sign of divine displeasure. Thus, the audience graps simultaneously the significance both of the immediate event and of its wider implications.

> *Rumble thy bellyful! Spit, fire! spout, rain!*
> *Nor rain, wind, thunder, fire are my daughters.*
> *I tax not you, you elements, with unkindness:*
> *I never gave you kingdom, called you children;*
> *You owe me no subscription. Then let fall*
> *Your horrible displeasure. Here I stand your slave,*
> *A poor, infirm, weak, and despised old man.*

Shakespeare often combines direct and indirect comparisons in a single passage. For example, both metaphors and similes are used to relate Lear's mental state to that of a tortured soul in hell.

> You do me wrong to take me out o'th'grave:
> Thou art a soul in bliss; but I am bound
> Upon a wheel of fire, that mine own tears
> Do scald like molten lead.

These examples, which only hint at the range of Shakespeare's figurative language, also illustrate how his poetic devices partially fulfill the same function as the constant visual representation of heaven and hell on the medieval stage. They relate human actions to the divine and demonic forces of the universe and treat man's affairs as significant to all creation.

Shakespeare's language makes special demands upon the actor. Figures of speech are apt to seem contrived and bombastic if the actor does not

A 1965 production of King Lear, *with Morris Carnovsky in the title role, at the American Shakespeare Theatre, Stratford, Conn. (Photo by Friedman-Abeles.)*

appear to be experiencing feelings sufficient to call forth such language spontaneously. All too frequently, Shakespeare's plays are damaged in performance when actors do not rise to the emotional demands of the poetry. Therefore, the very richness of expression can be a stumbling block for both performer and reader.

Spectacle and Sound. There are many opportunities for visual splendor in *King Lear*. The action occurs in a large number of places, and if all were depicted realistically, the stage would present a constantly changing aspect. Our knowledge of the Elizabethan stage, however, suggests that Shakespeare envisioned the spectacle in terms of stage properties, costumes, and the movement of actors.

Although scenery is not important, the frequent change of locale is. The forestage, discovery space, and upper stage would allow the necessary flow of one scene into the next. For example, the storm scene, which is set consecutively in an open space, before a hovel, and inside a farm house, would require only the forestage and the discovery space.

The relatively bare stage is enlivened by processions, numerous attendants, and constant physical movement. The opening scene, for example, is an important state occasion which would demand an elaborate procession of officials and courtiers, all of whom would be dressed in their finest garments. In later scenes, banners and heraldic devices would be used to distinguish Albany's and Cornwall's forces from those of the French. In almost every scene minor characters enrich the stage picture.

The actors' stage business also creates spectacle. Gloucester's eyes are put out, Kent is seized and placed in the stocks, Edgar and Edmund fight a duel, Lear dies. Nearly every scene offers physical action of this sort. (A comparison of the onstage action of *King Lear* with that of *Oedipus the King* helps to define a principal difference between Elizabethan and Greek tragedy.)

The costumes are an important visual element. In Shakespeare's day, most characters probably wore contemporary garments but the company's large wardrobe would provide much variety in color and line. During the performance some characters must change costumes several times. For example, Lear first appears in robes of state; in the following scenes, he wears the garments of a nobleman; after he goes mad, he appears in tattered garments entwined with weeds and flowers; and following his reunion with Cordelia, he is restored to clothes appropriate to his rank. Edgar changes from his gentleman's attire to rags, then to a peasant's garment, and finally to a suit of armor. Although most of the actors probably wore the same costumes throughout the play, the shifting combination of persons on stage would have lent constant variety to the picture.

Such sound effects as the storm, offstage fighting, and trumpet flourishes are important in *King Lear*. Music is used in a number of scenes. But most important is the sound of the actors' voices speaking Shakespeare's poetry.

King Lear, because of its combination of universal themes, a compelling story, powerful characters, great poetry, and interesting visual and aural effects, is one of the world's greatest plays. Although it embodies the values of its own period, it is timeless in appeal and transcends the limitations of a particular era. Thus, it continues to move audiences today as it has since its first presentation.

Shakespeare's Contemporaries and Successors

Shakespeare's greatness often diverts attention from his contemporaries and successors, many of whom are also among the world's finest dramatists. Of Shakespeare's contemporaries, Ben Jonson (1572–1637) was the most important. He began his career in the theatre as an actor (about 1597), but did not continue long in that profession. In 1598 he wrote *Every Man in His Humour* (in which Shakespeare acted), and soon became one of the most controversial authors of the day. He often accused his fellow playwrights of failing to understand the purposes and techniques of drama and of catering to the depraved taste of the "groundlings." Of all the authors of the period, Jonson was most attuned to

An eighteenth-century production of Ben Jonson's Alchemist. *David Garrick is seen at right in the role of Abel Drugger. (Culver Pictures.)*

classical ideas, and his work as a poet, playwright, and critic influenced many younger men to work for a more classical "regularity."

His most famous plays are *Volpone* (1606), *The Silent Woman* (1609), *The Alchemist* (1610), and *Bartholomew Fair* (1614)—all comedies. His tragedies were not well received. Jonson also wrote most of the masques (to be discussed later) presented at the courts of James I and Charles I.

Probably Jonson is best remembered for popularizing the *comedy of humours.* Since classical times it had been assumed that there were four bodily "humours," blood, phlegm, yellow bile, black bile, and that health depended upon the proper balance among these fluids. Too much of any one was said to lead to illness. The practice of medicine, therefore, consisted of two basic elements: purging (to eliminate excessive bile or phlegm) and bleeding (to eliminate excessive blood).

A number of Elizabethan authors applied this medical concept to human psychology, and Jonson, in particular, drew upon it in writing plays. He attributed the eccentricities of behavior to an imbalance of humours and created a wide range of character types based upon this scheme. The psychology of humours was much in vogue between 1598 and 1603, and, though it is seldom mentioned in plays after that time, many playwrights continued to base their characterizations on it. This approach to human behavior tended to produce character types rather than well-rounded individuals.

Jonson's most widely admired play is *Volpone.* The main character, Volpone, pretends to be rich and without heirs. Each of several persons is led to believe that he will inherit the fortune if he can stay in favor with Volpone. Consequently, each showers him with expensive gifts. At last, Volpone tires of his deception, makes a will leaving all his wealth to his servant, Mosca, and pretends to die. Later, when he tries to reclaim his property, Mosca refuses to give it up. Eventually Volpone, Mosca, and the would-be heirs are exposed and punished.

Most of the characters have been given the names of predatory animals, birds, or insects, such as Volpone (the fox), Voltore (the vulture), and Mosca (the fly), descriptive of the characters. Into this network of corruption, Jonson introduces two sympathetic figures, Celia and Bonario, who are almost sent to prison through the collusion of the others. This complication threatens to make the play serious, but the truth is revealed in time to prevent injustice and to maintain the high level of comedy.

Jonson frequently used comedy to denounce vice and foolish behavior. His consistent purpose of reforming conduct has led many to describe his plays as corrective comedies.

Francis Beaumont (c. 1584–1616) and John Fletcher (1579–1625), who wrote a number of plays in collaboration, were principally responsible for establishing the vogue of tragicomedy and romantic tragedy. Their chief works are *Philaster, The Maid's Tragedy, A King and No King,* and *The Scornful Lady,* all written between 1608 and 1613. (Tragicomedy and romantic tragedy are similar forms; both are essentially serious, but tragicomedy ends happily and romantic tragedy unhappily.) The subjects of Beaumont and Fletcher's plays were usually sensational. For example, in *The Maid's Tragedy* a wife tells her husband on their wedding night that she is the King's mistress and that she has married him only as a means of continuing her affair. The rest of the play develops from this sensational revelation. Both playwrights were particularly skilled in dramatic construction. They built complications to startling climaxes, alternated quiet and tumultuous episodes, and condensed complex material into far fewer scenes than Shakespeare employed. Their plays show more technical proficiency than Shakespeare's, but their subjects emphasized the shocking rather than the significant. Until well into the eighteenth century, their plays maintained a reputation equal to those of Shakespeare and Jonson and were performed regularly until the nineteenth century.

The work of Beaumont and Fletcher set the standard for the period between 1610 and 1642. Important writers of tragedy during these years include John Webster (?–c. 1630), whose *The White Devil* (1612) and *The Duchess of Malfi* (1614) are among the most powerful of English tragedies, and John Ford (1586–1639), who is best known for *'Tis Pity She's a Whore* (c. 1625–1633), in which a brother and sister are lovers. Since Ford treats this pair sympathetically, his play is frequently cited as evidence of decadence in English drama after the death of Shakespeare.

Other noteworthy playwrights of the time were Thomas Middleton (1580–1627), Philip Massinger (1583–1640), Thomas Heywood (c. 1574–1641), Thomas Dekker (c. 1572–c. 1632), Cyril Tourneur (c. 1580–1626), and James Shirley (1596–1666).

The Court Masque

When James I came to the English throne in 1603, he brought with him a taste for elaborate theatrical entertainment. He became the patron of Shakespeare's company, which was renamed the King's Men, and all other troupes were placed under the patronage of members of the royal family.

Unlike Elizabeth, who usually contented herself with performances by the public troupes, James also financed private court entertainments, called *masques*, which were performed on special occasions, such as weddings, briths, and visits from foreign dignitaries. The English masque was similar in all important respects to the Italian *intermezzo* and utilized Italian staging methods. The scripts for most of the masques were by Ben Jonson, while the settings and costumes were, with a few exceptions, designed by Inigo Jones (1573–1652), the court architect. Jones, who had studied in Italy, introduced Italian staging methods into England.

Under James I (reigned 1603–1625), an average of one masque each year was given, but under his successor, Charles I (reigned 1625–1649), two were usually presented annually. Other masques were produced by

Costume by Inigo Jones for Tethys or a Nymph in Daniel's Tethys Festival *(1610). (Devonshire Collection, Chatsworth. Reproduced by permission of the Trustees of the Chatsworth Settlement.)*

the Inns of Court and by noblemen. Great sums of money were spent. For example, James I expended more on a single masque in 1618 than on all the professional performances given at court during his entire reign.

The masque featured allegorical stories designed to honor a person or an occasion through a fanciful comparison with mythological or historical characters or situations. The speaking and singing roles were assumed by professional court musicians, while comic roles were played by professional actors. The major emphasis, however, was upon the courtier-dancers, who during the masque went into the auditorium to dance with selected spectators. Above all, the masque provided ample opportunity for elaborate spectacle and scenic display, and by 1640, when the last court masque was staged, Jones had introduced almost all of the scenic devices that had been popularized in Italy.

The influence of the masque was soon felt in the public theatres, where processions, music, allegorical scenes, and dances were employed with increasing frequency. For example, Shakespeare's *The Tempest* (1611) contains many masquelike elements. But the influence of the masque on scenery in the public theatre was not great until after 1660, when the proscenium arch and perspective settings became standard.

Closing of the English Theatres

Although the theatre was a thriving institution and was encouraged by the royal family, Puritan opposition to it grew throughout the first part of the seventeenth century. In 1642, when a power struggle between Charles I and parliament had led to civil war, the unsettled conditions were used as an excuse for closing all theatres. They were not to be reopened until Charles II was restored to the throne in 1660. Although there were surreptitious performances during the Commonwealth, the English theatre was virtually nonexistent during these years. When it was revived in 1660, it bore little resemblance to the theatre of Shakespeare, for it then embraced Italian staging conventions and the neoclassical ideal.

Spanish Theatre
and Drama in the Golden Age

As in England, the late sixteenth century brought a burst of activity in Spain. So fertile was the period between 1580 and 1680 that it has been designated the Golden Age of Spanish literature. Both the Spanish theatre and drama of this era have much in common with their English counterparts.

The first permanent public theatre (or *corrale*) was opened in Madrid

The frontispiece to Kirkman's The Wits, *published in 1673. The book contains a number of "drolls," short scenes extracted or altered from longer plays, which were probably performed during the Commonwealth. This illustration was long thought to represent the stage of the Red Bull, a public theatre used regularly from c. 1605 to 1642. More recently it has been argued that it represents a composite of the stages used for surreptitious performances during the Commonwealth. Note that the characters are drawn from a number of different plays. (From* Londina Illustrata, *Volume II, 1825.)*

in 1579. It was remodeled from an already existing courtyard formed by the walls of houses. The balconies and rooms of the surrounding buildings were used to seat spectators, while standing room and benches were provided in the courtyard. The stage was similar to that of the Elizabethan theatre in most respects: In back of a large forestage there was a permanent façade with an inner area that could be closed off by a curtain; on the second level of the facade a balcony served as an upper stage. Later Spanish theatres were to follow the same basic arrangement.

The connection between the church and the theatre remained close in Spain. Originally the corrales of Madrid were under the control of *cofradias,* or religious and charitable organizations. Even after the city assumed control of the theatres in 1638, its share of the revenue was used to support charities. Furthermore, nearly all playwrights of the Golden Age wrote plays (*autos sacramentales*) for religious festivals, and professional troupes performed them. Religious dramas were not forbidden in Spain until 1765.

Lope de Rueda (1510–1565), a dramatist, actor, and producer, is credited with establishing the professional theatre in Spain, but it did not flourish until after 1580. The two great playwrights of the Golden Age were Lope Felix de Vega Carpio, usually called Lope de Vega (1562–1635), and Pedro Calderón de la Barca (1600–1681).

Lope de Vega was a prolific playwright. Over four hundred extant

England
and Spain

119

works are attributed to him, and some accounts estimate his total output at more than 1800 plays. His subjects were drawn from the Bible, the lives of saints, mythology, history, romances, and other sources. Although he was an inventive and skillful writer, his dramas fail to achieve the profundity that marks Shakespeare's work. Like Shakespeare, he made considerable use of song and dance, and intermixed the comic and the serious. Some of his best known dramas are *The Sheep Well, The Gardener's Dog,* and *The King, the Greatest Alcalde.* Because of his great productivity and popularity, Lope de Vega influenced almost all subsequent Spanish dramatists; his position in Spain is comparable to Shakespeare's in England.

Although Calderón wrote many kinds of plays, he is best known for those that explore theological or philosophical ideas. He is said to have written more than two hundred works, of which about a hundred survive. Of these, the majority are autos sacramentales written for the Corpus Christi festivals of Madrid. Probably the best known are *The Great World Theatre* (c. 1645) and *The Devotion to the Cross* (1633), while his greatest secular play is *Life Is a Dream* (c. 1636), a philosophical allegory about the human situation and the mystery of life.

Other important playwrights of the Golden Age were Tirso de Molina (1584–1648), whose play *The Deceiver of Seville* is the first dramatic treatment of the Don Juan legend, and Juan Ruiz de Alarcón y Mendoza (c. 1581–1639). Unfortunately, with the death of Calderón, the Spanish theatre ceased to be a vital force.

A conjectural reconstruction of a Spanish corrale *as it might have appeared about 1660. (From Ricardo Sepulveda's* El Corral de La Pacheca. *Madrid, 1888.*

A reconstruction of a carro *or wagon for an* auto sacramentale. *From Sepulveda's* El Corral de La Pacheca.)

Thus, both England and Spain developed strong dramatic traditions before the new Italian ideas of writing and staging were widely adopted in either country. Their theatres and drama seem rather to be logical and gradual evolutions out of many earlier influences. In neither country was there a sharp division between theatrical entertainment designed for the court and that intended for the common people. Possibly the vigor of Spanish and English drama stemmed from the playwrights' desire to appeal to all classes and not merely to an aristocratic minority.

6

French Classicism

As in most other countries, the professional theatre in France evolved out of medieval practices. In some towns the plays were staged by trade guilds, whereas in others they were produced by associations created especially for that purpose. Of the latter group, the Confrérie de la Passion became the most important. Organized in 1402, by 1420 it was established in a permanent indoor theatre in Paris. Thereafter it was virtually the only producer of plays in that city.

In 1548 the Confrérie built a new theatre, the Hôtel de Bourgogne, which was to remain in use until 1783. Construction was barely underway, however, when the Confrérie was forbidden to produce religious plays, its primary function. In return, it was given a monopoly on all theatrical production in Paris. Unable to maintain audiences with secular plays, the Confrérie began to rent its theatre to traveling troupes. After 1598 its activities were confined solely to those of landlord, and each group desiring to perform in Paris had to pay the Confrérie a fee whether or not it played at the Hôtel de Bourgogne.

The French Theatre Between 1600 and 1625

Although many companies played in Paris in the late sixteenth and early seventeenth centuries, performances were sporadic. The best of the companies was that headed by Valleran-Lecomte (active 1592–1612), the first professional manager in France to achieve high quality in theatrical production. Valleran-Lecomte, who first appeared at the Hôtel de Bourgogne in 1598, dominated the Parisian theatre until 1612. Between 1612 and 1625 the most popular performers in Paris were the farce actors Turlupin, Gaultier-Garguille, and Gros-Guillaume.

The principal French playwright of the early seventeenth century was Alexandre Hardy (c. 1572–1632), who supplied Valleran-Lecomte with a large proportion of his plays. Hardy is said to have written about five hundred works (of which thirty-four still exist), and was probably the first French author to make a living by writing for the stage. Although his plays were of many types, the majority were tragicomedies. His emphasis

The court of France sponsored many spectacles similar to those of Italy. This illustration depicts Circe by Beaujoyeulx in 1581. The settings are by Jacques Patin. Note the galleries for spectators and the mansionlike arrangement of the scenery. The theatre was a hall in the Petit Bourbon and was later converted to conform to the Italian ideal by Torelli in 1645. Molière's company used the Petit Bourbon from 1658 to 1660, when the building was demolished. (From Germain Bapst's Essai sur l'Histoire du Théâtre, Paris, 1893.)

Farce actors at the Hôtel de Bourgogne around 1630. The three male figures at the center are Turlupin, Gaultier-Garguille, and Gros-Guillaume. Notice the commedia*like costumes. (From a comtemporary engraving by Bosse reprinted in Arsène Houssaye's* La Comédie Française, *1880.)*

was upon a continuous sweep of action similar to that found in novels of chivalry and adventure. Hardy was a very popular dramatist, but because his plays lacked depth, he was unable to establish in France a strong tradition of "irregular" drama such as was then current in England and Spain.

The staging of plays at the Hôtel de Bourgogne was quite different from contemporary practices in both Italy and England. From the beginning, the Confrérie had used an indoor stage erected at the end of a rectangular hall. At the Hôtel de Bourgogne the visible stage space was only about twenty-five feet wide (as compared with a typical outdoor stage of over a hundred feet). When the mansions were set up, therefore, they had to be arranged along the sides (one behind the other from front to back) and across the rear of the stage. The resulting picture superficially resembled Serlio's stage, but in Serlio's settings all of the elements were parts of a single location, while at the Hôtel de Bourgogne each structure represented a different place. The space in the middle of the stage was used as a generalized acting area in the manner of the medieval platea.

A number of designs by Laurent Mahelot for settings of this kind (the *décor simultanée,* or simultaneous setting) are still in existence. (See the illustration on page 125.) Simultaneous settings were used at the Hôtel de Bourgogne until around 1635, when the Italian style began to dominate. The simultaneous stage was appropriate to Hardy's dramatic method, but it was not well suited to the French classical drama which began to appear in the 1630s.

Changes in French Theatre, 1625–1650

The period from 1625 to 1650 brought sweeping changes to France because of more settled political conditions, a strong desire to raise the general cultural level, the importation of Italian ideas on staging and drama, and the appearance of strong native dramatisits.

France was embroiled in civil wars over religion from the 1560s until the 1620s. After Cardinal Richelieu became chief minister of France around 1625, however, the political situation grew more calm and he was able gradually to extend the central government's control over all phases of French life.

In the 1620s Richelieu and many other Frenchmen began to be concerned about France's cultural image and, in seeking to improve the status of literature and the arts, looked to Italy for guidance. Although Italian ideas had been current in France as early as 1550, they had been little known except among the educated classes. During the 1630s, however, they were to become a source of bitter controversy and consequently were soon widely known.

Until about 1625, the professional theatre maintained only a precarious footing in Paris. While the Hôtel de Bourgogne was occupied frequently, no company performed there continuously until 1623. By 1629, however, there were two professional companies in Paris.

During the 1630s both of the public theatres (the Hôtel de Bourgogne and the Théâtre de Marais) were still using simultaneous settings. Cardinal Richelieu was not happy with this kind of staging, which emphasized medieval rather than Renaissance ideals, and in 1641 he built in his palace a theatre of the Italian type with the first permanent proscenium

Mahelot's design for La Prise de Marsilly *at the Hôtel de Bourgogne in the 1630s. Note the simultaneous representation of a number of locales. (Courtesy Bibliothèque Nationale, Paris.)*

arch in France. This theatre, called the Palais-Royal after Richelieu's death, was to become the home of Molière's troupe.

When Richelieu died in 1642, Cardinal Mazarin, a native of Italy, succeeded him as prime minister. Mazarin's love of opera was responsible for bringing Torelli to Paris in 1645. By 1650 Torelli had established Italian scenic methods and theatre architecture at the French court.

The Italian ideal also came to dominate the public theatres. When the Théâtre de Marais was rebuilt in 1644, its stage was framed by a proscenium arch, and soon afterwards it began to emphasize spectacle in the Italian manner. In 1647 the Hôtel de Bourgogne was remodeled and given a proscenium arch for the first time. Thus, by 1650 Italian practices had largely replaced the staging conventions of the Middle Ages.

The Italian influence may also be seen in the formation of the French Academy, which originated about 1629 when a small group of men interested in literature and language began to meet informally. Richelieu encouraged them to form an official organization, which they did in 1636. This group, whose membership is restricted to forty at any one time (supposedly the outstanding men of French letters), still exists. It has always enjoyed considerable prestige, most conspicuously so in the seventeenth and eighteenth centuries, and has exerted a decided influence on French literature and drama. When the French Academy was formed it took as its province the principles and practice of literary composition and the rules governing the French language.

The Basic Principles of Neoclassicism

The French Academy inherited its standards of drama primarily from Italian critics. Since these standards undergird neoclassicism, the dominant artistic mode of the seventeenth and eighteenth centuries, they are important to any study of theatre and drama in that era. Neoclassical principles were a synthesis of ideas expressed by many men in many countries, but they were most consistently applied and defended in France. Italian critics of the sixteenth century (especially Minturno, Scaliger, and Castelvetro) laid the foundations upon which French critics of the seventeenth century (notably Chapelain, D'Aubignac, and Boileau) built. While there was, as in all movements, considerable variation in the ideas of individual writers, the basic principles of neoclassicism were sufficiently consistent to permit a general summary.

The neoclassicists were primarily concerned with a number of basic topics: the concept of verisimilitude, purity of dramatic types, the five-act form, decorum, the purposes of drama, and the three unities.

Verisimilitude, or "the appearance of truth," is a complex concept. To the neoclassicist, verisimilitude had three basic aspects: reality, morality, and generality or abstraction. The desire for "reality" required that the

In 1641 Cardinal Richelieu's new theatre contained the first permanent proscenium arch in France. The illustration shows the setting for the first production, Mirame. *Later this theatre was called the Palais-Royal and was used by Molière's troupe from 1660 to 1673, and after that time was the home of the Opera. From Pougin's* Dictionnaire Historique et Pittoresque..., *1885.)*

playwright rule out those things that could not actually happen in real life. It eliminated fantasy and supernatural occurrences unless they were an accepted part of a story (as in Greek myths or biblical material). Even then, however, the playwright was encouraged to minimize these features of a story. Such devices as the soliloquy and chorus were discouraged on the grounds that it is unnatural for characters to speak aloud while alone or to discuss private matters in the presence of a group. To replace these devices, each main character came to be given a trusted companion, or *confidant,* to whom he could reveal his innermost secrets. Violence was placed off-stage because of the difficulty of making it convincing.

This demand for faithfulness to reality was considerably modified by the insistence that drama must teach moral lessons. Consequently, the dramatist was asked not merely to copy life but to reveal its ideal moral patterns. Since God was thought to be both omnipotent and just, a play was expected to show wickedness punished and goodness rewarded. Those instances in which injustice seems to prevail in life were explained as a part of God's plan, which is often beyond human comprehension but inevitably just. Therefore, such apparent aberrations were considered unsuitable subjects for drama, for playwrights should depict that ultimate truth which is inseparable from morality and justice.

Both reality and morality were further modified by the principle of abstraction or generality. Rather than seek truth in a welter of peripheral details, the neoclassicist sought it in those attributes that are shared by all phenomena of a particular category. Those characteristics that are variable were considered to be accidental and therefore no essential part of truth. Thus, the truth was defined as those norms that are discoverable through the rational and systematic examination of phenomena, whether natural or man-made. Since these norms were considered the highest form of truth, which remains unchanged regardless of the period or locale,

French Classicism

127

rational men were expected to accept them as the basis for literary creation and critical judgment.

This conception of verisimilitude led to many lesser principles. The idea that truth is to be found in "norms" was extended to every aspect of dramatic composition. Drama itself was reduced to two basic types, tragedy and comedy, with others labeled inferior because they were *mixed forms.*

Tragedy and comedy were said to have their own individual normative patterns. According to the accepted theory, tragedy draws its characters from rulers or the nobility; its stories deal with affairs of state, the downfall of rulers, and similar events; its endings are always unhappy; and its style is lofty and poetic. Comedy, on the other hand, draws its characters from the middle or lower classes; its stories deal with domestic and private affairs; its endings are always happy; and its style is characterized by the use of ordinary speech. Such distinctions meant, among other things, that tragedy could not be written about the common man, and that comedy could not be written about the nobility. Each of these rules is somewhat arbitrary, though each bears some resemblance to actual Greek and Roman practice. The neoclassic critic, nevertheless, viewed these demands as necessary and inviolable, and dramatists were denounced when they deviated from them.

In actual practice there were many other dramatic types in the seventeenth and eighteenth centuries. The usual explanation of such deviations was that these forms were not serious efforts and were not worthy of critical consideration; they were said to be the products of poorly educated or tasteless writers and were labeled "irregular" or "illegitimate" dramas.

Deviant plays also usually violated the percept that all regular drama be divided into five acts. Horace had first stated this demand in Roman times (without offering any justification for it), and neoclassic critics adopted it, seemingly without ever questioning its basis. Despite the absence of a clear-cut rationale, however, the failure to observe the five-act rule was sufficient to mark any play as "illegitimate."

Perhaps most important to the dramatist was the belief that human nature has its own governing patterns that remain the same in all places and in all periods. The dramatist, therefore, was expected to confine himself to writing about the permanent aspects of humanity. This meant cutting away all qualities that might be attributed to a particular time, place, or personal peculiarity. In neoclassical plays, therefore, there is little concern with individualizing details and great emphasis upon the more universal aspects of character and situation.

These criteria are most easily seen at work in characterization. Each age group, rank, profession, and sex was said to have its own essence. The dramatist was expected to remain true to these norms in creating his characters, and the critic used them in judging the verisimilitude of the playwright's creations. This principle of character portrayal was termed *deco-*

rum, which in its broadest sense means "fittingness" or "appropriateness." Used in this broad sense, it is a helpful concept; but as employed by the neoclassicist, it was frequently synonymous with the set of behavioral standards approved at the time. Both verisimilitude and decorum are indicative of the neoclassical attempt to achieve complete universality in drama by cutting away everything that is not true of all human beings in all times and all places.

The humanist movement in the Renaissance had had a special problem in justifying literature as a legitimate study. In breaking away from the former preoccupation with theology, the easiest route was to urge the usefulness of drama for teaching moral lessons; this was the line taken by almost all theorists between 1500 and 1800 (and which many take even today). Most theorists argued that the purpose of drama is twofold: to teach and to please—although precedence was almost always given to teaching. If this teaching were to be clear (as it should be, according to many), the plays should show evil characters being punished and good characters rewarded for their behavior. (The term *poetic justice* was coined in the seventeenth century to indicate this meting out of justified rewards and punishments to the characters in a play.) Consequently, comedy was expected to ridicule behavior that should be avoided, and tragedy to show the horrible results of mistakes and misdeeds. Critics also believed that drama should please, for otherwise teaching would not be possible. This is sometimes called the "sugarcoated pill" function of art —entertainment used to sweeten a moral lesson.

Verisimilitude was also said to dictate adherence to the unities of action, time, and place. While unity of action has been demanded in almost every age, critics in the neoclassical period normally interpreted the rule to mean that a play should have only one action, and that there should be no subplots. Neoclassical theorists are the only ones who have placed great emphasis upon the unities of time and place. While Greek and Roman playwrights tended to observe these unities, there was no insistence by critics of the time that they were necessary to good drama. Castelvetro, writing in Italy around 1570, was the first theorist to set down the unities as they were to be accepted for the next two hundred years. He argued that since an audience knows that it has been in the theatre for only a few hours, an author cannot convince it that several days or years have passed. Therefore, the time that has passed in the play should be equal to the time the audience has spent in the theatre. Other critics were less severe, but few would allow time to exceed twenty-four hours. Likewise, Castelvetro argued that the audience knows that it has only been in one place and, therefore, it cannot be expected to accept a change in a play's locale from Rome to Athens, or to other widely separated places. The demand for unity of place was sometimes broadened by other critics to allow more than one location if all could be easily reached within the twenty-four-hour time limit. This utter confusion of clock time with fictional time and of actual place with fictional place is characteristic of the period and may be explained by that aspect of verisimilitude which demanded a close correspondence between reality and art.

These, then, are the basic principles of neoclassicism. They may seem artificial and arbitrary today, but to most persons in the seventeenth and eighteenth centuries they were meaningful concepts, and therefore they seriously affected both the writing and the staging of plays.

Corneille and Racine

The writer most closely associated with the transition to classicism in France is Pierre Corneille (1606–1684), who began writing plays in the late 1620s, but did not win great success until 1636 with *The Cid*. The production of this play set off a controversy that brought many issues about dramatic composition into focus, for the play adhered in part to neoclassical demands, but in the very observance of these rules it managed to raise serious questions about the validity of verisimilitude, decorum, and the unities.

The Cid is essentially a tragicomedy, for its serious action (centering around the rival demands of love and honor) is resolved happily. The unities are for the most part observed: The action is completed within twenty-four hours, the place is confined to the city of Seville, and there are no important subplots. But so many things happen in twenty-four hours (including a war that is fought and won) that credibility, or verisimilitude, is damaged. Furthermore, at the end of the play Chimène, the play's heroine, has agreed to marry Roderigue, who has killed Chimène's father in a duel less than twenty-four hours earlier. This ending both strains decorum and (since it is a happy one for the main characters) puts *The Cid* outside the neoclassical conception of pure tragedy.

A seventeenth-century performance of Le Cid, *(Culver Pictures.)*

The play was a great success in the theatre, nevertheless, and was both denounced and extravagantly praised. The newly formed French Academy was asked to arbitrate the dispute, and its decision, written by Jean Chapelain, the Academy's acknowledged leader (with Richelieu's help, it is sometimes said), sought to clarify the extent to which the play accorded with the neoclassical ideal. Chapelain decided that *The Cid* was not a tragedy, and that, while it had many things to recommend it, verisimilitude and decorum (the most important requirements) had been severely strained. The whole controversy seems somewhat ridiculous today, but at the time it served to make the public conscious of the neoclassical ideals which were shortly to dominate critical taste and dramatic writing. Corneille eventually accepted the judgment passed on *The Cid,* and his subsequent plays (the most famous of which are *Horace, Cinna,* and *Polyeucte*) adhered to the new demands and helped to establish French classicism. In 1647 he was elected to the French Academy, a clear indication that he was by then acceptable to that group.

Although he did not reach the heights that Racine was destined to achieve, it is Corneille who took the first important step toward a new drama. The most characteristic feature of his dramas is the hero with an indomitable will. While this character constantly grows in strength throughout a play, he does not grow in complexity. Since Corneille needs a great number of episodes to demonstrate this increase in strength, his plots are relatively complex while his characters are rather simple. Between 1652 and 1659 Corneille gave up writing; however, he resumed his career and continued to produce plays until 1674. But his late works never achieved the popularity of the early ones, and he lived to see himself eclipsed in critical esteem by Racine.

The work of Jean Racine (1639–1699) marks the peak of French classical tragedy. Racine's first play, *La Thébaïde,* was produced by Molière in 1664, and his reputation was firmly established in 1667 with *Andromaque.* His other works include *Britannicus* (1669), *Bérénice* (1670), *Bajazet* (1672), and *Phaedra* (1677). Racine's plays contain little external action; most concentrate upon a psychological conflict within a single character who wants to do the right thing but is prevented either by circumstances or by his own nature. The essential qualities of Racine's plays may best be seen by looking more closely at *Phaedra,* usually considered the greatest of French tragedies.

Phaedra

Plot and Structure. Against her will, Phaedra loves her stepson, Hippolytus. Although she is fully aware that this love is wrong, she is powerless to resist it. It is upon this conflict within Phaedra that Racine concentrates.

Most plays concerned with the conflict of good and evil have shown

Sarah Bernhardt (1844-1923) as Phaedra. The greatest French tragedienne of her time, an actress of immense charm and intensity, in a role contemporary critics considered particularly her own. (Courtesy Library and Museum of the Performing Arts, Lincoln Center.)

goodness at the mercy of some external evil or as the victim of forces set in motion by some ill-advised decision. In *Phaedra,* good and evil are bound up in the same personality. Herein lies the power of the play, for it shows a woman thoroughly moral in her convictions but whose willpower has been sapped by irrational emotional drives. Since the conflict is primarily an internal one, Racine needs little external action.

The opening act of the play reveals that Phaedra has been in love with Hippolytus for a long time and that her inner torment has at last driven her to the verge of suicide to avoid sacrificing her moral integrity. She is prevented from carrying out her decision, however, by the news that her husband, Theseus, has died. Oenone, Phaedra's nurse and companion, convinces Phaedra that it is now no longer shameful for her to love Hippolytus.

Phaedra declares her love to Hippolytus, who reacts with disgust. Phaedra is filled with shame and despair at her boldness. Her hopes are revived by Oenone, only to be completely dashed by the news that Theseus not only is alive but also has arrived in Troezen, the scene of the play's action.

When Theseus enters with Hippolytus, Phaedra is faced with a moral dilemma: How can she greet her husband in the presence of his son, to whom she has just declared her love? Her hasty departure arouses Theseus' suspicion, and Oenone, to save her mistress, accuses Hippolytus of having made advances to Phaedra. Theseus calls down a terrible curse upon Hippolytus and banishes him.

Phaedra is about to tell Theseus the truth when he unwittingly reveals that Hippolytus is in love with Aricia. Her good motive turns to jealousy, and she refrains from making the revelation that could save Hippolytus' life.

As Hippolytus leaves Troezen, a sea monster (sent by Poseidon, the sea god, to carry out Theseus' curse) frightens Hippolytus' horses and he is dragged to his death. Oenone commits suicide, and Phaedra, driven by grief, remorse, and self-digust, takes poison. Before she dies, however, she confesses her guilt to Theseus.

As this brief outline shows, the character relationships in *Phaedra* are complex, while the external action is simple. The plot complications are important only because of the emotional reactions they arouse in the characters. The crucial factor at almost every point is Phaedra's uncontrollable passion for Hippolytus; it is this passion that brings misery to all the characters in the play, since the deaths of Hippolytus, Oenone, and Phaedra and the desolation of Theseus and Aricia all stem from this single source.

Racine uses powerful contrasts in story and characters. For example, Phaedra's confession of love to Hippolytus is placed immediately after Hippolytus' similar confession to Aricia. As a result, the innocent love of Aricia and Hippolytus is set against the illicit love of Phaedra, and the sweetness and youth of Aricia serve to point up the torment and maturity of Phaedra.

Each complication sets in motion a chain of events that is irreversible and that leads inevitably to catastrophe. Finally, there comes a powerful obligatory scene in which Phaedra forces herself to come face to face with Theseus after both know the full truth. There are no unnecessary scenes; Racine achieves absolute clarity without any superfluous details.

Racine adheres to the neoclassical ideals of drama almost completely, but there is no sense of strain as a result of remaining within these bounds. The unity of time is clearly observed; a few hours at the most elapse during the course of the play. The place is unspecified (it is in or around the palace), but this is typical of neoclassical drama, since what happens to the characters does not depend upon where it happens. The action is focused almost entirely upon Phaedra's passion and its results. The story of Aricia forms a minor subplot, but it is a necessary part of the main action.

Racine based his play on Euripides' *Hippolytus,* but he made many significant changes. In Euripides' drama the emphasis is upon Hippolytus' self-righteous vow to remain chaste throughout his life. To punish him for denying her power, Aphrodite arouses Phaedra's passion. The results are much the same as in Racine's play, but the causes and the implications are entirely different. In Euripides' work, Hippolytus is not in love with someone else, and Phaedra is more or less an innocent tool of the gods.

Racine eleminated the gods as visible characters in his play and brought events into the realm of verisimilitude by showing only those occurrences that could happen in real life. The monster from the sea is the only supernatural element retained, and Racine could not omit it since this was a crucial part of a well-known myth. It is subordinated as much as possible, however, by placing the action offstage and carefully preparing for it.

Phaedra also departs obviously from its Greek model in eliminating the chorus and substituting *confidantes* for it. Each of the principal characters, except Theseus, has a confidant: Phaedra has Oenone, Hippolytus has Theramenes, and Aricia has Ismene. This device is an important one, for it realistically motivates the characters to voice their feelings and intentions. The characters speak very few passages when alone on stage, and these are either prayers or are uttered under extreme emotion. Both the use of the confidant and the elimination of soliloquies show the demand for verisimilitude at work.

Characterization and Acting. Phaedra has always been considered one of the most challenging roles in French drama; for a woman, it is a role

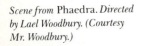

Scene from Phaedra. *Directed by Lael Woodbury. (Courtesy Mr. Woodbury.)*

comparable to that of Lear. It is difficult to perform, for there is little external action, and audience attention must be riveted on Phaedra's internal conflict. The subtleties and changes of emotional states must be clearly portrayed; therefore the ability to depict a wide range of emotional nuance is mandatory. Some of the demands can be seen by listing a few of Phaedra's major emotional responses: In the opening scene her quiet resignation turns to hope; she is then overcome by passion for Hippolytus; his rejection fills her with humiliation and rage; Theseus' return arouses abject shame and horror; she is overcome with jealousy when she learns of Hippolytus' love for Aricia; she turns on Oenone with bitterness and recrimination for the advice that has led to such a terrible situation; finally, on the point of death, she performs her duty with firm resolution. But this broad outline does not touch the gradations and subtle shifts of emotion within scenes that lay bare the heart and mind of a woman at the mercy of desires that are in conflict with her moral convictions. It is Phaedra's great capacity for moral feeling in conjunction with her uncontrollable love that makes her simultaneously both admirable and pitiable; her suffering and remorse redeem her in the minds of audiences.

While Phaedra is the center of concern, each of the other principal characters is also confronted with a psychological conflict of his own. Hippolytus, for example, is torn in the beginning between his love for Aricia and his duty to his father; later, he is torn between his desire to maintain his father's honor and to vindicate his own. Hippolytus, like Phaedra, loves against his will, so there is no question that he will return Phaedra's love. All the characters desire to act rationally, but each is swayed by irrational forces. Phaedra's is merely the most extreme of the cases.

Almost nothing is said about the age or physical appearance of the characters. The emphasis is entirely upon their psychological and moral states. Decorum of character is observed for the most part, and it is the departure from decorous behavior that brings doom. Broad strokes rather than minute details are used. The play depicts universals rather than the particularities of time and place and the idiosyncrasies of individuals.

Play Production in France, 1650–1675

The Parisian acting troupes in the time of Racine and Molière were organized on a sharing plan similar to that used by Shakespeare's company. They were democratic organizations in which each member had a vote. The French companies also included women, who had equal rights with the men and received comparable pay.

Since French plays were generally less complex than Elizabethan dramas, acting troupes were somewhat smaller. A French company was usually composed of from ten to fifteen members. As in the Elizabethan theatre, however, a number of persons were employed by the troupe as

In his early years Louis XIV was especially fond of the theatre. This engraving shows his costume for "Le Ballet de la Nuit" in 1653 in which he appeared as the "Sun King," an image which he cultivated for the rest of his life. (From Bapst's Essai sur l'Histoire du Théâtre, *1893.)*

supernumerary actors, ticket takers, musicians, scene painters, scene shifters, candle snuffers, and so on.

At the end of each performance the costs of production were deducted from the receipts and the remainder divided among the shareholders. Thus each actor's income depended upon the success of the company rather than upon a fixed salary. All of the leading groups in Paris at the time, however, received some money yearly from the crown although the sum was not large enough to guarantee them against loss.

Plays were selected by a vote of the troupe after hearing a reading of the work by its author. A play might be bought outright, but a more usual practice was to give the author a percentage of the receipts for a limited number of performances, after which the play belonged solely to the troupe. The playwright assisted in the original production of his work; thereafter the actors were presumed to be ready to perform it upon twenty-four hours' notice.

New plays were cast by their authors, while revivals required agreement among the troupe's members. This process was less complex than it might at first appear, however, since each actor normally played a limited range of roles. Thus, while there were occasional disagreements over casting, in most cases the troupe was in accord about the suitability of actors to portray certain kinds of parts. When a new actor came into a troupe, he learned his roles from the person whom he was replacing or from someone else in the company who was acquainted with the way in which the parts had been played before. Roles came to be played, therefore, in a traditional manner passed on from one actor to another.

While actors might play in both comedy and tragedy, they usually specialized in one or the other. Molière, for example, was never successful in tragedy, although he was considered to be the best comic actor of his day. One additional convention should be noted: ridiculous old women were usually play by men. Molière's brother-in-law, Louis Béjart, specialized in this kind of role.

Actors were expected to furnish their own costumes as a part of their professional equipment. For the most part costumes were contemporary garments, but, as on the Elizabethan stage, there were a number of conventionalized costumes. Classical, Near Eastern, and American Indian characters were usually played in elaborate and costly costumes quite unlike those worn in daily life. The typical dress of classical heroes was the *habit à la romaine*, an adaptation of Roman armor, tunic, and boots surmounted by a full-bottomed wig and plumed headdress. (See the illustration.)

The scenic demands were simple. Ordinarily, the setting represented a single place and even that was not indicated in detail because of the neoclassical quest for generality. Since place was not to be depicted with marked individualizing features, the same set (done in the Italian manner with wings, borders, and back-scenes) could be used for a number of different plays. Furthermore, by the second half of the seventeenth century spectators were seated regularly on the stage itself (on chairs or benches at either side), leaving an acting area only about fifteen feet wide. The actor, therefore, performed in the midst of spectators and in a very confined space. As a result, the majority of plays did not call for very much physical action, and little attention was paid to creating the illusion of a specific place. The stage, auditorium, and scenery resembled in all important respects those used in the Italian theatre.

The best season for plays was from November to Easter. The usual days of performance were Sunday, Tuesday, and Friday, although other days were used at times. Three o'clock was the announced time for performances, but actual starting time was later. The bill for each performance was composed of a long play, with a short play (usually a comedy or farce) serving as an afterpiece.

The tragic hero's costume as it developed during the seventeenth century and persisted through most of the eighteenth. An engraving after a painting by Watteau. (From Gillaumont's Costumes de la Comédie Française, *1884.)*

Molière

Just as French tragedy had achieved maturity with Racine, so French comedy was to reach its peak with Molière. Jean-Baptiste Poquelin, who assumed the name Molière (1622–1673), was the son of a prosperous upholsterer of Paris and had received a good education before entering the theatre in 1643. After his first venture, the Théâtre Illustre, failed,

Molière and his companions toured the provinces of France from 1646 to 1658. During those years the group obviously learned much, for when they returned to Paris they rapidly became second only to the Hôtel de Bourgogne troupe and they even surpassed that group in comedy. Molière was a favorite of Louis XIV, who allowed him to use the theatre Richelieu had built, the Palais-Royal, and protected him in many controversies.

Although Molière is noted today principally for his comedies of character and ideas, he wrote other kinds of plays as well. Greatly influenced by the commedia dell'arte, many of his plays are farces featuring the commedia character types. He also wrote a number of comedy ballets (comic plays with dances) for the court and tried his hand at tragedy. Throughout his career Molière borrowed as he saw fit from Plautus, Terence, the commedia, and from Spanish and Italian sources. Molière's work has retained a more universal appeal than that of his tragic contemporaries; his plays are still seen on the stages of almost every country, while those of Corneille and Racine are seldom produced outside of France.

Molière's most famous works are: *The School for Wives* (1662), *Tartuffe* (1664), *The Miser* (1668), *The Doctor in Spite of Himself* (1666), *The Misanthrope* (1666), *The Would-Be Gentleman* (1671), and *The Imaginary Invalid* (1673), *Tartuffe* will be examined here in some detail as an example of his comedy.

Molière was often called upon to provide entertainment at the court. Shown here is a scene from La Princesse d'Elide, *a comedy-ballet performed out of doors at Versailles in 1664. The scenery was real shrubbery. (From Pougin's* Dictionnaire..., *1885.*

Tartuffe

Tartuffe, or the Impostor was produced in a three-act version in 1664, in an altered form in 1667, and in its present five-act form in 1669. It has remained in the repertory almost continuously since its completion and has been performed more often than any other play by Molière.

Themes and Ideas. *Tartuffe* is obviously concerned with religious hypocrisy. While it is unwise to place too much emphasis on contemporary conditions, it may be helpful to look at historical events that clarify the play.

The most likely target of Molière's satire is the Company of the Holy Sacrament, a secret society formed in 1627 and by 1660 influential throughout France. Its purposes included the repression of heresy, the promotion of charity and missionary work, and the improvement of morals. In implementing the last of these aims, the society maintained "spiritual police" who spied upon the private lives of others. As one critic said of the group: "They had for their agents fanatics who to save souls recoiled from nothing, 'sanctifying by the purity of their intentions' what simple folk would call dirty actions."

Molère read *Tartuffe* to several persons before it was first produced in 1664, and the society immediately organized an attack upon it. The controversy became so heated that Louis XIV forbade further performances. Molière revised the play in 1667, hoping to remove some of the objections, only to have it withdrawn again. By 1669, when still another version was presented, the opposition was largely gone.

Whether Molière had the society in mind is not of great importance. It is clear that he was thinking of groups like the society who create conditions under which hypocrites can flourish. Molière, through the ending of the play, indicates that France would be better off without such groups, and that the King is able to tell truth from falsehood without their aid.

As in all of Molière's works, the balanced view of life is upheld in *Tar-*

French Classicism

tuffe. To Molière, true piety does not demand the abandonment of pleasure but the right use of it. The truly devout try to reform the world by actions that set a good example rather than by pious speeches or, as it is put in the play, "They don't espouse the interests of Heaven with greater zeal than does Heaven itself."

Another favorite topic with Molière is the forced marriage. In part, this motif is a convention inherited from past drama, especially Roman comedy and commedia dell'arte, in which plots frequently turn on the attempts of fathers to arrange marriages for their children without regard to suitability. Molière argues in his plays that most of the evils of marriage can be traced to forced unions. In *Tartuffe,* as elsewhere, he suggests that such marriages are apt to result in adultery. But in this play, marriage is an entirely secondary concern. The main theme is hypocrisy.

Plot, Structure, and Characterizations. The plot of *Tartuffe* can be divided into five stages: the demonstration of Tartuffe's complete hold over Orgon; the unmasking of Tartuffe; Tartuffe's attempted revenge; the foiling of Tartuffe's plan; and the happy resolution. There are three important reversals. The first (the unmasking of Tartuffe) brings all of the characters to an awareness of the true situation. The resulting happiness is quickly dispelled, however, when Orgon is shown to be at the mercy of Tartuffe. Since Orgon's credulity has placed him in this position, it would serve him justly to be punished, but innocent members of the family also are involved.

The first two reversals (turning the tables on Tartuffe, Tartuffe turning the tables on Orgon) have been carefully foreshadowed, but the final one and the play's resolution have not. The contrived ending (in which Tartuffe is suddenly discovered to be a notorious criminal) has been the subject of much criticism. It is an emotionally satisfying ending, in the sense that justice triumphs and normalcy is restored, but the contrivance cannot be explained away by accepted criteria of good dramatic construction.

Molière has also been criticized because of the long-delayed appearance of Tartuffe, who does not enter until the third act. This delay is not accidental, however, for Molière himself wrote:

> *I have employed . . . two entire acts to prepare for the entrance of my scoundrel. He does not fool the auditor for a single moment; one knows from the first the marks I have given him; and from one end to the other he says not a word and performs not an action which does not paint for the spectators the character of an evil man.*

That Molière was attempting to prevent any confusion about Tartuffe's true nature is further borne out by the inclusion in the first act of a lengthy argument by his "common-sense" character, Cléante (the character who most nearly represents Molière's point of view), in which true piety is distinguished from false. There is a similar discussion in most of Molière's plays, but as a rule it comes toward the end. The placement of

this argument in the first act of *Tartuffe* further indicates Molière's desire to make his purpose clear to the audience.

The structure of *Tartuffe* may also be clarified by examining the use made of various characters. Orgon's is the only role that is important in every act (in terms of onstage action). Cléante appears in Act I, where he performs his principal function—to present the common-sense point of view. He does not appear again until Act IV; in that act and in Act V he merely reinforces the ideas he has set forth in Act I. His presence in the play does not influence the action at all; it merely points up the theme.

While Dorine, the maid, appears in each act, her role is virtually completed after the beginning of Act III, even though she has been a major character up to that point. Her frankness and openness are used as a foil to show off Orgon's credulity, the lovers' petulance, and Tartuffe's false piety. It is she, with her wit and common sense, who sets their exaggerated behavior in proper perspective. After Tartuffe's entrance, she is no longer needed.

Even Tartuffe is given rather strange treatment when he finally makes his appearance after two acts of preparation. He has one of the most famous entrance lines ever written: "Laurent, put away my hair shirt and my scourge and pray heaven may ever enlighten you. If any one asks to see me, tell them I've gone to the prison to distribute the charity which others have given me."

But the major portion of his role is given over to his two "love scenes" with Elmire. Molière seems to take it for granted that the audience will accept the picture of Tartuffe painted earlier by the other characters and that the play need only show one aspect of his hypocrisy. Tartuffe's first speeches to Dorine (those in which he asks her to cover her bosom with

French Classicism

141

a handkerchief so as not to arouse evil thoughts in him) reveal his sensual nature, and it is this quality that is emphasized onstage.

Tartuffe displays another important side of his character when he is denounced by Damis. Rather than defend himself, he appears to accept the accusations with humility and as the lot of a pious man. This scene more than any other shows how Orgon has come to be taken in by Tartuffe.

While Act V shows Tartuffe's true nature, which has been masked under his hypocrisy, it is true, nevertheless, that most of what the audience knows of Tartuffe comes from what other characters say about him rather than through what he actually does onstage.

The lovers, Valère and Mariane, appear in Act II and are unimportant therafter. They serve merely to show how far Orgon has been influenced by Tartuffe, since Orgon is planning to marry his daughter Mariane to Tartuffe. The lovers' quarrel is a source of amusement but it is largely unrelated to the rest of the play. As in commedia, the lovers are handsome, upright, and admirable young people who deserve each other's love and who are being kept apart by a muddle-headed and perverse parent.

Elmire is also used when needed and ignored at other times. She appears in Act III (in which Tartuffe tries to seduce her), but she has only a few lines and most of these treat Tartuffe's suggestions with an air of frivolity. The bulk of her lines comes in Act IV, where she serves as the instrument for unmasking Tartuffe. This uneven distribution of the role has led to some confusion about her true nature, for some critics have argued that her moral character is questionable. It seems clear, however, that Molière had in mind a reasonably worldly but upright woman.

It is Orgon's role, however, that is most evenly distributed throughout the play. While the Tartuffes of the world are dangerous, they can exist only because of the Orgons, for the prosperity of the wicked depends upon the gullibility of the foolish. Just as Molière emphasizes Tartuffe's calculated piety, so too, he emphasizes Orgon's impulsiveness and stubbornness. Orgon is not a fool; he is a prosperous merchant with a substantial fortune. He errs in his judgment of Tartuffe largely because he acts without considering sufficient aspects of a question. When Tartuffe is finally unmasked, Orgon's character remains consistent, for, failing to see the difference between hypocrisy and piety, he says: "I give up all pious people. From now on I will hold them in utter contempt, and treat them worse than the devil himself." Thus, instead of returning to middle ground he assumes an equally exaggerated, though opposite, position.

Little indication is given of the age or physical appearance of the characters. Since Molière wrote with his own company in mind and directed the play, he did not need to specify every detail in his script. The role of Tartuffe was written for DuCroisy, a large man with a ruddy complexion. This, no doubt, was one of the sources of humor. All of Tartuffe's talk about scourges, hair shirts, and fasting was contradicted by his obvious plumpness, rosy health, and lecherousness. Orgon was played by Molière, noted for his expressive face and body, while Elmire was acted by Molière's wife, who was twenty-seven in 1669. Since Mme. Pernell was played by a man, the character was no doubt intended to be ridiculous in her exaggerated censure of everyone except Tartuffe and in her denunciation of pleasure. All of the characters are drawn from the middle or lower classes (in accordance with neoclassical theories of comedy).

Probably the least challenging roles for actors are those of Cléante and the lovers. Although meant to arouse audience sympathy, they seem mere cardboard figures. Tartuffe's role is difficult and the actor playing it must be wary of becoming too villainous, if the comedy is not to disappear under too great a threat. Orgon's is probably the best acting role, for not only is it the longest, it requires the greatest comic skill. One indication of the difficulty of the role is the scene in which Orgon conceals himself under the table and overhears Tartuffe's attempts to seduce Elmire. The success of the scene depends in large part upon a highly skilled pantomimic performance by the actor playing Orgon.

The unities of time and place are strictly observed in *Tartuffe*. Only a single room is required and even that need have only a table (under which Orgon can be concealed) and a closet (in which Damis can hide) for no specific use is made of the setting except in these two instances. The action is continuous, or nearly so, and occurs in a single day. All of the episodes, with the possible exception of the lovers' quarrel, are directly related to the main theme of the play. *Tartuffe* is clearly within the classical tradition.

Molière, nevertheless, has let dramatic need, rather than any preconceived notion of form, dictate his technique. In spite of all objections raised to it, *Tartuffe* has remained one of the most popular plays ever written. If it has flaws, it rises above them.

The Theatre After Molière's Death

Molière died in 1673. His life and death illustrate the status of the actor in France at that time, for, while he was highly admired as an author, his acting made him ineligible for many honors. For example, he could not be admitted to the French Academy, and upon his death he was forbidden a Christian burial, since the church's strictures against actors, issued in late Roman times, were still in effect. Most actors renounced their professions when death approached so that they might be accepted back into the church, but Molière died suddenly, having been taken ill during a performance; either he did not have time or refused to go through the usual formalities.

Only after the intercession of Louis XIV was Molière given a Christian burial, and then with minimal rites. Thus, while the actor's legal and economic status had improved by 1673, he was still in some senses an outcast.

Following Molière's death, French drama rapidly declined. Corneille

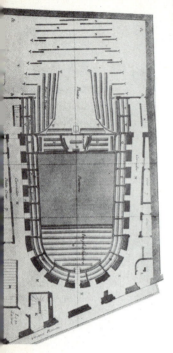

gave up writing in 1674, and Racine wrote no plays for the public stage after 1677. Thus, the great age of French playwriting was over by 1680.

The number of theatres also shrank steadily after 1673. At the time of Molière's death, five theatrical companies were playing in Paris: Molière's, the companies at the Hôtel de Bourgogne and the Marais, a company of Italian actors, and an opera troupe. In 1673, the director of the opera, Jean-Baptiste Lully, gained control of the Palais-Royal, and Molière's company was forced to move. Soon afterward Molière's troupe was amalgamated with the Marais company and, in 1680, this combined company was ordered to merge with the Hôtel de Bourgogne troupe.

This final merger is one of the most important events in French theatrical history, for it created the Comédie Française, the first national theatre in the world. This organization is still in existence, and more nearly

Ground plan of the theatre used by the Comédie Française between 1689 and 1770. Note the benches on the stage for spectators. (From Mantzius' History of Theatrical Art. *Vol. IV, 1905.*

The commedia dell'arte *troupe of the Hôtel de Bourgogne in 1689. (From* Almanach de l'An 1689.)

embodies a continuous theatrical tradition than any other single theatre.

The order that created the Comédie Française also laid down the rules under which it was to be governed. Like its predecessors, it was to be a shareholding company governed democratically by its members. Procedures were established for admitting actors to the company, for their retirements, for paying pensions, and for numerous other matters. A yearly subsidy was provided by the state.

After 1680, there were for some time three troupe in Paris: the Comédie Française, the Opéra, and an Italian commedia dell'arte company. When the Italian troupe was expelled in 1697 (after performing an alleged satire on Mme. de Maintenon, Louis XIV's second wife), the number was reduced to two.

In 1672, the Opéra had been awarded a monopoly on musical drama and other forms that utilized trained vocalists, more than six musicial instruments, or complex dance and spectacle. After the expulsion of the Italians, the Comédie Française achieved a similar monopoly on spoken drama. Thus, by the end of the seventeenth century, the Parisian theatre not only had shrunk but also the remaining troupes held entrenched positions which they were to defend against all encroachments throughout the eighteenth century.

The age of French classicism had brought the theatre of France to maturity. It produced three great playwrights, Corneille, Racine, and Molière, who have remained the primary models for French drama since that time. Unfortunately, the high point reached in the years between 1650 and 1680 would not be regained for several generations.

7

The Eighteenth Century

During the eighteenth century, the theatre expanded rapidly into geographical areas that previously had not had professional troupes. Dramatic forms also proliferated and theatrical practices underwent many changes, although the neoclassical mode remained dominant.

Government Regulation of the English Theatre

When Charles II was restored to the throne of England in 1660, the theatre reclaimed its place in English life. Since then, although the theatre has been closed briefly during natural disasters, periods of national mourning, and on similar occasions, its tradition has continued uninterruptedly.

When the theatre was reestablished in 1660, the king declared it illegal to produce plays without his patent (a monopolistic right that, like property ownership, could be sold or passed on to others). In the early 1660s, the king issued two patents—one to William D'Avenant (1606–1668), who

The Drury Lane Theatre, one of London's major theatres from the Restoration until the present time as it appeared in 1792. The present Drury Lane Theatre is used primarily for musicals. (From Wilkinson's Londina Illustrata, *1825.)*

organized a troupe known as the Duke's Men, and another to Thomas Killigrew (1612–1683), who established the King's Men. These two patents were to remain in effect thereafter until 1843.

During the first part of the eighteenth century many attempts were made to circumvent the patents, and eventually the violations, coupled with numerous productions satirizing government officials and policies, provoked the passage of the Licensing Act of 1737. This law reconfirmed the patents and further provided that, prior to production, each play had to be licensed by the Lord Chamberlain (a government official), who thus became the censor of all works intended for the stage. Although the strictness with which this law was enforced varied from time to time, for more than a century it did much to hamper the growth of the theatre in London, where only two theatres, Drury Lane and Covent Garden, were permitted to produce regular drama throughout the year. (After 1766, the Haymarket Theatre was licensed to perform during the summer months.) In the early nineteenth century, other theatres began to be licensed for limited periods to present "minor" forms such as melodrama and burletta, and it was owing in part to pressures from these theatres that the patents were finally rescinded in 1843. Since that time there has been no attempt to restrict the number of theatres in London. The provision for licensing plays, however, continued in effect until 1968.

English Theatre Architecture

When the English theatre reopened in 1660, performances were given at first in playhouses that had been built before 1642. Almost immediately, however, new playhouses, incorporating Italianate features, were built. The major difference between English and continental theatres involved the apron (that portion of the stage that extends forward of the proscenium arch), for though continental theatres had aprons, they were not used extensively for acting and did not have proscenium doors (that is, doors located forward of the proscenium arch and opening onto the apron). During the Restoration, there were sometimes as many as three proscenium doors on each side of the stage, although two were more usual. These doors permitted great flexibility in staging. For example, an actor might exit through one door and reenter immediately at another door on the same side, thus indicating a change in place or a passage of time. Thus, the apron stage was comparable in many ways both to the forestage of the Elizabethan theatre and to the platea of the medieval theatre.

Early in the eighteenth century the number of doors on either side was reduced to one, and thereafter the depth of the apron gradually diminished; but both features were retained until well into the nineteenth century, when the demand for greater realism motivated managers to abandon them and to place all action upstage of the proscenium arch. Because

Interior of the Covent Garden Theatre in 1794. One of the two main theatres of London from 1732 until 1843, the Covent Garden has been the home of opera since the mid-nineteenth century. (From Wilkinson's Londina Illustrata, *1825.)*

in the eighteenth century much of the action took place on the apron, the setting was principally a background rather than an environment for the actor, who performed, for the most part, forward of the proscenium where he could more easily establish rapport with the audience.

The auditorium of the English theatre, with its boxes, pit, and galleries, was similar in all important respects to those then in use on the continent. From the Restoration on, however, all spectators in the English pit were seated. Until 1762, spectators were also permitted to sit on the stage.

Scenery in the English Theatre

Scenery in the English theatre between 1660 and 1800 differed in no important respect from that used in Italy and France. Scenes were painted in perspective on wings, borders, and shutters. Since, in accord-

A scene from Elkanah Settle's The Empress of Morocco *(1673) at the Duke's Theatre in Dorset Garden, London. Although the forestage is not shown, a portion of the proscenium doors an stage boxes can be seen at the extreme sides. (From Wilkinson's* Londina Illustrata, *1825.)*

A sketch by Philippe Jacques de Louterbourg for the battle scenes in Shakespeare's Richard III. *This sketch was made about 1775 when the noted landscape, marine, and battle painter was engaged by David Garrick to superintend scene painting at the Drury Lane Theatre.*

ance with the neoclassical demand for universality, locales were generalized, a large number of settings were unnecessary. Plays were usually set in a palace, a garden, a prison, or another generalized place, and consequently the same setting was used for many different plays. Sometimes theatres even used a set of "neutral" wings which remained stationary throughout a play while only the back-scene was shifted to indicate a change in place. The "wing-and-groove" system was the standard method of shifting scenery in England.

Pantomimes, operas, and a few plays, however, demanded more detailed scenery and elaborate special effects. In these cases, new scenery was specially designed and prominently advertised. On such occasions, spectators might also be forbidden to sit on the stage. Until about 1750, theatres did not employ full-time scenic artists but commissioned scenery as needed from well-known painters. As the taste for spectacle grew in the last part of the eighteenth century, each theatre came to employ one or more scene painters, and new scenery appeared with greater frequency. At the same time, awakening interest in *local color* (picturesque locales and customs) led to increased emphasis upon specific times and places.

The most important eighteenth-century English scene designer was Philippe Jacques de Louterbourg (1740–1812), who began staging spectacular pieces (he seldom designed legitimate drama) for David Garrick at Drury Lane in the early 1770s. He complicated the stage picture by adding ground rows (profile pieces shaped and painted to represent rocks, mountains, grassy plots, fences and similar objects) to the traditional wing-border-drop settings. Since these could be placed almost anywhere on the stage, they increased the sense of naturalness and the illusion of space and distance. De Louterbourg also reproduced likenesses of actual places on stage and thereby helped to create a demand for greater scenic illusion. He improved stage lighting and was able to give the effect of natural light at different seasons, times of day, and in varying weather conditions by utilizing transparent backdrops behind which special lighting devices could achieve the semblance of a rising moon, a volcanic eruption, changes from fair to stormy weather, and similar effects. But, such practices were not to be exploited until the nineteenth century.

The English Acting Company

When the English theatre was reopened in 1660, its financial structure was considerably altered from that of Shakespeare's day. From the Restoration on, the theatre was to come more and more under the control of businessmen. After 1660, actors often served as managers of theatrical troupes, but the majority withdrew from the business affairs of the theatre. They became employees rather than active participants in management.

Typically, in the English theatre of the eighteenth century an actor was hired for a stated period, usually one or two years, at a specified salary with the additional guarantee of one or more "benefit" performances each year. At a benefit performance the receipts (after deduction of operating expenses) go to an actor, author, charitable group, or other designated source. The first benefit performance for an individual actor dates from about 1685, but after about 1710 every performer had at least one benefit each season, although a lesser actor often had to share his benefit with one or more of his fellows. While a benefit usually brought the actor additional income, it also offered the manager an excuse for paying him a relatively small salary during the rest of the year. Benefits often were occasions for great rejoicing, but, since they were tests of popularity, they could also be sources of embarrassment if attendance was small. Furthermore, an actor could lose money on a benefit if the receipts were not sufficient to cover the operating expenses of the theatre.

Although the English actor did not have the financial security enjoyed by his French contemporaries, his social status was higher: he was never excluded from the church; a number of actresses married into the nobility; and some actors were even buried in Westminster Abbey, an honor reserved for persons held in great esteem. On the other hand, the moral character of the actor continued to be questioned by the general populace.

Each actor or actress (actresses first appeared on the English stage in the 1660s and were accepted throughout Europe after that time) was usually employed for a *line of business*. This practice meant that each was hired to play a specific range of parts. If his line of business included the young lover, he typically played such roles regardless of age until he retired from the stage. While this sometimes led to incongruous casting, it also allowed the actor to develop considerable perfection in his specialty.

An actor learned his profession from experience rather than at a school. He might begin in a provincial company and later be taken into a London troupe, or, more rarely, he might learn a line of business while

The closet scene from Hamlet *as it appeared in the early eighteenth century. Note the contemporary dress worn by Hamlet and the Queen. (From Nicholas Rowe's edition of Shakespeare's works, Vol. V, 1709.)*

playing supernumerary roles in a London theatre. After a few years of apprenticeship, however, an actor's line of business was usually fixed for life.

Each actor also *possessed parts*. This meant that once he was given a particular role, it remained his until he left the company. An actor might be assigned up to a hundred roles, any one of which he could be expected to perform on twenty-four hours' notice.

Many of these practices were determined by the *repertory system* (under which a large number of plays were rotated with some regularity throughout the season). Between 1660 and 1800 the majority of any company's repertory was made up of standard plays from the past. A lesser part was composed of works from recent seasons. Usually these recent plays were not popular enough to retain in the repertory more than a few years. The smallest proportion of a company's offerings was made up of new plays. Those sufficiently popular were retained in the repertory, but many new plays were dropped after a single season or even after a single performance.

New plays were usually staged by their authors, while old plays were rehearsed by the "acting manager," usually a performer in the company who was given additional pay to assume these duties. Regardless of who

staged the plays, it was taken for granted that the actors were sufficiently
skilled to need little guidance. Thus, the acting manager usually
restricted himself to establishing where and when entrances and exists
were to be made, rehearsing difficult bits of stage business, and giving a
few hints about characterization or line readings. He probably spent very
little time on blocking (that it, positioning the actors on stage), for performers learned as part of their training to let the major actors have the
best stage positions and to move around them as inconspicuously as possible. The actor also learned to move to down center when his turn to
speak came and to direct his lines to the audience as much as to the characters on stage. The presence of the audience was constantly recognized
and emphasized by the practice of leaving the lights on in the auditorium
throughout a performance. Furthermore, since most of the action occurred
on the apron forward of the proscenium arch, the performer, in effect, was
in the auditorium with the spectators.

Rehearsals for plays not previously in the repertory normally extended
over a period of seven to twelve days. Meanwhile the actors were also performing nightly, and a short "refresher" rehearsal was probably held each
day for the play that was to be performed that evening. By modern standards rehearsal procedures were perfunctory. Thus, great reliance was
placed on the actor's stage presence and quick wit.

Actors often played more than one role on the same evening since the program was so complex. After 1720 a typical evening's bill, which usually lasted three or more hours, was arranged as follows: First, there was approximately a half hour of orchestral music; then came the prologue, followed by a full-length play; the intervals between the acts were filled with miscellaneous variety entertainment (such as singing and dancing monologues, feats of magic, ventriloquism, acrobatics, trained animals, and so on); subsequent to the main piece, an afterpiece (a pantomime, farce, or comic opera) was performed; the evening usually concluded with a song and dance. An actor often appeared in both the main piece and the afterpiece, and he might present one of the variety acts as well. An actor's versatility often determined his popularity.

Acting style was no doubt more conventionalized than modern taste would approve. The actor was said to base his acting on life, but to idealize what he found there rather than merely to copy it. Thus he selected, arranged, and considerably heightened elements based on typical human behavior and response. Periodically during the eighteenth century, actors supposedly reformed acting in the direction of a more natural style. But naturalism in acting is a relative matter, and the reforms probably merely softened the exaggerations. It seems unlikely that a performance would ever have been confused with real-life behavior.

In the eighteenth century, the actor, in terms of popularity and prestige, became the dominant artist of the theatre. For the most part, audiences went to see a particular actor perform a particular role. The appeal was comparable to that of opera today, for, since it frequently knew the

David Garrick and Mrs. Hannah Pritchard as Macbeth and Lady Macbeth. (From English Illustrated Magazine, *1776.)*

play already, the audience attended to see how the actor would perform his part. After each effective speech or scene the audience applauded as it does today when a singer finishes an operatic aria. This constant interaction between audience and actor made for a more intimate relationship than that typical in most theatres today.

The actors most admired in England between 1660 and 1800 were Thomas Betterton, Colley Cibber, James Quin, David Garrick, and Charles Macklin. Thomas Betterton (c. 1635–1710) dominated the English stage from about 1670 to 1710, during which time he played leading roles in almost all the standard plays in the repertory. He excelled in heroic and tragic parts, and his somewhat formal and elocutionary style became a model for many of his successors. Colley Cibber (1671–1757) is the best-known performer of the period from Betterton's death until the 1730s. Primarily a comic actor, he excelled in the role of the "fop," or fashionable man-about-town. His autobiography, published in 1740, is one of the principal sources of information about the English theatre from 1690 to 1735.

Between 1730 and 1740, James Quin (1692–1766), who was noted especially for his declamatory style, was considered England's best tragic actor. It was partially due to Quin's acting style that David Garrick (1717–1779) was said to have returned acting to a more natural mode when he came to prominence in the 1740s. Garrick was the major actor on the English stage between 1741 and 1776, as well as manager of the Drury Lane Theatre from 1747 to 1776. Through his sound judgment and taste, both in management and acting, he elevated the English theatre to a position of international esteem. Especially noted for his performance of Shakespearean roles, he is generally thought to have been the greatest of all English actors.

Charles Macklin (1699–1797) acted for approximately seventy years and was probably the most realistic actor of the eighteenth century. He was especially well known for his playing of irascible old men and for his revolutionary portrayal of Shylock in Shakespeare's *The Merchant of Venice,* a role previously performed by low comedians.

The actor in an established theatre company in London in the eighteenth century enjoyed a comfortable life, though his counterpart in the provincial company still led a hazardous existence. Even in London, however, there was as yet no pension system (as in France), and many actors ended their days in poverty.

Charles Macklin as Shylock. Macklin supposedly played Shylock as a semiserious character, departing from the earlier tradition of treating Shylock as a low comedy role. (From Doran's "His Majesty's Servants," 1897.)

English Playwriting

But the actor's position was more secure than that of the playwright. In the 1660s, writers of plays might be paid a fixed salary by companies, but this practice was soon replaced by benefits. Under this system, the author received the receipts of the third performance. If a play were especially

Mrs. Hartley as Cleopatra in Dryden's All for Love. *(Culver Pictures.)*

popular he might also receive benefits on the sixth, ninth, and each additional third night of the initial run of a play. As a rule, however, he was fortunate to receive one benefit. After the initial benefits, the play belonged to the company and the author received no further payment. It was not until well into the nineteenth century that the playwright could demand a royalty for each performance of his play.

The period from 1660 to 1700 is noted particularly for heroic tragedy and comedy of manners. The heroic play, written in rhymed couplets, usually concerned the necessity of choosing between love and honor (the relative merits of which were debated in lengthy and bombastic speeches), and abounded in violent action and startling reversals. Today these plays seem absurdly exaggerated, although they were extremely popular in their own period.

Alongside the heroic play another more vital strain of tragedy developed. Written in blank verse and more directly descended from the tragedies of Shakespeare, the outstanding examples are Thomas Otway's (1652–1685) *Venice Preserv'd* and *The Orphan,* both of which held the stage until the nineteenth century. Another example of this kind of Restoration tragedy is *All for Love,* by John Dryden (1631–1700), a reworking of Shakespeare's *Antony and Cleopatra* to make it conform to neoclassical rules.

The Restoration is principally noted, however, for the comedy of manners, in which characters and events are subordinate in interest to social values and customs. Readers have often been offended by the moral tone of Restoration comedy. Since 1700 most critics have interpreted these comedies as condoning or accepting behavior normally considered reprehensible. Many of these plays do waver between accepting and satirizing the age, but they should not be condemned too hastily on moral grounds. Before passing judgment on them, it is important to understand the basic view that underlies the plays.

Restoration comedies imply that man is corruptible but that the sophisticated observer will accept and tolerate deviations rather than become indignant or outraged about them. Restoration writers did not imply, however, that all forms of behavior are justified and that no distinctions are to be made among actions. The admirable man was thought to base his behavior on the maxim, "Know thyself," for this would lead him to assess his own qualities and capabilities and to respect them in his daily life. The plays, therefore, satirize persons who are either self-deceived or who are attempting to deceive others. The humor is directed against the fop, the pretender at wit and sophistication, the old woman who is trying to be young, the old man who marries a young wife, and other similar types. The norm is embodied in those characters who are truly witty and sophisticated, who see others and themselves clearly, and who act accordingly. These characters are tolerant of almost all behavior, however, and for this reason the plays have often given the impression of condoning immoral behavior. In a few plays immoral behavior is accepted, but in the majority the rewards and punishments are meted out according to how well the characters live up to the ideal of self-knowledge.

Restoration comedy originated with such works as George Etherege's (1634–1691) *Love in a Tub* (1664), *The Man of Mode* (1676, and *She Would If She Could* (1668), and reached its perfection in the plays of William Congreve (1670–1729), especially *Love for Love* (1695), and *The Way of the World* (1700).

The Restoration comedy of manners was not calculated to please the Puritan elements in English society. After the return of Charles II in 1660 Puritan influence, which had dominated England during the Commonwealth, was little felt for some time. Furthermore, from 1660 to about 1690 theatre audiences were largely drawn from the upper classes or from the more liberal elements of the middle class. But change set in after 1689, when William and Mary were crowned rulers of England. Under the patronage of these monarchs, the merchant class came to wield considerable power, and from the 1690s onward, when it attended the theatre in sizable numbers, it exerted pressure for reform.

The rise of the middle class coincided with a resurgence of Puritan protests against the theatre, the most powerful statement of which came in Jeremy Collier's *A Short View of the Immorality and Profaneness of the English Stage* (1698). In this work Collier attacked current plays, particularly the comedies of manners. While many dramatists of the day defended their own works and those of others, Collier was sufficiently persuasive that many playwrights reconsidered their views. Various influences, then, combined to bring about a change in the subject matter and spirit of English drama after 1700.

The transition to a new outlook can be seen most clearly in the comedies of George Farquhar (1678–1707), whose *The Recruiting Officer* and *The Beaux' Stratagem* are among the best English plays of the early eighteenth century. The new drama put greater emphasis on a clearcut set of moral standards, the settings were more frequently placed outside of London, and the characters were less apt to be drawn from fashionable society.

English Sentimental Drama

While neoclassical tragedy continued to be written throughout the eighteenth century (the best-known example is *Cato* by Joseph Addison), the most important dramatic types were to be sentimental comedy and domestic tragedy. The appearance of these forms can be explained in part by the desire of the middle class to see itself and its ideals depicted on the stage.

The term *sentimental* is sometimes used as a label for almost all drama of the eighteenth century. It indicates basically an overemphasis on arousing sympathetic response to the misfortunes of others. Even comedy became preoccupied with the ordeals of sympathetic characters, and humorous scenes were reserved for minor characters, usually servants. Many plays could be called comedies largely because they ended happily rather than because of subject matter or treatment. The expressed aim of the dramatist was to draw forth a smile and a tear, or, as one writer put

A scene from The Conscious Lovers *by Sir Richard Steele. From an edition of the play published in 1816. (Culver Pictures.)*

it, to produce "a pleasure too exquisite for laughter." The refined protagonists of these plays voice many noble sentiments; they are oppressed by circumstances that they bear bravely and from which they eventually are rescued; and they are handsomely rewarded for their moral fortitude.

Today these plays seem highly exaggerated in their depiction of human nature. The characters appear too good and noble and the circumstances too contrived to be convincing. But these plays attracted large audiences who were reduced to tears and who accepted the works as realistic pictures of human motivations. To understand the appeal of the plays, therefore, it is necessary to examine the view of human psychology prevalent at that time.

The eighteenth century conceived of humans as basically good. To remain good, a person needed only to listen to his instincts and to follow their promptings. Evil behavior was thought to result from unfortunate circumstances or the failure to follow dictates of the heart. Consequently, the person who fell into evil ways might be reformed, sometimes even in a moment's time, through an appeal to his basic goodnesss. To endure ordeals and resist temptations were looked upon as tests of true virtue, and to reward those who met these tests successfully was considered the logical and necessary outcome.

One other factor—the attitude toward emotional display—helps to explain the appeal of sentimental drama in the eighteenth century. Man was viewed as subject to all sorts of pressures from without, against which he must exert counteracting pressures from within if he is not to be overwhelmed. The chief form of outwardly directed pressure was considered to be emotion. The display of emotion, then, became both the sign of a healthy mind and a means of maintaining health. Furthermore, the ideal emotions were thought to be those sympathetic responses aroused when witnessing the suffering of innocent beings. Emotional display, therefore, was proof of a virtuous nature (one properly moved at the sight of suffering), and, at the same time, this response helped to maintain health. To weep and to feel deeply, then, were desirable, and playwrights labored to fulfill the needs.

Eighteenth-century sentimental comedy received its first full expression in *The Conscious Lovers* (1722) by Sir Richard Steele (1672–1729). In it, the penniless heroine, Indiana, after withstanding many trials, is discovered to be the daughter of a rich merchant, thus making her marriage to the hero acceptable to his father. Later sentimental comedy is best exemplified in Hugh Kelly's (1739–1777) *False Delicacy* (1768), which shows how three unsuited lovers are disentangled and the virtuous rewarded.

Sentimental comedy had its serious counterpart in domestic tragedy, which deliberately avoided the kings and nobility of traditional tragedy and chose its characters from everyday life (principally the merchant class). It usually painted the horrible outcome of giving in to sin, just as sentimental comedy showed the rewards of resisting sin.

George Lillo (1693–1739) established the vogue for domestic tragedy with *The London Merchant* (1731), a play that shows an apprentice who, led astray by a depraved woman, robs his employer and murders his uncle. It is clearly indicated that had the apprentice resisted temptation, he could have married his employer's daughter and become a prosperous merchant. The play praises the virtues of the merchant class and denounces sin in the most obvious terms. Today *The London Merchant* seems overly simple, but it exerted great power over audience throughout the eighteenth century and was a major influence on the drama of France and Germany. Although others followed in Lillo's steps, *The Gamester* (1753), a play by Edward Moore (1712–1757) about the evils of gambling, is the only other notable English play of the type.

Sentimental comedy and domestic tragedy are indicative of the weakening of neoclassical standards. Each represents a considerable departure from the "pure" dramatic forms demanded by critics, for they mingled elements formerly associated wholly with comedy or tragedy.

Ballad Opera, Burlesque, and Pantomime

Still other departures from the neoclassical ideal occurred during the eighteenth century as new "illegitimate" forms appeared. The most im-

Macheath with Lucy and Polly in Gay's The Beggar's Opera. *(Culver Pictures.)*

portant of the new forms were ballad opera, burlesque, and pantomime.

The emergence of ballad opera can be explained in part by the popularity in England of Italian opera. In the early years of the Restoration, a debate began between champions of Italian opera and of native English opera. Supporters of the Italian style triumphed, and in the early years of the eighteenth century opera became enormously popular. The vogue reached its peak with the works of George Frideric Handel (1685–1759), who worked in England after 1710. The ballad opera built on this enthusiasm.

In *ballad opera*, sections of dialogue alternate with lyrics set to existing popular that the producers ran it continuously for sixty performances, was *The Beggar's Opera* (1728) by John Gay (1685–1732). It was so popularl that the producers ran it continuously for sixty performances, one of the first long runs in theatrical history. Its popularity spawned many imitations between 1728 and 1737.

While *The Beggar's Opera* treated Italian opera humorously, it did much more, for it also satirized the contemporary political situation in England. At the end of the work one of the characters observes that it is difficult to tell whether the robbers are imitating the ruling classes or whether the ruling classes are imitating the robbers. The moral is said to lie in the demonstration that the lower classes, like the upper, have their vices, but that, unlike the upper classes, the lower orders are punished for their wrongdoings. The ballad opera eventually gave way to the sentimental operetta, or comic opera. The principal writer of this form was Isaac Bickerstaffe (1735–1812), whose most popular works were *Love in a Village* (1762) and *The Maid of the Mill* (1765), the titles of which suggest both the content and tone.

During the 1730s Henry Fielding (1707–1754) turned to writing farces that burlesqued much of the drama of the day and frequently satirized the ruling classes more severely than Gay had. Fielding's *The Tragedy of Tragedies, or, The Life and Death of Tom Thumb the Great* (1730) travesties the tragedies of the time, while his *Pasquin* and *The Historical Register for 1736* ridicule contemporary politics and social conditions. The combination of ballad opera and burlesque did much to assure passage of the Licensing Act of 1737.

The most popular new form in the eighteenth century, however, was *pantomime*. It came into being around 1715 and was perfected by John Rich (c. 1682–1761), manager of one of the patent companies. The pantomime was composed of dancing, silent mimicry and some spoken passages performed to musical accompaniment and set against elaborate senery and special effects. Typically, comic and serious scenes alternated. The comic plot usually involved Harlequin, who by some device has obtained a magic wand by means of which he can transform places, objects, and persons at will. Normally, the serious plot was derived from a mythological or historical subject already known to the audience.

Pantomime, which served as afterpieces to full-lenth plays, made its

A design by Cipriani and Richards for Charles Dibdin's pantomime, The Mirror, or, Harlequin Everywhere, *at Covent Garden in 1779. (From* The Magazine of Art, *1895.)*

appeal largely to the eye, and great expense and much time were lavished on producing it. But the investment was repaid by increased attendance. It was largely because of the visual requirements of opera and pantomime that stage machinery and scenery became increasingly elaborate in England.

Goldsmith and Sheridan

By the 1770s sentimentalism (in the form of comedy, domestic tragedy, comic opera, and pantomime) dominated the English stage. At this time two dramatists, Goldsmith and Sheridan, endeavored to reform public taste.

Oliver Goldsmith (1730–1774) through his plays, *The Good-Natured Man* (1768) and *She Stoops to Conquer* (1773), attempted to reestablish what he called "laughing" comedy. His plays are in the tradition of Jonson's more boisterous works or Shakespeare's farces. The plays of Richard Brinsley Sheridan (1751–1816), on the other hand, are in the vein of Restoration comedy but free from its ambiguous moral tone. His most famous plays are *The Rivals* (1775), *The Critic* (1779), and *The School for Scandal* (1777), the last frequently called the greatest comedy of manners in the English language. It will be examined here in some detail as an example of eighteenth-century drama.

The School for Scandal

Themes and Ideas. On the surface, *The School for Scandal* and *Tartuffe* have striking parallels. These may be seen especially in the unmasking of the hypocrite, and in the means used to make the husband realize that he has been deceived.

The differences between Molière's and Sheridan's plays, however, are greater than their similarities. *Tartuffe*, for example, is more restricted in its action and number of characters. But the greatest difference is in tone: *Tartuffe* shows the threat of religious hypocrisy to individual freedom and morality: *The School for Scandal* is largely confined to satirizing sentimental comedy and scandalmongering. Unlike Tartuffe, Joseph Surface never becomes a serious threat to the welfare of admirable characters, and the "school" of scandalmongers tampers, for the most part, with the reputations of persons never seen by the audience. As a result, Sheridan's play is more lighthearted in tone and seems far less serious in purpose than does Molière's work.

The School for Scandal is a comedy of manners, for it is primarily concerned with depicting the fashions and customs of the day. The main action is set against the background of a "school for scandal" which embodies contemporary social norms. The shallowness of this group allows hypocrites such as Joseph Surface to flourish, since it cannot distinguish between pious statement and virtuous action. Furthermore, the group's own shallowness prevents its members from perceiving depth of character in others. Trifling with reputations, consequently, has become a game for those who are unable to distinguish between fashionable behavior and true character.

Sheridan places much of the blame for this state of affairs on the vogue for sentimentalism, and his principal unsympathetic character, Joseph Surface, is made a "man of sentiment"—that is, one who mouths moral maxims. His pious statements are accepted as proof of a virtuous character, while the frank and natural behavior of his brother, Charles, is taken as the sign of a lost soul. Sheridan is ultimately concerned with the distinction between true virtue and pious remarks—between ingrained character and superficial "sentiment." His sophisticated and humorous treatment of this theme, however, never allows its serious aspects to come to the fore, for he concentrates on the comic results of human shortsightedness and frailty. Much of the humor in the play results from the way in which the plans and methods of the rascals serve as traps in which they themselves are caught.

While Sheridan satirizes sentimental comedy, he has not been able to free his own play from many of its traits. His admirable characters are themselves inclined to moralize or fall into "sentiments," as, for example, Maria does ("Wit loses its respect with me when I see it in company with malice"); and the play as a whole illustrates the typical lesson of sentimental comedy (true virtue will be rewarded—and with a sizable fortune). Furthermore, characters have been divided into the truly virtuous, who act according to the dictates of their hearts, and the misguided, who behave according to current fashion. Lady Teazle's actions demonstrate at first the results of following fashion; her reform is brought about by listening to the dictates of her heart.

Plot and Structure. *The School for Scandal* has both a Prologue and an Epilogue, as did almost every play written during the Restoration and eighteenth century. The Prologue is used to put the audience in the right frame of mind and to suggest the mood of the play, while the Epilogue contains an appeal for audience favor along with a summation of the play's basic intention. Both Prologue and Epilogue are short and neither is essential for understanding the play.

The School for Scandal is structurally complex since it weaves together the schemes, desires, and cross-purposes of so many characters: the underhanded machinations of Joseph Surface and Lady Sneerwell; the cross-purposes of Sir Peter and Lady Teazle; the attempts by Sir Oliver to discover to whom he should leave his money; the desires of Charles and Maria to marry each other; and the rather generalized desire of the scandalmongers to interfere in the affairs of everyone else.

Sheridan has solved his problem in part through the relationship he has established among the characters. All move within the same social circle in London and all know each other well. Furthermore, Sir Peter is the guardian of Maria and has been the best friend of the now-deceased father of Charles and Joseph Surface. These close ties allow Sheridan to maneuver his characters more freely and to motivate their appearance whenever they are needed by the action. They also allow him to bring together logically the various strands of the plot as the play progresses.

The scandalmongers are among the least important characters, but they are used to great advantage in the play's structure. First, Sheridan establishes the social context by showing the school in action. Second, the school is used for expository purposes, for their gossip reveals many important facts and sets up the conditions out of which the conflicts arise. Third, their gossip and intrigues affect the other characters. It is they who have almost ruined Charles Surface's reputation with Sir Peter and Maria, and it is Snake's defection from the group that eventually clears the final obstacle from the path of Charles and Maria. Fourth, the school is one of the principal sources of comedy through its witty and malicious conversations. It is a mark of Sheridan's greatness as a comic writer that the group always remains ridiculous and, while complicating the action, never seriously threatens the welfare of the sympathetic characters.

Sheridan's structural methods often resemble the technique used by Shakespeare. The similarity is especially evident in the way the subplot and the main plot are integrated. In *The School for Scandal* the Sir Peter–Lady Teazle story in the beginning has little connection with the Joseph–Maria–Charles story. As the play progresses, however, the two sto-

The screen scene from the original production of The School for Scandal, *1777. Note the forestage, proscenium doors, stage boxes, clearly defined wings, and the similarity of the actors' costumes to those worn by the spectators. (Courtesy Yale University Library.)*

ries move closer and closer together, and in the "screen" scene the revelation of Joseph's relationship with Lady Teazle leads to the resolution of both the subplot and the main plot. Sheridan, like Shakespeare, also moves the place of action in accordance with the needs of his story. *The School for Scandal* has fourteen scenes which occur in four different houses. This freedom of movement makes the complex plotting much easier, for it would be almost impossible for all of the events to occur believably in a single place.

Sheridan, like both Shakespeare and Molière, constantly strives for clarity in characterization and situation. For example, in the opening scene he makes it quite plain that Joseph Surface is a hypocrite who is attempting to ruin his brother. The situation between Sir Peter and Lady Teazle is made equally clear in the second scene. Asides to the audience are used throughout the play whenever an action or a motivation might otherwise be ambiguous. In addition, many of the characters have been given names which point to their basic natures: Snake, Sir Benjamin Backbite, Lady Sneerwell, and so on.

While Sheridan makes the action completely lucid at any moment, he does not let the audience forsee the way in which it will be resolved. He arouses expectations that Joseph Surface will be unmasked, that the school will be put to rout, that Lady Teazle will be brought to her senses, and that Maria will be made happy, but the play's complications serve to keep the truth sufficiently concealed from the characters to make the outcome doubtful. Thus, Sheridan achieves clarity and suspense simultaneously.

The high point of the play is the screen sequence, one of the most skillfully constructed scenes ever written, since it brings to a climax almost all of the preceding conflicts and uses them to build a series of increasingly important comic reversals that culminate in the discovery of Lady Teazle behind the screen. This discovery leads to an obligatory scene that serves to bring Lady Teazle to her senses and to unmask Joseph's hypocrisy. This is the decisive moment in the play, for it makes possible the unwinding of all the complications.

The unities of both time and place (as interpreted by English critics) are observed, since all action occurs within twenty-four hours and all places are within easy reach of each other. The close connection between the main plot and the subplot creates unity of action also. *The School for Scandal* is a good example of English neoclassicism, which was considerably more liberal than its French counterpart.

Characters and Acting. In accordance with the neoclassical notion of decorum, the characters in *The School for Scandal* are drawn largely as types. Charles Surface is the natural young man who does those things appropriate to youth. He is frank, honest, rash, unthinking, hasty, and fundamentally good-natured. Joseph, on the other hand, pretends to have the characteristics of the older, mature person and thus is unnatural and ludicrous. Except in his marriage to a young woman, Sir Peter observes the proper decorum for a man of his age, and it is for this lapse that he is made to suffer. Maria, Sir Oliver, and Rowley represent the ideal standard of behavior, and their conduct is vindicated in the resolution. On the other hand, the school of scandalmongers and Joseph Surface clearly deviate from the ideal pattern and are punished. Charles, Lady Teazle, and Sir Peter deviate only in a few respects and, at the end of the play, acknowledge their shortcomings and declare their intentions to reform.

Sheridan uses only a few broad strokes to differentiate his characters. For example, the scandalmongers are distinguished from each other principally through age, sex, and methods of gossip. Sir Benjamin and Crabtree differ from each other primarily through age and from the other members of the school by sex. Mrs. Candour is unlike Lady Sneerwell mainly because of her distinctive method of murdering reputations.

All of the characters—except Old Rowley, Moses, and the servants—are drawn from the leisure class. None is concerned about making a living. Charles and his companions worry about getting enough money to live pleasurably, but they do not consider working for it. The characters' world, therefore, is that of the aristocracy. They are preoccupied with such matters as marriages, the making of proper impressions, the maintenance and destruction of reputations. To live pleasurably is the ideal.

Sheridan satirizes those who murder reputations and those who are hypocrites, but he does not raise any doubts about the essential rightness of the social system itself. This restricted concern gives the play a tone of lightness and frivolity that is only slightly modified by the moralizing of Maria and Sir Oliver and by the play's ending.

The actors, therefore, must create a sense of sophistication and urbanity. The members of the school must display an artificiality that contrasts sharply with the down-to-earth qualities of Sir Oliver, Sir Peter, and Old Rowley. Maria's straightforwardness contrasts with Lady Teazler's unthinking behavior, and Charles' frank enjoyment of life with Joseph's pretense of sobriety. All of the roles, with the possible exception of Maria's and Old Rowley's, and the minor roles of the servants and Charles' companions, offer considerable challenge. Most of the characters are allowed to be delightfully malicious, to undertake a series of disguises, or to undergo experiences that demand a wide range of responses. Maria, however, remains constant throughout the play and serves more than any other character as the ideal against which the others are judged.

Visual and Aural Appeals. *The School for Scandal* is set in the London of its own time (1777). This is reflected especially in the costumes—those of the upper class of the day. A contemporary engraving of the "screen" scene (see page 241) shows the production's costumes and setting, the theatre's apron stage, proscenium doors, and members of the audience seated in boxes. The actors' dress corresponds closely with that worn by the audience, and the division of the scenery into two sets of wings and a back scene is evident.

By the 1770s spectators had been banished from the stage and more emphasis was being placed on the settings, of which several are required for *The School for Scandal*. Most of the places are not specific in their requirements, but are designated merely as a room in Sir Peter's house, at Lady Sneerwell's, and so on. More specific settings are required for the scene in which Charles sells the family portraits and for the screen scene. All of the settings would have been changed in full view of the audience.

The School for Scandal contains a considerable amount of rather precisely specified business. For example, at Charles Surface's house a supper is in progress during which toasts are drunk and songs are sung. This is followed by an auction of the pictures. Many other scenes are equally detailed. Much of the action probably took place on the forestage, and many exits and entrances were undoubtedly made through the proscenium doors. The use of the forestage kept the action close to the audience and made the asides more acceptable.

One of the strongest appeals of *The School for Scandal* is its language. Sheridan follows in the tradition of the Restoration by making his characters speak with polish and wit, a kind of idealized conversation in which each turn of phrase seems exactly right, though spontaneous. The dialogue is sophisticated and sparkling; it reflects the same detachment from socioeconomic concerns as the subject matter; it is English at its best in conversational usage. Sheridan's polished prose demands a precise delivery, which should be a source of special delight for an audience.

The School for Scandal has been more consistently popular than any other comedy in the English language. Its story, its wit, and its comic inventiveness have kept it understandable and thoroughly enjoyable to successive generations.

France

Although today the English theatre of the eighteenth century may seem more interesting than that of other countries, at the time, the French theatre dominated Europe. Throughout the eighteenth century, France was both the political and cultural center of the Western world.

By 1700 the neoclassical ideal, as embodied in the tragedies of Corneille and Racine and the comedies of Moliére, had become the standard against which European drama was judged. In tragedy the insistence upon remaining true to the ideal established by Racine did much to freeze dramatic invention. The only French tragic writer of note in the

A scene from Beaumarchais' The Marriage of Figaro. (*An engraving in the original edition of the play, 1785.*)

eighteenth century was Voltaire (1694–1778), who began writing plays in 1718. After spending a few years in England in the 1720s, Voltaire decided that French drama should be liberalized, and he attempted several innovations, such as the use of crowds and ghosts, more spectacle, greater realism in acting and costuming, and a limited amount of violence on stage. But Voltaire's reforms seem slight today, and his influence operated principally to preserve the ideals of Racine. His best plays are *Zaïre* (1732) and *Alzire* (1736).

But while tragedy remained rather close to the Racinian mold, comedy departed considerably from Molière's pattern as the eighteenth century progressed. The changes parallel rather closely those then underway in England.

The works of Pierre Carlet de Chamblain de Marivaux (1688–1763) are important forerunners of sentimental comedy. Marivaux wrote principally for the Italian players who, after the death of Louis XIV in 1715, were allowed to return to France. This troupe played at first in Italian, but, finding this unprofitable, soon turned to plays in French. It was restricted in the kinds of plays it could do, however, since the Comédie Française had a monopoly on regular drama. The Italians, therefore, performed short plays and "irregular" dramas. Many of Marivaux' plays were written in three acts to conform to this demand, since all regular dramas of the period employed the five-act form.

The dominant theme of Marivaux' plays is the awakening of love. Typically, the main characters are a man and a woman who are skeptical about both love and marriage. Gradual and subtle changes are traced as the characters are brought to a point at which they must confess the love that has overcome them. Earlier comedy had typically treated characters already firmly in love when the plays opened; the complications arose from their attempts to overcome the opposition of parents or some other external force. In Marivaux' plays, however, the obstacles are psychological and internal.

Marivaux' works are written in a polished, carefully wrought, subtle style which has come to be called *marivaudage*. The most famous of the works are *The Surprise of Love* (1722), *The Game of Love and Chance* (1730), and *False Confidences* (1737). Although they contain many sentimental elements, they concentrate primarily upon the revelation of universal psychological states. For this reason, in France today Marivaux' works are among the most frequently produced comedies from the past.

True sentimental comedy appeared first in the works of Pierre Claude Nivelle de La Chaussée (1692–1754), whose plays *The False Antipathy* (1733) and *The Fashionable Prejudice* (1735) established the vogue for *comédie larmoyante* (tearful comedy). These plays differed from their English counterparts only by being written in verse, but even this distinction was not maintained by many of La Chaussée's successors.

Domestic tragedy had no strong advocate in France until Denis Diderot (1713–1784) espoused it in the 1750s. Diderot argued that the traditional

Left: *Marie-Françoise Dumesnil in Racine's* Athalie. *In spite of the play's Biblical setting, Dumesnil is wearing an eighteenth-century court dress. (From Pougin's* Dictionnaire Historique et Pittoresque, *1885.)*
Right: *Costume worn by Mlle. Clairon in* The Orphan of China *(1755). This costume supposedly marked a change toward greater authenticity, although from a modern point of view it is still clearly influenced by eighteenth-century taste. (From a contemporary print.)*

classifications of drama into tragedy and comedy should be supplemented by two *middle genres* (which correspond roughly to sentimental comedy and domestic tragedy). It was the middle genres that interested Diderot most, and he advocated many reforms in contemporary staging to increase the appeal of these dramatic types. He believed that the best drama is that which arouses the greatest emotional response in the audience, and that the degree of emotion aroused is determined by how fully the illusion of reality is created. He, therefore, argued for the use of dialogue written in prose and for characters and situations drawn from everyday life. Diderot also advocated the "fourth wall" approach, in which the stage is treated as a room with one transparent wall through which the audience looks. The actors then supposedly act as they would in an actual room without taking any cognizance of the audience. Diderot argued that, to achieve this effect, the stage picture must be conceived in terms of complete naturalness. Although Diderot's idea of the fourth wall was not to be carried out consistently until the late nineteenth century, it is an important landmark in the movement toward realism.

Diderot also wrote an important treatise on acting, *The Paradox of the Actor*. In it he argues that on stage the actor should feel nothing himself but should render the external signs of emotion so compellingly that the audience is convinced of the reality of the fictional situation. He declares that the actor's emotional involvement in a dramatic situation should make him lose control over his performance.

Although Diderot's ideas have remained important, they exerted little influence on his contemporaries. His plays, *The Illegitimate Son* (1757) and *The Father of a Family* (1758), were not successful, although they did help to establish the term *drame* as a designation for serious plays which do not fall into the category of traditional tragedy.

The most important French playwright of the late eighteenth century is Pierre Augustin Caron de Beaumarchais (1732–1799), who wrote some *drames* in the fashion of Diderot, but who is remembered primarily for two comedies, *The Barber of Seville* (1775), and *The Marriage of Figaro* (1784). Both center around the character of Figaro. In the first play he is a barber and the epitome of all the clever servants of comedy as he aids Count Almaviva to marry Rosina, the ward of Doctor Bartholo, who wishes to marry Rosina himself. The scene in which the Count, disguised as a music master, gives Rosina a lesson while Figaro shaves *Doctor Bartholo* is comparable in quality to the screen scene in *The School for Scandal*.

While social satire plays only a small part in *The Barber of Seville,* it is of considerable importance in *The Marriage of Figaro*. In the latter play Figaro is in Count Almaviva's service and about to marry Suzanna, a serving girl in the household. The Count is tiring of Rosina and is attempting to seduce Suzanna. The action of the play is principally taken up with uncovering and thwarting the Count's schemes, which offer many opportunities for comment on the relative worth of the aristocracy and the lower classes.

The auditorium and stage of the theatre that was to become the home of the Comédie Française in 1799. When this drawing was made in 1789, the theatre was being used by one of the minor troupes. (From L'Ancienne France, *1887.*

Comic opera also developed in France in the eighteenth century. Alain René LeSage (1668–1747), its originator, began his career by writing for the Comédie Française, which produced his great comedy of manners, *Turcaret,* in 1709. A disagreement with the Comédie, however, left him without an outlet for his plays, since there was no other legitimate theatre in Paris at that time. He turned, therefore, to the small theatres which had been set up at the Fairs. These theatres, which defied the monopoly held by the Comédie Française, managed to remain in operation, nevertheless, throughout the eighteenth century. For them, LeSage wrote short pieces in which spoken dialogue alternated with songs set to popular tunes (just as Gay was to do later in the English ballad opera); the characters were the stock commedia figures and the subject matter was frequently topical and satirical. These short pieces gradually evolved into comic opera.

In the 1740s comic opera came under the sentimentalizing influences of the eighteenth century. The new trend can best be seen in the works of Charles Simon Favart (1710–1792), who not only dispensed with commedia characters but also used original music and subject matter similar to that in sentimental comedy. In this new guise, comic opera was taken over in 1762 by the Italian troupe (a state-subsidized company since 1723), who thereafter made it a major part of its repertory.

France produced a number of outstanding actors in the eighteenth century, the most famous of whom were Clairon, Dumesnil, and Lekain. Claire Hippolyte Clairon (1723–1803) played in a number of theatres before making her debut at the Comédie Française in 1743 in the role of Phaedra. Her success was immediate and lasting. Diderot thought her the ideal actress; she was also a favorite of Voltaire, who worked with her in making many of his reforms in acting and costuming. Her acting was the essence of the carefully planned, controlled, "natural" style.

Diderot states that Clairon's approach was the opposite of that used by Marie Françoise Dumesnil (1713–1803), who made her debut at the Comédie Française in 1737. Dumesnil excelled in emotional roles but lacked the control of Clairon. She had no interest in reforming the stage and thought the actor should always be magnificently dressed regardless of the part. Her great emotional intensity led many to rank her above Clairon.

Henri Louis Lekain (1729–1778) made his debut at the Comédie Française in 1750 and eventually was acclaimed the greatest tragic actor of his age. Although he had a rough voice, was small and not handsome, he overcame these handicaps through diligent work. He was closely associated with Clairon in making reforms in acting and costume.

In addition to championing a more realistic acting style, Clairon and Lekain abandoned the traditional costumes in favor of others that reflected (although not always accurately) the historical period of the action. These reforms, begun in the 1750s, are symptomatic of innovations which were to undermine neoclassicism. After spectators were removed from the stage at the Comédie Française in 1759, scenic display also increased and began to include elements of local color. Perhaps owing to the growing emphasis on spectacle, the old theatre buildings began to seem inadequate. The Palais-Royal (home of the Opéra) burned in 1763, the Comédie Française abandoned its theatre in 1770, and the Hôtel de Bourgogne was not used after 1783. In their places rose buildings that made better provisions for the audience and provided larger stages and more complex machinery. Perhaps because of the French Revolution the innovations were not fully exploited until after 1800.

During the Revolution the monopolies held by the Comédie Française, the Comédie Italienne, and the Opéra were abolished, and for the first time since the fifteenth century, governmental restraints were removed. But the 1790s was a time of chaos in the theatre as in politics. Order was not restored until Napoleon came to power in 1799, but he soon reinstated governmental control over the theatre and used his influence to perpetuate neoclassical standards. Not until after 1815, therefore, was romanticism to break the hold of neoclassicism, which had dominated the French stage since the mid-seventeenth century.

Italy

During the eighteenth century, Italy continued to be preoccupied with opera, and as this form became popular elsewhere, composers, singers, and designers were exported to other countries. Largely because of the vogue for opera, Italian theatrical architecture and scenic design continued to dominate throughout Europe.

In the course of the eighteenth century, design underwent a number of significant changes. Of these, perhaps the most important was the introduction and perfection of angle perspective. In angle perspective, the vanishing point is placed at either one or both sides. The viewer appears to see the object at an angle, therefore, and a sense of space is created by suggesting the continuation of vistas offstage on either side. The development of angle perspective is usually credited to the Bibiena family, of which at least seven members in the seventeenth and eighteenth centuries were scene designers in the principal theatrical centers of Italy, Austria, Germany, Sweden, Russia, Spain, and Portugal.

The Bibienas were also instrumental in popularizing settings conceived on an enormous scale. During the seventeenth century, the stage had been treated as an extension of the auditorium and the scenery had been proportioned accordingly, but in the eighteenth century the wings near the front of the stage were painted as though they were merely the lower portion of structures too large to be contained on the stage. Consequently, settings by the Bibienas and their contemporaries often create a mood of fantasy and unreality through vastness. The Bibienas also continued the trend toward excessive ornamentation which had begun in the seven-

*A design of 1719 by Giuseppe
Galli da Bibiena (1696-1757) for
an opera. (Courtesy the Metropolitan Museum of Art, Dick
Fund, 1931.)*

teenth century. Columns were twisted and entwined with garlands, S-
curved supports were added to beams and pediments, encrustations
abounded everywhere.

During the last half of the eighteenth century still other changes
occurred. As comic opera developed, domestic and rustic scenes became
common, while interest in more specific settings led to the inclusion of
"local color" details. The rediscovery of Pompeii in 1748 captured the
imagination of Europe and aroused interest in classical ruins. As a result,
classical buildings, formerly depicted in pristine condition, were frequently represented in a state of decay and overgrown with vines or
shrubs. Under the influence of Gian Battista Piranesi (1720–1778), who
emphasized extremes of light and shadow in his engravings of prisons and
ruins, designers also began to be aware of mood and to depict picturesque
places as seen by moonlight or interiors illuminated by only a few shafts
of light. Thus, during the eighteenth century, scenic design underwent
many changes in visual style, although the basic arrangement of wings,
drops, and borders continued unchanged.

But if the Bibienas are the best known of eighteenth-century Italian
designers, they had many rivals. Among these were Filippo Juvarra
(1676–1736), the Mauro family (who flourished from the 1650s until the
1820s), the Quaglio family (who worked as designers from about 1650

until 1942), and the Galliari family (who worked from the early eighteenth century until 1823).

In addition to opera, commedia dell'arte continued to be popular in the eighteenth century. But, by the 1730s commedia had become repetitious and somewhat vulgar and decadent, and its emphasis upon farce had begun to be out of tune with the new taste for sentimental drama. Consequently, two of Italy's playwrights, Goldoni and Gozzi, attempted to reform the commedia, and for a time they injected new life into it.

Carlo Goldoni (1707–1793) began writing plays for a commedia troupe in his native city of Venice in 1734. He soon came to the conclusion that commedia should be reformed and set out to substitute written scrips for improvised action. At first he wrote out only a single part, but soon he was able to persuade the actors to accept plays in which all speeches were set. Although he continued to use traditional characters, he sentimentalized them and removed all indecency. *The Servant of Two Masters,* the title of which suggests the basic comic situation, is a good example of Goldoni's commedia plays.

Had Goldoni's work been restricted to commedia, he probably would not now be remembered, but he also wrote many other kinds of plays, including comedies, comic operas, and tragedies. Today he is considered Italy's greatest comic writer of the eighteenth century. Goldoni's comedies usually concern women (who are much more sensible than Goldoni's men) and the middle and lower classes (who are almost invariably depicted as superior to the upper class). Sentimentalism pervades most of

One of Piranesi's engravings for his Differentes Vues…de l'Ancienne Ville de Pesto *(1777–78). Note the ruined architectural detail and the dramatic use of light and shade, features which influenced scene design of the period.*

The Eighteenth Century
175

his work, but a spirit of fun and lightheartedness keeps it from being cloyingly sentimental. Many of his plays are still highly regarded and frequently performed; the most notable are *The Mistress of the Inn* (1753) and *The Fan* (1764). Goldoni's last years were spent in France, and a number of his more than 250 plays were written for the Comédie Italienne in Paris.

Carlo Gozzi (1720–1806) was bitterly opposed to Goldoni's reforms in the commedia and to his satirical picture of the aristocracy. Many of Gozzi's works were calculated to counteract Goldoni's influence; the best known are fairy tales in which imagination is given free rein, and in which many events and practices of the day are satirized. Gozzi wrote out some scenes in their entirety, but others were left to be improvised. Because they are incomplete and topical, it is now difficult to appreciate Gozzi's plays. Neither Gozzi nor Goldoni was long able to stop the decline of commedia, and by 1800 this form, one of the most interesting the theatre has produced, had virtually come to an end.

The most important writer of tragedy in eighteenth-century Italy was Vittorio Amedeo Alfieri (1749–1803). Born in Turin of a wealthy and noble family, he spent most of his early life traveling about Europe without any fixed purpose. But in 1775 he turned to writing plays and rapidly became Italy's greatest tragic writer. Alfieri's plays mingle social consciousness with classical subjects and form. Most deal with questions of freedom, equality, and political responsibility, but these themes are embodied in stories taken from classical or biblical sources. In an attempt

Scene from one of Goldoni's plays. Note the commedia *costume at right. (From the edition of Goldoni's plays published in Venice, 1789.)*

to recapture the spirit of Greek drama, Alfieri cut away every detail that was not absolutely essential. He employed very few characters, used no chorus, and strictly observed the unities. His *Saul* (1784) and *Mirra* (1786) have great power because they concentrate upon the dilemma of a single individual in a compelling situation. Saul shows the biblical character at the end of his life, aware of his decline in power and jealous of David's strength. He alternates between exerting his authority autocratically and being led by others; in his vacillations between madness and sanity, he is both pathetic and terrifying. The interest of the play is centered in the role of Saul, considered in Italy to be the ultimate test of the tragic actor.

But Alfieri was writing at the end of the neoclassical tradition. Although his plays helped to revive the national consciousness in Italy, they had little influence on subsequent dramatists.

In spite of its large role in shaping the European theatre, by the end of the eighteenth century Italy had ceased to develop vital new ideas. In the nineteenth century it remained the center of the operatic world but played little part in the development of theatre and drama.

Northern and Eastern Europe

The eighteenth century saw the development of theatre in Russia and throughout northern Europe. Prior to 1750, there had been only sporadic theatrical performances in Russia. Although there were some church dramas in the medieval period, a few "school" dramas, and occasional performances at court, as an institution the Russian theatre dates from the mid-eighteenth century. The first dramatist of note was Alexei Petrovich Sumarokov (1718–1777), whose tragedy *Khorev*, written in the neoclassical style, was first performed in 1749 by cadets at the Academy of the Nobility. At about the same time Fyodor Volkov (1729–1763) and his brother achieved some success with an acting company in Yaroslavl. Hearing of their work, the Empress Elizabeth summoned them to St. Petersburg in 1752, where they remained to become the core of the state troupe established in 1756. But, though the Russian public theatre dates from the 1750s, it was not to produce any outstanding drama until the nineteenth century.

Theatre and drama also came to prominence in northern Europe for the first time in the eighteenth century. The history of drama in Norway and Denmark is one and the same until the nineteenth century, since the two countries were united from the fourteenth century until 1814 and Danish was the official language of both. No drama of note was written in Norwegian until the nineteenth century. Denmark's drama went through many of the same stages as that of other countries: religious drama in the Middle Ages (though little evidence of it remains) and school drama in the sixteenth century. But no plays were written in the Danish language until the eighteenth century. The cultural standards of Denmark were largely derived from France; the language of polite society was French and the academic language was Latin, while Danish was used only in business and other daily transactions.

The theatre in Denmark at the beginning of the eighteenth century was restricted to a resident French company at court and to small touring groups from Germany that played at fairs or on special occasions. In 1720 Frederick IV dismissed his French actors, but the leader of the troupe, René Magnon de Montaigu, who had been in Denmark for thirty-five years, was granted permission to open a public theatre. The Danish theatre may be dated from the launching of this venture in 1722. Since there were no plays in the Danish language at this time, Montaigu commissioned Ludwig Holberg (1684–1754) to supply him with a repertory. Holberg, born in Norway, was well-educated and widely traveled. He became a professor at the University of Copenhagen in 1718, and in 1719 he began writing satires which are usually considered the beginnings of literature written in Danish. Holberg, thus, was a natural choice when a need arose for Danish-language plays. He wrote a large number of comedies, the most famous of which are *Jeppe of the Hill* and *Erasmus Montanus*. Much of his work still seems fresh in its treatment of Danish types and farcical situations.

Sweden also developed drama in the medieval period, a school drama in the sixteenth century, and a professional theatre in the seventeenth century. But it did not produce a dramatist of any stature until Strindberg began writing at the end of the nineteenth century. Sweden's theatre and drama up to that time were primarily reflections of foreign influences. While there was a public theatre in Sweden as early as 1690, it was not until the reign of Gustav III (1746–1792) that it flourished. A national theatre was established in 1773, and since that time the Swedish theatre has been a relatively vigorous institution.

Gustav III also built a theatre at Drottingholm (a summer residence of the court) which was closed at his death in 1792 and left unused until it was rediscovered in the 1920s. It is now one of the world's great theatrical museums, since it is one of the few eighteenth-century theatres that has not been altered; even its eighteenth-century scenery and machinery are intact.

America

The theatre in America is also a product of the eighteenth century. Although there was sporadic theatrical activity from the seventeenth century on, the professional theatre in America can be said to date from 1752, when Lewis Hallam (1714–1756) brought a company of actors to America. Playing first in Williamsburg, Virginia, they went on to perform

in the major cities along the Atlantic seaboard. Many later groups were offshoots of this company.

The theatre in America encountered considerable opposition, but it was beginning to be accepted when the American Revolution put an end to all theatrical activities in 1774. In the 1780s it was revived and by the end of the century was firmly established from Charleston, South Carolina, to Boston. After this time the theatre followed the westward movement of American settlers, and actors soon traveled to any area that could support even a few performances.

A scene from Royall Tyler's The
Contrast (1787), the first comedy
by an American to be profession-
ally produced. (From the first edition of the play, published in
Philadelphia, 1790.)

The American theatre was a frank imitation of the English system, and most of its early workers came from England. The first important native figure was William Dunlap (1766–1839), playwright and manager, who worked principally in New York and did much to establish a theatre of importance there. His *History of the American Theatre*, written in 1832, has remained an important source of information about the early theatre in the United States.

Germany

The most striking changes in the eighteenth-century theatre occurred in Germany. In 1700 Germany was composed of many small states divided by religious and political differences. The Thirty Years' War (1618–1648) had depleted both Germany's population and its resources, leaving few large cities and little wealth. The theatre was divided between private court productions and public traveling companies, with little connection between the two.

Court theatres arose under the influence of Italian opera. The first opera in German-speaking territories was given at Salzburg in 1618, but it was not until after 1650 that the vogue spread. After 1652 the court at Vienna became one of the major operatic centers of Europe, and its example was imitated throughout Germany, where each court maintained—as well as its financial condition would allow—an opera company patterned after those of Italy.

But touring companies were the true founders of the spoken drama in Germany. The first traveling players in Germany came from England around 1590. Gradually, the English actors were replaced by Germans, and by 1630 there were some all-German companies, although the conditions under which they worked did not change essentially after 1725. None of the troupes had a permanent home, since no town could as yet support a professional theatre. Touring, therefore, was necessary but costly and time-consuming. Companies varied their programs as much as possible so as to exert maximum appeal to the limited audience in each town. For example, one company in 1735 performed seventy-five different full-length plays and ninety-three one-act plays in a period of eight months. The working conditions and the pay were poor, and the troupes were generally scorned by the educated classes. Actors, therefore, were frequently persons who had no other work open to them. The low state of the theatre was reflected in the plays, which featured violent action, exaggerated characters, and bombastic dialogue. Hanswurst, a character based on Harlequin of the commedia dell'arte, played a major role in all plays, even serious ones.

All these factors conspired to keep the German theatre in low repute until about 1725 when Johann Christoph Gottsched (1700–1766) and Carolina Neuber (1697–1760) made the first serious effort to reform the

German stage. Gottsched, who was interested in improving the quality of German literature and in elevating taste and morals, saw in drama one means for reaching the poorly educated classes, and, to implement his ideas, he formed a liaison with the acting troupe headed by Carolina Neuber. Gottsched's standards were derived primarily from French neoclassical drama, which was completely unknown to the audiences of popular German theatres. Nevertheless, Gottsched and his associates set out to provide a new repertory, much of it either translated or adapted from the French.

Carolina Neuber tried to raise the level of acting and the reputation of the theatrical profession by insisting upon careful rehearsals and a high level of personal morality. She banished Hanswurst from her theatre and revised her repertory to bring it into closer accord with Gottsched's aims. In none of her attempts was she entirely successful.

Although Gottsched and Neuber never fully achieved their goals, their work marks the turning point in the history of German theatre. From their time on, there was a steady rise in the fortunes of the theatrical profession and by the end of the eighteenth century, German drama and theatre could be compared favorably with that found anywhere in the world.

Germany's first important dramatist was Gotthold Ephraim Lessing (1729–1781), who turned attention away from French neoclassicism to

A wandering troupe of German players in the eighteenth century. The actors are preparing for a performance. (Courtesy Bild-Archivs der Osterreichischen Nationalbibliothek.)

Friedrich Ludwig Schroeder as Falstaff. (From Literatur und Theaterzeitung, *1780.)*

English drama as more compatible with German tastes. His *Miss Sara Sampson* (1755), which is set in England, established the vogue for domestic tragedy in Germany. His most popular play is *Minna von Barnhelm* (1767), a comedy that shows how a rich young girl maneuvers an officer into marriage, although he wishes to decline because he has lost his wealth and therefore feels unworthy of her. It has much in common with the sentimental comedy of the period, but, like the works of Goldoni, is saved from the extremes of the type by its overall good humor and spirit of fun. *Nathan the Wise* (1779) was conceived as a dramatic poem rather than as a stage play, but it has enjoyed a continuous career in the theatre. It brings together Christian, Moslem, and Jewish characters to illustrate that the best religion is one that achieves the most humanitarian results. Its argument for religious tolerance has helped to insure its lasting reputation.

Lessing's plays employ a strict cause-to-effect structure in which each event grows naturally out of the one preceding it. With them he promoted a return to what he called "true" classicism (as opposed to the "false" classicism of the French).

Lessing's critical writings, especially the *Hamburg Dramaturgy* (1767–1768), also helped to turn attention away from French drama, but with results that he did not foresee or approve. Many young writers concluded from his arguments that all rules were meaningless, unncessary, and contrary to German needs. As a result, much German drama of the late eighteenth century is chaotic in thought and structure. The best-known group of playwrights is usually labeled the "Storm and Stress" school because of its emphasis on controversial ideas and its emotional outbursts. But their experiments were harbingers of the romanticism that was to develop around 1800.

Just as German drama found more adequate expression through the works of Lessing, so too the acting profession grew in prestige through the efforts of several key performers. One of the important pioneers was Johann Friedrich Schoenemann (1704–1782), who acted with Neuber before forming his own troupe. Into his company he took Ekhof, Ackermann, and Sophie Schroeder, all prominent figures in the German theatre. Konrad Ekhof (1720–1778), who joined Schoenemann's company in 1740, perhaps did more than any other German actor of the eighteenth century to establish the respectability of the acting profession. He reformed acting style in the direction of greater naturalness, ran a short-lived training school for actors, and influenced most of the other principal performers of the day.

Konrad Ackermann (1710–1771) and Sophie Schroeder (1714–1792), eventually husband and wife, began their acting careers in Schoenemann's company and then formed their own troupe, which played throughout Germany and in Russia and Switzerland. Ackermann's good nature made him a favorite with audiences and his managerial skill kept the company in good financial condition.

Hanswurst, the clownish character who appeared in most German plays of the early eighteenth century. (From an eighteenth-century engraving; courtesy University of Iowa Library.)

Friedrich Ludwig Schroeder (1744–1816), the son of Sophie Schroeder by an early marriage, is generally considered the greatest German actor of the eighteenth century and perhaps of all time. He grew up in the Ackermann troupe, but it was from Ekhof that he learned most. Schroeder did more than any other actor to popularize the new drama that came into vogue after Lessing, and it was he who introduced Shakespeare to the German stage. Because of his acting, his managerial skill, and his personal charm, he was for many years considered to be the head of the theatrical profession in Germany.

During the last quarter of the eighteenth century, the prestige of the German theatre grew rapidly. The breach between the court and public theatres was bridged with the formation of subsidized state troupes that served both court and public. The first of the national theatres was formed at Gotha in 1775, and it was soon followed by others at Vienna, Mannheim, Cologne, Weimar, Berlin, and elsewhere. By 1800 almost every Germanic capital had a state theatre organized along lines similar to the Comédie Française.

Although by no means the most prosperous, the best-known state troupe at the end of the eighteenth century was probably that at Weimar. Here Johann Wolfgang von Goethe, using autocratic methods of directing, welded a company of second-rate actors into the finest ensemble then to be seen in Germany. Goethe's reputation as Germany's greatest poet also served to attract attention to the Weimar theatre, which reached its peak between 1798 and 1805 with productions of Friedrich Schiller's plays. Goethe emphasized grace, harmony, and balance in movement and speech, and sought in every element of production to achieve an idealized beauty. The company's style was to exert strong influence on German theatrical production until well into the nineteenth century.

Thus, by 1800 the German theatre had undergone a revolution. Permanent theatres now housed resident companies, the acting profession was respected, and German drama was beginning to assume international importance. Furthermore, Germany was already in the process of developing a romantic drama that would overthrow those neoclassical ideals that had dominated the stages of Europe for more than a century and a half.

8

The Nineteenth Century

Romanticism

By the beginning of the nineteenth century a number of earlier trends had coalesced in what is now usually called romanticism. As with most movements, many of the traits of romanticism may be found in other periods as well, most notably in Shakespeare's age. Nevertheless, as a term, *the romantic movement* usually refers to artistic and social trends in the years between 1800 and 1850.

Most of the ideas that helped to shape romanticism had gradually come to the fore during the eighteenth century. Neoclassicism had been based in large part on the belief that human beings can, through rational analysis, discover adequate explanations for everything in life and art. During the eighteenth century, however, faith in reason was gradually supplanted by trust in natural instinct as the best guide to right feeling and action.

Furthermore, the rise in prestige of the middle class during the eighteenth century prompted a reconsideration of those social and political

Design by Alessandro Sanquirico (1780–1849) for L'Allunno della Giumenta, *a ballet presented at La Scala, Milan, in 1812. Sanquirico was one of Italy's leading designers in the early nineteenth century. (From Sanquirico's* Raccolta di Varie Decorazioni Sceniche. *Milan, 1810–1828.)*

theories that had led to a class structure under which the majority were subservient to the nobility. Gradually, primitive society, as a state in which humans had been free to follow the dictates of their own conscience without political and economic strictures, came to be idealized. Equality among human beings and freedom of conscience and action became watchwords of the new ideology. (Both the American and French revolutions were motivated in part by these emerging views.)

Equally important, the earlier belief that truth is to be defined in terms of "norms" gradually gave way to the conviction that truth can only be discovered in the infinite variety of creation. According to many romanticists, the universe has been created by God out of Himself so that He may more easily contemplate Himself. Therefore, everything in existence is a part of everything else, for all have a common origin in God. To know ultimate truth, then, one must include as much of creation as possible. Consequently, rather than eliminate details so as to arrive at norms, one should seek to encompass the infinite variety of existence.

Since all creation has a common origin, however, a thorough and perceptive examination of any part may provide insight into the whole. Thus nature (forests, rivers, mountains, and so on) reflect something of humanity, just as humanity reflects nature. The more unspoiled a thing is —that is, the less it deviates from its natural state—the more suitable it is for use in the search for truth. This view helps to explain why romantic writers show a marked preference for poetry about landscapes and other aspects of nature and for drama about unspoiled man living in primitive times or in rebellion against the restraints imposed by society.

Nevertheless, because truth is infinite, it is ultimately beyond total comprehension by the human mind. Thus, no matter how hard a writer may strive to embody truth in his works, he is doomed to fail, at least in part, because of the impossibility of his task. The romanticists, however, believed that, despite these limitations, a few rare beings—the geniuses—can perceive far more of the truth than is ever revealed to ordinary human beings. Genius was said to involve an innate capacity to grasp intuitively the complexity and immensity of the universe. But, this capacity that sets the genius off from other humans, who, keeping their eyes on the material world, are unaware of ultimate reality, frequently makes him appear strange (even dangerous), and thus he is often treated as an outcast. Genius, then, is both a gift and a curse.

This conception of genius had evolved slowly during the eighteenth century. Originally, the neoclassicists had implied that if a writer follows the rules he can produce good plays. But, in the eighteenth century, a need for something more was expressed (a quality for a time called *taste* and later *genius*). At first, genius was thought merely to supplement the rules (which were still considered necessary to good art), but eventually it was said to conflict with the rules because rules restrict genius, which must be free to make its own laws.

According to the romanticists, then, the genius did not need to be concerned with norms and precepts laid down by others but only with how to express his own perceptions of truth and reality. Despite such declarations of freedom, however, the romanticists soon came to view Shakespeare's plays as ideal models (much as the Renaissance had viewed Greek and Roman plays, and the neoclassicists had the works of Racine and Molière). They frequently saw in Shakespeare's works, nevertheless, only freedom from restraint. As a result, they adopted a loose structure in which the unities (sometimes even of action) were abandoned. Since authors frequently ignored the requirements of the stage (because genius was thought incapable of being confined by such practical demands), many of the plays were never produced and others had to be adapted before they could be staged. About much of the dramatic writing of the period there is an air of impracticality. On the other hand, the new outlook freed writers from the often arbitrary demands of neoclassicism.

With the coming of romanticism, the neoclassical doctrine of verisimilitude was firmly rejected. Whereas neoclassicism had sought to eliminate everything that could not logically happen in real life, romanticism often emphasized the supernatural and mysterious as essential parts of the totality of existence. Thus, ghosts and witches, prophecies and curses, coincidence and providence were basic elements in many romantic dramas. Subjects also were chosen from many sources previously ignored, and Greek myths gave way to medieval tales, national or local legends, and stories about folk heroes or rebellions against social or moral codes. These were used to embody themes showing man's attempts to achieve freedom of ideals or behavior, to find peace of mind or the secret of all being. This fusion of new forms, subject matter, themes, and techniques created a drama quite unlike that of the neoclassical age.

The Nineteenth Century

Major Romantic Dramatists

Although the romantic ideal was first fully expressed by German theorists around 1800, most of the concepts that went into it can be traced to England. Nevertheless, England never experienced a romantic "revolution," as many other countires did, probably because the changes in outlook and practice there evolved so slowly as to be almost imperceptible. Furthermore, in England the neoclassical ideal was never so fully entrenched as it was in France, and therefore the transition to romanticism was more easily made.

In England, romanticism produced few dramas of lasting value. The lack was little felt, however, since in Shakespeare it already had the period's ideal romantic writer. But Shakespeare's influence was not always beneficial, for many promising writers spent their lives turning out imitations of his work. Perhaps the most successful of the English romantic playwrights was James Sheridan Knowles (1784–1862), originally an actor, who for a time won phenomenal popularity with such works as *Virginius* (1820), *William Tell* (1825), and *The Hunchback* (1832), all of which mingle pseudo-Shakespearean verse and techniques with melodra-

Coronation scene from Schiller's The Maid of Orleans *as presented at the Royal Theatre, Berlin, in 1801. About 200 actors appeared in this scene. (From, Weddigen's* Geschichte der Theater Deutschland, *1904.)*

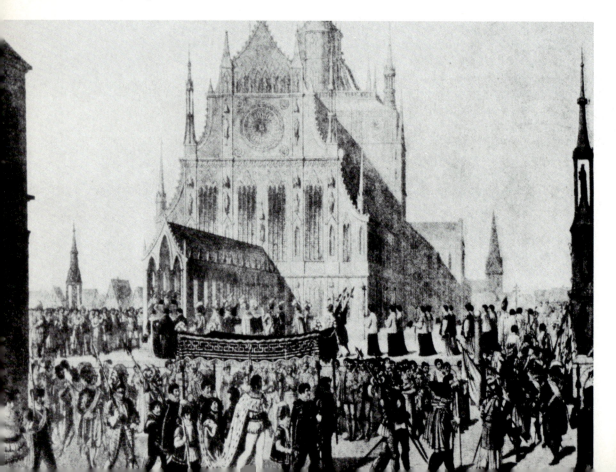

matic stories. In addition, all of the major English romantic poets—Coleridge, Wordsworth, Byron, Keats, and Shelley—wrote plays, but, though some of the works were produced, they were seldom well received and thus made little impact on the theatre.

Germany was more fortunate than England, for its romantic playwrights were to produce plays of more lasting value. Two of the dramatists who contributed most to German romanticism—Schiller and Goethe—denied any affinity with the movement and preferred instead to be called classicists. Nevertheless, both wrote plays that embody romantic ideals, and to both other romanticists often acknowledged their indebtedness.

Friedrich Schiller (1759–1805) began his playwriting career as a member of the Storm and Stress school in 1782 with *The Robbers*, a typically romantic work about a good man who is forced by evils around him to become an outlaw. This play was a favorite throughout the world until the end of the nineteenth century. Beginning with *Don Carlos* (1787), Schiller turned for his subject matter to moments of crisis in history. *Don Carlos* deals with the awakening aspirations of a Spanish prince to free the Netherlands from Spain and to encourage freedom throughout the world. He is opposed by the court and church, and eventually his father, Philip, gives him up to the Inquisition for punishment. Schiller used English history in *Maria Stuart*, French history in *The Maid of Orleans*, Swiss history in *William Tell*, and German history in his Wallenstein trilogy. Few dramatists have combined such a sweep of historical material with such theatrical power. If he falls short of Shakespeare it is because of his too obvious attempt to express philosophical ideas.

Johann Wolfgang von Goethe (1749–1832) is to German literature what Shakespeare is to English, for he is universally considered to be the greatest of German writers. His first play, *Götz von Berlichingen* (1773), deals with the attempts of a German knight of the sixteenth century to remain free in the midst of political and religious intrigues. Around him swirls the life of the times presented much in the manner of a modern movie scenario. Goethe did not write *Götz* with stage presentation in mind, but the play, which contains fifty-four scenes with over forty named characters (in addition to soldiers, peasants, gypsies, judges, jailers, courtiers, and so on), was soon adapted for the theatre, nevertheless. Its enormous popularity on stage established a vogue for dramas of chivalry.

Goethe underwent a change in the 1780s. Concluding that true greatness lies in an idealized art similar to that of the Greeks, he wrote some plays in the classical manner, the most famous of which is *Iphigenia in Tauris*. But Goethe is best known today for *Faust*, which, like *Götz*, was not conceived with the stage in mind, although it was soon adapted for theatrical presentation and has been performed frequently since the early nineteenth century. Although romanticism is so complex as a movement that it is difficult to choose one work as typical, *Faust*, Part I, has been selected for extended discussion here because it embodies so many features characteristic of romantic drama.

Faust

Because *Faust* is considered the greatest literary work in the German language, it is impossible to do justice to it in a short discussion. Still, its major characteristics can be explored. Goethe worked on *Faust* throughout his life, beginning Part I in the 1780s and completing it only in 1808; Part II was not published until 1831. It is, therefore, a partial record of Goethe's own growth and change as well as a reflection of the attitudes of his age. A "dramatic poem" conceived on a scale too vast for the theatre, *Faust* must be adapted and condensed when it is produced.

Themes and Ideas. *Faust* is a play about man's aspirations and capabilities, a hymn to his essential greatness and ability to work out his own salvation.

The "Prologue in Heaven" establishes the basic theme when God states that man cannot avoid making mistakes in his search for fulfillment, but that continuous striving will lead him to the truth. The scenes that follow dramatize the search itself. Before the search begins, however, Mephistopheles makes a pact to aid Faust in return for Faust's agreement that

George Alexander as Faust (in Scene XIV), in a late-nineteenth-century English production of Goethe's play. (New York Public Library Picture Collection.)

Mephistopheles can take his soul whenever he finds a moment about which he says: "O stay! thou art so wondrous fair!" This will be the moment of fulfillment toward which Faust has directed all of his energies and beyond which there will be no point in living.

Part I shows Faust's discontent, his pact with Mephistopheles, and his search for fulfillment in physical pleasures. This is the clearest and most dramatic part of the work. Part II becomes more difficult to understand, but it shows the completion of Faust's striving. Having found sensual pleasure inadequate in Part I, Faust then seeks meaning in ideal loveliness and poetry; eventually he finds the moment for which he has been searching when he renounces his own selfish interests for service to others. But Mephistopheles is thwarted when he comes to take Faust's soul, for Faust has been led to salvation and truth through that very striving for fulfillment in which Mephistopheles has aided him.

Goethe is concerned in Part I with only the first phase of this story. The beginning depicts Faust's deep discontent and his longing to encompass the infinite meaning and activity of life. Faust then makes his pact with Mephistopheles, who sets out to show him pleasure. Faust falls in love with Margarete; she is disgraced and dies; Faust and Mephistopheles

Faust's first meeting with Marguerite, Act II, Scene I, in an English production. (New York Public Library Picture Collection.)

flee. This rather straightforward story is complicated by a number of scenes that on the surface may seem irrelevant. Each scene, however, contributes to Goethe's purpose, for his main concern is the philosophical and spiritual development of Faust.

The second scene is an excellent illustration of Goethe's methods and interests. It shows a day of revelry in which a cross-section of humanity participates. Faust's psychological state is delineated through a pointed contrast between Faust, a group of peasants, and Wagner, the scholar. Faust admires the peasants, who are at peace with their world and can find pleasure in music, dance, and drink. But Faust knows that these pleasures are fleeting; he wants to find lasting and complete satisfaction. Wagner, on the other hand, seeks his pleasures in books and in the past. Faust wants to live life intensely as the peasant does, he wants to encompass knowledge as the scholar does, but he is also searching for something more, something indefinable. The scene serves principally, therefore, as a means of outlining Faust's psychological state rather than as a means of forwarding a dramatic action. It is a moment suspended in time and analyzed with care, but it does not arouse the kind of expectations of future developments that are typical of dramatic composition. *Faust* alternates such static scenes with more dynamic ones.

Goethe is also concerned with man's relationship to good and evil. At one point, Mephistopheles says that God lives in eternal light, that the witches and evil spirits live in eternal darkness, and that man lives in both light and darkness. Man thus exists somewhere between good and evil and though he longs for eternal light, his own nature and circumstances keep him in partial darkness. It is not surprising then that many of the scenes in the play use night and day symbolically. For example, the Walpurgis Night scene points up Faust's dilemma as a man who has given himself up to darkness in his attempt to achieve the light.

Darkness is related to Faust's false search for fulfillment in sensual pleasures, which are part of man's animal nature. Such physical pleasures are also essentially selfish. For example, Faust's love for Margarete is primarily carnal, and he displays no real concern for her welfare until it is too late. He does not talk of marrying her, he only strives to possess her. Her death and the dilemma of Faust at the end of Part I show the limitations of sensuality as a way of life. Mephistopheles, furthermore, is the very incarnation of a sadistic sensuality, which Faust accepts as his guide throughout Part I, although he is continually tormented by the difference between the ideal he had set out to find and the actuality.

The Walpurgis Night scene illustrates in part the darker side of man's nature, and in part the range of creation. Everything has been created out of God (it is he who has separated the light and the darkness) and everything is part of his plan. The witches and evil spirits, then, are part of Faust; they represent sensuality without moral standards, unrestrained whim and selfishness.

Goethe shows that sensuality is eventually self-defeating. At the end of

A nineteenth-century setting for Faust. (From Bapst's Essai sur l'Histoire du Théâtre, 1893.)

Part 1, Faust is left more dissatisfied than when he began his search. A higher power can save Margarete, but Faust can only stand by helplessly. He must search elsewhere for the answer.

Plot and Structure. The structure of *Faust* is extremely loose. Although it bears certain superficial resemblances to Elizabethan drama, *Faust* does not have the economy of Shakespeare's plays and it lacks any compelling unity of action. For example, Shakespeare always makes his basic dramatic situation clear in the opening scene, but it is not until the fourth scene of *Faust* that the pact with Mephistopheles sets the action in motion. If the two Prologues are included, almost one fourth of Part 1 is taken up with introductory material.

The principal dramatic questions raised in the play concern Faust's ability to find completion and to save his immortal soul. These questions hold the play together, but the nature of the first is such that Faust may look anywhere for its answer. Goethe chooses to have Faust seek first for fulfillment in material and sensual pleasures, but this is not a necessary development out of what has gone before. Any other choice could have been made, though Goethe's is not illogical. Furthermore, any phase of Faust's search might be illustrated at length or briefly.

The only sequence developed in terms of a clear cause-to-effect relationship is the Faust–Margarete story. But even this sequence is broken up by the insertion of scenes that illustrate Faust's psychological and philosophical attitudes. Although all of the scenes are thematically related, they are by no means all dramatic. Many could be eliminated without any confusion to an audience, and their removal might actually lead to

The Nineteenth Century

193

greater clarity in performance. The major source of unity, then, is thought rather than incident.

Part I does not complete the story of Faust. It concludes the sequence showing Faust's search for fulfillment in pleasure, but the central questions remain unresolved and are continued in Part II. Thus, while Part I develops and resolves one phase of the story, it marks only the beginning of Faust's search.

Part I consists of twenty-five scenes (plus two prologues) and takes place in about sixteen different locals. Time and place change rapidly, and many special effects are demanded (such as a dog that grows in size and is transformed into Mephistopheles, the Walpurgis Night scenes, the Witch's Kitchen in which monkeys stir potions, and so on). Its production stretches the demands of the stage as far as they have ever been extended, but these demands are a clear outgrowth of Goethe's aims to encompass as much of creation as possible and to dramatize man's search for meaning, his varying states of mind, and the vastness of his aims and abilities. The constant variety keeps the work from becoming boring, but it Goethe's purposes are not understood, *Faust* may appear to be a jumble of disconnected scenes. It is a lofty conception that requires a special effort from the reader for comprehension and a very high degree of interpretive and technical skill from the director.

Characters and Acting. The cast of characters in *Faust*, Part I is too vast to count, for it is composed in large part of crowds, choruses, unspecified numbers of witches, wizards, and spirits. Those given any degree of psychological development are few: Faust, Mephistopheles, Wagner, Margarete, Martha, Valentine, and Lieschen. The rest are types or abstrac-

A scene from Goethe's Faust, *Part I, at Yale University. Directed by Frank MacMullan; designed by Frank Bevan; lighting by Stanley McCandless. (Courtesy Yale University School of Drama.)*

tions. For example, in scene 2 a large number of people are celebrating a holiday outside the city walls, but these are designated only as soldiers, peasants, maids, apprentices, students, and the like.

Goethe is interested in the range of creation but he is not concerned with individuals except in a few cases. His principal effort has gone into Faust, and it is only as the other characters illustrate his condition that they are important to the play. It is evident that the role of Faust is the most difficult one for an actor, not only because of Faust's central position, but also because the role consists so much in the expression of longing, of dissatisfaction, of unbounded aims. An actor in this role may easily become bombastic and ridiculous since what Faust wants is so intangible and is expressed in such lofty speeches.

Mephistopheles' role is much easier to encompass. It consists largely of displays of cynicism, cunning, and deprecation. It offers an actor considerable scope in which to display his talents, nevertheless, since it must embody the threat to Faust's success.

Margarete is primarily the young and innocent girl brought to ruin by her own too-loving and credulous nature. She is required to display a wide range of emotions, however, for she goes from awakening love, to happiness, to shame, to madness and death. Hers is the most clearly projected role in the play.

The actors portraying the type characters must bring to the play extensive talents—for movement, dance, song, and pantomime. The "extras" in this play make the difference between a good and bad production, for they supply a background for the action and illustrate the complexity of creation and of Goethe's philosophical concerns.

Visual and Aural Appeals. There is probably no play that allows designers to utilize their gifts so thoroughly as does *Faust*. The costumer must create suitable garments for will-o'-the-wisps, witches, monkeys, wizards, personifications of abstract qualities and evil spirits, in addition to those for human characters. The lighting designer must suggest the ranges of night and day and the wonders of Walpurgis Night. The scene designer must either provide a single setting capable of suggesting the great variety of places or numerous backgrounds that can be changed rapidly.

The audience's senses are assaulted through all possible means: the spoken word, song, music, dance, natural and supernatural visions, witches' frolics, folk festivals, and disembodied voices. There is an almost endless variety of attractions. The proper staging and coordination of all these elements strain the powers of any director, even with the full assistance of choreographer, musicians, costumer, lighting designer, and set designer. The task is stupendous, but if properly done *Faust* shows the theatre in its fullest splendor, for it extends the resources of the stage to their breaking point. In its attempt to embody the infinite variety of creation and man's longing for filfillment, *Faust* is an outstanding example of romanticism.

Other Dramatists

Although never a conscious part of the romantic movement, Heinrich von Kleist (1777–1811) is perhaps the best German dramatist of the early nineteenth century. Kleist never saw any of his plays produced. They were not published until 1821, and they did not find their way into theatrical repertories until the late nineteenth century. Today Kleist is remembered principally for one comedy, *The Broken Jug* (1806), and two tragedies, *Penthesilea* (1808) and *The Prince of Homburg* (1810). The last play, one of the best of the German romantic era, concerns a young officer who is so bent upon gaining renown that he defies military orders when he sees the chance of winning a victory. Although successful, he has endangered the entire army, and therefore is sentenced to die. He is reprieved only after he comes to recognize that his personal goals must be subordinated to the greater good that is to be found in self-renunciation and service. It is a compact and moving drama.

By 1815 the strength of the romantic movement in Germany had receded, a decline that may be attributed in part to the contemporary political climate. The excesses of the French Revolution had called into doubt many of the social and political ideas that had given rise to romanticism, and the doubts were increased when Napoleon set out to unite all of Europe under his leadership. As the belief in the possibility of unselfish service to others was shaken, pessimism began to replace the former optimism. This disillusionment is well illustrated in the plays of Georg Büchner (1813–1837). His *Danton's Death* (1835) concerns an idealist who, seeing his highest ideals debased by the pettiness of his fellow men, comes to question the ideals themselves. Unable to decide whether life has any meaning, he goes to his death with dignity but still in doubt. *Woyzeck* concerns a man who, little better than an animal, is led inevitably to his downfall by the social circumstances under which he is forced to live. Both plays are pessimistic in outlook and peculiarly modern in their views of human psychology.

Like many of his contemporaries, Friedrich Hebbel (1813–1863) underwent a serious crisis in belief after first accepting the romantic view. Unlike Büchner, however, who never passed beyond pessimism, Hebbel found consolation in philosophy derived from Georg W. F. Hegel. He came to view history as a series of conflicts between old and new ideals through which absolute spirit (or God) works toward perfection. Consequently, in his plays the main characters are representatives of the old and new orders. Since the old has the power of established authority behind it, the new usually suffers, although the suffering foreshadows the triumph of the ideal that has seemingly been defeated. In this way Hebbel reconciled the world's imperfections with a vision of future improvement. His most famous play, *Maria Magdalena* (1844), is now usually read as a forerunner of realism, since its characters are drawn from ordinary life, its dialogue is in prose, and its story ends in the suicide of the heroine, a victim of society's narrow-mindedness. Nevertheless, like Hebbel's other plays, it embodies the conflict of old and new values and suggests that change is on its way. With Hebbel's death in 1863, German drama entered a period of decline from which it did not recover until after 1890.

Romanticism in both England and Germany was already declining before it gained acceptance in France. Although many strictures on the theatre were removed by the Revolution, Napoleon reinstituted censorship in 1804 and openly favored neoclassical drama. In 1807 he issued a decree which established four state theatres (one for major dramatic forms, one for minor dramatic forms, one for comic opera, and one for opera). In many ways Napoleon actually reinstated the condition that had existed before 1790. There was one important difference, however— Napoleon allowed private theatres, although the number and repertory were carefully controlled. These nonstate theatres, located largely on the Boulevard du Temple, are the ancestors of today's popular Parisian houses, which are still referred to as "boulevard" theatres.

Despite Napoleon's strictures, romanticism made headway in France. Its basic premises were given currency primarily through *On Germany* by Mme. de Staël, an enemy of Napoleon who spent her years of exile in Germany. Published in 1810, the book was suppressed almost immediately, but, when Napoleon was overthrown in 1814, it was quickly reissued and widely circulated. Nevertheless, it was not until Victor Hugo (1802–1885) published the Preface to his play *Cromwell* in 1827 that the aims and ideas of the French romanticists were clearly set forth, and romanticism did not triumph in France until Hugo's *Hernani* was produced at the Comédie Française in 1830.

The French plays of the new movement differ considerably from their German counterparts, and in actuality are more closely related to the melodramas of the day. *Hernani* and many other romantic dramas make use of such melodramatic devices as disguises, overheard secrets, hidden staircases, and hairbreadth escapes. They differ from melodramas primarily in their greater depth of characterization, the use of verse and the five-act form, and a preference for unhappy endings.

Hernani concerns a man who has become an outlaw because his father has been unjustly accused of treason and his lands confiscated. Hernani loves Doña Sol, who is also loved by her guardian, Don Ruy Gomez, and by Don Carlos, the future Holy Roman Emperor. Don Carlos comes searching for Hernani while he is a guest in the house of Don Ruy. When he cannot find Hernani, who is hidden in a secret chamber behind a portrait, Don Carlos takes Doña Sol away as a hostage. Before Hernani sets out to rescue Doña Sol, he gives Don Ruy a horn and promises that, if his life is ever needed, Don Ruy need only blow the horn. In the final act, which takes place on the wedding day of Doña Sol and Hernani (now forgiven and no longer an outlaw), Don Ruy, filled with jealousy, blows the horn. Hernani drinks poison, as does Doña Sol, and Don Ruy then kills himself. It is a plot in which love and honor are pushed to the extreme, but it is also a play filled with melodramatic devices, suspense, and powerful poetry.

Other important French romantic dramatists were Alexandre Dumas, Alfred de Vigny, and Alfred de Musset. Alexandre Dumas *père* (1803–1870) is remembered today chiefly for his novels, *The Count of Monte Cristo* and *The Three Musketeers,* but in the 1830s he was famous as a dramatist of the new romantic school. He wrote a number of plays, among them *Henri III and His Court* and *The Tower of Nesle,* which display the same essential characteristics as those of Hugo.

Alfred de Vigny (1797–1863) translated many of Shakespeare's plays into French and helped to popularize them. But he is best remembered today for his play *Chatterton* (1835), which depicts a poet who is too delicate and refined in spirit to find happiness in the materialistic world into which he is thrown. He eventually dies rather than compromise his values. In many ways Chatterton embodies the romantic genius at war with a world he refuses to accept.

The works of Alfred de Musset (1810–1857) are almost totally unlike those of his French contemporaries. Musset was concerned with the psychology of characters, especially lovers. Self-protection is the source of complications in most of the plays. Musset frequently writes of two people in love (or who think they are in love), each of whom is so afraid of being hurt that he disguises his true feelings; in turn, this disguise serves only to wound the other person, who strikes back in a way that widens the breach. Sometimes the breach can be healed to permit a happy resolution, but sometimes it cannot and disaster results. Probably because the psychological orientation of Musset's plays has kept them fresh for modern audiences, they are still widely produced in France and are the most universally admired of French romantic dramas. Musset's best-known plays are *No Trifling with Love, A Door Should Either Be Shut or Open,* and *Lorenzaccio.*

Melodrama

Even as romantic drama was developing, melodrama was also emerging; it was eventually to become the most popular form of the nineteenth century. It appealed to a much wider audience than romantic drama and continued to develop and to hold the stage long after the romantic movement had ended.

Plays have exhibited melodramatic qualities since the earliest times, and examples may be found in every period. But it was not until the eighteenth century that various elements came together to create the conditions out of which a form called melodrama was to emerge.

Perhaps the most important feature of melodrama is its observance of strict moral justice. No matter how terrible the trials of the virtuous char-

Setting by Gué for one of Pixérécourt's melodramas. The play is set in Scotland in the sixteenth century. (From Ginisty's Le Mélodrame, *1901.)*

acters or how powerful the villainous, the good are rewarded and the evil are punished. The world depicted is one in which deeds and characters are separated by clear-cut moral distinctions. The emotional appeals are basic: the arousal of pity and indignation at the wrongful oppression of good people and intense dislike for wicked oppressors. A melodrama also typically brings in comic relief through a minor character, usually a rather simpleminded or severely frank one. The action, which progresses almost entirely through the machinations of the villain, is generally simple in outline, for too many subtleties would lessen the moral distinctions. Normally, it is composed of incidents that show the hero or heroine undergoing superhuman trials at the hands of one or more totally unscrupulous characters. Suspense is emphasized, and the reversal at the end of the play is extreme (from almost certain death to safety, from near disgrace to complete vindication, from poverty to wealth, and so on). Usually a series of unexpected discoveries or of hairbreadth escapes (frequently utilizing concealed hiding places or disguises) keeps the plot moving. The melodrama of the nineteenth century developed a set of stock characters that appeared in almost every play: the hero, the heroine, the comic character, and the villain. Since the characters change little psychologically or morally, interest is centered on the manipulation of events. Although specific traits and circumstances differed from play to play, melodrama remained remarkably constant in its handling of characterization and action.

The term *melodrama* means a combination of music and drama, and during much of the nineteenth century this type of play was accompanied by a musical score just as a movie is today. Underlining the emotional qualities of scenes, music helped to achieve the desired response from the audience. Most melodramas included incidental songs and dances as well and, according to the capabilities of the actors, these portions were expanded or contracted from one production to another.

Most of the characteristic features of melodrama were present in such eighteenth-century forms as sentimental comedy, drame, and pantomime, although they had not yet been synthesized. It merely remained for elements to be recombined in a distinct way to create a recognized form. Credit for the formalization of melodrama goes to two men: August Friedrich Ferdinand von Kotzebue (1761–1819) and René Charles Guilbert de Pixérécourt (1773–1844). Kotzebue, a German, wrote over two hundred plays, the most famous of which are *Misanthropy and Repentance* (played throughout the English-speaking world as *The Stranger*) and *The Spaniards in Peru*. A Kotzebue craze swept the world between 1790 and 1825. Kotzebue was a master of sensationalism, with which he mixed sentimental philosophizing and startling theatrical effects. His success led to many imitations.

But it was Pixérécourt, a Frenchman, who first consciously fashioned his plays in what was to become the accepted mode of melodrama. His first full-length play, *Victor, or The Child of the Forest* (1798), established both his success in the theatre and melodrama as a type. He wrote over one hundred plays, almost all of which were enormously popular, and intended, as he put it, for a public that could not read. He did not labor so much over the dialogue, therefore, as over easily identified character types and startling theatrical effects. His plays brought vast new audiences into the theatre. Although in his own day he was enormously successful, Pixérécourt's fame was not truly lasting, for others learned to manipulate the same kinds of effects and to invent even more startling stage tricks. Melodrama soon surpassed all other forms in box office appeal.

The fortunes of melodrama throughout the world cannot be traced here, but, since the basic pattern was much the same everywhere, the English experience can be cited as reasonably typical. Until the 1820s the majority of melodramas were rather exotic, either because they were set in some remote time or place or because they featured the supernatural or highly unusual. In the 1820s the form took a new turn, however, when increased emphasis was placed on familiar backgrounds and subject matter: Pierce Egan's *Tom and Jerry, or Life in London* (1821) featured a number of well-known places in London and told a story based on everyday events; J. B. Buckstone's *Luke the Labourer* (1826) helped to popularize domestic themes; Douglas William Jerrold's *Black-Eyed Susan* (1829) started a vogue for nautical melodramas; and Edward Fitzball's *Jonathan Bradford* (1833) was the first of many works based on actual crimes.

Then, in the 1830s, melodrama began to acquire a more elevated tone as well-known writers were attracted to the theatre. Edward George Bulwer-Lytton (1803–1873), already famous as a novelist, helped to establish "gentlemanly" melodrama with *The Lady of Lyons* (1838) and *Richelieu* (1839); both held the stage through the remainder of the century. From about 1840, melodrama attracted playgoers of all ranks. Probably the most suc-

Dion Boucicaults' Colleen
Bawn. *(From an acting edition
of the play, c. 1865.)*

cessful of the later English writers was Dion Boucicault (1822–1890), whose
The Corsican Brothers (1852), *The Octoroon* (1859), *The Colleen Bawn*
(1860), *The Shaughraun* (1874), and numerous other plays combine sentiment, wit, local color, and such sensational and spectacular endings that
they tax the full resources of the theatre.

Uncle Tom's Cabin

The most popular melodrama of the nineteenth century was *Uncle
Tom's Cabin*, an adaptation of Harriet Beecher Stowe's novel, which was
published in 1852. Mrs. Stowe opposed the adaptation of her work for the
stage, but was unable to prevent it because the inadequate copyright laws
of the time did not allow her to do so. Despite the enormous popularity
of the numerous stage versions of her novel, she never received any financial remuneration from them.

Although a number of dramatizations were made of *Uncle Tom's
Cabin,* that by George L. Aiken, an actor who later became a prolific
writer of pulp fiction, was the most popular. His adaptation was produced at Troy, New York, in September 1852. Aiken first constructed a
three-act play that ended with the death of Little Eva, and then wrote a
second play that continued the story until the death of Uncle Tom. They
were soon combined to form the six-act play that was presented after that
time. When the six-act version was produced in New York in 1853, it
played for 325 performances, a phenomenal run for the period. The play
was so long that it was presented without the usual afterpiece, an innova-

tion that helped to establish the single-play entertainment that was later to become standard.

Themes and Ideas. Since Mrs. Stowe was principally concerned with the plight of blacks, her novel was in large part a plea for the abolition of slavery. Much of this is retained in the play. It can best be seen in the story of George Harris and Eliza, which shows how slave owners (even the best of them) separated families by selling members, and how the black was forced to become a fugitive if he rebelled against his status as a piece of property. The black's plight is also shown in the story of Uncle Tom, who also is parted from his family (although this is not emphasized), and who eventually dies at the hands of the inhumanly cruel Simon Legree.

The rights of slave owners versus the natural rights of human beings is debated sporadically in the play. The institution of slavery is shown to be evil, even though all slave owners are not. The precariousness of the black's position is demonstrated by St. Clare's death, for this relatively good slave owner has planned to free Uncle Tom but fails to do so in time, and consequently Uncle Tom must endure a terrible fate under Simon Legree's brutality.

Uncle Tom's Cabin is also concerned with religion. (Mrs. Stowe was married to a minister and came from a family famous in religious circles.) Uncle Tom is sustained in his trials by his faith, which is used to explain his trustworthiness and perfection as an individual. He teaches his religion to Little Eva, aids in St. Clare's conversion, and comforts Cassy with his picture of God's love. This emphasis culminates in the final tableau in which Little Eva, riding on a "milk white dove" among clouds bright with sunlight, blesses the kneeling figures of St. Clare and

Eliza crossing the frozen river in Uncle Tom's Cabin. *Produced by William Brady at the Academy of Music, New York, 1901. (Courtesy Harvard Theatre Collection.)*

Uncle Tom. This final scene seems to suggest that religious faith, patience, and goodness will bring about eternal salvation. It also serves as a happy ending to what would otherwise be an atypical melodrama.

Along with religion, love plays a large part. Topsy is reclaimed by love, St. Clare is reformed by his love for Little Eva, Eliza and George are made strong by love, and Phineas Fletcher is converted to abolitionism through his love for a Quaker girl. The evil characters are depicted as lacking in love for others.

But the ideas are decidedly subordinate causes for the play's appeal. Ultimately, it is the spectacle of good and evil in conflict that accounts for the strong emotional response that this melodrama elicited from generations of playgoers.

Plot and Structure. *Uncle Tom's Cabin* is composed of a number of loosely connected stories. For example, the subplot dealing with Eliza and George Harris is related to the main plot only because Eliza and Uncle Tom are owned by the same family. The decision to sell Eliza's child and Uncle Tom to a slave dealer initiates both plots, but the two are unrelated thereafter except thematically. The looseness of the plot may also be illustrated in other ways. Even in the main plot Uncle Tom's life with Little Eva and his fate under Simon Legree are connected only through the character of Uncle Tom. Other scenes, such as those between Miss Ophelia and Deacon Perry, have no discernible purpose except as comic relief.

The organization of *Uncle Tom's Cabin*, therefore, is not always that of a cause-to-effect relationship among the various parts (although this kind of organization is often found within the individual subplots), but is largely determined by the play's themes and by a desire for variety. The parts are held together by fortunate coincidences—the characters meet at just the right moment, and their personal lives are manipulated as needed for the story with little attempt to justify the startling fluctuations (for example, apparently Shelby loses and regains his money, and Little Eva and St. Clare die primarily because these events are needed to motivate plot complications).

But the sprawling form and the poorly motivated occurrences obviously did not detract from the play's appeal. The variety was in itself one of the chief sources of attraction: the story of Topsy serves as an antidote to what today seems Little Eva's almost cloying perfection; George and Eliza are suitable contrasts to Uncle Tom in their attitudes toward slavery; and Simon Legree is strikingly different from St. Clare and Shelby as slave owners. Variety is also achieved through the alteration of comic and serious tone, of quiet and bustling scenes, and in the many reversals of fortune.

Although the unity of the play is to be found in its themes and characters, the range of appeal is sufficiently wide to reach all segments of the audience. The goodness of Little Eva and Uncle Tom is balanced by the rebelliousness of George and Eliza; the comic and pathetic actions of

Topsy and the schemes of Gumption Cute are contrasted with the villainy and punishment of Simon Legree.

The play's six acts are subdivided into thirty scenes, a number of which are tableaux (posed scenes without words), the most striking of which is the final moment when Little Eva blesses Uncle Tom and St. Clare. (Advocated by Diderot in the eighteenth century, the *tableau* was widely used in minor entertainments by the end of that century; it was especially popular in the nineteenth century when no play was considered complete without a series of striking tableaux.)

Uncle Tom's Cabin ignores the unities of time and place. It is set in Kentucky, Ohio, Louisiana, and Vermont, and it is obvious that much time has elapsed between the first and last scenes. It uses many of the same devices as *Faust*, but in a more accessible form.

Characters and Acting. *Uncle Tom's Cabin* includes approximately twenty-five characters, although a number of additional ones could be used to advantage in such scenes as the slave auction. While this is a large cast, it probably would be even larger if coincidences did not bring the same characters together so frequently, even though the scene may change from Kentucky to Louisiana or Vermont. Since many characters disappear for scenes at a time, roles can be doubled with ease.

All of the characters are types. (The names Uncle Tom and Simon Legree have passed into popular usage as descriptions of types of behavior.) The demands on the actor, therefore, are not great, for each needs to show only a few specific characteristics. Uncle Tom never wavers in his loyalty and convictions; Little Eva is constantly good; George Harris is always rebellious; and, though she becomes less rambunctious, Topsy remains essentially the same throughout the play. St. Clare is said to have reformed but, since he is never shown to be intoxicated on stage, this assertion has little meaning to an audience.

The character of Simon Legree demonstrates one of the chief differences between nineteenth-century melodrama and that of today. Although the totally brutal Legree shows fear of damnation in one scene, the psychological causes behind his behavior are never explored. In a modern play such a scene would probably explain the bases for the brutality. This difference in characterization marks the principal change in present-day melodrama from the earlier version.

Interesting hints are given about two characters who remain undeveloped in the play. Marie, Little Eva's mother, is petulant, has frequent headaches, and displays other signs of being demanding and childish. After one scene she is completely neglected, however, and no action stems from these characteristics. Similarly, Cassy is shown to be relatively complex. She has abandoned her principles, but still knows the difference between right and wrong. She seems to have some strange power over Simon Legree and torments him, but she remains a minor character, for these hints are never developed. Audiences in the nineteenth century probably supplied missing information, however, since these two characters are developed more fully in the novel, with which almost every reader of the time was familiar.

The characters, then, as is typical of melodrama, are simple. They are characterized physiologically, sociologically, and in terms of basic attitudes. Much is made of physical appearance, and the division into white and black is important to the play's theme. Furthermore, the characters have "significant looks" about them: Little Eva is said to have an unworldly appearance; George Harris is spoken of as having a look of courage and conviction; Topsy's comic appearance is an important element in her characterization. Sociological factors are also emphasized, since the division into slaves and free men, owners and overseers, workers and the leisure class is important. The chief concern, however, is with the fundamental attitudes of each character. But these attitudes are confined largely to clear-cut moral stances—either good or bad. No character needs to deliberate about what he should do, for his choice is predetermined by his basic moral nature. The characters remain uncomplicated, therefore, but clear.

Language. By the mid-nineteenth century, prose was being used increasingly in serious drama. Melodrama employed simple, straightforward dialogue in which characters openly state their feelings and motives. In fact, characters frequently seem unduly self-conscious about their own moral qualities—the good people appear self-satisfied and pious, while the bad seem thoroughly aware of their own evil natures. Though the result is clarity of character, such stilted statements of moral purpose make nineteenth-century melodrama easy to parody.

But if the language is simple, it is also capable of arousing intense emotional response. Uncle Tom's death is still touching, and the plight of Eliza and George still arouses indignation and admiration.

The language of melodrama helped to establish the standard of our own time under which everyday speech is imitated rather than idealized. After 1850, poetry was increasingly supplanted by conversational prose.

Visual and Aural Elements. Melodrama, like romantic drama, placed considerable emphasis upon spectacle. The settings for *Uncle Tom's Cabin* range from the comfortable interiors of wealthy homes to rough cabins; from the idealized landscape of St. Clare's garden to the ice-filled river over which Eliza escapes; from city streets to desolate country scenes. The contrast is made more evident by the rapid changes, for no act of the play has fewer than four scenes. Quiet and restrained scenes such as the idyllic life of Uncle Tom and Little Eva contrast sharply with the flight of Eliza and George, a slave auction, and the beating of Uncle Tom.

The basic scenic elements were still wings and drops with special pieces added as needed. The illusion of reality was sought, however, and considerable effort was spent in making such scenes as that in which Eliza crosses the ice seem as realistic as possible. The popularity of the play led many companies to mount rival productions in which they sought to outdo each other with realistic stage effects. Mules, horses, and bloodhounds were added in the pursuit of Eliza and George, and the terrible plight of the characters was constantly underlined by spectacle. Melodrama greatly extended the physical demands on staging. Motion pictures were later to capitalize so successfully on the tastes created by melodrama that they supplanted the stage as the principal purveyor of spectacle.

Costumes in *Uncle Tom's Cabin* were contemporary dress but modified to emphasize the particular qualities of the individual characters. For example, Simon Legree was made terrible in part because of his appearance, and no doubt Little Eva was costumed as the nineteenth-century idea of perfection.

Uncle Tom's Cabin was accompanied by an orchestral score, and at various points songs were inserted. During the peak of the play's popularity, producers sought to surpass each other in the amount of incidental entertainment added to the play. Undoubtedly, spectacle, music and dance, coupled with a strong, simple, emotional story, explains in large part the success of *Uncle Tom's Cabin* (as well as that of many other melodramas of the nineteenth century).

Melodrama combined the demands upon staging made by romantic drama with the simplistic moral outlook of eighteenth-century drama. Thus it popularized most of the trends of the preceding century. While melodrama is frequently associated principally with the nineteenth-century, it remains the most popular form today, since the majority of motion picture and television dramas are of this type.

Major Trends in Nineteenth-Century Theatre

During the nineteenth century the theatre continued to expand, although its growth was at first inhibited by political and economic forces. The Napoleonic wars, which involved all of Europe during the first part of the century, were followed after 1815 by an economic depression that lasted until about 1840. Despite these obstacles, an ever-increasing demand for theatrical entertainment, created primarily by the industrial revolution and the consequent growth in urban population, was to lead in the second half of the century to an era of financial prosperity for the theatre.

The Repertory Company

Until late in the nineteenth century, the typical producing organization continued to be the resident company performing a large repertory of plays each season. Nevertheless, the system underwent significant changes during the course of the century under the impact of visiting stars, the rise of touring companies, and the increase of long runs.

Repertory companies had always had their leading players, and the most powerful companies were able to attract the best actors, but the deliberate exploitation of stars was largely an innovation of the nineteenth century. For example, after 1810 English actors with great reputations began to tour America in starring engagements, performing their most famous roles with the resident companies they visited. Originally the star system lifted the level of local productions, since touring actors were those of the first rank, but after 1830 performers with lesser talent also began to tour, and as the frequency of visits increased, members of the local troupes became merely supporting players. This, in turn, led the better local actors to try their fortunes on the touring circuit. After a time managers found it difficult to maintain a first-rate company. By 1850 the

One of the favorite entertainments in America during the nineteenth century was the minstrel show. This sheet music shows some figures associated with one of the best-known troupes, Christy's Minstrels. (Courtesy University of Iowa Library.)

craze for visiting celebrities was universal, and many of the most renowned performers made round-the-world tours.

The resident troupes were even more seriously undermined by the rise of traveling productions, made feasible by the expanding network of railroads. In America, the railroad system extended from coast to coast by 1870 and continued to grow thereafter, offering reasonably dependable transportation to almost any place in the United States. A comparable growth occurred in other countries, so that by the last half of the nineteenth century almost every town of importance was served by a railroad line. Largely because transportation was now dependable, the star system gradually gave way after 1860 to the *combination company,* a term used to describe groups that toured with stars, a complete cast, sets, costumes, and properties. A combination company normally performed only one play rather than a repertory of attractions. By 1886, there were 282 touring companies in America. The impact of the new system is indicated by the rapid decline of resident companies. In America, the fifty resident companies of 1870 had been reduced to twenty in 1878, to eight in 1880, and to four in 1887. A similar change can be noted elsewhere. In England and France, provincial troupes virtually disappeared. Germany, with its network of state theatres, was perhaps the country least affected.

The companies undermined by touring groups were, for the most part, provincial resident troupes. Repertory companies in large cities, on the other hand, were little affected by the combination companies. Nevertheless, they too declined, but for another reason—increasingly long runs. Before 1850 successful new plays had usually been performed an average of seven to fifteen times and then placed in the repertory to alternate with other plays. Occasionally a piece was so popular that it was kept running longer, but this was unusual. After 1850, however, the length of runs increased steadily and rapidly, while the size of each theatre's repertory was reduced accordingly, since fewer plays were needed to fill out a season. For example, Wallack's Theatre in New York during the season of 1855–1856 performed sixty plays, but by the mid-1870s it was performing only fifteen to twenty, and by the mid-1880s only five to ten. This change is explained in part by the enlarged potential audience in urban areas, but it is also attributable to growing costs of production, for plays had to be performed enough times to recover the investment made in them. Ultimately, the fate of the repertory system was sealed when it became evident to managers that seasonal contracts with performers were no longer economically sound, since not all members of a company were needed for each play and therefore some were idle during long runs though still being paid. The obvious solution (and the one adopted) was to abandon the company altogether and to employ actors as needed for the run of a play. Thus, by 1900 most producers had given up the repertory system in favor of a single-play, long-run policy. The actor, in turn, had to seek a new engagement each time a play closed. Consequently, while the new arrangement solved many of the producer's problems, it greatly increased those of the actor.

The demise of the repertory system did not signal a decrease in theatrical activity, however, for in quantity productions continued to increase until well into the twentieth century. The growth in touring, on the other hand, did create many new problems. In America, for example, New York rapidly became the center of production from which all companies originated. Actors, therefore had to go to New York to seek employment, just as local managers did to book attractions for their theatres. By the 1890s the booking of productions was extremely chaotic, since to fill up a season a local manager might have to negotiate with as many as forty different producers, each of whom was simultaneously dealing with countless other local managers. Often, touring companies defaulted on their contracts, leaving theatres without attractions for several days at a time.

Out of this situation the Theatrical Syndicate grew when six theatre managers and booking agents joined together in 1896 for the purpose of gaining a monopoly on "the road." The Syndicate promised local theatres a full season of plays, complete with stars, on the condition that they book exclusively through it. Although many local managers welcomed the new stability, others resisted the attempted monopoly. In these cases, the Syndicate bought, rented, or built rival houses and gradually drove the recalcitrant managers out of business. Because they controlled a majority of key theatres, the Syndicate could also force New York producers to sign exclusive contracts with them, since otherwise road companies would find it difficult to obtain enough bookings to make tours profitable. Through such devices, the Syndicate dominated theatrical production in America between 1896 and 1915. It also did much to elevate commercial above artistic motives, an attitude from which the American theatre has not yet fully recovered.

Audiences

The eighteenth century had seen the middle classes flock to the theatre, and to this group the nineteenth century added the lower classes. A number of factors—the industrial revolution (which greatly enlarged the urban population), the expansion of public education, the belief in democracy and equality—served to bring into the theatre many persons who had not previously attended.

The increased demand for theatrical entertainment was met in several ways. First, the number of theatres grew significantly. For example, in London, where there had been only three theatres in the late eighteenth century, there were twenty-one by 1843 and thirty by 1870. In Paris there were eight theatres in 1810 and twenty-eight in 1855. Second, theatre

One of the many theatres built in London between 1810 and 1840, the Royal Coburg as it looked when it opened in 1818. It later came to be called the Old Vic and as such is still in use. (From Wilkinson, Londina Illustrata, 1825.)

auditoriums were enlarged to hold more spectators. For example, in London the Drury Lane and Covent Garden theatres each held about 2000 prior to 1790, but later reconstructions gave them seating capacities of more than 3000. It is often said that managers were forced to emphasize spectacle in such theatres, since subtlety in acting was impossible. Third, most theatres enlarged the range of entertainment so as to appeal to the varied tastes of audiences. Sometimes as many as three full-length plays, plus numerous variety acts, were offered on the same evening. Often a program required five or six hours of playing time. But with this quantity went a decline in quality. After 1815 many playgoers with relatively sophisticated tastes ceased to attend. They were not to return until after 1850.

After the mid-century, the situation began to change. First, regular drama was gradually separated from the variety-hall atmosphere. Theatres came to specialize in a particular kind of entertainment and regular drama became again the province of a more sophisticated group, a trend that was accelerated in the twentieth century by the development of motion pictures, which consciously attempted to attract that mass audience that had constituted a large part of the nineteenth-century theatregoing public.

Second, as theatres began to specialize in a particular kind of entertainment, the bill for each evening became less complex. Theatres offering drama turned more and more to a single play as the sole attraction. The length of performances changed correspondingly, and by 1900, programs lasted only two to three hours.

Third, changes in programming led to alteration in the auditorium. After 1860 there was a trend toward smaller houses and consequently toward improved sightlines and acoustics. Seating patterns were also altered as boxes were abandoned in favor of the orchestra. This change was brought about by two factors: the general increase in democratic sentiment, which made the mingling of classes more acceptable than when the box, pit, and gallery plan had originated; and the trend toward homogeneity within each audience, which was encouraged by programming that limited the audience to those with similar tastes. The result was that in the pit comfortable arm chairs gradually replaced the benches previously used there; at the same time the area was retitled the orchestra. In theatres built in the late nineteenth century boxes were often omitted and the space formerly occupied by them was devoted to mezzanine or balcony seating.

Staging

Developments in staging during the nineteenth century may be attributed primarily to increased interest in historical accuracy and illusionism. Prior to the late eighteenth century, history was not considered relevant to art, since universal truth, independent of time and place, was said to be the province of drama. In general, neoclassicism was almost totally antihistorical in outlook. During the eighteenth century, however, a concern for the circumstances of time and place began to appear. As a result, the successive changes and developments of society became as important as those that had remained constant. Interest began to shift from ideal

Left: *Ground plan of the Drury Lane Theatre, London, 1808. (From Wilkinson's* Londina Illustrata, *1825.) Right: Interior of the Drury Lane Theatre in 1808. Note the five tiers of boxes. (Courtesy Metropolitan Museum of Art, Dick Fund.)*

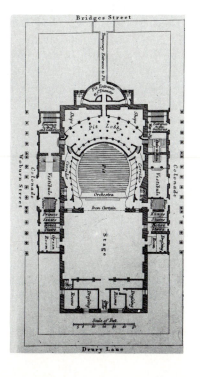

Costume designs by J. R. Planché for Shakespeare's King John, *produced at Covent Garden in 1823. This production is supposedly the first in England to use historically accurate costumes for all characters. Shown here are costumes for Philip Falconbridge and Hubert de Burgh. (Courtesy Stark Collection, University of Texas Library.)*

and universal qualities to the individualizing details of man's existence. National and historical differences in architecture, literature, dress, and social customs began to be studied with enthusiasm. The first history of costume appeared about 1775 and antiquarianism in general increased thereafter.

The interest in time and place extended to the unusual or exotic. Authentic dances and costumes of other countries began to creep into plays, and unusual or picturesque settings became popular. This kind of background detail came to be called *local color,* since it rendered the characteristic and individual features of a specific locale.

At first, historically accurate details and local color were used only sporadically and inconsistently. Charles Kemble's production of Shakespeare's *King John* (produced in London in 1823) was the first in England to claim complete historical accuracy in every detail of costuming, a principle extended to scenery in *Henry IV, Part I* in 1824. Both of these productions were designed by J. R. Planché (1796–1880) who, through his productions and through his histories of costume and other antiquarian studies, did more than anyone else in England to forward the movement toward historical accuracy in the theatre.

In Germany, historical accuracy was used as early as 1801 in a production of Schiller's *The Maid of Orleans* in Berlin. The state theatre in Berlin especially after 1814 under the management of Count Karl Bruhl, was to be a major force in popularizing antiquarianism throughout Germany. In France, local color was a standard part of melodrama after 1800, but it was the romantic dramatists, especially Hugo and Dumas *père,* who first insisted upon historically accurate settings and costumes. Nevertheless, throughout the world antiquarianism was inconsistently employed until about 1850, by which time it was becoming a point of pride to offer productions certified to be completely accurate in every detail.

Quite frequently the historically accurate details and local color were used only as interesting visual embellishments that had no effect upon the action of the play. It did not bother audiences or producers that historical accuracy was most often irrelevant to the spirit of the plays themselves. Nevertheless, it was through such visual details that realism began to enter the theatre, but realism in subject matter and characterization were not to be fully exploited until after 1850.

Once realism of spectacle had been accepted as a standard, the wing-and-drop setting no longer seemed adequate for representing interiors. Consequently, it was gradually replaced by the *box set,* consisting of three walls and a ceiling. The first steps toward the box set were taken in the late eighteenth century, when flats were occasionally used to fill the space between wings. Gradually the entire setting came to be enclosed, although the precise stages of this process cannot be dated. By the early nineteenth century, the box set seems to have been in use on the continent, but it was not introduced in England until the 1830s. It was not to be used consistently anywhere, however, until the late nineteenth century.

The demand for illusionism also led to the leveling of the stage floor
(which, since the Renaissance, had sloped upward toward the rear).
During the nineteenth century, it became increasingly difficult to achieve
the desired realistic effects solely through wings and drops (which normally had to be erected parallel to the front of the stage) and also
increasingly frustrating to maneuver set-pieces around the grooves on a
sloping floor. Eventually the old methods of handling scenery (chariot-
and-pole and sliding grooves) were abandoned as too restrictive, and
around 1875 stages began to be remodeled, the floor leveled and the
machinery for handling wings removed. Thereafter, scenic units could be
placed at any angle and wherever desired, but new methods of shifting
scenery had to be devised. The most usual solution was a large number of
stagehands who moved units manually, but toward the end of the century
such devices as the revolving stage, the elevator stage, and the rolling platform stage were introduced. (A *revolving stage* is created by mounting a
large circular segment of the stage floor on a central pivot. A number of

The Nineteenth Century

213

Steele Mackaye (1842–1894) was an American playwright, actor, director, inventor, and reformer. Shown here is his Madison Square Theatre, which opened in 1880. It featured a double stage, one above the other, on elevators. Settings could be changed in less than one minute. (From The Scientific American, *April 5, 1884.)*

settings may then be mounted on this portion of the stage floor, and scene changes can be effected by merely rotating the stage until a new setting comes into view. On an *elevator stage,* parts or all of the floor may be raised or lowered. For example, scenery may be mounted on a segment of this floor while it is in the basement and then raised to stage level. A *rolling platform stage* is mounted on tracks parallel to the front of the stage. Entire settings may be erected on the platforms in the wings and then rolled onstage. The revolving stage, the elevator stage, and the rolling platform stage are only three of the many mechanical devices that have been used to shift scenery since the late nineteenth century.)

The trend toward realism also brought changes in other theatrical practices. For example, in the last part of the nineteenth century, the front curtain began to be closed regularly to mask scene changes. Several factors account for this change. The increasing complexity of settings demanded that stagehands do much of their work onstage and their visible presence would have been distracting. Probably more important, however, was the growing demand for illusionism, easily destroyed for most audiences if settings are assembled before their eyes. Diderot's theory of the fourth wall also began to be applied with some consistency, as actors came to perform more and more inside the proscenium (rather than on the apron) and to behave as though they were in real rooms in real houses.

Innovations in stage lighting also aided the development of realism. By 1820, gas had begun to replace candles and oil lamps and was in use almost everywhere by the 1840s. For the first time since the theatre had moved indoors the stage could be lighted as brilliantly as desired. Furthermore, by 1850 the *gas table,* a central panel of gas valves, permitted complete and instantaneous control over all of the stage lights. This new power led to numerous experiments with realistic effects. The perfection of the lime light and the carbon arc, forerunners of the follow spot, aided in these experiments since with them concentrated beams of light could be focused on the stage for the first time. Both were exploited beginning around 1850, at first for such special effects as rays of sunlight or moonlight but gradually for lighting the acting areas as well. After 1880, electricity rapidly replaced gas as the standard illuminant. It offered great flexibility without the constant danger of fire, the chief drawback of gas.

Brighter light, which came with the introduction of gas, emphasized the artificialty of the painted scenery and props, and by the 1830s three-dimensional details began to appear. Door knobs were added to doors, real molding was attached to the walls, carpets were laid over the floors, and artificial fires glowed in fireplaces. Such details began to be demanded by the action of plays, and by 1870 actors were being required to perform such everyday tasks as boiling water, brewing, serving and drinking tea.

The Actor

The increased concern for realism carried over into acting as well. Many of the developments can best be seen by surveying briefly the careers of a few outstanding English actors of the nineteenth century.

The English stage of the early nineteenth century was dominated by the Kemble family, whose most famous members were John Philip Kemble (1757–1823) and his sister, Mrs. Sarah Siddons (1755–1831). Kemble made his London debut at Drury Lane in 1783 as Hamlet, and remained on the stage until 1817. Mrs. Siddons, frequently said to be the greatest English tragic actress of all time, was established in the London theatre by 1782 and retired in 1812. The Kembles aimed at grace, dignity, and beauty in movement, gesture, and voice. Thus, they tended to idealize characters.

By 1820, however, the classical style of the Kembles was being chal-

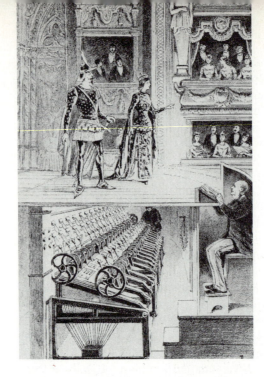

A lighting control board of the late nineteenth century. Note also the prompter at the front of the stage. (From Moynett's La Machinerie Théâtrale, 1893.)

Backstage at Booth's Theatre, New York, in 1870. Note the use of traps on hydraulic lifts to raise and lower heavy props and pieces of scenery. This was one of the first theatres to have a level floor and dispense with grooves. Note the use of stage braces to support the scenery now that grooves are no longer available for that purpose. (From Appleton's Journal, Vol. 3, May 28, 1870.)

lenged by the romantic ideal, epitomized in the acting of Edmund Kean (1787–1833), who made his London debut at Drury Lane in 1814 and remained on the stage thereafter until his death. Kean often sacrificed dignity and beauty to the depiction of intense emotion. On the other hand, he sometimes so neglected the quiet moments in a play that he was inaudible. This alternation of intensity with indifference led Coleridge to remark that to see Kean act was like reading Shakespeare by flashes of lightning. Nevertheless, Kean could magnetize audiences and his style became so widely accepted that it set the standard for actors who succeeded him.

William Charles Macready (1793–1873) made his debut in 1810 and retired in 1851. His acting style was a compromise between those of Kemble and Kean, since he worked for beauty and dignity combined with emotional intensity. He planned each detail of his characterizations carefully, and as a theatre manager insisted on painstaking rehearsals. He also did much to popularize historical accuracy in scenery and costumes.

Mme. Lucia Elizabeth Vestris (1797–1856), after achieving fame as a performer in light comedy and musical entertainments, managed the Olympic Theatre in London from 1831 to 1838. With her husband, Charles Mathews (1803–1873), she did much to turn comic acting away from broad effects to a more natural style. She is also said to have introduced the box set in England, to have employed real (rather than fake) properties, to have abandoned the practice of costuming comic characters in ludicrous garments, and to have shortened the program so that audi-

Edmund Kean as Othello. (From Strang, Vol. I, 1902.)

ences could be out of the theatre by eleven. Most of her changes moved the theatre in the direction of greater realism.

With his wife, Ellen Tree (1806–1880), Charles Kean (1811–1868), son of Edmund Kean, achieved fame as an actor and manager, principally through his Shakespearean productions at the Princess's Theatre in London between 1850 and 1859. Kean prided himself on the historical accuracy of every detail of his settings, costumes, and properties. It is his productions above all that mark the triumph of historical accuracy in English staging. The patronage of Queen Victoria further served to elevate Kean's work in the eyes of the English public and to bring aristocratic audiences back to the theatre again after a long absence.

Squire Bancroft (1841–1926) and his wife, Marie Effie Bancroft (1839–1921), are noted for the many reforms they popularized at the

William Charles Macready in the gravedigger scene from Hamlet. *(The Illustrated London News, 1846.)*

Henry Irving's production of King Lear. *A sketch by Hawes Craven. (From the souvenir program.)*

Prince of Wales's Theatre between 1865 and 1880. They concentrated upon plays of contemporary life, especially those by Tom Robertson (1829–1871), to which they applied rigorous standards of realism in every element of production. Just as Charles Kean triumphed with the realism of history, the Bancrofts established the realism of modern life. Their practices helped to popularize the box set and realistic costumes, properties, and acting. Furthermore, they gained acceptance of orchestra seating and helped to popularize matinee performances.

Henry Irving (1838–1905) was the first English actor to be knighted, a sign that the acting profession was at last socially acceptable. With Ellen Terry (1847–1928) he achieved great renown during the final decades of the century in his productions of Shakespeare's plays, romantic drama, and melodrama. Irving was also a theatrical manager, and was the first in England to abandon the groove method of shifting scenery. He placed scenic units onstage whenever needed and employed a vast number of stagehands to make the necessary changes. He was also the first English manager who consistently concealed scene changes from the audience. More than any other producer, Irving synthesized earlier trends toward complexity and realism in staging.

This survey of English actors by no means exhausts the list of great performers of the nineteenth century. Others include: François Joseph Talma (1763–1826), Rachel (1821–1858), Constant Benoit Coquelin

Top: *François-Joseph Talma as Titus in Voltaire's* Brutus. *(From Jullien's* Histoire du Costume du Théâtre, *1880.)* Right: *Edwin Booth as Hamlet. (From Strang's* Players and Plays of the Last Quarter Century, *Vol. I, 1902.)* Left: *Edwin Forrest as King Lear. (Strang, Vol. I.)*

(1841–1909), and Sarah Bernhardt (1845–1923) in France; Mikhail Shchepkin (1788–1863) and Prov Sadovsky (1818–1872) in Russia; Tommaso Salvini (1829–1916), Adelaide Ristori (1822–1906), and Eleanora Duse (1859–1924) in Italy; Ludwig Devrient (1784–1832), Friedrich Haase (1827–1911), and Fanny Janauschek (1830–1904) in Germany; Bogumil Dawison (1818–1872) and Helena Modjeska (1844–1909) in Poland; and Edwin Forrest (1806–1872), Charlotte Cushman (1816–1876), and Edwin Booth (1833–1893) in America.

The Playwright

The nineteenth century brought great improvements in the playwright's financial position. Previously, the writer had lost all control over the production of his plays after their initial performances. The *royalty system* of paying authors (a payment either of a fixed sum or of a percentage of the receipts for each performance) had been introduced in France in the late eighteenth century, but it was not universally adopted until the last quarter of the nineteenth century.

The first copyright law designed to give the dramatist control over the production of his plays was passed in France in 1791. By 1829, the French Society of Dramatic Authors was able to establish the rate of payments to authors, provide a pension system, and secure many additional privileges for dramatists. In England, a copyright law was enacted in 1833. Such laws, however, could not insure the dramatist's rights beyond the boundaries of his own country. Thus, an American might produce an English play without paying its author any fee, or he might translate a play and claim it as his own. More effective protection came after 1887 when under the provisions of an international copyright agreement all countries subscribing to it promised to protect the rights of foreign as well as native authors. Therefore, with rare exceptions, playwrights throughout the world had been accorded legal protection by 1900. The dramatist might still have difficulty getting his plays produced, but when they appeared, either on the stage or in print, his rights were guaranteed by law.

Typically, the culmination of one trend signals the beginning of another. And so it was in the nineteenth century, for romantic drama, melodrama, and realism of stage spectacle laid the groundwork for that movement—realism—which is usually said to mark the beginning of the modern theatre. By the last half of the nineteenth century those ideas and practices that characterize the modern era were already emerging and were merely waiting to be exploited.

9

The Oriental Theatre

While one theatrical tradition was developing in Europe, a quite different one was emerging in the Far East. The two did not make significant contact, however, until the end of the nineteenth century. Although they have exerted some influence upon each other in the twentieth century, they have continued along essentially different lines.

Almost every Asian country has a rich dramatic heritage, and each deserves extensive treatment, but only a few can be considered here. Because the theatres of India, China, and Japan have exerted the greatest influence, both upon other Asian countries and upon the West, they have been selected for discussion.

The Oriental theatre is almost as old as that of the West. But the review of its history and conventions has been delayed until this point because space permits only brief treatment of them as an adjunct to this study of Western theatre, on which Oriental practices made no impact until the modern era.

Theatre and Drama in India

The origins of the Indian theatre are obscure, for the surviving records are vague about chronology. According to Hindu legend, Brahma taught the art of drama to the sage Bharata, author of *Natyasastra* (*The Science of Dramaturgy*) written sometime between 200 B.C. and 200 A.D. Since this work gives detailed descriptions of acting, dance, costume, and makeup, these arts must have been highly developed by that time.

The first important Oriental dramas were those written in Sanskrit. The majority of the plays are based on two epics, *Mahabharata* and *Ramayana,* both dating from sometime between 500 B.C. and 320 A.D. About twenty-five plays and numerous fragments written between the second and the ninth centuries A.D. have survived. Thus, Indian drama reached its peak in those years when Western drama was at its lowest ebb.

Sanskrit plays differ markedly from their Western counterparts. They are not classified as comedy, tragedy, or melodrama, and are little concerned with characterization or philosophical issues. Rather, they are organized around fundamental moods, or *rasas*. There are nine rasas: erotic, comic, pathetic, furious, heroic, terrible, odious, marvelous, and peaceful. Although a play may employ many rasas, incompatible ones are avoided. All plays end happily, for Sanskrit drama aims to leave the spectator in a state of harmony. Violence and death are kept offstage, good and evil are clearly differentiated, and good is always triumphant.

Sanskrit drama is composed of diverse elements. The plots usually center around one principal story, but to it a number of subplots, ranging from the serious to the farcical, may be joined. The dialogue is a mixture of prose and verse (which is used in moments of intense emotion or for heightened expression), and of Sanskrit (the learned language, spoken in the plays by gods, kings, ministers, generals and sages) and Prakrit (the everyday language, spoken in the plays by soldiers, peasants, servants, women and children). Characters range through many social ranks and psychological types. For example, the hero (almost always a ruler or member of the aristocracy) usually has as his companion a dwarfish, gluttonous clown, who serves not only as comic relief in the serious story but also as confidant to the hero.

In many respects, Sanskrit plays resemble epic poems, for narrative passages, alternating with dialogue, establish the situation and relate events that have occurred offstage. As in novels, characters often describe their innermost feelings. Place changes freely. In length, Sanskrit plays vary from one to ten acts. According to the accepted rules, the events shown in a single act should all occur within twenty-four hours, while no more than one year should elapse between successive acts. Bharata lists ten kinds of plays, ranging through monologues, farces, operatic pieces, social plays, and heroic dramas. Of these, the heroic is considered the most important. Based upon history or mythology, it shows an idealized hero defending a righteous cause. Usually there is also a love story, in which the lovers are kept apart by some evil force until the end of the play.

In staging, realism was avoided. Each performance was preceded by a ritual designed to please the gods and to put both actors and spectators in the right frame of mind. Plays were given only on special occasions (such as marriages, festivals, victories, coronations, and important visits). Performances lasted four or five hours. The majority of the audience was drawn from the aristocracy.

Little is known about the playhouses of ancient India. Bharata states that most performances occur in palaces or temples but that when theatres are set up, they should adhere to the following rules: The theatre should be ninety-six feet long by forty eight-feet wide and divided into two equal parts (auditorium and stage). Four pillars (white, red, yellow, and blue) indicate where members of the social castes are to sit (although in most instances the audience was probably restricted to the upper castes). The total seating capacity was only about 400. A curtain divided the stage area into two equal parts, the front half to be used for the dramatic action and the rear half as dressing rooms and offstage space. The stage may have had two levels; the lower was used for most scenes while the upper was reserved for scenes set in heaven, in a tower, or in another high place.

Since no scenery was used (although the stage was decorated with paintings and carvings as a decorative background), place could shift rapidly to permit a continuous flow of action. Both place and situation were established at the opening of each scene through narrative and pantomime. During episodes, stylized movement and gesture suggested climbing a hill, riding a horse, crossing a stream, driving a chariot, and myriad other actions. Thus, through words and pantomime, the actor stimulated the audience to imagine whatever the drama required.

The Hindu theatre depended most upon the actor. Nevertheless, judging by contemporary references, actors did not rank high in social status or moral esteem. They led a wandering existence, moving about seeking engagements. Each troupe worked under a leader, who supervised the production as a whole. Both men and women acted.

The actor was considered to have four basic resources at his disposal: movement and gesture; speech and song; costume and makeup; and psychological insight. By the period in which the great Sanskrit dramas were written, movement and gesture had become rigidly conventionalized. Gestures were classified according to the parts of the body and inner feelings. There were thirteen movements of the head, thirty-six of the eyes, seven of the eyebrows, six of the cheek, six of the nose, nine of the neck, five of the chest, twenty-four of each hand, thirty-two of the feet. These were combined according to situation, mood, and character to create a sign language as complex as the spoken word.

Similarly, speech and music were regulated according to intonation, pitch, and tempo, and were mingled as situation, mood, and character demanded. The drama was accompanied throughout by instrumental music played on a drum and stringed instruments. The drum was considered essential, since it followed the speakers' voices closely and underscored rhythms. Through sung passages, especially upon the entrance or exit of characters, the musicians also indicated changes in mood and provided information about situation or character.

Costumes and makeup also followed strictly prescribed conventions. Color was used symbolically: High-caste characters were indicated by red, low-caste characters by blue; gold was used for the Sun and Brahma, orange for the gods; and so on. Ornaments, such as belts, necklaces, bracelets, and headdresses differentiated characters within the same basic type. Makeup was so conventionalized that it could indicate a character's place of birth, social position, and historical period. Properties were also used symbolically. For example, if an actor carried a whip it indicated that he was riding in a chariot; a bit indicated that he was on horseback; the presence of an elephant was indicated by a goad.

For purposes of psychological characterization, roles were divided into a number of clearly differentiated categories. For example, the hero might be one of four types: quiet, gallant, impetuous, or sublime. Such classifications extended to a number of other character types, each with several subdivisions, and all differentiated by rigidly prescribed costumes,

Scene from Shakuntala *as performed by the Brahman Sabha, Bombay, in 1954. (Courtesy Information Service of India.)*

makeup, and gestures. Furthermore, emotions were divided into nine categories: quietude, wonder, digust, fear, energy, anger, pathos, laughter, and love. It was the actors' task to blend these rigidly codified emotions, character types, costumes, makeup, intonations, gestures, and movements into a totality capable of arousing the appropriate rasa.

Of the Sanskrit plays that have survived, some of the most famous are King Harsha's (seventh century A.D.) *The Pearl Necklace, The Lost Princess,* and *Nagananda;* Bhavabhuti's (late seventh century) *The Later Story of Rama, The Story of the Great Hero,* and *The Stolen Marriage;* and Vishakhadatta's (ninth century) *The Ring of Rakshasa.* By far the best of the plays are *The Little Clay Cart,* attributed to King Shudraka (probably of the fourth century), and *Shakuntala.* The plot of *The Little Clay Cart* is entirely invented. It is primarily concerned with the love of a Brahmin for a courtesan, although there are a number of other subplots, all of which come together at the end of the ten acts when the true prince, previously befriended by the courtesan, recaptures his throne and unites the Brahmin and courtesan, who have narrowly escaped death at the hands of the evil prince.

But *Shakuntala,* written by Kalidasa in the late fourth or early fifth century, is the acknowledged masterpiece of Sanskrit drama. *Shakuntala* is divided into seven acts, each separately titled and each marking an important stage in the story's development. In Act I, entitled "The Hunt," King Dushyanta, following a deer, comes riding into the forest in a chariot. Upon being informed that he is near a hermitage, he halts the

Members of the Kerala Kalamandalam Kathakali Dance Theatre of India being made up for performance. Following tradition, all roles are played by men. (Courtesy Kazuko Hillyer International.)

chase. Entering the hermitage, he sees a number of young women, among them Shakuntala, daughter of the sage Kanva, and falls in love with her. Much of Act II, entitled "Keeping the Story Secret," is taken up with the clown's complaints and jokes. The King dissuades his party from hunting and later orders them to disperse the demons who are said to be disturbing the quiet of the hermitage. In Act III, entitled "The Enjoyment of Love," the King eavesdrops on Shakuntala and her friends, discovers that Shakuntala loves him, reveals himself, and eventually wins her. At the opening of Act IV, called "Shakuntala's Departure," the King has returned to the court, leaving Shakuntala with a ring as a token of their marriage by mutual consent. An ill-tempered ascetic, Durvasas, believing that he has been insulted, places a curse on Shakuntala, declaring that the King will forget her. When he is reproached, he relents suffiencly to say that the King will remember her when he sees the ring. Kanva now discovers that Shakuntala is pregnant and insists that she go to join her husband. Act V, called "Shakuntala's Rejection," shows Shakuntala's arrival at the court. Unfortunately, while bathing in a river during her journey, she has lost the ring and the King has no memory of her. The King's chaplain finally suggests that Shakuntala stay at his house until the truth can be investigated, but before the act ends, he reports that a spirit has flown away with Shakuntala. In Act VI, entitled "Separation from Shakuntala," a fisherman is charged with stealing a ring belonging to the King, although he insists that he has found it in the belly of a fish. When the King sees it, his memory returns and he is stricken with remorse. While he is sorrowing over Shakuntala's disappearance, he is summoned to assist the gods in destroying demons. The final act opens with the King flying through the air, the demons now having been destroyed. He lands in a hermitage, where he encounters a young boy, who, through a series of signs, is revealed to be his own son. When the mother is summoned, it is Shakuntala. They are reunited and all ends happily.

As this brief summary indicates, the action of *Shakuntala* takes place over a number of years and in several places. It mingles the natural and the supernatural, the serious and the comic. The basic emphasis, however, is upon the love story, for the majority of the text is devoted to evoking the emotions of awakening love, doubt and yearning, fulfillment, the sorrows of rejection and loss, and the bliss of reunion now tempered with parental love. Thus, the basic rasa is love.

Shakuntala is famous for its powerful evocation of the forest, the fleeing deer, the sense of place and emotion—all achieved through language. Kalidasa, a master of simile and metaphor, has won universal praise for his overall harmony of style. But despite its sensual charms, *Shakuntala* illustrates well the Hindu search for peace of soul, rest after struggle, and happiness after trial and submission to fate. Its love story and the struggle of admirable characters against unfriendly powers give *Shakuntala* universal appeal, even though the Hindu setting and outlook may seem strange to Westerners. As the first Oriental drama known in

Chhau, a masked dance from Bengal in northeastern India. (Courtesy Performing Arts Program of the Asia Society.)

Europe, it was responsible for stimulating interest in the theatre of the Orient. Following the Mohammedan invasions of India during the twelfth and thirteenth centuries. Sanskrit drama retreated to a few temples.

The history of Indian dance is similar. More ancient than drama, dance was well developed by the time Bharata wrote *Natyasastra*, in which he describes 108 dance positions. Dance probably reached its peak during the fourth and fifth centuries A.D., and, after the Mohammedan invasions, it was preserved primarily by temple dancers in the state of Madras. As Indian nationalism emerged in the late nineteenth century, classical dance came to be highly prized as a heritage of the past. The principal form today, usually called Bharatanatyam, is a solo dance for women noted for its grace. Classical dance has also survived in other forms, most notably the Kathak, characterized by intricate footwork and precise rhythms, and the Manipuri, noted for its swaying and gliding movements.

Today, the best known dance-drama of India is probably Kathakali, now about three hundred years old. Like Sanskrit drama, Kathakali is based on Hindu epics, but, perhaps because it is pantomimic, it exaggerates many features subordinated in the dramas. Violence and death are brought on stage; major emphasis is placed on the passions and furies of gods and demons or on the loves and hates of superhuman characters. Good and evil engage in desperate struggles, but good always wins.

The Kathakali actor-dancers rely entirely upon mime, costume, and makeup, although musicians help to tell the story through song and instrumental accompaniment. Gestures are conventionalized into about five hundred separate signs. Characters are divided into seven basic types, each with its own costume and makeup, which takes hours to apply. Kathakali is performed entirely by men and boys.

These dance-dramas are presented in a temple courtyard (or other open space) on a stage about sixteen feet square covered with a flower-decked roof and lighted by torches. Performances last all night. The appeal of Kathakali is so special, depending as it does on a rather thorough knowledge of its conventions, that few attempts were made to perform it outside of India until 1967, when a troupe was seen in Paris, London, and Montreal. Since then it has become increasingly well known in the West.

In addition to classical drama and dance, India boasts many other dramatic types, some probably dating back to the earliest times. Among these types, one of the most popular today is the folk play, which varies in form according to the region. Some are operatic, others are light farces, dance dramas, or devotional plays. Despite this variety, most folk plays have many common characteristics. A narrator usually sets the scene, summons characters as needed, and describes the events occurring offstage. Music accompanies the action throughout. The plays are performed on open stages surrounded on three sides by spectators. No scenery is used; the acting is stylized. Differing from one area to another, the conventions are clearly understood by the local audiences. Most performances go on all night.

A Western-style drama, descended from plays brought by the British when they arrived in the eighteenth century, has also been prominent in modern India. Few Indian authors, however, have been markedly successful with Western forms. Perhaps the best has been Rabindrinath Tagore (1861–1941), who won considerable fame with his blending of Indian

Performers in another Kathakali dance-drama. (Courtesy Information Service of India.)

and Western conventions in such plays as *The King of the Dark Chamber* (1914) and *The Cycle of Spring* (1917).

India has been hampered in developing a native drama by its lack of a national language. Within India, fifteen major languages and about five hundred dialects are in common use. This diversity of speech, combined with differences in local customs, has served to divide the country and to encourage drama with local appeal. Today productions range from ancient Sanskrit drama to folk plays and realistic works in the Western manner. But, though the Indian theatre is diverse, its influence on the rest of the world still derives primarily from the Sanskrit dramas written between the fourth and twelfth centuries and traditional dance-drama such as Kathakali.

Theatre in Southeast Asia

The theatre of Southeast Asia is related to that of India, perhaps because the peoples of that area share the heritage of Hinduism and Buddhism. Dance-drama, especially, is highly developed in Indonesia, Thailand, Cambodia, Laos, and Burma. But there are as well many other

Shadow puppet from Malaysia representing Hanuman (the monkey king). (From the private collection of Ruth and Walter Meserve.)

The Oriental Theatre

theatrical forms—folk drama, operetta, spoken drama, pantomime, improvised plays, shadow puppet plays, doll puppet plays, and Western-style drama. Perhaps the most distinctive form is the shadow play, which in numerous local variations, is widely performed in Indonesia, Malaysia, and Thailand.

The shadow play seems to have been cultivated most fully on the island of Java in Indonesia, where it is called *wayang kulit*. It is unclear when or where it originated. Some scholars argue that it is purely indigenous, others that it came from India, and still others that it came from China. Regardless of its origin, by the eleventh century A.D. it had developed into a highly complex art quite unlike the forms seen in India or China.

The Indonesian shadow plays, like Sanskrit drama, take their subjects primarily from the *Mahabharata* and *Ramayana*. In performance, flat leather puppets act out the events, while the puppet master chants the story, manipulates the puppets (which are attached to wooden sticks), directs the music and sound effects. Performances often last as long as ten hours, consuming an entire night. They are accompanied by music played by an orchestra composed primarily of percussion instruments. The stories usually center around the struggles between good and evil characters, the good always winning.

A number of dramatic types have been derived from the *wayang kulit*. One variation (*wayang golek*) uses three-dimensional doll puppets. Another (*wayang orang*) uses human performers, as does *wayang topeng*, a masked dance-drama that draws on stories from many sources. The variations in dramatic type are extremely numerous.

Theatre and Drama in China

Just as drama and dance in India and Southeast Asia may be said to constitute one major strand of Oriental tradition, those of China form another strand. As in India, ritual dance in China is of ancient origin, possibly going back to the Shang Dynasty (c. 1500–1027 B.C.). A few secular elements, in the form of pantomime, jests, and songs seem to have crept into these rituals and into court festivals during the Chou Dynasty (c. 1027–256 B.C.). Thereafter, various types of incidental entertainment flourished: acrobatics, dances, music, pantomimes, and other displays. Eventually these came to be called the "hundred plays."

Chinese actors traditionally date their origin from 714 A.D., when Emperor Hsuan Tsung established the "Pear Garden" as a training school for performers of music and dance. (Chinese actors are still often called "Students of the Pear Garden.") During the Sung Dynasty (960–1279) tales based on history were intermingled with choreographed dances and songs to create a semidramatic form. It is now usual to consider *Chang Hsieh, The Doctor of Letters*, which dates from this era, to

Shadow puppet from Malaysia representing Seri Rama (the hero). (From the private collection of Ruth and Walter Meserve.)

be the oldest extant Chinese play. It includes a prologue (which summarizes the action) and a main story told through dialogue and songs.

During the Sung Dynasty the best performers were recruited for the court. Others played wherever they could. They banded together into troupes of five to seven members and played in villages or cities, in teahouses or impromptu theatres. In the cities, playhouses were situated in special areas, or "title districts." According to contemporary accounts, theatres were fenced enclosures, above which flags and banners flew; the stage was a roofed platform open on three sides; at ground level there was a large area where people might stand; and around this there might be raised stands or balconies.

But it was not until the Yuan Dynasty (1279–1368) that Chinese drama first flourished. Through most of the Yuan period the best drama-

Chinese shadow puppets made of skin. Shadow puppet plays can be traced back to the 2d century B.C. in China. (Courtesy the Performing Arts Program of the Asia Society, New York.)

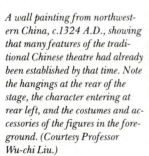

A wall painting from northwestern China, c.1324 A.D., showing that many features of the traditional Chinese theatre had already been established by that time. Note the hangings at the rear of the stage, the character entering at rear left, and the costumes and accessories of the figures in the foreground. (Courtesy Professor Wu-chi Liu.)

The Oriental Theatre

tist lived in northern China, where they developed a style usually labeled "northern." Each play in this style consisted of four acts with from ten to twenty songs or arias, all sung by the protagonist. The rest of the characters spoke or recited their lines. If the dramatic action could not be represented in four acts, a "wedge" could be added as a prologue or interlude. The wedge was short, with no more than two arias, which might be sung by some character other than the protagonist. The simple unadorned accompaniment used a seven-tone scale.

It is unclear how many plays were written during the Yuan period, but more than 700 titles are recorded; about 170 have survived. Some of the best known "northern" plays are *The Injustice Done to Maid Tou* by Kuan Han-ch'ing (sometimes called the father of Chinese drama), *Romance of the Western Chamber* by Wang Shih-fu, and *The Story of the Chalk Circle* by Li Ch'ien-fu. In "northern" plays the action typically extends over months or years; only rarely is it confined to one place; and it occasionally ends unhappily, although poetic justice usually prevails.

Before the middle of the fourteenth century, a "southern" school of drama began to emerge in the area around Hangchow. The best known of these plays is *Lute Song* (c. 1350) by Kao Ming. Under the Ming Dynasty (1368–1644) the "southern" style came to dominate. By 1600 its characteristic features had become relatively fixed. A "southern" play may have as many as fifty or more acts, each with its own title. In the opening act, usually called the argument or prologue, a secondary character sets forth the purpose and explains the story. Succeeding acts introduce many plot strands; all are happily resolved in the final scene. Any of the characters may sing, and there are solos, duets, and even choruses. The music is composed for a five-tone scale (except when tunes were borrowed from northern plays). Although northern dramas continued to be written after 1600, they were mainly poetic exercises.

Southern drama too gradually became mere closet drama. The scripts were often too long to be produced in their totality; the language was too formal and filled with allusions to be understood by anyone except scholars; and the writers followed rules so slavishly that spontaneity disappeared. Nevertheless, the southern style continued to dominate dramatic writing until the nineteenth century.

Peking Opera, the dominant theatrical form in China since the mid-nineteenth century, came to the fore only gradually. As the southern style lost its vitality and appeal, a number of local styles emerged, most of them mingling traditional stories with melodies based on folk tunes. In 1790, to celebrate the Emperor's birthday, the best performers from various regions were brought to Peking. Many remained and features from various regional styles gradually amalgamated to become Peking Opera.

Unlike its predecessors, Peking Opera was primarily a theatrical rather than a literary form; its emphasis was upon rigidly controlled conventions of acting, dancing, and singing rather than upon the text. Instead of a single work, an evening's program in Peking Opera is usually made up of

A scene from Romance of the Western Chamber, *one of the most popular of Yuan dramas. From an edition published during the Ming dynasty. (Courtesy Professor Wu-chi Liu.)*

a series of short pieces, many of them acts or portions of longer works (including traditional southern and northern plays), intermingled with acrobatic displays. There are no intermissions and usually the scenes are arranged to ensure that the best performers are saved for the final episodes.

The plays of Peking Opera are usually classified under two headings: civil plays (dealing with social and domestic themes) and military plays (involving the adventures of warriors or brigands), although the two are often mingled. The dramas are derived from earlier literary plays, novels, history, legend, mythology, folklore, and romance. All end happily. The text of a work is seldom strictly followed, for all great actors make

A typical Peking opera orchestra. Musical instruments from left to right: hsiao-lo *(small gong),* nao-po *(cymbals),* ta-lo *(big gong)* tan-p'i-ku *and* pan *(single-skin-drum and wooden-clapper),* san-hsien *(three-stringed banjo),* erh-hu *(second fiddle),* yüeh-ch'ing *(moon guitar), and* ching-hu *(first fiddle). The orchestra is led by the drum player, sitting in the center. Formerly the orchestra was placed downstage left in full view of the audience. Today, it is often concealed behind a stage-left wing or in the orchestra pit. A standard orchestra consists of eight to ten musicians. In some elaborate contemporary productions more than twenty musicians are employed. (From Siao and Alley,* Peking Opera. *Peking: New World Press, 1957. Photo and notes supplied by Daniel S. P. Yang.)*

changes at certain points, and each troupe has its own version of standard works. The dramatic action in a Peking Opera is often obscure because beginnings and endings are neglected, for the primary interest lies in the high points of the story. A play, however, is merely an outline for a performance, and the audience goes to see a production rather than to hear a literary text. The names of dramatists are not even listed on the programs.

Above all, Peking Opera is characterized by the conventions it inherited from earlier periods and developed into a strict system. Many traditional practices are best understood in relation to the stage and its equipment. The Chinese stage still preserves features derived from its earliest form—a temple porch with a roof. Thus, the traditional stage is an open, almost-square platform surmounted by a roof supported by columns. Raised a few feet above the auditorium, it is surrounded by a wooden railing about two feet high. The stage is equipped simply. There are two doors in the rear wall (the one on stage right is used for all entrances and the one on stage left for all exits); between them hangs a large embroidered curtain; the floor is carpeted; the permanent furnishings are restricted to a wooden table and a few chairs.

The place of the dramatic action may be indicated in a number of ways. The audience may be told through speech or song what the stage represents. Pantomime may be used to establish place or changes of place. For example, actors pantomime knocking at gates, climbing stairs, or entering rooms; a circle around the stage indicates a long journey. Place may be indicated by the arrangement of the table and chairs. Depending upon the arrangement, the stage may become a law court, banqueting hall, or other room; the addition of an incense tripod indicates a palace, an official seal indicates an office, and an embroidered curtain hung from a pole indicates a general's tent, Emperor's chamber, or a bride's bedroom, depending upon the arrangement of the table and chairs and other properties. A wall is created by placing the chairs back to back, a bridge by placing the back of the chairs against the ends of the table; a single chair may stand for a tree or a door; the table used alone may represent a hill, cloud, or some other high place.

Additional properties may be used to indicate place or to clarify the action. A cloth upon which a wall is painted may be used to represent a fort, city gate, or mountain pass; a banner with a fish design indicates water; four pieces of cloth carried by a running actor signifies the wind; a whip symbolizes riding a horse; flags upon which wheels are painted signify a chariot or wagon; a stylized paddle is used to pantomime rowing. Weapons are semirealistic in appearance but are made of bamboo, wood, or rattan.

For full appreciation of the pantomime and properties, a spectator must be familiar with the conventions of the Chinese theatre. The intention is to stimulate the imagination but not to give an illusion of reality. To many commentators, the approach is best exemplified by the *property men,* or stage assistants, who bring on, rearrange, and remove properties as needed. No attempt is made to disguise their presence; they wear ordinary street clothes, often extremely informal ones. But while they are ever present, they are not considered to be a part of the stage picture; they are merely a part of the conventions they help to create.

General Lien P'u (played by the noted actor Ch'iu Sheng-jung) strikes a magnificent pose in The Reconciliation between the General and the Minister, *one of the first Peking operas written after 1949. The character belongs to the role of* ching *(painted face). Symmetrically painted facial design of red, black, and white suggest a loyal, straightforward but hot-tempered character. Note the exaggerated length of the beard. (From* Peking Opera. *Photo and notes supplied by Daniel S. P. Yang.)*

Chinese actor Mei Lan-fang in a ch'ing-i *(virtuous woman) role. The role can be compared to that of the soprano in Western opera because of its strong emphasis on singing. Peking opera acting is highly stylized, as exemplified here in the delicate pointing of the fingers and the manner of holding a tea tray. (From Arlington and Acton,* Famous Chinese Plays. *Peiping: Henri Vetch, 1937. Photo and notes supplied by Daniel S. P. Yang.)*

The noted comic actor Ma Fu-lu in the role of Chiang Kan in Meeting of the League of Heroes. *The role belongs to the category* wen-ch'ou *or "comic scholar." Note the white patch of make-up around the nose and eyes, the trade-mark of a clown on the Peking opera stage. (From* Famous Chinese Plays. *Photo and notes supplied by Daniel S. P. Yang.)*

The Oriental Theatre

The musicians are treated much like the property men. They also remain in full view throughout the performance and are dressed in ordinary street clothes. They come and go freely and are never considered to be part of the stage picture. (In many theatres of present-day China, however, the musicians have been removed from the stage and placed in an orchestra pit.)

Music is indispensable in the Chinese theatre. It establishes atmosphere, controls timing and movement, accompanies the many sung portions, and welds the entire performance into a rhythmical unity. Most of the music for Peking Opera is borrowed from already existing sources and recombined according to the needs of particular plays. It is usually worked out collaboratively among the actors and musicians. Since Chinese musical notation is extremely imprecise, the musicians must memorize their parts.

The instruments used in the Chinese theatre have no exact counterparts in the West. The leader of the orchestra plays a kind of drum, which establishes tempo and accentuates rhythms. Gongs, cymbals, brass cups, flutes, strings and other instruments complete the orchestra. The entrances and exits of all characters are signaled by deafening percussion passages. Sung portions are accompanied only by flute and strings. Much of the action is performed against a musical background.

The focal point of the Chinese theatre, however, is the actor, for the simplified stage focuses all attention upon him. Acting roles are divided into four main types: male, female, painted face, and comic. The male (or *sheng*) roles range from young to old and from fops to warriors. They include statesmen, scholars, lovers, and other heroic types. The roles are subdivided according to whether they involve acrobatics and fighting or whether they are restricted to singing and dancing. Actors playing these roles wear simple makeup and, with the exception of young heroes, beards. The female (or *tan*) roles are subdivided into six kinds: the virtuous wife or lover; coquettes; warrior maidens; young unmarried girls; evil women; and old women. Although originally all tan roles were played by women, actresses were banned from the stage from the late eighteenth until the twentieth century. After 1911 actresses returned to the theatre and have now largely replaced the male tan actors. The "painted face" (or *ching*) roles are distinguished by the elaborate painted facial makeup worn by the actors. The ching roles include gods and other supernatural beings, courtiers, warriors, and bandits, but the basic characteristic of all is swagger and exaggerated strength. They are subdivided according to whether they are good or evil or whether they must engage in fighting and gymnastics. The clown (or *ch'ou*) roles are the most realistic. They speak in everyday language and are free to joke and improvise. They may be servants, businessmen, jailers, matchmakers, shrewish mothers-in-law, or soldiers. The clown must be a good mimic and acrobat.

Makeup is an important part of the Chinese theatre. Bearded sheng

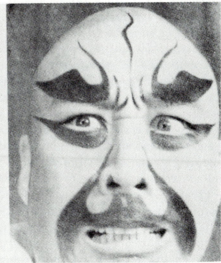

Examples of face painting in Peking Opera. From top left, clockwise: The King Hsiang Fu, a heroic face; an unstable character; a fierce but stupid general; a dragon character in "Disturbance in Heaven."

The Oriental Theatre

actors and old women wear little makeup. For most tan roles the face is painted white and the eyes surrounded by a deep red shading into pink. A similar makeup, but with less contrast, is used for the unbearded sheng actors. For the ching roles, the entire face is painted in bold patterns symbolic of the character's traits. Realism is completely ignored. The clown's distinguishing feature is a white patch around each eye. The types of clowns are differentiated by a variety of black patterns painted on the face.

Typically, costumes are vivid in color and heavily patterned. There are more than three hundred articles of costume, each designed to indicate the wearer's character-type, age, and social status. Colors, motifs, ornaments, and accessories are combined according to an elaborate system of conventions. Color is always used symbolically: yellow signifies royalty, red loyalty and high social position, dark crimson a barbarian or military advisor. The tiger motif means power and masculinity, the plum blossom long life and feminine charm; the dragon motif is associated with the Emperor. There are more than a hundred varieties of headdress, each symbolic. Most costumes are made of rich materials regardless of the character's social position, although clowns and very poor persons sometimes wear linen or cotton garments.

Speech and movement are also highly stylized. Upon entering, each important character describes his own basic attributes and appearance in a half-chanted, half-spoken passage. He may then explain the situation or give other information. In this way, the dramatist quickly supplies essential exposition leaving the major part of the scene for the high point of a situation or emotion.

All stage movement is related to dance, for it is symbolic, pantomimic, and rhythmical. Every word of the text is accompanied by movement intended to clarify or heighten meaning. Thus, stage gesture is completely conventionalized. There are seven basic hand movements, more than twenty different pointing gestures, about twelve special leg movements, many special arm movements, and a great many sleeve and beard movements. The method to be used in walking or running is specified for each role. In creating a part, the actor must combine the prescribed gestures and movements according to the situation, mood, and character.

Vocal delivery is also controlled by rigid conventions. Each role has its own pitch and timbre. Prescribed rhythmical patterns often require that syllables or words be distorted. Even spoken passages must observe conventionalized tempos and rhythms. In addition, chanted or sung passages are freely inserted into spoken portions.

The character of the Chinese theatre also owes much to the audience. Probably because many early theatres were teahouses, the ground floor of the traditional Chinese theatre was furnished with tables and stools at which spectators were served tea as they watched the play. Poorer spectators sat on benches placed on a raised platform which extended along the sides and back of the auditorium. A balcony, divided into sections much

Setting for a Peking opera. An embroidered satin backdrop and two curtained doorways serve as the basic setting. The door on stage right is used for entrances, that on stage left for exits. The different locales of the action are suggested by the table and chairs, which are arranged by the property man in full view of the audience. This setting was used for Twice a Bride, *a full-length Peking opera staged at the University of Hawaii in 1963. Directed and designed by Daniel S. P. Yang. (Photo by Camera Hawaii.)*

like the boxes of Western theatres, was later added; in some periods it was used by wealthy persons, in others it was reserved for women.

Since 1911, this arrangement has been modified. Now most theatres are furnished with Western-style seating. Nevertheless, the audience's behavior has changed little. Spectators come and go freely, eat and drink, carry on conversations. Each member has his favorite passages, to which he attends carefully only to ignore others. Like the dramatists, the spectators seem more interested in the high points of a story or performance than in unified effect.

Since the Communists assumed control over the Chinese mainland in 1949, a number of changes have been made in Peking Opera. The reforms are designed primarily to make subjects and ideas conform to Communist goals, but they also extend to some theatrical conventions. To clarify its standards, the government has caused to be produced a number of "model" works to serve as guides. In its traditional form, Peking Opera is now most fully preserved on Taiwan and in Hong Kong and Singapore.

Western-style drama has also made considerable impact in China since 1911. It is usually called "spoken drama" to distinguish it from the operatic mode of the traditional form. A number of writers have attempted the style, but the most successful has been Ts'ao Yu (1910–   ), whose works, such as *Thunderstorm* (1933), *Sunrise* (1935), and *The Bridge* (1945), deal with contemporary social problems. Since 1949, the majority of Chinese spoken drama has dealt with ideology. In these melodramas, characters are usually divided into heroes or villains on the basis of political conviction and invariably the enemy is exposed and routed.

In the West, knowledge of Chinese art and drama has grown slowly since the eighteenth century, when increasing trade precipitated a vogue for Chinese decorative motifs throughout Europe. Nevertheless, it was not until the twentieth century that the Chinese theatre became widely known in the West. Even then, Chinese drama was seen primarily in such adaptations as Benrimo's *The Yellow Jacket* (1913), Klabund's *The Circle of Chalk* (1923), and Hsiung's *Lady Precious Stream* (1938). Since World War II, the appearance of Peking Opera troupes in the West and the wide dissemination of filmed performances have done much to increase direct knowledge. The impact of Chinese drama on the West is best exemplified in the work of Meyerhold, Brecht, and others, who, impressed by the simplicity and anti-illusionistic conventions of the Chinese theatre, adapted many of its techniques.

Theatre and Drama in Japan

Today, the Japanese theatre is more widely known in the West than that of any other Oriental country, for until recently China has been isolated from the rest of the world, while India's classical theatre is no longer vital. Furthermore, the traditional forms still figure prominently in the active Japanese repertory. Because Westerners have become increasingly familiar with Japan and its traditions, to them the Oriental theatre is above all the Japanese theatre.

As in other Asian countries, the theatre in Japan descended from ritual dance, which dates from no later than the early Christian era. When Buddhism was introduced into Japan during the sixth century A.D., dance plays set to music came with it. One form of this early dance drama, *bugaku,* is still performed at the imperial court on important state occasions by dancers whose art has been passed down through generations of families with hereditary rights to the form.

Between the tenth and thirteenth centuries, several kinds of entertainment were common. Of these, the most important historically are *dengaku* (which had its origins in native harvest rituals) and *sarugaku* (which grew out of ritualistic elements imported from China). Both were medleys of disconnected songs, dances, and short sketches. It was out of *sarugaku* that Noh, one of Japan's most important theatrical forms, evolved. It first attained eminence through the innovations of Kannami Kiyotsugu (1333–1384), who fused dance with mimicry. Noh reached its highest point with Kannami's son, Zeami Motokiyo (1363–1443). Of the approximately 240 plays still in the active repertory, more than 100 were written by Zeami. It was also Zeami who formulated the principles of Noh drama, acting, and production, recording them in the *Kadensho,* a book considered to be as important to Oriental drama as Aristotle's *Poetics* is for Western drama.

Because Noh is rooted in the fourteenth- and fifteenth-century Japanese culture, one needs to know something about conditions of that era. Kannami and Zeami lived at a period in Japan's "middle ages" (1192–1868)

A Noh production of Aoi no Ue (The Lady Aoi) *by Zeami Motokiyo. (Courtesy Kokusai Bunka Shinkokai, Tokyo.)*

when a new political and social structure had taken shape and the arts were flourishing. In 1192 the Emperor had ceded his secular powers to a *shogun,* or military dictator, who thereafter ruled in his name. The shogunate lasted until 1868, when the Emperor resumed his powers. Under the shogunate an elabororate feudal system was maintained and strict codes of honor and behavior were required. The most important group was the *samurai,* or hereditary warrior class, beneath whom were ranked the other classes, each with clearly prescribed functions, dress, and style of living. This feudal system was not abolished until 1871. During the early middle ages there was much confusion in the arts because of the conflict between the ideals of the earlier aristocratic culture and the new warrior outlook, and between the native cultural heritage and that imported from China (which had been dominant with the aristocrats). By the time Kannami and Zeami appeared, these conflicts were being resolved and synthesized to create forms that are still considered the high point in Japanese artistic expression.

The major influence on Noh was Zen Buddhism. From this spiritual source Zeami adopted the conviction that beauty lies in suggestion, simplicity, subtlety, and restraint. Virtually all of his premises are summed up in the complex term *yūgen,* which, most simply, means gentle gracefulness, the mysterious beauty of impermanence in which elegance is always accompanied by awareness of its fragility. In later years Zeami extended his conception of *yūgen* to include the feeling of tranquil loneliness and the peaceful acceptance of old age. It is the qualities summed up in *yūgen* that Noh seeks to capture.

The Oriental Theatre
241

Most Noh traditions were fixed by 1650. Although originally Noh had appealed to all classes, it became more aristocratic under the shoguns. In the seventeenth century, Noh actors were granted *samurai* status and a stipend raised by a system of national requisitions. Five branches of Noh were recognized and the headship of each was made hereditary. These five schools still exist. After 1868, Noh lost its privileged position and survived in the difficult period immediately following primarily through the patronage of special societies. Since World War II it has been recognized as a national treasure and given support which places it on a more secure footing. It has also gained in popular esteem.

Nevertheless, Noh's appeal is limited, since its form was fixed long ago. The language, based on aristocratic speech of the fourteenth century, is unintelligible to most persons today. Many spectators bring scripts to performances so they may follow the plays. The majority of lines, some in prose and some in verse, are sung or intoned. The few spoken passages—typically fewer than one-third of the text—are recited in a highly stylized manner. Ordinary speech is heard only between the parts of a two-act piece when a player comes onstage to summarize what has happened in the first part.

Noh is essentially a dance-drama in which the script serves to create a setting for choreographic movement. It is not primarily concerned with dramatic action; rather, it seeks to express a situation in lyrical form. All Noh plays reach their fulfillment in a dance; the lines that precede the climactic dance serve primarily to establish the circumstances that motivates

A Japanese Noh stage as it appears today. (Reprinted with permission from The Traditional Music of Japan *by Shigeo Kishibe, Tokyo: Kokusai Bunka Shinkokai, 1966.)*

it. A chorus sings the actor's lines while he is dancing and narrates much of the story. The script of a Noh drama is usually shorter than that of a Western one-act play.

Noh plays are classified into five types: *kamimono,* or plays praising the gods; *shuramono,* plays about warriors; *kazuromono,* plays about women; *kuruimono,* miscellaneous plays, most often about mad persons or spirits but sometimes about unmasked "living persons"; and *kirinomono,* plays about demons, devils, or other supernatural beings. Traditionally, a program was made up of one play of each type performed in the order listed above. In recent years, however, it has become common to have programs composed of only two or three plays.

The Noh plays on a program are separated by *kyogen,* or short farcical pieces. Kyogen do not use musical accompaniment; all of the dialogue, except for a few short, chanted passages, is spoken. In kyogen, actors seldom wear masks. Most plays require no more than three actors, although occasionally more are needed. Essentially humorous and pantomimic, kyogen plays are, nevertheless, performed according to rigidly controlled patterns.

One of the most popular of Noh plays is *Atsumori* by Zeami. It includes only four characters, two very minor. It tells of the warrior Kumagai, who has killed Atsumori, a young nobleman, in battle. Kumagai is so grieved that he has become a priest, Rensei, so that he may pray for Atsumori's soul. On his way to Atsumori's grave, he encounters some reapers. When one of the reapers declares that he is a member of Atsumori's family, Rensei kneels to pray. This ends the first of the two acts. In the interlude between the acts, the events surrounding Atsumori's death are narrated. At the beginning of the second part, the ghost of Atsumori (the reaper of the first act) now appears dressed as a young warrior and identifies himself to Rensei. The remainder of the play is largely a narrative that establishes the background of the battle in which Atsumori perished. The play culminates in the re-creation of the fight in a dance with narrative accompaniment by the chorus. At the climactic moment, the ghost of Atsumori hovers over Rensei ready to deliver a death blow, but Rensei's prayers have been effective. The play ends with Atsumori saluting Rensei with "pray for me again, oh pray for me again." The entire script occupies only about nine pages in print.

All Noh performers are male. The principal character is called *shite,* the secondary character *waki.* Each may have a companion, although many plays include only two characters. Seldom does a cast extend beyond six characters. There are occasional noble child roles *(kokata)* and commoners. *Kyogen* actors sometimes appear as peasants, servants, or boatmen to add an everyday or occasionally humorous touch.

The shite and his companions wear masks made of painted wood. Other characters are unmasked. Masks may be divided into five basic kinds: aged, male, female, gods, and monsters. These types have many variations, and occasionally special masks are required.

Costumes are based upon the ceremonial dress of several centuries ago, although adapted to achieve a sense of grandeur and to increase the performer's apparent stature. Garments are rich in color and design; most are made of silk and are elaborately embroidered. They are never gaudy, however, as the costumes of the Chinese theatre are. Articles of dress may be divided into four categories: outer garments; indoor clothing or garments worn without overdress; lower garments, such as divided skirts; and headdresses. Within each category there are many variations, but the same garments may be combined with others for use in several different roles. Thus, costumes are less rigidly conventionalized in color and design than in the Chinese theatre.

Only a few, highly conventionalized hand properties are used. The most important is the fan, which can suggest the rising moon, falling rain, rippling water, and blowing wind, as well as a variety of emotional responses. The meaning of the fan is indicated by the actor's pantomime and the musical accompaniment.

Stage furnishings are also simple. A simple, miniaturized wooden or bamboo stand may symbolize a mountain, palace, bedroom or other place, depending upon how it is decorated. Usually no more than one or two stage properties are present at once. Each is highly stylized; there is no scenery or stage machinery.

The design of the stage itself has been fixed since about 1615. There are two principal parts: the bridge (*hashigakari*) and the main acting

A character in the Noh play
Yuya. (*Courtesy Kokusai Bunka Shinkokai, Tokyo.*)

area (*butai*). Both are roofed. The roof over the main stage is supported by four columns, each with its own name. The upstage right pillar is called *shitebashira* ("principal character's pillar"), for here the shite pauses as he enters to announce his name and to give other pertinent information. While reciting, he faces the downstage right pillar (the *metsukebashira*). The downstage left pillar is called *wakibashira*, because of its association with the secondary character (or alternatively the *daijinbashira*, or "minister's pillar," because of the role often played by the waki). The upstage left pillar, beside which the flute player sits, is called the *fuebashira* (or "flute pillar").

The main platform is divided into three areas, although the only architectural barriers are the four pillars. The largest part, used for the main action, is enclosed within the four pillars. It is about nineteen feet square. The floor of this area is constructed of special wood and sounding jars are placed underneath to make the rhythmic and emphatic stamping of feet, a distinctive feature of Noh, more effective. To stage left of the main area is the *wakiza*, used primarily for the six- to ten-member chorus, which narrates much of the story. Back of the upstage pillars is the *atoza*, occupied by the orchestra composed of two or three drummers and a flute player.

The principal entrance to the stage is the bridge (*hashigakari*), a railed gangway extending from thirty-three to fifty-two feet in length and about six feet in width. It joins the stage to the dressing rooms. It is used for all important entrances. In front of it are planted three small pine trees, symbolizing man, earth, and heaven. In the upstage left corner of the atoza is located a second entrance, the "hurry door," used by subordinate characters or those who have died, stage assistants, chorus, and musicians. It is only about three feet high. Another door, the "noble's door," is located upstage of the wakiza, but nowadays is never used and thus is purely decorative.

The rear wall of the stage and bridge are made of wood. On the portion behind the atoza are painted pine trees and on the stage left wall bamboo, probably to recall the natural setting which formed the background for the original Noh performances. The audience views the stage from two sides: from the front and the stage-right side of the main platform.

The object of a Noh performance is to capture the essence of a situation or emotion. Every episode is drawn out, often to great length. The high points take the form of extremely stylized static gestures or bodily attitudes held for some time. During a performance, every movement of hands and feet, every intonation must follow set rules. The orchestra furnishes the musical setting and establishes the timing of every gesture. Noh is one of the world's most carefully controlled theatrical experiences. The over-all effect is that of an elaborate ceremony or ritual.

Puppets have also played a significant role in Japanese theatrical life. Puppet performances may be traced back to the Heian period (781–1185

Kumagai, a noted general of the Genji clan, as portrayed in a puppet theatre production of Kumagai Jinya. (Courtesy Kokusai Bunka Shinkokai, Tokyo.)

A puppet theatre production showing a scene along the road in Yoshitsune Sembon Zakura (Yoshitsune and the Thousand Cherry Trees). (Courtesy Kokusai Bunka Shinkokai, Tokyo.)

A.D.), but the *puppet theatre* did not emerge until the Keicho era (1596–1614). It was given its definitive form by Takemoto Gidayu (1650–1714). Its characteristic plays were written by Chikamatsu Monzaemon (1653–1724), usually considered Japan's greatest playwright, who worked for many years with Takemoto at his puppet theatre in Osaka.

The puppets themselves have undergone many changes. Originally, only a head was used, but by 1678 full figures, with hands and feet, were common. During the eighteenth century, devices were developed to permit the puppets to move their eyes, fingers, and eyebrows. By 1736 they had been enlarged to their present height of three or four feet. Thus, the figures became ever more lifelike. As puppets became more complex, more operators were required. Originally, one operator, completely hidden from view, was sufficient. By the 1730s three men, all completely visible, were required for each principal puppet. One manipulated the head and right arm, another the left arm, and the third the feet.

The stage also became more complex. Unlike Noh, puppet theatre used scenery, and the desire to change the background motivated the invention of stage machinery that would be unknown in the West until much later. Elevator traps were introduced in 1727 to raise scenery to stage level, and after 1758 they were used to create different stage-floor levels.

The conventions of puppet theatre were fixed during the eighteenth century, the peak of its popularity. After this time, it was overshadowed by the Kabuki. Today it survives primarily in one company, the Bunraku of Osaka.

A performance in puppet theatre begins with the appearance of an announcer, clad in black and wearing a hood (the dress of all stage assist-

ants except the principal puppet handlers, musicians, and narrator). He announces the name of the piece, the *samisen* player, and the narrator. The instrumentalists and singers sit on a raised platform at stage left; the *samisen* player and narrator are located on a small turntable downstage left (at the end of each act the turntable is revolved to bring on a new *samisen* player and narrator).

The *samisen* is a three-stringed instrument with a drumlike base. It is simultaneously plucked with a large pick and struck with the hand or fingers. Samisen accompaniment is considered essential in puppet theatre, for it follows the rise and fall of the voice and gives special emphasis as needed. Since puppet handlers do not speak, the narrator tells the story, speaks the dialogue, and expresses the emotions of each puppet. He may weep, laugh, draw back in astonishment or fear as he reacts to the changing situation.

The stage is long and shallow. A low partition across the front represents the level upon which the puppets supposedly walk. Back of this, the puppet operators act out the story. All locales are represented scenically and are changed as the story demands. Numerous properties are also used.

The puppets vary somewhat in size and complexity according to their function in the drama. Supernumeraries do not have movable eyes or fingers and are usually operated by a single handler. Female puppets, even major characters, do not usually have feet, although they are suggested by the way the costume is held. Puppets representing important characters are equipped with extremely complex mechanisms. Only the principal handlers are clothed in formal kimonos; subordinate handlers wear the black dress of stage assistants. The handlers attempt to absorb themselves in the drama and to become one with the puppets they manipulate. The Bunraku is probably the most complex puppet theatre in the world intended for an adult audience.

Today, Kabuki is the most vital of the traditional Japanese forms, for it has remained sensitive to change. But for this reason, many critics consider it "impure," since it has borrowed freely from Noh, puppet theatre, and other sources. Perhaps because it has remained sensitive to change, Kabuki is the Japanese form most easily understood by Western audiences.

Kabuki originated around 1600 when Okuni, a ceremonial dancer, began to give public performances in Kyoto. Although it soon attained great popularity, the shoguns sought to restrict its growth. In 1629, women were forbidden to appear on the stage, and in 1652 young men's Kabuki was banned. Thus, it was men's Kabuki that persisted. Until the end of the eighteenth century, Kabuki borrowed heavily from puppet theatre, taking over many of its plays, as well as its stage machinery and architecture. After 1780 it eclipsed puppet theatre in popularity. Since the fall of the shoguns, in 1868, it has been Japan's major dramatic form.

Kabuki plays began as simple sketches incorporated into danced performances. The first two-act piece was not given until 1644. The first

The Oriental Theatre

A Kabuki production of Gedatsu (The Release of Kagekiyo's Soul), *originally produced in 1744 and revised in 1914 and 1953. The scene shows the Todaiji Temple at Kamakura. (Courtesy Kokusai Bunka Shinkokai, Tokyo.)*

important writer of this form was Chikamatsu, who worked for Kabuki troupes before turning to puppet theatre. Many of Chikamatsu's puppet plays were later adapted for Kabuki performance. Next to Chikamatsu, the most famous Kabuki dramatist is Takeda Izumo (1691–1756), Chikamatsu's successor as playwright to the Osaka puppet theatre. He is remembered primarily for *Chushingura* (1748), the most popular of all Kabuki plays. Eleven acts long, *Chushingura* requires a full day in performance. It is based upon an actual event in which forty-seven faithful followers avenged the wrongs done to their master. Only one writer after Izumo, Kawatake Mokuami (1816–1893), has won lasting fame, being especially noted for his low-life characters. Today, almost every Kabuki program includes a selection from one of his approximately fifty plays.

Kabuki plays are divided into three types: *jidaimono,* or plays with a historical background; *sewamono,* or plays with a domestic or low-life background; and *shosagoto,* or dance-plays. Within these categories there is much variety, for the Japanese do not have precisely defined dramatic forms. A Kabuki play often mingles the comic and the serious. There are few purely comic works, however, and these are dance plays in one act. Some longer works are called comedies because they end happily. The majority of plays are essentially melodramas. Kabuki scripts concentrate upon climactic moments rather than upon a clearly articulated story. Thus, there are many strong scenes but the connection between them is sometimes vague. The habit of writing relatively complete episodes probably explains the modern practice of making up Kabuki programs from parts of plays, or even parts of acts.

Kabuki programs are long. In the eighteenth century they lasted all day. In 1868 the maximum length was set at eight hours. Since World War II, it has been usual to give two performances a day, each about five hours long.

Many critics consider dance to be the basis of Kabuki, for choreographic movement is a fundamental part of every performance. Kabuki dance distills the essence of real emotions and actions into stylized gestures, movement, and postures.

Kabuki roles are divided into such basic types as *tachiyaku,* loyal and courageous men; *katakiyaku,* villains; *wakashukata,* young men, who may be called *nimaime* if they are of mild disposition; *dokekata,* comic roles; *koyaku,* children's roles; and *onnagata,* women's roles, all played by men.

Because Kabuki acting is based upon conventions, it requires long and careful study. The actor usually begins his training at the age of six or seven; he appears on stage in children's roles from the very beginning. Thus, his work combines study and practice. Since acting is largely a hereditary profession, most of the actors come from a few families. Each family has its own system of stage names, some of which are so honored that they can be assumed only by undisputed masters of their art. A Kabuki actor is seldom considered mature until middle age.

Kabuki does not make use of masks. Some roles, however, require boldly patterned makeup. Typically, the makeup is composed of a white base upon which patterns of red, black, blue, or brown are painted. The onnagata leaves the face completely white except for false eyebrows and rouging at the corners of the eyes and to shape the mouth. The makeup of each character symbolizes and describes his role.

Every role also requires a conventionalized costume. Most garments are based upon historical dress, but altered for dramatic purposes. Since accuracy is of little importance, several historical periods may be used in the same play. Patterns and colors are usually subdued. Some costumes weigh as much as fifty pounds and must be rearranged frequently with the assistance of stage attendants. The attendants wear black and are considered to be invisible.

Every scene is accompanied by music. Because Kabuki has borrowed from many sources, the placement of the musicians on stage varies: For plays based on Noh, the musicians are placed upstage; for those borrowed from puppet theatre, the musicians are at stage left; for still other plays, the musicians are seated on stage right. In addition to the onstage musicians, others are placed behind a screen on stage right to provide special effects. As in puppet theatre, the most essential instrument is the *samisen,* which accompanies the singing and narration. The visible musicians are dressed in *kamishimo* (divided skirt, kimono, stiff horizontal shoulder

Famous actor Mitsugoro Bando plays the aged warrior Ikyu in "Sukeroku," one of the most popular Kabuki plays. (Courtesy Consulate General of Japan, New York.)

pieces), the formal dress of the nobility in the eighteenth century. When not performing, the musicians sit upright and motionless. There is none of the informality of the Chinese theatre.

Since the Kabuki actor does not sing, a narrator and chorus are often prominent, especially in those plays adapted from Noh and puppet theatre. The narrator may set the scene, speak part of the dialogue, or comment on the action. Even in those plays written for Kabuki, the narrator recites many passages, especially during complex dances or strenuous action. Even spoken passages are related to music, for they follow conventionalized intonational patterns.

The visual style of Kabuki lies somewhere between the extreme stylization of Noh and the illusionism of the Western theatre. This compromise can be seen in the stage, scenery, and properties.

Originally Kabuki used the Noh stage. As it came under the influence of puppet theatre, however, it adopted many staging devices from that form. In 1753 a large elevator stage was introduced, and in 1758 the first revolving stage anywhere in the world was installed. After 1827, the revolving stage was built in two sections, one inside the other, which revolved independently. A forestage was added in the eighteenth century and became the principal acting area after 1745. Around 1725, one of the Kabuki's most distinctive features, the *hanamichi,* appeared. A raised gangway leading from a small room at the rear of the auditorium to the stage, the hanamichi is used for all important entrances as well as for many important scenes. This innovation was so popular that a second hanamichi was added by 1780.

By 1830 the Kabuki stage had reached its characteristic form. The Noh roof had been abandoned and the stage enlarged until it occupied the entire width of the auditorium. The auditorium was divided into numerous square enclosures, or floor boxes, in which spectators sat on mats. After 1868 many changes occurred as Western influence increased. The proscenium arch was introduced in 1908 and after 1920 both the proscenium arch and Western-style seating became standard. The second hanamichi was abandoned, although it is still installed temporarily for pieces requiring it. In 1878 gas lighting was introduced and evening performances began. Since the late nineteeenth century, the Kabuki theatre has welcome all new developments in stage lighting. Nevertheless, Kabuki relies for the most part on glaring white light except in scenes, such as nighttime, when special effects are required.

Western influence has not altered the basic characteristics of the Kabuki stage, however, for, although the proscenium arch is now used, the proportions are unlike those found in the West. For example, in the present Kabuki-za in Tokyo the proscenium arch is ninety feet wide but only twenty feet tall. The auditorium is also proportioned differently. In the Kabuki-za, it is only six feet deep and about one hundred feet wide.

Unlike Noh, Kabuki represents every locale scenically. The scenery is changed in full view of the audience by means of the revolving stage, elevators, grooves, or by stage attendants. Most settings emphasize lateral composition. Perhaps for this reason, no more than two sets are erected on the revolving stage at once; settings are never triangular. Painted scenery is seldom purely representational. For example, the rear of the stage is often enclosed by flats showing a distant view; the painting is not illusionistic, however, for the cracks between the flats show and the top of the view is cut off with black curtains. Sometimes relatively realistic buildings are erected on stage, but they are almost always combined with symbolic pieces. Furthermore, some scenic pieces are conventionalized. White mats may represent snow, blue mats water, gray mats ground; different kinds of trees may indicate a change in locale.

Similarly, properties range from the symbolic to the realistic. The fan is used, as in Noh, to indicate riding a horse, shooting an arrow, opening a door, the rising of the moon, the falling of rain, and many other actions. Scarves serve equally diverse purposes. Other properties are partially representational. Perhaps the Kabuki horse best summarizes the mixture of realism and convention. A wooden framework, shaped like a horse, is covered with velvet and equipped with saddle and bridle. The upper part is representational. But this framework is mounted on the back of two actors, whose legs clearly show. Other properties—such as armor, swords, human heads, animals, and household goods—are treated in much the same manner. It is this mingling of the conventional with the realistic that makes Kabuki more easily accessible to the Western viewer than any of the other traditional Oriental forms.

Perhaps a short discussion of a Kabuki play will further clarify the form. Since Chikamatsu is universally considered the greatest of Japanese playwrights, his *The Battles of Coxinga* (1715), a history or jidaimono play, has been selected. This was Chikamatsu's most popular work, originally played for seventeen months and revived frequently thereafter.

The Battles of Coxinga is divided into five acts and twelve scenes; in time, it covers a period of six or seven years beginning in 1644. The basic story may be summarized briefly. The evil minister, Ri Toten, betrays his country (China) to the Tartars, who capture the palace and behead the Emperor. The Empress, about to bear a child, flees but is killed. A faithful minister rips open her womb and rescues the child. The Emperor's sister, cast adrift in a boat, floats to Japan where she is rescued by Watonai (later called Coxinga), the son of an exiled Chinese official. Watonai and his parents decide to return to China and to lead an uprising. After a

Kabuki stage at Edo as it appeared in 1806. (Courtesy Tsubouchi Memorial Theatre Collection, Waseda University, Tokyo.)

series of exploits, many magical, Coxinga recaptures the palace and restores the young Emperor to the throne.

Each act develops a different phase of the story and each builds to a high point of action. Act I shows the betrayal, battle, deaths of the rulers, and the escape of the Princess (made possible by a female attendant who fights off an army of pursuers). Act II tells of the arrival of the Princess in Japan, Coxinga's return to China, and his incredible fight with a tiger in the forest. Act III shows Coxinga's attempts to recruit followers, eventually made possible by the suicides of his mother and half-sister, both of whom kill themselves on stage. Act IV shows the progress of the struggle and the escape of the child Emperor from the Tartars (made possible by a cloud bridge created by the gods). Act V relates the end of the struggle, with the recapture of the palace, the flaying of the Tartar prince and the beheading of Ri Toten. Thus, each act builds to a strong scene allowing the actors to display their special skills.

The characters are divided into the good and the evil. They are differentiated primarily on the basis of age, sex, rank, and degrees of strength or self-sacrifice. The cast includes twenty-three principal actors and a number of supernumerary characters.

The place shifts often. Locales include the palace, a seacoast in Japan, the exterior of an armed fort, a forest, the mountains, various interiors, and the open sea. At least twelve settings are required. It would be almost impossible to stage this play if illusionism were sought. The task is simplified because the narrator speaks a large part of the text. (This play was originally written for puppet theatre.) The narrative provides exposition, summarizes action that has occurred between scenes, reports the internal feelings of the characters, and describes the action during climactic scenes. Although the actors are assigned many lines, they are more involved in pantomimic dance. Thus, the battles, suicides, beheadings, and other vio-

The Oriental Theatre

253

lent deeds are rendered as choreographed movement communicating the essence of deeds without any attempt at realism. Just as the story is larger than life, its rendition lies somewhere between fantasy and reality; its stylized action, speech, and music create a spectacle of great beauty.

In addition to the classic forms, newer styles of drama developed. The earliest of these, *shimpa,* began about 1888 and grew out of the desire to portray contemporary ideas and events realistically. It reached its peak about 1905 and then declined. In 1909 the Free Theatre Society was formed and thereafter did much to familiarize Japanese audiences with Western drama. Another offspring from westernization is *shingeki* (new theatre), long committed to realism in writing and to Stanislavsky's approach in acting. In recent years, however, it has become more attuned to other modes and is now sensitive to all major trends.

Despite these new forms it is the traditional arts of Noh, puppet theatre, and Kabuki that continue to command the greatest respect both at home and abroad.

Eastern Influence in the West

Awareness of the Oriental theatre developed only gradually in the West. The first major impression was made in 1789, when Sir William Jones translated *Shakuntala* into English. In 1791 this version was translated into German and in 1803 into French. *Shakuntala* made an enormous impression on Europeans, perhaps because it came at a time when romanticism was emerging.

Interest in Oriental drama had little effect upon the theatre until the end of the nineteenth century, for at first there was little appreciation of Asian theatrical conventions, so markedly different from the illusionistic techniques then standard in the West. Not until the revolt against realism began in the 1890s did Oriental theatrical practices begin to attract Western directors.

Considerable interest was aroused by a Chinese troupe that played in Paris in 1895 and by a Japanese group that appeared in London in 1900. During the early twentieth century a number of individual performers toured widely in the West. Nevertheless, it was not until such directors as Lugné-Poë, Meyerhold, Brecht, and Artaud began to champion Oriental practices as antidotes to realism that Eastern conventions had any real impact. Innovations were at first considered merely perverse, but since World War II they have aroused increasing sympathy. Although it is doubtful that many Westerners even now truly understand the Oriental theatre (beyond a few of its conventions), the Eastern and Western theatres are in closer contact today than at any time in the past. Many developments in the modern theatre are more easily understood if the awakening interest in Oriental conventions is remembered.

10

The Beginnings of the Modern Theatre, 1875–1915

By the mid-nineteenth century romanticism had lost much of its appeal, for the belief in humanity's idealistic nature had received many setbacks. For example, after the downfall of Napoleon in 1815, most European countries had reinstated political conditions as oppressive as those of the eighteenth century. The ideals of liberty, equality, and fraternity seemed to have been forgotten. Furthermore, the general misery of a large part of humanity was emphasized by the industrial revolution, as a result of which workers poured into urban centers where living conditions were daily more inadequate. Crime and poverty were prevalent.

The Backgrounds of Realism

In the face of these political and economic conditions, the romanticist's longing for some idealized realm seemed both too vague and too impractical. Many persons came to argue that dreams must be abandoned for a systematic inquiry into actual conditions and for solutions based on verifiable facts. Observation, prediction, and control of behavior became new goals.

Among the major influences on the changed outlook was Auguste Comte (1798–1857), whose philosophy came to be called *positivism*. In his writings, published between 1830 and 1854, Comte argued that sociology is the highest form of science and that all knowledge should ultimately be used for the improvement of society. He stated that the key to knowledge lies in precise observation and experimentation, since all events must be understood in terms of natural cause and effect. Comte's philosophy placed primary emphasis on phenomena that can be experienced through the five senses, and thus focused attention upon the observation of contemporary events.

Positivism was soon reinforced by Charles Darwin's *Origin of Species* (1859). Darwin's evidence was used to support two main theses: (1) all forms of life have developed gradually from a common ancestry; and (2) the evolution of species is explained by the "survival of the fittest."

Darwin's theories have several significant implications. First, they make heredity and environment the determinants of existence. Everything that humans are or can be is attributed to the physical makeup with which they are born or the conditions under which they live. Second, heredity and environment become explanations for all character traits and actions. Furthermore, since behavior is determined by factors largely beyond the individual's control, he cannot truly be held responsible for it. If blame is to be assigned, much of it must go to the society that has allowed undesirable hereditary and environmental factors to exist. (While until recently few persons have sought to control heredity, many have turned their attention to the improvement of environment.)

Third, Darwin's theses cast considerable doubt on the existence of God as traditionally conceived. If He exists, according to the new view, it is as an impersonal force. The idea of immortality was seriously challenged at the same time. If there is no future life, a human being can reach fulfillment only in the present one, and, to many, science seemed to offer the greatest possibilities of achieving the maximum good.

Fourth, Darwin's theories strengthened the idea of progress. If humans have evolved from an infinitesimal grain of being to the complex creature they now are, improvement and progress appear to be inevitable. Nevertheless, it was argued, progress can be channeled and hastened by the consistent application of scientific method to social problems.

Fifth, humankind is reduced to the status of a natural object. Prior to the nineteenth century human beings had been set apart from the rest of creation and treated as superior to it. Now they lost their privileged status and became merely another object for study and control.

Like most movements, then, realism sought to improve the lot of humankind by coming to grips with its perception of truth. The new school, however, tended to limit its definition of truth to knowledge gained through the five senses (sight, hearing, taste, smell, and touch). This marked change in view inevitably influenced conceptions of art, including theatre.

Realism in the Theatre

By 1850 a conscious movement toward realism in theatre was emerging. It developed first in France, and by 1860 its advocates had proclaimed the following precepts: The playwright should strive for a truthful depiction of the real world; since he may know the real world only through direct observation, he should write about the society around him; and he should strive to be as objective as possible.

Given such an outlook, it was only natural that playwrights came to emphasize the details of contemporary life and to avoid historical subject matter and idealized human motives and deeds. Many writers turned to themes not previously treated on the stage, and conservative critics charged that the theatre had become little better than a tavern or sewer. To such charges of immorality and decadence, the supporters of realism replied that the plays, as truthful depictions of life, were moral, since truth is the highest form of morality, and that to present an idealized picture of life would be to elevate falsehood over truth and thereby become truly immoral. Furthermore, the supporters of realism suggested, if audiences do not like the pictures of contemporary life shown on the stage, they should strive to change the society that has furnished the models rather than denounce the playwright who has been fearless in his treatment of what he sees around him.

The visual elements of staging were easily brought into accord with the new demands, for the groundwork had already been laid by romantic drama and melodrama, both of which had presented with ever-increasing accuracy details of dress and setting. Until after 1850 however, spectacle was used primarily to idealize place, historical period, or characters. It was a simple task to extend these earlier practices to meet the demands of realism.

A suitable dramatic form was also available in the *well-made* play. Although all its elements may be found before the nineteenth century, the well-made play was perfected by Eugène Scribe (1791–1861), one of the most prolific and successful writers of his day. Scribe's plays, numbering over four hundred, lack depth of insight but are important because they epitomize the dramatic structure adopted by the new realistic school of writers.

The basic characteristics of the well-made play are: clear exposition of situation; careful preparation for future events; unexpected but logical reversals; continuous and mounting suspense; an obligatory scene; and a logical resolution. This structural pattern was not unique with Scribe,

Final scene from The Lady of the Camellias. *(From* Théâtre Contemporain Illustré, *1867.)*

but he reduced it to near formula and combined it with absorbing situations in which character and thought were sacrificed to suspense. Nevertheless, the well-made play was easily adapted by the realists because of its careful exposition and its clear cause-to-effect arrangement.

While earlier movements supplied dramatic techniques and an approach to spectacle, both of which were readily adaptable to the realistic mode, they did not provide equally helpful guidance in subject matter and characterization. It remained for two French playwrights, Alexandre Dumas *fils* (1824–1895) and Emile Augier (1820–1889), to direct attention consistently to contemporary social problems as subjects for dramatic treatment.

Dumas *fils* came to public attention in 1847 with a novel, *The Lady of the Camellias,* which he dramatized in 1849. Because of its subject matter, however, the play was not granted a license for production until 1852. One of Dumas' biographers has said of the play:

> *Now came a young man who dared to depict not a courtesan of historical legend, not an adventuress surrounded by a halo of poetic symbolism, but a "kept woman" of everyday contemporary life, and this author made his subject even more realistic by writing in ordinary prose.*

The play, generally known today as *Camille,* was extraordinarily popular, and its heroine, who dies of tuberculosis, has become an almost legendary character. But while its language and subject show a trend toward realism, the overall tone makes the play now seem merely another romanticization of the "prostitute with a heart of gold."

Dumas soon became dissatisfied with his work and sought to treat his subjects more realistically. In 1855 he wrote *The Demi-Monde,* which denounces the same kind of characters he treats sympathetically in *Camille.*

After this time he attempted to establish a *theatre of social utility* by writing plays about contemporary social problems, such as divorce, unscrupulous business practices, and the plight of illegitimate children. But as Dumas became more and more concerned with social problems he also became increasingly the moralist. As a result, his plays are now usually called *pièces à thèse* (or thesis plays). Dumas' works seem dated because of changes in the society about which he wrote and because of excessive moralizing in the plays, but they probably did more than any other dramas of the age to establish concern for contemporary social problems.

Augier is noted principally for his political and social dramas about contemporary French conditions. Many of his plays deal in a less didactic way with the same problems treated by Dumas: the power of money, the dangers of churchmen in politics, and fallen women. The dramatic power of Augier's plays, such as *Youth* (1858) and *Giboyer's Son* (1862), did much to popularize the new style of playwriting.

Ibsen

But it is to Ibsen that credit must go for the ultimate triumph of the new methods. *Modern* drama is usually dated from the late 1870s, when Ibsen began to write in the realistic mode.

Henrik Ibsen (1828–1906), Norway's first important dramatist, began writing plays about 1850. His early work, much of which is based on Nor-

Ibsen's Rosmersholm *at the Norwegian National Theatre, Oslo, 1906. (From* Bühne und Welt, *1906.)*

wegian legends, is clearly related to romantic drama, but in 1877 Ibsen turned to the problem play with *The Pillars of Society* and continued in that vein with *A Doll's House* (1879), *Ghosts* (1881), and *An Enemy of the People* (1882). With these plays, Ibsen established his reputation as a radical thinker and controversial dramatist. *Ghosts*, especially, became a storm center, for in it Mrs. Alving, against her better instincts, has remained with a depraved husband out of conformity to traditional morality only to have her son go mad, presumably from syphilis passed on to him by his father. To audiences and critics of the late nineteenth century, *Ghosts* empitomized the "sewer" into which the drama had sunk. Ibsen soon moved away from social problems, and beginning with *The Wild Duck* (1884) concentrated upon personal relationships in such plays as *Rosmersholm* (1886), *Hedda Gabler* (1890), *The Master Builder* (1892), and *When We Dead Awaken* (1899).

Despite the changes in subject matter and style, Ibsen's basic theme remained constant: the struggle for integrity, the conflict between duty to oneself and duty to others. In his many variations on this central concern, Ibsen brought together trends that are both the culmination of nineteenth-century movements and the beginning of modern drama.

Much of Ibsen's work contributed to realism. He discards asides and soliloquies and is careful to motivate all exposition. All scenes are causally related and lead logically to the dénouement. Dialogue, settings, costumes, and business are selected to reveal character and milieu and are clearly described in stage directions. Each role is conceived as a personality whose behavior is attributable to hereditary and environmental forces.

Ibsen's final plays, which differed considerably from the earlier pieces, were to influence nonrealistic drama as extensively as the prose plays did realistic works. In them, symbols enlarge the implications of the action and many of the plays border on fantasy. Symbolist playwrights at the end of the century, partially under Ibsen's influence, developed much more fully the theme of mysterious forces at work in human destiny.

Almost all later playwrights, whether realists or idealists, were to be affected by Ibsen's conviction that drama should be a source of insight, a creator of discussion, a conveyor of ideas, something more than mere entertainment. He gave dramatists a new vision of their role.

The many strands of Ibsen's work are probably brought together most effectively in *The Wild Duck*.

The Wild Duck

In *The Wild Duck,* Gregers Werle returns home after an absence of fifteen years, decides that the lives of all his acquaintances are based on lies, and determines to make them face the truth. His efforts lead to catastrophe.

The principal characters are Old Werle (Gregers' father), Hjalmar

Ekdal (Gregers' childhood friend), and Old Ekdal, Gina, and Hedwig (Hjalmar's father, wife, and daughter). Old Werle is prosperous, while the Ekdals live in comparative poverty, although years ago Werle and Ekdal were business partners before Ekdal was sent to prison for illegal dealings. Gregers suspects that his father let Ekdal accept blame that was partially his. Gregers also believes that Old Werle arranged Hjalmar's marriage to Gina, a former maid in the Werle household, because Gina was pregnant by Werle. Thus, he thinks that Hedwig is not Hjalmar's child.

Gregers takes a room at the Ekdals, in spite of Gina's protest, so that he may force them to face the reality which he believes all are avoiding. Through insinuation and leading questions, Gregers gradually brings his "truth" into the open. After Hjalmar rejects Hedwig, she decides, with a child's simplicity of reasoning, that only some great sacrifice can prove her love for Hjalmar; consequently, she kills herself.

Essentially, *The Wild Duck* is a play about the necessity of illusions. Dr. Relling, another tenant in the Ekdal house, says that most persons need "a saving lie" upon which to base their lives if they are to retain a degree of self-respect and a sense of purpose.

All of the play's characters serve to illustrate this theme, but the opposing positions are most obviously represented by Relling (who believes in the necessity of illusion) and Gregers Werle (who believes that everyone must be forced to face the truth). Relling appears more nearly to represent Ibsen's own point of view, for Greger's self-righteous meddling brings only disaster to others.

Ibsen has strengthened his theme through the symbolism of the wild duck. The wild duck is a living creature, but around it cluster a series of relationships and concepts that suggest wider meanings than would be possible without it. The symbolism of the duck pervades the entire play, and to appreciate it fully the stages in the duck's existence must be recalled. First, the duck, happy and carefree, lives in a wild state. Then it is wounded by a hunter. In its pain and desire to hide, the duck dives to the bottom of the sea but is brought to the surface by a dog. The duck survives but does not thrive in the hunter's house. It is given to another family who construct an artificial environment for it, and, though crippled, it now appears to be as happy as in its wild state.

Ibsen seems to suggest that the wild duck's experiences parallel those of humankind. In his early years an individual may live a relatively carefree existence; then one day, wounded by circumstances, he tries to run away, to hide, or to die because of his feelings of inadequacy and disgrace; but he is forced to return to his daily existence, and consequently he constructs a set of delusions by means of which he can regain self-respect and a sense of purpose. He then becomes relatively happy in this artificial realm of illusion. Every major event and character in *The Wild Duck* can be related to this pattern, although exact correspondences are few.

Characters and Acting. The Ekdal family is reflected in the wild duck,

since all in a sense are victims of Old Werle (the hunter), while Gregers corresponds in part to the dog, for he insists on dragging all the characters above the surface of illusion and into the bright light of truth. The house in which the Ekdals live is somewhat like the ocean depths into which the wounded duck dives, since each of its occupants, with the exception of Hedwig, is seeking to hide within his own particular illusion.

Old Ekdal has lived in an illusory state so long that it has become an integral part of his being. It is implied that he has always been childish, that when he was in business with Werle he spent most of his time hunting. This neglect of responsibility helped to bring about his disgrace. Since his release from prison he has reconstructed his life around the attic, which he treats as a "forest," complete with "wild life" (the duck and rabbits). He prefers the safety of this make-believe world to the real one. Like the wild duck, he too has been wounded and now lives in an artificial environment.

Gina is probably the most enigmatic character in the play, for the truth about her past remains unclear. She is also the one most capable of accepting her fate and of living life moment by moment without worry either about the past or the future. She is stolid and down-to-earth, but she too is one of Werle's victims.

Ibsen has drawn a number of interesting parallels and contrasts between Old Werle and Hedwig. It is possible that Hedwig is the daughter of Old Werle (this is never clarified), both have weak eyesight, both try to make amends to others. But Old Werle has treated life as though it were the sport of hunting, and when he wounds he makes amends through such material compensations as money and arranged marriages. On the other hand, Hedwig responds to life with her whole being and rather than wound others kills herself. She is open, frank, and without artifice. Unlike Old Werle, who shot the wild duck in sport (just as he had unthinkingly seduced Gina and used others all his life), Hedwig shoots herself in earnest, for hers is an act of sacrifice performed out of love. Old Werle faces up to his shortcomings at the end of the play, but he still believes that money and material gifts can atone for the wounds he has inflicted on others.

Ibsen's principal effort has gone into the roles of Hjalmar and Gregers. Hjalmar speaks as though he were sensitive, ambitious, and idealistic, but his actions show that he is insensitive, lazy, and self-centered. Gina manages the photographic studio; she and Hedwig sacrifice every comfort for Hjalmar. Old Ekdal's disgrace is to Hjalmar an excuse for easy sentiment, just as Hedwig's death will be in the future. But Hjalmar is perfectly happy in his illusions, for he can indulge himself and, at the same time, find excuses for being ineffectual.

That Gregers accepts Hjalmar as a hero demonstrates his own impracticality and lack of experience. He has hidden away from the world for fifteen years, has thought much about life, but has avoided becoming involved in it. Although he never attempts to change his own life, he feels free to meddle in the affairs of others.

Relling is used as a foil for Gregers. His ability to anesthetize the pain of disillusionment is demonstrated in Molvik, the theology student who rationalizes his failures under the belief that he is "demonic." Relling, the doctor, has administered to the psychic wounds of the characters by providing them with "saving lies," while Gregers destroys the illusions that have made life tolerable.

But in spite of the obvious use of characters to illustrate ideas, Ibsen employs realistic techniques in creating roles. Every important characteristic is shown through action. For example, Hjalmar's character is built up through a series of contrasts between actions and statements. The audience sees his awkwardness at the dinner party and then hears his self-glorifying account of it; he leaves the picture retouching to Hedwig in spite of her weak eyes and his previously expressed anxiety about her eyesight. Similarly, the traits of all the other characters are brought out through well-motivated and lifelike speech or action. The audience learns about the characters as it would in a real-life situation; there is seldom any feeling of contrivance.

Ibsen has been careful to fill in the sociological backgrounds of his characters, and each attitude and trait is grounded in particular social circumstances. For example, Hjalmar's selfishness is explained in part by his indulgent upbringing by two maiden aunts.

Ibsen has also made his characters complex personalities by showing both good and bad aspects of each. None is without flaws (with the possible exception of Hedwig), but none is villainous. This complexity makes each role challenging to actors, and requires subtlety in playing.

Plot and Structure. In his dramas, Ibsen used many techniques of the well-made play, but was able to overcome the sense of artificiality by avoiding asides, concealed hiding places, overheard conversations, the fortuitous arrival of letters, and similar devices. He retained careful preparation and developed action logically out of previous occurrences and clearly demonstrated character traits. A sense of reality is created by the meticulous selection and arrangement of details.

Ibsen typically used a late point of attack, and in most plays no more than two or three days elapse, for the stage action is the culmination of past events. In *The Wild Duck* the most important antecedent action has occurred at least fifteen years before the play begins. This demands careful handling of exposition, since the past is essential as an explanation of the present. Ibsen's favorite device for motivating exposition is the return of a character who has been absent for a considerable time. In *The Wild Duck* Gregers Werle has returned home after a fifteen-year absence, during which he has lived in virtual isolation. Thus, he can believably inquire about the past. At the same time, however, Gregers' attitude and his purposeful air arouse curiosity about his motives and create suspicion that the truth is being concealed. Consequently, as the past is revealed, expectations about future developments are also evoked.

Although exposition is scattered throughout *The Wild Duck*, it is especially prominent in the first two acts. Many of Ibsen's plays are written in four acts, but *The Wild Duck* has five, in part because these two are required to establish the situation out of which the succeeding three acts grow. Ibsen's need for two acts of preparation is also illustrated by the use of two settings to contrast Old Werle's and the Ekdals' living conditions. By the end of the second act, both situation and characters have been clarified, the symbolism of the wild duck has been introduced, and Gregers has indicated his intention of rectifying the errors of the past. The final three acts grow logically out of the first two.

Ibsen's skill can be seen in his economy. There are no extraneous scenes and almost nothing could be removed without destroying clarity. At the same time, there is no feeling of haste, for each event seems to develop as it might in real life. Nevertheless, each of the acts is built through a series of complications leading to a high point of suspense near the end of the act, while the play as a whole builds to the climactic scene of Hedwig's death. Ibsen thus achieves great dramatic power (which results from masterful craftsmanship) while giving the effect of naturalness.

Although it might be argued that there are a number of plot strands—perhaps one for each character—all are so woven together that the action is one. It is the effect of each character on all the others that motivates the action and leads to its logical and believable outcome.

Visual and Aural Effects. Ibsen's realistic technique can also be seen in the visual elements of *The Wild Duck*. Detailed descriptions of the settings are given in stage directions. Furthermore, unlike most earlier plays, the setting plays an important role in the action. The influence of environment upon the characters is made clear in part through an accurate representation of the surroundings. The characters seem to live in the settings, for they do everything there that they would in a real room. In the studio they eat, retouch photographs, entertain friends, and carry on their daily existence in countless ways. The settings, never mere additions, are vital to the action.

Although environment helps to create character, the characters in turn help to create environment. The garret, for example, has been remodeled into an artificial forest to meet the psychological needs of its inhabitants. Unlike a neoclassical play in which settings are generalized, *The Wild Duck* demands a stage environment singularly its own—one determined by the specific action and characters. Instead of merely supplying a typical and normative background, the set designer is now asked to create a clearly individualized environment.

Because the actions performed in *The Wild Duck* are such as might be seen in daily life, the audience is inclined to judge their believability according to how well daily life is recreated. For example, in the third act a table is set, and a meal is served and eaten. Although onstage not everything is done exactly as in real life, it must correspond closely with normal action or much of the play's effect will be undermined. Stage production in such plays as *The Wild Duck*, therefore, must be based in part upon a direct observation of life. The aim is to create an illusion of reality through the accumulation of details.

The same realistic ideal is reflected in the language of *The Wild Duck*. Gina lapses into her lower-class speech in moments of stress, while under similar circumstances Old Ekdal is inclined to express himself more formally. Hjalmar alternates between flights of fancy and mundane expression. Thus, Ibsen has tried to capture an illusion of daily speech colored by individualizing characteristics.

The Wild Duck, with its subject matter drawn from contemporary life, closely observed detail, and avoidance of contrivance, illustrates well the realistic mode. At the same time, its symbolism anticipates developments in nonrealistic drama.

England

The spirit of realism soon spread throughout the world. For example, in England the works of such playwrights as Arthur Wing Pinero (1855–1934), Henry Arthur Jones (1851–1929), John Galsworthy (1867–1933), and George Bernard Shaw (1856–1950) show in varying degrees the influence of the new trend.

Pinero began his career by writing farces and sentimental plays, but turned to realism around 1889. His best-remembered play, *The Second Mrs. Tanqueray* (1893), although it concerns a "woman with a past," helped to break down the strictures against frank subject matter, since its ending, in which the woman is punished, upheld the moral code of conservative audiences. Thus, it was simultaneously daring and reassuring.

Jones started writing plays in the 1870s but made his principal impression in the 1880s and 1890s. He was a didactic and somewhat melodra-

matic playwright who, along with Pinero, helped to pave the way for more realistic drama and his *Saints and Sinners* (1884), *Michael and His Lost Angel* (1896), and *Mrs. Dane's Defense* (1900).

Galsworthy, who won fame first as a novelist, did not begin writing plays until 1906 with *The Silver Box,* in which the justice meted out to a poor and a rich man for similar crimes is contrasted. His later plays, among them *Strife* (1909), *Justice* (1910), and *Loyalties* (1922), are all objective treatments of social problems and demonstrate Galsworthy's considerable gift for creating clear-cut conflicts and natural dialogue. They also depict characters as victims of the social system. Probably more than any other English playwright of his time, Galsworthy adhered to the major tenets of realism.

George Bernard Shaw was probably the most vociferous and important of Ibsen's admirers. But Shaw's approach differs markedly from Ibsen's, for while his plays are serious in their intention of influencing human behavior, they use comic devices to make serious points. In his treatment of problems, Shaw begins with what he thinks is the accepted attitude and then demolishes it before proposing his own solution. Shaw also delighted in using paradoxes to make both characters and audiences reassess their values. Thus, *Arms and the Man* (1894) punctures romantic notions about war and love, and *Major Barbara* (1905) depicts a munitions maker as more humanitarian than the Salvation Army, for the former provides his workers with the means whereby to improve their lot whereas the Salvation Army only prolongs the status quo. Ultimately,

Shaw wished through his plays to demonstrate the possibility of gradually solving human problems through education, better living conditions, and common sense. But Shaw was no mere propagandist, for his plays are theatrically effective and entertaining. It is not as a thinker that Shaw will be remembered but as a playwright who used thought as a basis for dramatic conflict. Among his many plays, some of the finest are *Candida* (1895), *Caesar and Cleopatra* (1899), *Man and Superman* (1903), *Heartbreak House* (1919), and *Saint Joan* (1923). Perhaps his most popular play is *Pygmalion* (1913), the story of an illiterate flower girl who is transformed by her mentor so thoroughly that she is mistaken for a duchess.

Russia

Another writer of the late nineteenth century, Anton Chekhov (1860–1904), was to be almost as influential as Ibsen. Unlike Ibsen, however, whose plays built on those of Scribe. Augier, and Dumas *fils*, Chekhov built on the work of such native Russian playwrights as Gogol, Ostrovsky, and Turgenev.

Nikolai Gogol (1809–1852) began the movement toward realism in Russia with *The Inspector General* (1836), a grotesque, farcical satire on corruption among government officials in provincial Russia. This beginning was advanced by Alexander Ostrovsky (1823–1886) and Ivan Turgenev (1818–1883). Ostrovsky was the first Russian writer to confine himself solely to drama; his forty-eight plays are credited with creating a Russian drama free from Western European influence. In his dramas about the merchant class and lower aristocracy, Ostrovsky copied the speech and

Act I of the first production of The Cherry Orchard, *1904. (From* Moscow Art Theatre, 1898-1917, *1955)*

manners of everyday life to create a sense of closely observed reality. He also used symbols in much the same manner as Ibsen and Chekhov were to do later. His work is probably seen at its best in *The Thunderstorm* and *The Forest*.

As a dramatist, Turgenev is remembered almost solely for *A Month in the Country* (written in 1850 but not produced until 1872). As the title suggests, the action takes place on a remote country estate. Partially out of boredom, Natalya, the protagonist, falls in love with the young tutor of her son. But Natalya's young ward is also in love with the tutor, and still another man loves Natalya. The play is a study in jealousy, heartbreak, and compromise. The characters, in no sense heroic, are portrayed with deep understanding, for Turgenev concentrates upon the inner motivations of each. In the end, all are disappointed, but each has achieved a measure of self-understanding. It is a quiet but intense drama.

Chekhov began by writing short stories and humorous sketches, and moved on to vaudeville skits and one-act farces. The long plays, which he began to write in 1887, met little success until 1898 when *The Sea Gull* was presented by the Moscow Art Theatre, which went on to produce his *Uncle Vanya, The Three Sisters,* and *The Cherry Orchard.* It is on these four plays that Chekhov's reputation rests.

Many qualities relate Chekhov's dramas to the realistic school. The subject matter and themes, drawn from contemporary Russian life, show how the daily routine gradually shrinks the spirit and drains the will. The characters long for happiness and wish to live useful and full lives, but they are constantly thwarted by circumstances and their own personalities. Frustration and compromise are the lot of most of Chekhov's characters.

Chekhov's realism is further seen in his dramatic form, for the plays have an air of aimlessness which matches that of the characters' lives. There is no sense of hurry, of theatrical trickery, or even of normal dramatic structure. All violent deeds and emotional climaxes occur offstage. Thus, the action is kept in the background while the foreground is occupied by a number of seemingly commonplace details. But, since the characters do not fully understand their own feelings and since they seek to conceal as much as to reveal their responses, it is in the seeming trivia that one must seek the undercurrents that make up the dramatic action. Untimately what happens to each character is a direct result of the kind of person he is. Thus, character and fate are one. Chekhov treats all of his characters with tolerance and compassion, but he also makes them both sympathetic and ridiculous. Therefore, the pathetic and the comic are intertwined and often are evident simultaneously.

But Chekhov is not entirely a realistic writer, for like Ibsen he also makes considerable use of symbolism, perhaps most obviously in *The Sea Gull* and *The Cherry Orchard.* In the latter, the orchard is a symbol of the Old Russia and the aristocracy. Though it no longer yields fruit, the orchard is clung to by its owners when its sale would save the rest of the estate they so dearly love. In the end, the orchard is bought by a newly rich peasant and is subdivided for a housing development, an action that illustrates the changing social order in which the useless, though decorative aristocracy is being displaced by the callous but pragmatic middle class. The orchard thus enlarges and extends the meaning of *The Cherry Orchard* just as the duck does in Ibsen's *The Wild Duck*.

Chekhov's plays have exerted a strong and lasting influence on succeeding playwrights. Some critics see all modern realistic drama as being derived from the joint influence of Ibsen and Chekhov.

Naturalism

Thus far only realism has been considered. But, while realism was developing, another, more extreme movement, naturalism, was also emerging. Realism and naturalism are closely related because both demand a truthful depiction of life and are based on the belief that ultimate reality is discoverable only through the five senses. The naturalists, however, insisted that art must become scientific in its methods and must depict behavior as being determined by heredity and environment.

The major spokesman of the naturalistic school was Emile Zola (1840–1902), who argued that art, if it is not to perish, must emulate science both in choosing subjects and in treating them. According to Zola, subjects may be of two kinds: those based on scientific findings and those that faithfully record events observed in real life. Using the first type, the dramatist sets up characters and situation and then lets them interact according to the inevitable laws of heredity and environment. About the second approach, Zola states:

Instead of imagining an adventure, complicating it, preparing stage surprises, which from scene to scene will bring it to a final conclusion, one simply takes from life the history of a being, or of a group of beings, whose acts one faithfully records.

The playwright is thus restricted either to dramatizing "scientific" theories and laws or recording case studies.

Zola also argued that the writer should remain detached and never allow his own prejudices to intrude. The dramatist should observe, record, and experiment with the sole aim of demonstrating the truth. Because the dramatist should be objective about his subject matter, he must be free to treat whatever seems most fruitful for arriving at truth. In practice, naturalism tended to emphasize the more degraded aspects of lower-class life. Just as dramatists of the eighteenth century had turned to the middle class for its subjects, so those of the late nineteenth century turned to the lower classes. But whereas the life of the middle class had been idealized, the life of the lower classes was most often depicted as debased. As a result, much naturalistic drama was preoccupied with

The Beginnings of the Modern Theatre, 1875–1915

269

A naturalistic production at the Théâtre Antoine, Paris, in 1902. The play is Menessier's adaptation of Zola's novel The Earth. *Note the hayloft in the background and the chickens in the foreground. (From* Le Théâtre, *1902.)*

human maladies. Zola was fond of comparing naturalistic art with medicine; he stated that the dramatist should have the same interest in examining and defining human social illnesses as the doctor does in physical ailments.

Zola and his followers also sought a completely objective dramatic method. They were especially opposed to the "well-made" play because to them its emphasis on exposition, complication, suspense, crisis, and resolution subordinated truth to theatrical effect. Zola wrote, "The word *art* displeases me; it contains I know not what ideas of necessary arrangement." One member of the movement suggested that a play should be a *slice of life*—that a dramatist should transfer to the stage as faithfully as possible a segment of reality.

Because of the emphasis upon environment as a determinant of character and action, the stage setting was given greater importance under naturalism than in any previous movement. Every detail was reproduced accurately onstage so as to create the milieu that has influenced the characters and their actions. This care also extended to costumes, furniture, properties, stage business and acting. Zola stated that actors should "not *play*, but rather *live*, before the audience." He wished the stage to be arranged as much like a room in a real house as possible and the actors to speak and move as they would in real life.

The extreme demands of naturalism lost sight of the differences between art and life. A dramatist must select, arrange, and heighten his material if he is to hold the interest of an audience. Transferred to the stage, reality is seldom interesting. Thus, though naturalism attracted considerable attention in the late nineteenth century, it produced few dramatists of note. Even Zola was much more successful as a theorist and novelist than as a playwright. As a dramatist, he is best known for *Thérèse Raquin* (1873), an adaptation of one of his early novels, which shows the deterioration and suicide of a couple who have murdered the woman's former husband so they may marry.

A more successful French dramatist in the naturalistic vein (though he denied any allegiance to the movement) was Henri Becque (1837–1899), especially with *The Vultures* (1882), which shows the fleecing of a group of women by their supposed friends after the death of the family's head, and *La Parisienne* (1885), in which a completely amoral woman rationalizes her extramarital affairs as a means of forwarding her husband's career.

As a conscious literary movement, naturalism, like realism, began in France but soon spread to other countries. Unlike realism, however, naturalism attracted few outstanding dramatists elsewhere and in most cases even they eventually defected to less extreme movements. Of the writers in other countries who wrote some naturalisic plays, perhaps the best are Gerhart Hauptmann (1862–1946) in Germany and Maxim Gorky (1868–1936) in Russia. Hauptmann, usually said to be the first important modern German dramatist, is probably best known for *The Weavers* (1892), which shows an uprising among starving Silesian weavers; it is remarkable in part because it has a group (rather than an individual) as protagonist. Gorky is especially remembered for *The Lower Depths* (1902), set in a flophouse peopled with human wrecks whose backgrounds, characters, and illusions are gradually revealed.

As a conscious movement, naturalism had for the most part run its course by 1900. Nevertheless, it had been instrumental in focusing attention on the need for accurate, firsthand observation of life, in pointing out relationships between environment and behavior, and in encouraging greater attention to the details of stage production. In its insistence that reality be reproduced onstage, however, naturalism was unsuccessful. As its more extreme demands were abandoned, naturalism gradually merged with the larger and more acceptable realistic movement.

The Emergence of the Director

The same forces that produced realism and naturalism also led to corresponding changes in the theatre arts. By 1850, historical realism and local color had already been accepted and the wing-and-drop setting was giving way to the box set. But the realism of 1850 merely added nonessential details to scripts. For example, although Shakespeare's plays were acted in

Antony's oration over the body of Caesar in Saxe-Meiningen's production of Julius Caesar. *(From* Die Gartenlaube, *1879.)*

historically accurate settings, this did not make them realistic—it merely added realistic spectacle to nonrealistic dramas. True realism had to wait for plays which made the background a necessary part of the action.

As the demand increased for greater realism in all aspects of theatrical production, so did the need for more careful rehearsals and better coordination of all elements. As a result, the director gradually assumed full authority over production.

The modern director is usually traced from Georg II, Duke of Saxe-Meiningen (1826–1914), the ruler of a small German state, whose troupe came to public attention through a series of tours between 1874 and 1890. The superior quality of his presentations demonstrated the importance of the director to effective theatrical production.

Saxe-Meiningen's troupe, the Meiningen Players, performed the same standard plays (such as those by Shakespeare and Schiller) seen in the repertory of almost every German company of the day. Nevertheless, this troupe, composed almost solely of unknown actors, gave performances of such power that it eclipsed the work of the major theatres. It became clear that the reason for the Meiningen troupe's success was its director's staging methods.

The most important elements of the Duke's approach were his complete control over every aspect of production and his long and careful rehearsals. Rather than utilizing stars, he subordinated all performers to the overall effect, insisted on absolute obedience and drilled his troupe in lengthy rehearsals. He paid careful attention to the crowds and supernumerary parts as well as to the principal roles. A painter and a draftsman, Saxe-Meiningen designed the scenery, costumes, and properties to suit the action, and meticulously worked out the total stage picture as it developed moment by moment.

The artistic superiority of his productions stimulated the imagination of several future leaders. Saxe-Meiningen's realism, however, was largely restricted to pictorial elements, for he was little interested in the new realistic plays. Nevertheless, he demonstrated how scenic environment and stage action can be integrated to achieve powerful effects.

Few well-established acting troupes adopted Saxe-Meiningen's methods immediately, however, for most depended on stars who were unwilling to subordinate themselves to the demands of a director. Furthermore, the long rehearsals needed for perfection were too costly. Nevertheless, by the 1880s a few groups were emulating Saxe-Meiningen's methods. After that time the director steadily gained artistic control over theatrical production and has retained that power to the present day.

The Independent Theatre Movement

By the late 1880s both a realistic–naturalistic drama and realistic staging under the supervision of a demanding director had emerged. The new drama was rarely being performed, however, and the staging methods were being applied primarily to traditional plays. It remained, therefore, to bring the two together. Still, this was difficult to do because in most countries strict censorship forbade the production of such plays as *Ghosts* on the grounds of moral offensiveness. Eventually the challenge was met by "independent theatres," which began to be established in the 1880s. Since these organizations were private, being open only to members (although anyone could join) they were not subject to censorship and therefore could perform plays forbidden to more established theatres. These groups were also more willing to accept an authoritarian director because for the most part their actors were amateurs or little-known professionals rather than stars. Therefore, independent theatres were able to accomplish what the more important theatres had not, for these newer groups exploited and developed the new staging techniques and gave the new drama its chance to be heard.

The first of the independent theatres was the Théâtre Libre, founded in Paris in 1887 by André Antoine (1858–1943), a clerk in a gas company who began his work with amateur actors and with stage furniture taken from his own home. An enthusiastic follower of Zola and Saxe-Meiningen, Antoine sought absolute fidelity to real life. He worked out every detail of background and action with great care. He designed interior settings as though they were real rooms, arranged everything as in real life, and only then decided which wall should be removed for stage presentation. He did not always rearrange furniture to accommodate the audience's view, but rather tried to achieve absolute naturalness in the stage picture. He used real properties (such as carcasses of beef, bottles of wine, and running water) and tried to reproduce every detail of an environment. Applying the same standards to the actors' movements and speech, he held long and painstaking rehearsals to achieve the effects for which he was striving.

Many realistic and naturalistic plays (among them *Ghosts* and *The Wild Duck*) were first seen in Paris at Antoine's theatre, and it was to such plays that his approach was most suited, although he produced a number of poetic dramas as well. Antoine's original audience was a rather special one, but the fame of the Théâtre Libre rapidly grew and soon others wished to see productions of this kind. By 1900 most of the old barriers against realistic plays and staging had been broken down and Antoine's methods were being adopted by previously conservative theatres.

Antoine's was only the first of a number of important independent theatres. In 1889 the Freie Bühne was founded in Berlin by a group headed by Otto Brahm (1856–1912). It made no significant innovations in staging but concentrated instead on presenting plays denied a public hearing by the censor. It was especially instrumental in launching Gerhart Hauptmann as a major dramatist. By 1894, when Brahm assumed the direction of a commercial theatre, the new drama was being assimilated into the popular theatre throughout Germany.

In London the Independent Theatre, founded by J. T. Grein (1862–1935), opened in 1891 with Ibsen's *Ghosts*, long banned from the English public stage. The Independent Theatre was organized to produce plays of a "literary and artistic rather than a commercial value," and was not as concerned with the new realistic and naturalistic drama as most of the other independent theatres were. Nevertheless, it paved the way for the new drama, and launched Shaw as a playwright.

There were also a number of other independent theatres, but these are the most important. Not only did they meet an important need at the time, they provided a permanent lesson, for since the late nineteenth century whenever the established theatre has become insufficiently responsive to new demands, a solution has been sought in some variation on the independent-theatre idea—the "art" theatre, the "little" theatre, Off-Broadway, Off-Off-Broadway, and so on.

In addition to the independent theatres, another group—the Moscow Art Theatre—was to play a significant role in revitalizing the theatre at the turn of the century. Although it shared many artistic ideals with the independent theatres, it was from the first a fully professional troupe playing for the general public.

The Moscow Art Theatre was founded in 1898 by Konstantin Stanislavsky (1865–1938) and Vladimir Nemerovich-Danchenko (1859–1943), partially under the inspiration of the Meiningen company. Like the German troupe, the Moscow Art Theatre had few experienced actors and tried to compensate for this lack through long rehearsals and careful attention to

Interior of the Moscow Art Theatre about 1910. (From Moscow Art Theatre, 1898-1917, *1955.)*

detail both in acting and in spectacle. Their first major success was won with the plays of Chekhov.

As time went by, Stanislavsky became more and more concerned with the problems of the actor, and eventually evolved an approach that was to be one of the most influential ever proposed. This system has been disseminated throughout the world by Stanislavsky's books, *My Life in Art* (1924), *An Actor Prepares* (1936), *Building a Character* (1949), and *Creating a Role* (1961).

Although there has been much disagreement over the essence of Stanislavsky's teachings, basically they consist of the following principles:

(1) The actor's body and voice must be thoroughly trained and flexible so that they can respond instantly to all demands.

(2) The actor must be skilled in observing reality so that he can build his role truthfully through the careful selection of lifelike action, business, and speech.

(3) The actor needs to be thoroughly trained in stage technique so that he can project his characterization without any sense of artificiality.

(4) The actor must undergo psychological training of a rather complex nature so that he may imagine himself in the situation of the character he is playing. In doing so he may call on *emotion memory* (the ability to recall emotional responses comparable to those required in the dramatic situation).

(5) If the actor is not merely to play himself on the stage, however, he must have a thorough knowledge of the script. The actor, therefore, needs

to define clearly his character's basic desires and motivations in each scene, in the play as a whole, and in relation to other characters. The character's primary goal or motivation is called the *through-line* since the rest of the characterization must be built on it. The actor must understand his role so thoroughly (every detail of background, feeling, and action) and he can believe in its truth. To make the character thoroughly comprehensive and believable, the actor at times may have to fill in or invent details omitted from the script.

(6) A complete understanding of the play should lead the actor to subordinate his own role to the demands of the whole and to cooperate in achieving an ensemble effect for the entire troupe.

(7) All of his work onstage should be welded together through concentration. The actor must focus his entire attention upon the unfolding events moment by moment and strive to convince the audience that he is involved in a situation that is occurring spontaneously and for the first time. To do this, he should concentrate upon imagining, feeling, and projecting the truth of the stage situation.

(8) The actor must be willing to work continuously to perfect himself as an instrument and to perfect his performance in each play.

Stanislavsky's entire system urges the need for devoted and constant effort on the part of the actor. In Stanislavsky's view a performer is successful only when he can convince the audience of the truth of the stage situation, and this conviction results only from intense training and endless striving for perfection. Nevertheless, Stanislavsky was never fully satisfied with his system and he often cautioned others against trying to take it over without allowing for differences in artistic needs and cultural backgrounds.

But if today Stanislavsky's system seems the most important product of the Moscow Art Theatre, one should not forget that the company's productions were responsible for demonstrating the effectiveness of Stanislavsky's approach. Since the 1930s the Moscow Art Theatre has been recognized by the Russian government as the leading company of the Soviet Union.

Alterations in Realism

By 1900 realism had become the dominant mode in dramatic writing and in theatrical production almost everywhere. It was to remain dominant until around 1950, even though it underwent many alterations and withstood many challenges from other movements.

Many of the alterations in realism can be traced to the influence of Sigmund Freud (1856–1939), whose psychoanalytic theories provided a scientific explanation for much human behavior with previously had been attributed to instinct or supernatural forces and which had thus been placed outside the scope of realism. Freud's conception of the mind (as a faculty that telescopes experience, sublimates and suppresses desires, and often works irrationally) made it possible for dramatists to depart considerably from the early techniques of realism without departing from a scientific outlook. These departures, in turn, moved realism in the direction of the many nonrealistic styles that appeared after 1890 and made it ever easier for it to assimilate techniques that had originated in revolts against realism.

Symbolism

Although realism came to dominate the theatre, it was not universally accepted. Revolts against it began in the late nineteenth century and continued thereafter. Most protests were short-lived, though each probably served to weaken its target.

The first important revolt against realism is usually called symbolism (or alternatively neoromanticism, idealism, or aestheticism). As a conscious movement, it appeared in France in the 1880s and had largely expired by 1900. Symbolism is antirealistic in denying that ultimate truth is to be found in evidence supplied by the five senses or by rational thought. Instead, it holds that truth is to be grasped intuitively.

Since it cannot be logically understood, truth cannot be expressed directly. It can only be suggested through symbols that evoke feelings and states of mind, corresponding, though imprecisely, to the dramtist's intuitions. The surface dialogue and action in a symbolist play, therefore, are not of primary importance. As Maeterlinck put it:

Side by side with the necessary dialogue you will almost always find another dialogue that seems superfluous; but examine it carefully, and it will be borne home to you that this is the only one that the soul can listen to profoundly, for here alone it is the soul that is being addressed.

He went on to say:

Great drama, if we observe it closely, is made up of three principal elements: first, verbal beauty; then the contemplation and passionate portrayal of what actually exists about us and within us, that is to say nature and our sentiments; and, finally enveloping the whole work and creating the atmosphere proper to it, the idea which the poet forms of the unknown in which float about the beings and things which he evokes, the mystery which dominates them, judges them, and presides over their destinies. I have no doubt that this last is the most important element.

Thus, while a play portrays human actions, its ultimate aim is to convey intuitions about a higher truth that cannot be adequately expressed in words and that can only be suggested through symbols.

Unlike the realists, the symbolists chose their subject matter from the past or the realm of fancy, and avoided any attempt to deal with social problems or to recreate the physical environment of its characters. Like the neoclassicists, they aimed to suggest a universal truth independent of time and place. Unlike the neoclassicists, however, the symbolists did not believe that truth can be logically defined or rationally expressed. A symbolist drama, consequently, tends to be vague, mysterious, and ambiguous.

By far the most famous symbolist playwright was Maurice Maeterlinck (1862–1949), a Belgian who spent most of his life in France. His more important works are those written in the 1890s during his association with the symbolist school. Since his *Pelléas and Mélisande* (1892) is often said to be the best symbolist drama of its time, it will be examined here in some detail.

Pelléas and Mélisande

On the surface, *Pelléas and Mélisande* is the melodramatic story of a young wife who falls in love with her husband's younger brother. The husband kills his brother and the young wife dies of grief. This simple story of awakening love and its consequences holds the play together, but the ideas and feelings behind this façade are of the most interest to Maeterlinck.

Fate, presentiment, and an air of mystery dominate each scene. The characters are puppetlike, for they do not understand their own actions or motivations. Their backgrounds are never filled in, the precise time and place of the action is left unspecified, and events are not causally related. Instead of realistic and logical action growing out of character and situation, the play depicts a fairy-tale world in which inexplicable forces control human destinies.

Maeterlinck suggests that life is impenetrably mysterious. Rather than stating his beliefs directly, he implies them through recurring motifs and symbols. Because ideas are only suggested, it is impossible to isolate them definitely, although some uses of the more obvious motifs—water, light and darkness, height and depth—can be examined.

Water plays a part in almost every scene. Mélisande is first discovered by a pool; she and Pelléas play by a fountain in which she loses her wedding ring; later Pelléas and Mélisande declare their love for each other and Pelléas is killed by the same fountain; they search for her ring in a grotto, which must be approached by a narrow path between two lakes; Pelléas and Golaud find bottomless pits filled with water under the castle; the sea is referred to in almost every scene; and the women try in vain to wash away the stains on the threshold of the castle.

Pools of water are used to suggest many different things. The characters try to see the bottom of the pools, just as they try to peer into the depths of each other's souls; in neither case can they penetrate the mystery. A fountain is also used to indicate the difference between Mélisande's feelings for Golaud and for Pelléas: she has been discovered by Golaud at a fountain in a dark forest; she comes to Pelléas by a fountain in an open park and in full moonlight.

In each scene some important use is also made of light or darkness. The forests surrounding the castle are dark, and light may be seen only by looking toward the sea; characters sit in darkness or try to find a pool of light; lamps refuse to stay lighted.

Low and high places are also used symbolically. Mélisande sits in a tower; Pelléas and Golaud penetrate into the bowels of the castle to investigate the stench that arises; soaring towers or bottomless pits recur in almost every scene.

It is impossible to assign a definite meaning to each of these motifs or symbols. Rather, one must consider the connotations suggested by the context in which the symbols occur. The sea, for example, seems to represent the only avenue of escape, unlike the forest which is constantly encroaching on the castle. The sea is also associated with light, just as the forest is with darkness. Light is used to suggest frankness, the known truth, light-heartedness, and happiness. Darkness, on the other hand, implies secrets, the unknown, untruths, and unexpressed thoughts and fears. Throughout the play, love, happiness, and light struggle with fate, misery, and darkness.

Behind all the happenings, however, there is a sense of mystery and fate. Love comes to Pelléas and Mélisande against their wills, just as the sheep are led to slaughter against theirs; doors will not stay open and lamps will not stay lighted in rooms when Pelléas and Mélisande are alone. They are led by forces greater than themsleves.

The powers of love and light are pitted against those of fate and darkness. At the end of the play both the enigma of the human soul and the meaning of life remain as mysterious as when the play began. Arkël, speaking of Mélisande and her baby, makes it clear that this mystery is the essence of life and will continue to be so.

> 'Twas a little being, so quiet, so fearful, and so silent. . . . 'Twas a poor little mysterious being, like everybody. . . . I shall never understand it at all. . . . Come; the child must not stay here in this room. . . . She must live now in her place. . . . It is the poor little one's turn.

Thus, while rebelling against the outlook of the realists and naturalists, Maeterlinck is as deterministic as any of his opponents. His characters are at the mercy of forces just as destructive and far more mysterious than those of heredity and environment. In many ways, Maeterlinck's world is more frightening than that of Zola, for it is both unknowable and uncontrollable.

Plot and Structure. *Pelléas and Mélisande* has sometimes been termed Shakespearean because of its free use of time and place and its lack of specificity about setting. These surface similarities, however, almost exhaust the likenesses between Maeterlinck and Shakespeare, for Shakespeare always told a coherent story in thoroughly understandable terms, while

The Beginnings of the Modern Theatre, 1875–1915

279

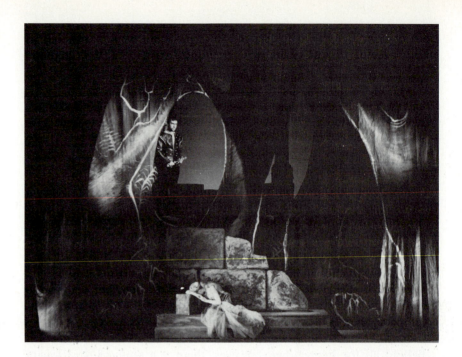

Pelléas and Mélisande *at the Belgian National Theatre. (Photo by Carl Hensler, Brussels.)*

Maeterlinck merely uses a story as a means for suggesting intuitions about life and the soul.

Pelléas and Mélisande is a love story organized around certain themes and ideas. Many scenes are only loosely connected with the main story line. For example, the opening scene in which the women try to wash the stains from the castle steps sets a mood of mystery and hopelessness, but has nothing to do with the story's action. Likewise, such scenes as that in which the sheep are led to slaughter are extraneous to the main plot. Mood and theme, therefore, are as important as action in the play's structure.

Furthermore, the number of scenes between the first meeting of Pelléas and Mélisande and their deaths could be expanded or contracted without seriously affecting the story. Awakening love is suggested early, but its existence is denied until the moment before Pelléas is killed. Thus, while all the scenes are connected, they do not develop through a clear chain of cause and effect.

Although Maeterlinck has used the five-act form, his act divisions are entirely arbitrary since they do not mark important breaks in the action or high points of suspense. Rather, the individual scene is the major structural unit.

Premonition is used to build and maintain suspense. There is a continual hint of some mystery behind the events which will be revealed. The characters seem to be led on toward some important discovery that is never forthcoming. They meet death but they are not enlightened. Even the audience is led only to the conclusion that life is mysterious and will remain so.

Characters and Acting. The characters are almost as vague as the ideas. They yearn, love, and die without knowing why.

All of the main characters are of the ruling class, but this fact has little effect upon their personalities or the action of the play. Their ages and physical appearance are also of little importance: Arkël is an old man; Genevieve is his daughter and the mother of Golaud and Pelléas; Golaud's hair is beginning to turn gray; Yniold is a child; it is implied that both Pelléas and Mélisande are young and attractive. All of this information is pertinent but slight in amount.

Psychological attributes are vague as well. The compassionate Arkël constantly attempts to look into the depths of being. Genevieve wants everyone to be happy. Golaud is a hunter, a man of action who loves quickly and steadfastly; he has a deep sense of honor that drives him to kill Pelléas. Neither Pelléas nor Mélisande performs any positive action or displays any positive psychological traits prior to the scene in which Pelléas dies. Until that time, they sigh, they resist love and preserve a sense of propriety. None of the characters fully understand his own motivations, and each is driven by forces stronger than himself.

Maeterlinck, therefore, is less interested in portraying lifelike characters than in suggesting states of feeling that come upon characters mysteriously and lead to mysterious consequences. His concept is further illustrated by the original production of the play in 1893. The actors chanted their lines and used angular gestures to emphasize the gulf between everyday behavior and the events presented in the play. It is not the texture of daily living that is important, but the relam of the spirit that lies beyond physical existence.

Visual and Aural Effects. In its simplicity and repetitiveness, the language of *Pelléas and Mélisande* suggests a beginner's textbook in reading. But this repetitiveness helps to emphasize the recurring motifs, and the simplicity is designed to prevent too much interest in surface reality. The very lack of complexity suggests that the audience needs to look beneath the surface.

Antirealism was emphasized in the original production through a number of devices. The stage lighting, very low in intensity, came from directly overhead. A gauze curtain, hung at the front of the stage, made it appear that the entire action was occurring in a mist. The scenery was painted in grayed tones to increase the effect of distance and mistiness. The actors wore costumes based on the paintings of Memling, who lived in the fifteenth century. These departures from realism were underscored by a sing-song delivery of lines and the use of unnatural gestures. The entire production was designed to remove the action from the world of everyday life; it was as unlike the productions of the realists as possible.

Pelléas and Mélisande, thus, was not concerned with contemporary problems and did not render truth through a depiction of the external

Scene from Maeterlinck's The Blue Bird *at the Théâtre Rejane, Paris, 1911. The scenery, by V.E. Egorov, was loaned by the Moscow Art Theatre, for whom it was originally designed. (From* Le Théâtre, *1911.)*

details of daily life. Rather, it dealt with such universal (but broad) themes as love, life, and death, and embodied them in symbols and motifs. Because the symbolists were interested primarily in mysterious spiritual forces, they had to use means quite different from those employed by the realists. Perhaps because of its lack of concreteness, symbolism appealed only to a limited audience and produced few plays of lasting interest.

Many attributes of symbolism may be found in the work of such later writers as Claudel, Andreyev, and Yeats. Paul Claudel (1868–1955) depicted the struggle between the flesh and the spirit, always ending in the triumph of religious faith, in such plays as *Break of Noon* (1906), *The Tidings Brought to Mary* (1912), and *The Satin Slipper* (1930). His fame was grown steadily since Jean-Louis Barrault staged *The Satin Slipper* with great critical success in 1943. In Russia, the foremost symbolist playwright was Leonid Andreyev (1871–1919), whose *The Life of Man* (1906) is an allegory of human existence from birth to death and of defeat by a cruel and whimsical universe. Peopled with such characters as The Man, His Wife, and Someone in Gray, *The Life of Man* combines the characteristics of a medieval morality play with those of Maeterlinck's works. In Ireland, William Butler Yeats (1865–1939) combined simple stories, complex ideas, and powerful poetry in such plays as *Cathleen ni Houlihan* (1902), *On Baile's Strand* (1904), *At the Hawk's Well* (1916), and *Purgatory* (1938).

Antirealistic Theatre

The revolt against realism also brought new attitudes toward the theatre. The symbolists drew much inspiration from the work of Richard Wagner (1813–1883), who sought to fuse all the arts into a master work: music drama. Opposed to realism, Wagner argued that music is necessary to the finest drama, which should be "distanced" from actual life. Furthermore, according to Wagner, music offers a means whereby the dramatist-composer may control the performance of the actor–singer, since music can dictate the pitch, duration, and tempo of the words. Wagner also believed that the master artist should retain complete control over the scenery, costumes, lighting, and all other theatrical elements. Thus, he was one of the first advocates of unified production and a strong director.

Wagner argued that the greatest truths cannot be approached through realism and that the theatre should lift the audience out of its humdrum daily existence through an idealized drama "dipped in the magic fountain of music." To evoke the proper esthetic distance, Wagner used a double proscenium, a curtain of steam, and a darkened auditorium to create a "mystic chasm" between spectators and performers. Perhaps because he too sought to depict an idealized world, Wagner exerted considerable influence on the symbolists.

The symbolists encountered many of the same difficulties in getting their plays performed as the realists and naturalists had, and they too had to establish independent theatres to gain a hearing. The first of these, the Théâtre d'Art, founded by Paul Fort in 1890, was succeeded by the Théâtre de l'Oeuvre in 1892. Under the direction of Aurélien-Marie Lugné-Poë (1869–1940), the Théâtre de l'Oeuvre opened with *Pelléas and Mélisande*. Until 1897 Lugné-Poë staged all plays in a highly stylized manner. Although he later adopted a more eclectic approach, continuing his theatre until 1929, he is remembered primarily for his work with sym-

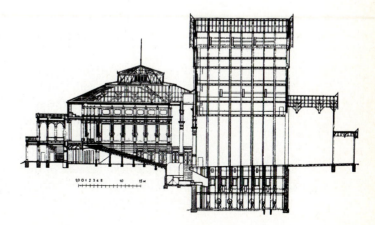

Cross section of Wagner's theatre at Bayreuth, which opened in 1876. (From Sachs' Modern Opera Houses and Theatres. London, 1896-1898.)

Stage and auditorium of the Bayreuth Festival Theatre. Note the steeply raked auditorium, the double proscenium, and the absence of a center aisle and side boxes. (From Barkhin's Architectura Teatra. *Moscow, 1947.)*

bolist plays. Lugné-Poë did not attempt to create the illusion of reality, seeking instead a unity of mood and style. His approach in the 1890s is summed up in the phrase, "the word creates the decor."

The symbolists believed that scenery should be confined to draperies or undefined forms that evoke a sense of infinite space and time. Historical detail was avoided because it tied plays to specific periods and places rather than bringing out their timeless qualities. Therefore, decor was reduced to elements giving a generalized impression appropriate to the ideas and atmosphere of a play. Similarly, costumes were usually simple, draped garments of no particular period or place; colors were dictated by the play's mood.

The symbolists thus advocated simplicity of setting and costume. The physical elements of production were subordinated so that attention might be concentrated upon the words of the playwright. For the most part, symbolist productions were too determinedly nonrealistic to attract a wide following. Nevertheless, they laid the foundations for several subsequent developments.

Appia and Craig

Although not of the symbolist school, two major theorists, Adolphe Appia (1862–1928) and Gordon Craig (1872–1966) were clearly in the tradition of Wagner and the symbolists.

Appia's desire to embody Wagner's ideas led him to articulate for the first time many of the now accepted ideals of theatrical production. Appia began with the notion that artistic unity is fundamental, but declared it difficult to achieve because of the diverse visual elements used in the theatre: the moving actor, the horizontal floor, and the perpendicular scenery. Appia's search for unity led him to demand many changes in theatrical production. Rejecting flat, painted scenery, he insisted that three-dimensional structures are the only proper environment for the three-dimensional actor if unity is to be attained. To reveal the shape and three-dimensionality of the scenery and the actor, light, from various angles and directions, is required. Furthermore, light must change as action and mood change. Constantly changing light fuses the various elements into a unified whole, for it reveals and reflects shifting emotions and ideas. In this way, light becomes the visual equivalent of music, since it welds the elements together visually just as music does aurally.

Appia suggested that the producer begin with a search for the essential qualities of a script and then for the means to embody them in theatrical terms. Since a unified and artistic performance is the goal, the entire production must be conceived by one person—the director. Appia thus reinforced the trend toward elevating the director to a position of dominance.

Although few of Appia's designs ever reached the stage, his ideas were expressed in a number of books and sketches. His designs are simple, all unnecessary details having been removed. They use mood, light and shade, mass and line to interpret the essential character of a scene. His theory and practice have exerted a pervasive influence on modern staging.

Craig believed in many of the same ideas as Appia but was much more militant in his statements and did a great deal more to popularize the theories. He denied that the theatre is a collection of subsidiary arts; rather, he argued, the master theatre artist creates his own autonomous product out of action, words, line, color, and rhythm, just as artists in other fields use the elements appropriate to their art. Because there can

Design by Adolphe Appia for the sacred forest in Wagner's Parsifal, *1896.*

only be one master artist in the theatre, Craig once suggested that the actor should be replaced by the marionette, since the marionette cannot inject its own personality into the work and thwart the director's conception.

Opposed to realism, which he called "the theatre of sermons and epigrams," Craig wanted to create works that would appeal directly to the senses and transform the theatre into "a place for visions." Like Appia, Craig stood for extreme simplicity in scenery, costume, and lighting, and depended upon line, mass, and color for his effects rather than upon historical accuracy or detailed ornamentation. Also like Appia, he helped to promote the director as the supreme theatre artist.

Craig realized that his work would not find immediate acceptance in the commercial theatre and sought other places in which to experiment. He established a school in Florence, Italy, in 1913, but his work was interrupted by World War I. He also expounded his ideas in his magazine, *The Mask,* and in a number of books. As with Appia, few of Craig's scene designs were ever carried to completion, but his writing inspired many theatre workers and has had untold influence on the modern stage.

In addition to Appia and Craig, several other producers of the early twentieth century—perhaps most notably Fuchs and Diaghilev—encouraged departures from realism in theatrical production.

In two books, *The Theatre of the Future* (1905) and *Revolution in the Theatre* (1909), Georg Fuchs (1868–1949) declared pictorial illusionism outmoded and set out to "retheatricalize the theatre." In 1907, with Fritz Erler (1868–1940) he founded the Munich Art Theatre to implement his ideas. In their theatre, the size of the proscenium opening could be changed by an adjustable inner proscenium; the stage floor was broken into sections, each mounted on an elevator, so that it could be arranged into levels; the acting area was surrounded by four cycloramas, each of a different color, which could be changed electrically; and the orchestra pit could be covered over to create a forestage. For decor, Fuchs and Erler depended almost entirely upon levels, a few set pieces, and lighting; they sought to fuse all elements through rhythm, which Fuchs called the "primal" theatrical force. Ultimately they hoped to reestablish that sense of communion between audience and performer that had characterized the Greek theatre and had been lost with the emphasis on illusionism. Like Appia and Craig, Fuchs demanded a simplified staging that captured the spirit of a work without regard for surface realism.

In Russia several groups turned to nonrealistic staging in the early twentieth century. Probably the most important of these was the Ballets Russes, which under the direction of Sergei Diaghilev (1872–1929) and Mikhail Fokine (1880–1942) made an enormous impression in Western Europe after 1909, especially with its pictorial style. Its impact did not come from any new technical devices, for it relied almost exclusively on painted wings and drops, but from its stylized decor—primarily decorative motifs, color, and line—that reflected moods and themes rather than

Craig's setting for Hamlet *at the Moscow Art Theatre in 1911. (From* Moscow Art Theatre, 1898-1917, *1955.)*

specific periods and places. The costumes also exaggerated line, color, and mass. The Ballets Russes' designers, especially Leon Bakst (1866–1924) and Alexandre Benois (1876–1960), were to exert incalculable influence on the theatre between 1910 and 1930.

Eclecticism in Theatrical Production

Around 1900 it began to be suggested that each type of play, and even each individual play, has its own style which demands a distinctive stage treatment. This idea was revolutionary in many ways, for in each period prior to this time a single standard was applied to all productions. For example, in 1850 a Greek drama, a play by Shakespeare, and a melodrama would all have been given the same kind of settings and would have been acted in much the same style. Although after 1890 there was much debate over the relative merits of realism and antirealism, each director still tended to adopt a single approach and to use it for all plays.

But others at the time began to argue that the style of a production should be determined by the style of the script and by the theatrical conventions and actor–audience spatial relationships in use at the time when the play was written. If he accepted this argument, a director then needed to use a great number of approaches to staging, for each new production

Design by Norman Bel Geddes for Reinhardt's production of The Miracle. *The theatre was transformed to resemble a cathedral. (Courtesy of the Bel Geddes Collection, a gift of the Tobin Foundation, Hoblitzelle Theatre Arts Library, University of Texas.)*

became a new problem requiring a solution somewhat different from that applicable to any other. This eclectic approach, which eventually triumphed, was to be one of the distinguishing marks of twentieth-century directing.

As sometimes practiced, however, eclecticism was merely another version of historical realism, for some directors slavishly based productions on knowledge about earlier theatrical conventions (for example, they might stage a play by Shakespeare as nearly as possible as it would have been done in the Elizabethan period) rather than, as had been usual in the nineteenth century, using costumes and settings that reflected the historical period of the play's action. This kind of approach was taken by William Poel (1852–1934), who, working with the Elizabethan Stage Society between 1894 and 1905, staged a number of Elizabethan plays. Although he did not always use the same solution, Poel is now remembered almost entirely for his attempts to reconstruct the Elizabethan public stage. He also popularized several conventions: dressing the actors in Elizabethan garments to reflect Shakespeare's own day rather than the historical epoch of the dramatic action; using costumed pages to draw the curtains of the inner stage and to arrange properties and furniture; and an onstage audience to emphasize the audience–actor relationship of the Elizabethan era. But Poel's major emphasis was on continuity and rapidity in both action and speech. Although his productions did not generate widespread enthusiasm, they demonstrated the advantages of unbroken playing and of concentrating attention on the actors. In France, Antoine used a similar approach in staging several French plays of the seventeenth century (that is, he sought to recreate the staging conventions in use at the time when the plays were written).

But true eclecticism owes most to Max Reinhardt (1873–1943), who began his career as an actor under Otto Brahm before taking up directing around 1900. Thereafter, Reinhardt produced plays from all periods and of all types and in a great variety of styles. He believed that some plays require large theatres, whereas others fare best in small houses. (He was one of the first directors to have a small experimental theatre attached to a larger theatre.) He often remodeled spaces to fit the needs of a particular kind of play. For example, for a medieval pageant drama, he transformed a theatre into a cathedral; to house Greek drama, he remodeled a circus building; and for eighteenth-century plays, he acquired a hall of state in an eighteenth-century palace. He also experimented with all kinds of stage machinery, theatrical devices, and visual motifs in an attempt to create the right atmosphere for each work.

With this eclecticism, Reinhardt coupled the belief that the director is the supreme artist of the theatre. He always made a *Regiebuch,* or prompt book, in which every detail of movement, lighting, scenery, costume, and sound was recorded with exactness. He coached his actors carefully and controlled each element of his productions. A script was for him an outline offered by the playwright for completion by the director.

Reinhardt popularized many ideas that were to be widely accepted and practiced in the twentieth century: the need for a different approach to each play; an awareness of the interdependence of theatre architecture and dramatic styles; the need for a detailed prompt book prepared before rehearsals begin; the acceptance of the director as the supreme artist of the theatre and as the completer of the playwright's work. Reinhardt's continuing influence may be seen in contemporary experiments with theatres-in-the-round, open stages, and other audience-actor relationships. Between 1900 and 1933 Reinhardt was one of the world's most prolific and famous directors.

But if Reinhardt was the primary popularizer of eclecticism, he was aided by many others. In England, Harley Granville Barker (1877–1946), especially through his work at the Royal Court Theatre between 1904 and 1907, did much to establish the new ideal with plays by authors ranging from Euripides to Shaw. (More than any other producer, Barker won acceptance for Shaw's plays in England.) In France, Jacques Rouché (1862–1957) promoted the eclectic idea at his Théâtre des Arts between 1910 and 1913. By the time World War I began in 1914, eclecticism had been disseminated throughout Europe, although it had not prevailed everywhere.

By 1915, Ibsen, Shaw, Zola, and others had done much to make drama once more a medium for the pursuit of truth and not merely a source of entertainment. Furthermore, producers almost everywhere had been forcefully reminded that theatre is an art, and they had been provoked into debates over its principles, purposes, and techniques. After having been intitiated by realism and naturalism, the modern theatre began to assume that pattern of rapidly changing modes which has characterized it ever since.

11

The Theatre from 1915 to 1940

Between the first and second world wars, realism continued to be the most popular mode with unsophisticated audiences, but it was embraced by few major artists, who participated instead in one or more of the numerous artistic movements that came into being during these years. Most of these movements were short-lived, but each left permanent marks on the theatre.

Expressionism

Of the movements, the first to make a deep impression was expressionism. As a label, *expressionism* was coined in France to distinguish the kind of painting done by Van Gogh and Gauguin from that of the impressionists. Around 1910 it was introduced into Germany, where soon it was being applied to almost any work that deviated from traditional modes. Thus, it is not surprising that many diverse artists were grouped under its banner. The first true expressionist play—*The Beggar* by Reinhard Johannes Sorge (1892–1916)—was published in 1912. Thereafter expressionistic drama grew steadily in popularity with the reading public, although few works, because of the strict censorship then in effect, were performed before the war ended in 1918. Expressionism reached the peak of its popularity between 1919 and 1923 and then rapidly declined. By 1925 it had virtually ended as an organized movement.

Because expressionism was used rather loosely as a label, it is difficult to define. Nevertheless, its basic tenets can be summarized. The expressionists believed that fundamental truth is to be found within humankind—its spirit, soul, desires, and visions—and that external reality should be reshaped until it is brought into harmony with these inner attributes so that the human spirit may realize its aspirations. Many writers sought merely to express their perceptions of this inner spirit, but others wished to transform society. Consequently, some historians have divided the expressionists into two groups: the mystics and the activists. The latter were especially antipathetic toward materialism and industrialism, which they saw as the chief blocks to the expressionist goals and as the major destroyers (or warpers) of the soul. Some expressionists called for the destruction of the old society and all its materialistic trappings. Almost all adherents of the movement spoke of the "regeneration of man" and the "creation of the new man." Ultimately, most hoped to build a world

Final scene from Wedekind's Spring's Awakening. *Translated and directed by Gary Gaiser. Costumes by Leon Brauner. Setting by Frank Silberstein. Lighting by Joan Sullivan. (Courtesy Indiana University Theatre.)*

free from war, hypocrisy and hate, where individuals could express themselves freely, and in which humanitarianism would replace materialism.

Most expressionists were opposed to realism and naturalism because those movements glorified science, the major support of the technical society it so deplored. In addition, they disliked realism's emphasis on external appearance, which they considered a secondary aspect of truth. They also were contemptuous of symbolism because of its flight from contemporary problems.

Expressionist drama tended toward one of two types. Many plays concentrated on the negative aspects of the present in an attempt to show how false ideas have distorted man's spirit until he is little better than a machine. Other plays look forward to transforming society and to achieving harmony between man's environment and his spirit. Because the plays are message-centered, they are episodic; many take the form of a search or pilgrimage. Since truth is said to lie in internal vision, the external appearance of things is often distorted. Shape may be exaggerated or altered, color may be abnormal, movement may be mechanical, speech may be reduced to short phrases or single words, All these devices are employed to project a vision quite unlike that of the realists or the symbolists.

Expressionist Dramatists

Among the major influences on expressionist drama are the works of Strindberg and Wedekind. August Strindberg (1849–1912), the first Swedish playwright to achieve international fame and one of the major dramatists of the modern world, wrote over fifty plays, in addition to novels and nonfictional works. Up to about 1895 his writing is essentially realistic. *The Father* (1887) and *Miss Julie* (1888) are among the best works of the time. But when personal crises drove Strindberg to the edge of insanity, his outlook on life and art underwent profound changes. In the late 1890s he began to write a series of plays usually considered to be forerunners of expressionism. These include *The Dream Play* (1902) and *The Ghost Sonata* (1907). In his Preface to *The Dream Play*, Strindberg states:

The author has tried to imitate the disconnected but seemingly logical form of the dream. Anything may happen; everything is possible and probable. Time and space do not exist. On an insignificant background of reality, imagination designs and embroiders novel patterns: a medley of memories, experiences, free fancies, absurdities and improvisations.

In other words, in *The Dream Play* Strindberg tries to destroy the limitations of time, place, and logical sequence by adopting the viewpoint of the dreamer. One event flows into another without logical explanation, characters dissolve or are transformed into other characters, and widely separated places and times blend to tell a story of tortured and alienated humankind in search of meaning that will explain or justify suffering.

Franz Wedekind (1864–1918), like Strindberg, moves from starkest realism to symbolic abstraction. Sometimes he paints the world as we know it, but at others he depicts the most subjective nightmares, often within a single work. His *Spring's Awakening* (1891) tells the story of two adolescents' struggles with sexual awareness in a puritanical society; much of the play is straightforwardly realistic, but the final scene passes over into pure fantasy. One boy has committed suicide and his ghost urges the other to do likewise but is thwarted by the symbolic Man in the Mask. This mixture of styles and the preoccupation with sexual themes continued throughout Wedekind's work, seen at its best in *Earth Spirit* (1895) and *Pandora's Box* (1904) (which are now sometimes produced together as *Lulu*). It was to Wedekind and Strindberg that the expressionists turned for many of their dramatic techniques.

After 1912 Germany produced many expressionist playwrights, but the most widely known are Ernst Toller (1893–1939) and Georg Kaiser (1878–1945). Toller's first play, *Transfiguration* (1918), written while he was in prison for pacifism, is an antiwar drama. Of his later works the most important is *Man and the Masses* (1921), which shows how the machine and factories have come to dominate the lives of human beings. Toller realizes that the machine is here to stay, but argues that the soul of man must conquer the factories so that the machine may become the servant of man rather than man of the machine. More importantly, *Man and the Masses* shows a heroine, who stands for the expressionistic ideals, betrayed by the Nameless One, who is more interested in winning a victory over capitalism than in serving humankind. She is interested in Man, he in the Masses. The play points out the great gap between the ideal and actuality. But while the play is pessimistic in its outcome, it still looks forward hopefully to the day when the workers will be ready for a better life.

Kaiser began writing in 1911, but his early work is principally satirical and without any strong conviction. World War I, however, made him question the whole foundation of a society that could generate such acts of destruction. In the process of questioning he wrote some of the most powerful of expressionistic plays.

Among Kaiser's best known works is his trilogy—composed of *The Coral* (1917), *Gas I* (1918), and *Gas II* (1920). In *The Coral* and *Gas I*, the expressionist vision fares much as it does in *Man and the Masses* (it is defeated, but hope is expressed for the future). By the time he wrote *Gas II*, however, Kaiser had abandoned his belief in the ideal and was predicting humankind's ultimate destruction. Perhaps the best of all expressionist plays is Kaiser's *From Morn till Midnight*, which will be examined here in detail. Written in 1912, it was published in 1916 and first produced (privately) in Munich in 1917.

From Morn till Midnight

From Morn till Midnight has much in common with medieval drama. Some critics have stated that it shows the "stations of martydom" in the life of modern man. The play's central character, the Cashier, may be viewed as an Everyman of the modern world, and the time of the action, from morn to midnight, suggests the span of human life.

The play is also related to *Faust,* since both are concerned with human beings' search for meaning and fulfillment. Like Faust, the Cashier ultimately finds an answer, but unlike Faust, he becomes a martyr because of the debasement of modern life.

From Morn till Midnight shows humans reduced to a machinelike existence, devoid of any purpose except material gain. The Cashier is jarred out of this pattern by the exotic and sensual appeal of the Lady from Italy, and he comes to realize for the first time that he has been dehumanized. Consequently, he sets out to find some meaning in existence. Along the way he makes several stops: one involving home and family, another symbolic of society and the state (the racetrack scene), another of sensual pleasure, and one of religion. He ultimately recognizes the rightness of the soul's claims, but the debasement of the masses is such that they are not ready for his answer.

While the ending is pessimistic, it suggests that since "the new man" has emerged in the Cashier, it might also emerge in the masses. Were this to occur, a rebirth of society would ensue.

Plot and Structure. The seven scenes of *From Morn till Midnight* are held together by the presence of the Cashier in each and by themes and ideas. Everything is focused upon the central character's search for fulfillment.

The first two scenes are primarily preparatory and expository. Scene I establishes the dehumanizing effects of materialism and demonstrates the system of values that underlies the action. The bank is symbolic of

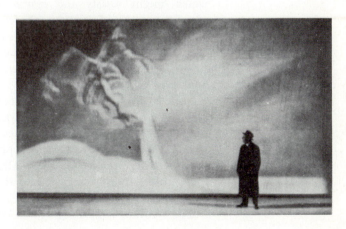

Scene 3 of From Morn till Midnight *as presented by the Theatre Guild in 1922. Note the tree which has turned into a skeleton. Directed by Frank Reicher; settings by Lee Simonson; (Photo by Francis Bruguiere. Courtesy Lincoln Center Library of the Performing Arts.)*

society, since the accumulation of wealth is the primary goal of material-ism. The Stout Gentleman and the Bank Manager, representatives of the established order, are convinced that in money lies the answer to all of human beings' problems.

The effect of such values on the common man is seen in the Cashier. He does not speak until the end of the first scene, but functions like a robot: he raps when he wants attention, he takes in and pays out money, he enters sums in a book. For all practical purposes he has become a soulless machine.

But this routine is broken by the appearance of the Lady from Italy, whose strangeness jars the Cashier out of his machinelike state. In his desire to possess her, he responds as his society has conditioned him to act —since money is the key to success, he steals an amount that should be sufficient to accomplish his aim, the possession of the Lady.

Scene 2 shows that the Cashier's view of the road to happiness is erroneous. The Lady is respectable, and the Cashier has irrevocably lost his old place in society.

Scene 3 marks the major transition from the old to the new life. The Cashier cannot go back, and therefore must decide upon a course of action. For the first time he realizes the emptiness of the past, and he is eager to explore what he has been missing: "I have reason to expect great discoveries." He still believes that his stolen money will be the key to success.

Scene 3 also prepares for those to follow, for it is out of his decision to search for the meaning of life that each of the succeeding scenes grows. The scheme of the play is seen further in the appearance of Death. The Cashier declines Death's invitation to go with him by saying, "Call me up around midnight," and, "Before nightfall, I'll have to meet a number of obligations." In the scenes that follow the Cashier makes several visits, and then at midnight reencounters Death.

Although Scene 4 shows the first of his stops, it is still related to the past since it involves the Cashier's own home and family. But the home, which might satisfy the search for happiness, has been as completely mechanized as the bank, for here even sentiment has been thoroughly standardized. The Cashier's decision to leave the house before he eats lunch seems such a disruption of order that his mother dies. It is not surprising then that the Cashier decides that the home "does not meet the final test."

Scene 5 shows the Cashier's attempt to find meaning in the political and social structure of society, symbolized in the racetrack. Here the people assemble to watch the contestants, who, no matter how tired they may be, race whenever a monetary prize is offered: the higher the prize the more exciting the race becomes. All eyes in the stadium (except those of the Cashier) are on the races and the prizes. The race becomes a symbol of the drive for monetary gain.

The stadium is also segregated in terms of social classes and feeling.

"In three rings placed on top of each other, bursting with spectators—the magic works. In the first gallery, discipline is maintained by the higher class audience. . . . Higher up, the bodies begin to move. Exclamations are heard. Second gallery. At the very top, all restraint is abandoned. Fanatic shouts. Naked screams. The gallery of passion." The Cashier sets out to break down all the barriers of class and feeling by offering the highest prize ever heard of. "Fusion of all rings. Utter dissolution of the individual results in the densest core: passion. To reach that point is the greatest experience."

At this stage in his search, then, the Cashier is attempting to break down class barriers and to achieve a universal brotherhood of man. By inducing the fullest expression of emotion, he thinks that he can break down the regimentation of society. But just as the Cashier is about to succeed, the ruler arrives and the spectators resume their conditioned responses. The Cashier has still been using the lure of money as the key to happiness. He has not yet been able to rid himself of the values of his society.

Scene 6 explores the search for happiness through sensual pleasures. The most exotic foods, plus the suggestion of sexual orgy, are used to represent this goal. This road, too, proves to lead nowhere. When the Cashier lifts the mask of one of the women she is so ugly that he is repulsed, and another proves to have a wooden leg. The anticipated joys of the flesh turn into disgust and the Cashier rushes out. Kaiser emphasizes the emptiness and soullessness of material pleasure through the complete selfishness of the cabaret's customers. Since they steal the money left by the Cashier, the poor and tubercular waiter must pay the bill himself.

Scene 7 brings the Cashier to the end of his journey as he searches for fulfillment in religion. He has been brought to a Salvation Army hall by the same Salvation Lass who has appeared fleetingly in Scenes 5 and 6, in both of which she has gone about her business as mechanically as the Cashier did in Scene 1. It is not surprising, therefore, that she too turns out to be as corrupt as the rest of society.

The Cashier has come to the Salvation Army hall because he has lost all sense of purpose. In the meeting that follows, the testimonials of repentant sinners sum up the Cashier's experiences in the play and each makes the Cashier see himself more clearly.

Finally, he realizes that the call of the soul is the true road to happiness. But when he repents of his past and scatters his stolen money about him, the materialism of society is reconfirmed. The supposedly repentant sinners become beasts striving to tear the money from each other. Since the Salvation Army Lass does not enter the fight, the Cashier thinks that he has found his true mate. But she is merely more cunning than the others, for she turns him over to the police for the reward.

The final moments sum up the play's message. In the darkness of the hall a tangle of wires outlines the skeleton of Death, whom the Cashier had eluded in Scene 3. "From morning till midnight I race in a circle. Now his finger shows a way—toward what goal?" He dies with his arms outstretched on a cross and his dying sigh echoes words associated with Christ, *Ecce Homo* (Behold the Man). The lamps explode, and the Policeman says, "We've had a short circuit"—a remark that the audience should interpret as referring to society.

Although the Cashier has seen the way to truth, the people (as in the history of Jesus) are blind to his values and prefer materialism to his spirituality. He has changed nothing, but he has shown the way. Kaiser expected his audience to see the difference between two sets of values, and to prefer those of the Cashier.

Characters and Acting. Each of the characters in *From Morn till Midnight* is given only a social designation or "type" name. Each is intended to embody the characteristics of a group rather than an individual. Most speeches are made up of clichés and the characters perform only sterotyped actions. This machinelike quality, essential to Kaiser's attitude toward modern life, should be reflected in the acting.

Only the Cashier (beginning in Scene 3) and the Lady escape stereotyping. The Lady is from another world, and it is her unusualness that jars the Cashier out of the mold into which he has been forced.

The play centers around the Cashier. He is the only truly articulate character and the only one who is able to escape from that machinelike existence that dominates the lives of the others. His speech and action must undergo a change beginning in Scene 3, therefore, and must contrast with those of the other characters. He should grow in humanity and strength as his search comes nearer and nearer to fulfillment. Only if his role is made sympathetic and his search meaningful can Kaiser's intentions be realized. A mechanical quality must be achieved with all characters except the Lady and the Cashier. On the other hand, the Cashier's universal qualities must be brought out, for he represents humankind seeking to escape the stultifying results of modern life.

Visual and Aural Factors. Mechanical qualities also should be reflected in the scenery, lighting, and costumes, and each of these must represent modern life in its most stereotyped form. Scene 3 offers a clue to the proper approach to spectacle. In that scene a tree turns into a skeleton and then reassumes its normal appearance. The visual elements, therefore, are intended to express the Cashier's vision of reality, rather than to reflect the everyday appearance of objects.

In their efforts to embody their themes visually, the expressionists frequently used fragmentary rather than full-stage sets. The scenic elements often were given jagged lines, the walls were made to tilt or lean, unnatural color was used; details were enlarged or diminished in size to emphasize the relative importance of each to the play's ideas. Appearances, thus, were distorted to express feelings and ideas.

Costumes, lighting, and stage properties were treated in similar fashion. Many characters often were dressed identically so as to emphasize the uniformity of modern human beings. (See, for example, the treatment of the Jewish Gentlemen in the racetrack scene of *From Morn till Midnight*.)

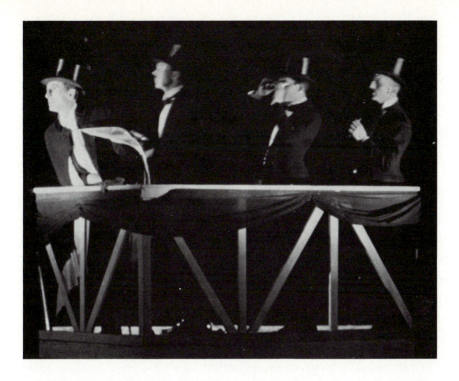

Unnatural color, angle, or intensity in lighting might be used to parallel the distortion of human values depicted in the scripts.

From Morn till Midnight attempts to express the playwright's vision of modern humanity: the mechanization of feelings and activities and the subjugation of the human spirit. It demonstrates the results and suggests a way out of the dilemma. As with much modern art, *From Morn till Midnight* requires a special intellectual effort for comprehension. Once the scheme is understood, the play's intention is relatively clear, although today it may seem oversimplified in its analysis of human ills and in its recommendations for a better future.

Expressionism in the Postwar Years

When the German government fell in 1918 only a few expressionist plays had been seen on the stage. Even these had been mounted rather traditionally. Thus, both the public performance of the plays and the development of a theatrical style appropriate to them had to await the end of the war. Then, beginning in 1919, expressionist drama suddenly came into vogue and a new style of production developed rapidly. Two German directors, Leopold Jessner (1878–1948) and Jurgen Fehling (1890–1968), were especially instrumental in developing and popularizing expressionist production techniques. Jessner, working in Berlin after

1919, won international fame for his imaginative use of flights of steps (*Jessnertreppen*) as a major scenic and compositional device. He also manipulated color and lighting to reflect the inner feelings of characters and reversals of situation. Jessner worked primarily with older plays, to which he gave new life through his visual approach. Fehling, on the other hand, made his reputation by staging expressionist plays. He experimented with a wide range of devices (such as dances set to the sound of cash registers, constantly shifting colored lights, and distorted shapes) to reflect the emotional qualities found in the scripts. As the work of Jessner and Fehling became widely known, their practices were adopted elsewhere.

Expressionism in the theatre seems to have reached its peak in 1923. Its desire to transform the world into a place where humanity's highest spiritual potential might be realized had raised high hopes, but these had been dissipated by the wranglings over peace settlements and the aftermath. As optimism gave way to the suspicion that humans are basically selfish and destructive, the foundations of expressionism were undermined, and by 1925 the movement had ceased to be productive.

Expressionism was for the most part a German phenomenon (perhaps because the hostilities of World War I discouraged the spread of the movement or the use of the term in countries opposed to Germany). During the 1920s, however, expressionism for a time exerted considerable influence elsewhere. In America, dramas indebted to it include Elmer Rice's *The Adding Machine*, Eugene O'Neill's *The Hairy Ape* and *The Great God Brown*, and Marc Connelly and George Kaufman's *Beggar on Horseback*, all written in the 1920s. One of the most famous of all expressionist plays is *R. U. R.* (1921) by the Czech playwright, Karel Čapek (1890–1938).

But, though expressionism as a movement had virtually disappeared by 1925, many of its techniques continued to be used. Its later influence is to be seen largely in a freer treatment of visual elements, the introduction of

Trial scene from Elmer Rice's The Adding Machine. *Directed by Gregory Foley.*

dream sequences into otherwise realistic plays, and in other devices that permit free manipulation of time, place, and appearance. Its dramatic and staging techniques have been absorbed into the general eclecticism of the twentieth-century theatre.

Futurism, Dadaism, and Surrealism

While expressionism was developing in Germany, other movements were emerging elsewhere. One of the first was futurism, launched in 1909 by the Italian poet, Filippo Tommaso Marinetti (1876–1944). Like the expressionists, the futurists rejected the past and wished to transform humankind. But whereas the expressionists associated the past with soul-destroying materialism and industrialism, the futurists glorified the energy and speed of the machine age and sought to make these the basis of their art. Beginning in 1910, they gave performances during which they proclaimed their manifestos, gave concerts, read poems, performed plays, and exhibited works of visual art—sometimes several of these simultaneously. They denounced the theatre of the past and declared music halls, nightclubs, and circuses to be better models on which to base future forms. They found earlier drama too lengthy, analytic, and static and proposed intead a "synthetic drama" that would compress into a moment or two the essence of a dramatic situation. Although interest in futurism declined in the 1920s and it was never a major movement in the theatre, it pioneered innovations that would be revived and extended in the 1950s and 1960s, among them: direct confrontation and intermingling of performers and audiences, the exploitation of technology to create multimedia productions, and the use of simultaneity and multiple focus in performances.

Another movement, dadaism, was launched in Switzerland in 1916. Its principal spokesman was Tristan Tzara (1896–1963), who published seven manifestos between 1916 and 1920. Dadaism was grounded in thoroughgoing skepticism about a world that could produce a global war. Since insanity seemed to them the world's true state, the dadaists sought to replace logic and reason with calculated madness. Rather than suggesting programs to improve the world, they called all programs into question. They presented a number of productions composed of lectures, recitations, dances, visual art, and short plays. Often several things were going on simultaneously. At the end of the war, the dadaists dispersed, and by 1920 the movement had lost its impetus. Although it left few lasting works, much of what it stood for was to resurface in the 1960s under other names.

In France, dadaism was absorbed into surrealism, which was launched in 1924 with a manifesto written by André Breton (1896–1966), the movement's principal spokesman. Breton defined surrealism as "pure psychic automatism, by which is intended to express, verbally in writing,

or by other means, the real process of thought. Thought's dictation, in the absence of all control exercised by the reason and outside all esthetic or moral preoccupation." Thus, Breton, under the influence of Freud, makes the subconscious mind the source of the artist's most significant perceptions, for he argues that truth is most apt to surface when the superego's censorship and the ego's logic have been neutralized.

Surrealist artists and writers gained their effects by mingling the familiar and the strange. In surrealist drama, familiar human situations occur in unusual (often mythical) surroundings, and seemingly unrelated scenes are juxtaposed. Such techniques break the bonds of ordinary reality and create associational patterns that lead the mind to novel but significant perceptions.

Surrealism had little direct impact on the theatre. The most effective use of its techniques were made by Jean Cocteau (1892–1963), never an acknowledged member of the school, in a series of scenarios for ballets and in such dramas as *Orpheus* (1926) and *The Infernal Machine* (1934). Many of its devices, however, were to be taken over by the postwar absurdists, and several scene designers were to borrow from its visual conventions.

Artaud

Surrealism influenced the theatre indirectly through Antonin Artaud (1895–1948), a surrealist before being expelled from that movement. Artaud began his career in the theatre in 1921 and worked for a number of producers in Paris before serving as a director of the Théâtre Alfred Jarry from 1926 to 1929. In 1931, inspired by a troupe of Balinese dancers at the Colonial Exposition in Paris, he began to write the theoretical essays (published in 1938 as *The Theatre and Its Double*) from which stems his considerable influence on the contemporary theatre.

According to Artaud, the theatre in the Western world has been devoted to a very narrow range of human experience, primarily the psychological problems of individuals and the social problems of groups, whereas the more important aspects of existence are those submerged in the unconscious mind. Artaud called this Western use of the theatre mistaken, and he recommended that of the Orient as an antidote.

Artaud considered the theatre's true mission to be the expulsion of all those things that cause divisions within humankind and between individuals and thus lead to hatred, violence, and disaster. As Artaud put it, "The theatre has been created to drain abscesses collectively." The ultimate goal is a harmonious society.

To reach this goal, Artaud prescribed certain remedies. He was certain that it could not be reached through appeals to the rational mind, which has been conditioned by society to sublimate many fundamental human impulses. He was also convinced that it could not be done through language, for that is the primary tool of rational thought. He sometimes called his a "theatre of cruelty," since in order to achieve its ends it would have to force the audience to confront itself. To do this, he sought to break down the audience's defenses by operating directly on the sensory apparatus in a way that bypasses the conscious, rational mind. He declared that the audience "cannot resist effects of physical surprise, the dynamism of cries and violent movements . . . used to act in a direct manner on the physical sensitivity of the spectators." But, according to Artaud, this approach requires a new "language of the theatre." He recommended replacing traditional theatre buildings with remodeled barns, factories, or airplane hangars, and locating acting areas in corners, on overhead catwalks, and along the walls. In lighting, he called for a "vibrating, shredded" effect, and in sound he favored shrillness, abrupt changes in volume, and the use of the human voice to create harmonies and dissonances. Thus, Artaud wanted to assault the audience, to break down its resistance, to purge it morally and spiritually.

Artaud was a visionary and at first was little appreciated. But after World War II, as the conception of man darkened, his influence steadily increased. It was to be especially strong during the 1960s, when many of his techniques came into common use.

Copeau and the Cartel

Although the dadaists, surrealists, and Artaud were perhaps the major innovators in the French theatre between the wars, they enjoyed little critical esteem at the time. Rather, the acknowledged leaders were Copeau and the members of the Cartel.

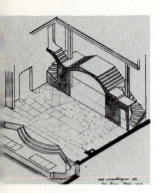

An isometric drawing of Jacques Copeau's stage, the Vieux Colombier, in 1919. (From Theatre Arts, *1920.)*

Jacques Copeau (1879–1949) began his career as a critic, but in 1913 founded his own theatre, the Vieux-Colombier. At that time he declared that the salvation of the theatre lies in a renovated drama rather than in innovative visual reforms (the means then being attempted by most directors). Copeau argued that the director's primary task is to translate faithfully the dramatist's script into a "poetry of the theatre." Furthermore, he stated that the actor, as the "living presence of the author," is the only essential element, and that the rejuvenation of the drama can best be served by a return to the bare platform stage. Consequently, at the Théâtre de Vieux-Colombier he removed the proscenium arch to create an open platform, at the rear of which he erected an alcove surmounted by a balcony reached by steps. This basic structure, which could be altered somewhat by the addition of curtains and set pieces, was used for all productions. Forced by World War I to close his theatre, Copeau reopened it in 1919 and continued until 1924, when he retreated to the provinces to perfect his art and to train actors.

Copeau's single-minded devotion to excellence, in which scenic investiture is subordinated to acting, was to dominate theatrical production in France between the two world wars. With variations, his work was carried on by Louis Jouvet (1887–1951), Charles Dullin (1885–1949), Georges Pitoëff (1884–1939), and Gaston Baty (1882–1951), the most prestigious of French directors in the 1920s and 1930s. In 1927 they formed an association, usually called the Cartel des Quatre, to assist each other and to promote common ideals. While no member of the Cartel used as simplified a stage as Copeau's, all were opposed to realism and all but Baty accepted Copeau's view of the director's function.

Copeau's influence continues to be felt, perhaps more so in England and America than in France, because his actor-training techniques were so widely disseminated by his nephew, Michel Saint-Denis (1897–1971). After working with Copeau from 1919 to 1931, Saint-Denis headed the Campagnie des Quinze (which built on Copeau's practice), and in 1936 he was persuaded by a number of influential English directors to open an acting school in England. After that time, much of his career was devoted to developing actor-training programs in the English-speaking world. He founded the Old Vic's theatre school in London, worked with the Royal Shakespeare Company, and helped to plan the curriculum for the national theatre school of Canada and the Julliard School in New York.

The United States

The innovations in playwriting and production that had been introduced in the late nineteenth century were widely accepted in Europe before they were known in America, partially because until 1915 the conservative Theatrical Syndicate maintained control of theatrical production. Nevertheless, around 1910 the new spirit of the European theatre was beginning to be felt in the United States. The *new stagecraft,* as the European approach was called in America, was imported primarily

through the efforts of a few young men who, after traveling and studying in Europe, were determined to transform the American theatre. The most influential were Robert Edmond Jones (1887–1954) and Lee Simonson (1888–1967), major designers between 1915 and 1940.

The new stagecraft was embraced first by the little theatre movement, which blossomed between 1910 and 1920. Noncommercial organizations more interested in artistic excellence than financial success, the little theatres combined the European notion of an independent theatre with acceptance of the all-powerful director (perhaps because the actors were usually amateurs) and the new staging techniques. The most important of these early groups were: the Little Theatre of Chicago, founded in 1912 by Maurice Brown; the Toy Theatre of Boston, founded by Mrs. Lyman W. Gale in 1912; the Washington Square Players of New York, founded in 1915; the Provincetown Players, founded in Provincetown, Massachusetts, in 1915 but later moved to New York; and the Arts and Crafts Theatre of Detroit, founded in 1916.

A few of these groups were especially influential. At the Arts and Crafts Theatre, Sheldon Cheney in 1916 launched *Theatre Arts Monthly,* which soon became the forum for the new movement in America, popularizing its ideals and keeping Americans abreast of developments both at home and abroad. Until 1948 it was to be one of the major voices of the American theatre. The Provincetown Players made its impact by encouraging

Macbeth *as presented by Arthur Hopkins in 1921. Setting by Robert Edmond Jones. The entire production was done in an expressionistic style. Note the three masks suspended above the stage; the arches of the setting reportedly tilted ever more precariously as the action progressed. (From* Theatre Arts, *1921.)*

The Theatre from 1915 to 1940

305

new American playwrights. It was this group that first recognized the talent of Eugene O'Neill (1888–1953), generally considered to be America's foremost dramatist. Even after O'Neill achieved popular success with such plays as *Beyond the Horizon* (1920), *Anna Christie* (1921), and *The Hairy Ape* (1922), the Provincetown Players continued to present those works, such as *Welded* (1924) and *The Fountain* (1925), that were unacceptable to commercial producers. The Provincetown Players offered opportunities for experimentation rarely found elsewhere.

Following World War I the impact of the new stagecraft began to be felt in the professional theatre. In 1919 the Theatre Guild was founded with the goal of presenting the best American and European drama. Through its choice of plays and production techniques, it did more than any other company to demonstrate the effectiveness of the new stagecraft. The influence of the little theatres and the Theatre Guild was reinforced by Arthur Hopkins (1878–1950), a commercial producer who, in collaboration with Robert Edmond Jones, championed both the new drama and the new visual mode. The success of these pioneering organizations had by 1925 won acceptance for the new stagecraft (especially its visual conventions).

A new generation of playwrights also appeared after World War I. It included, in addition to O'Neill, Maxwell Anderson (1888–1959), Elmer Rice (1892–1967), Sidney Howard (1891–1939), Thornton Wilder (1897–1975), and Paul Green (1894–   ). All are related to their European counterparts in their dedication to a drama that was more than entertainment, although none was committed to any particular movement. Thus, their work ranged through many styles.

A scene from the original production of Awake and Sing *by Clifford Odets, with Morris Carnovsky, John Garfield (standing), Art Smith, Stella Adler, and Phoebe Brand in the cast. Setting, Boris Aronson. (Photo–Vandamm Collection, courtesy Library and Museum of the Performing Arts, Lincoln Center.)*

In the 1930s the most prestigious American organization was the Group Theatre, which grew out of a workshop at the Theatre Guild and developed into an independent company in 1931. A repertory company modeled on the Moscow Art Theatre, the Group Theatre attempted to apply the Sanislavsky method to acting and stage production. During the 1930s it produced some of the finest plays seen in New York, and was especially successful with such works of Clifford Odets (1906–1963) as *Waiting for Lefty* (1935), *Awake and Sing* (1935), and *Golden Boy* (1937). The Group Theatre also fostered the talents of a number of important directors (among them Harold Clurman and Elia Kazan) and actors (such as Lee J. Cobb, John Garfield, and Morris Carnovsky). Members of this troupe were to be the principal popularizers of the Stanislavsky system of acting in America; some former members such as Lee Strasberg (at the Actors Studio) and Stella Adler (at her own studio in New York) have continued to teach this method.

Russia

The Revolution of 1917 signaled a sharp break with the Russian past, but, since the new Communist leaders were for some time preoccupied with political, social, and economic problems, they did not seek to impose conformity on the theatre until the late 1920s. Thus, during the first ten years of the Soviet regime the arts enjoyed considerable freedom. Further-

Meyerhold's set during production.

more, many of the most enthusiastic supporters of the Revolution were futurists or members of other avant-garde movements who welcomed the new regime as an opportunity to break completely with the past and to create new artistic forms. Of this group, Vsevelod Meyerhold (1874–1940) became and remained the leader in the theatre until around 1930.

Meyerhold was one of the original members of the Moscow Art Theatre, but he soon left it out of dissatisfaction over its dedication to realism. Nevertheless, in 1905 Stanislavsky appointed him director of an experimental group seeking alternatives to the company's methods. But Meyerhold's subordination of actors to his own directorial concept led to friction and he soon left once more. Between 1905 and 1917, he worked with many groups exploring the limits of the theatre as an artistic medium. In many ways, his work paralleled trends in painting at the time, especially toward abstractionism.

After 1917, Meyerhold sought to develop methods that would serve the needs of a revolutionary society. The most important of his experiments were those with biomechanics and constructivism.

Biomechanics refers to a system of acting through which Meyerhold hoped to bring the performer into line with the needs of the new age by making him as efficient as a machine in carrying out his assignment. Basically what Meyerhold had in mind is a variation on the James-Lange theory: particular emotions may be elicited by particular patterns of muscular activity. Thus, the actor, to arouse within himself or the audience a desired emotional response, need only enact the appropriate kinetic pattern. Through such methods Meyerhold sought to replace Stanislavsky's emphasis on internal motivation with one on physical and emotional reflexes. To create a feeling of exuberant joy, Meyerhold thought it more efficient for the actor to plummet down a slide, swing on a trapeze, or turn a somersault than to restrict himself to behavior considered appropriate by realistic standards.

Design for one of Meyerhold's constructivist productions.

Constructivism was Meyerhold's attempt to arrive at a setting that would be a "machine for acting" without any superfluous details. The term was taken over from the visual arts, where since about 1912 it had been used to describe abstract sculpture composed of intersecting planes and masses. Thus, in both acting and setting Meyerhold was seeking forms appropriate to the new society. He was most persistent in this search between 1922 and 1925, after which he softened his approach until the late 1920s when his productions had become at least partially representational.

Meyerhold's directing is probably seen at its best in *The Inspector General* (1926), his adaptation of Gogol's play. He transferred the scene to a large city, reshaped the characters, and introduced several new ones. The costumes, scenery, and properties were based on nineteenth-century visual motifs, and most of the action was set to period music. Perhaps the most striking scene was that in which officials emerged simultaneously from each of the fifteen doors that surrounded the stage to offer the supposed Inspector a bribe.

Another influential but less radical post-Revolution director was Yevgeny Vakhtangov (1883–1922), who began as a faithful follower of Stanislavsky and then sought to blend Stanislavsky's and Meyerhold's approaches. From Stanislavsky he preserved the emphasis on concentration, the exploration of each character's biography, and the search for hidden meanings; with this he combined stylized movement and scenic elements not unlike those used by the expressionists. Vakhtangov called his approach "fantastic realism." Perhaps because he insisted that his actors find some justification for whatever they did on stage, his productions always appeared unified and coherent, even when they departed from traditional modes. Not only did he win a large following during his lifetime, his influence continues to be strong because so many of his coworkers and students became leading directors and passed his methods on to others.

Next to Meyerhold, the most experimental director of the 1920s was Alexander Tairov (1885–1950), who headed the Kamerny Theatre in Moscow from 1914 until his death. Tairov argued that there is no relationship between art and life, that the theatre is comparable to the sacred dances of an ancient temple. To him, the text was an excuse for creativity. Like Fuchs, he thought rhythm the most important element in the theatre and orchestrated his productions almost as if they were musical compositions; speech was a compromise between declamation and song; movement always tended toward dance. The overall effect was nearer to ritual than to the usual dramatic performance. Because of his emphasis upon rhythm, Tairov's settings were often composed primarily of steps and levels to enhance variety in movement and tempo. Although Tairov was to modify his approach somewhat after 1930, he remained the Russian director most concerned with a theatrical art independent of social or political ideologies.

After Stalin assumed full power in the late 1920s, theatrical workers began to encounter pressures to uphold the ideology of the Party and to use techniques easily comprehensible to the common man. Soon innovators such as Meyerhold and Tairov were being denounced as "formalists" who failed to understand the people's needs. In 1934, "socialist realism" was proclaimed the appropriate style for all writing. This meant that dramatists not only were expected to reflect the approved ideology but to include in their works a positive hero who points the way toward the total triumph of communism. Most subsequent plays are melodramas that denounce opponents of the Party and glorify its supporters.

The demand for realism also extended to staging. As the prestige of Meyerhold and Tairov declined, that of the Moscow Art Theatre rose. Following the Revolution, the Moscow Art Theatre at first seemed to hesitate about the appropriate path to take, but after 1925 it began to add

Soviet plays to its repertory and to stage them with great effectiveness according to realistic standards. Consequently, the government regarded the troupe with increasing favor, and by the late 1930s had declared its methods the standard by which all others were to be judged.

During the 1930s the Russian theatre was reduced to conformity and in the process lost the vitality that had been so evident throughout the preceding decade. It has yet to recover fully.

Brecht and Epic Theatre

During the 1920s still another movement—*epic theatre*—took shape in Germany. Prior to World War II, it was little appreciated, but after 1945 its influence steadily grew. Epic theatre is associated above all with Bertolt Brecht (1898–1956), who began his career in the theatre when the expressionists were at the peak of their popularity. Much of his early writing is indebted to that school, but beginning around 1925 he broke away and thereafter gradually formulated the theories that undergrid his dramatic writing.

Brecht called his work *epic* to distinguish it from the *dramatic* theatre against which he was in revolt. He stated that the old theatre has outlived its usefulness since it reduces the spectator to a role of complete passivity. In it, according to Brecht, events are presented as fixed and unchangeable, for even historical subjects are treated from a present-day point of view; this approach encourages the audience to believe that things have always been the same. Furthermore, realistic staging gives the action an air of stability which contributes to the idea that an entrenched position cannot be altered. The spectator, therefore, can only watch in a hypnotized and uncritical way; his senses are lulled, and he cannot participate "productively" in the theatrical event.

In the place of this old theatre, Brecht envisioned a new theatre in which the spectator would become a vital part. To bring about this change, Brecht sought to alter both drama and theatrical production. In describing his ideal theatre, Brecht used three key terms: *historification, alienation,* and *epic*.

Scene from Brecht's Mother Courage. *Directed by Gary Gaiser; designed by James French; lighting by Margaret Heymann; costumes by Sigrid Insull. (Courtesy Indiana University Theatre.)*

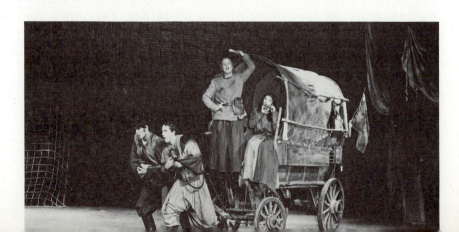

Unlike the realists, Brecht thought that the theatre should not treat contemporary subject matter in a lifelike manner. Rather, the theatre should "make strange" the actions it presents. One avenue to estrangement lies in *historification,* which ordinarily means using material drawn from other times or places. Contrary to old theatrical practices, which depict historical material in today's pattern, Brecht argued that the dramatist should emphasize "pastness"—the removal of events from the present. The playwright should make the spectator feel that, if he had been living under the conditions shown in the play, he would have taken some positive action. The audience should then go on to see that, since things have changed, it is possible to make desirable social reforms in the present.

Historification is part of the larger concept of *alienation.* (Although alienation is not a precise translation of Brecht's original term, *verfremdungseffekt,* it is the one that has been popularized in America. More accurately it means "to make strange.") In addition to historification, the playwright may use other means for making things strange. He may deliberately call the audience's attention to the make-believe nature of the work (rather than trying to convince the audience of the play's reality). Songs, narrative passages, filmed sequences, and other devices may be used for this purpose. The audience should never be allowed to confuse what it sees on the stage with reality. Rather, the play must always be thought of as a comment upon life—something to be watched and judged critically.

Although Brecht always insisted that the theatre should bring pleasure, he argued that the greatest pleasure comes from "productive participation," in which the spectator actively judges and applies what he sees on the stage to conditions outside the theatre. Some critics have interpreted Brecht's concept of alienation to mean that the audience should be in a continuous state of objective detachment. In actuality, Brecht manipulated esthetic distance to involve the spectator emotionally and then jar him out of his empathic response so that he may contemplate and judge what he has experienced.

Each element of production should contribute to alienation. Brecht did not envision, as most twentieth-century theorists have, a synthesis of all the arts in the theatre, but rather the independence of each. Music, for example, should make a comment upon the action rather than merely underscore the meaning of the words. For example, in *Mother Courage* the satirically bitter words of a song which tell of the gradual moral degradation of a character are set to a consciously lighthearted tune. The contrast between words and music achieves alienation, for it forces the spectator to consider the song's significance.

Likewise, scenery is not intended to create the illusion of place. It may suggest a locale, but it does not depict it in detail. Brecht advocated the use of projections, fragmentary set pieces, and similar devices for indicating the location of action, but in each case the elements should comment on the action as well.

As a further aid in alienation, Brecht wished to let the mechanics of the theatre remain visible. He suggested mounting the lighting instruments where they may be seen, changing the scenery in view of the audience, and placing the musicians onstage. Such devices prevent a production from lulling the audience into a feeling of security and timelessness, and engage the spectator's judgment in such a way as to arouse his social consciousness.

Brecht called his plays *epic* because he thought they resembled epic poems more than traditional drama. The epic poem, composed of alternating sections of dialogue and narration, presents a story from the viewpoint of a single storyteller. The epic also may freely change place and time; it narrates some scenes and shows others; it bridges passages of time with a single sentence or a brief passage; it may easily cover the sweep of a historical period. (It is easier to understand Brecht's point if such a work as *The Iliad* is compared with traditional dramatic works.)

Epic theatre seeks its ultimate effect outside the theatre. By stirring up thought and inciting the spectator to act for desirable social reforms, a play escapes becoming an opiate and assumes a vital and productive role in men's lives.

Many of the staging techniques used by the epic theatre were first employed by Erwin Piscator (1893–1966) in Berlin in the 1920s. The most famous of his productions, *The Good Soldier Schweik* (1927), is a bitter satire on the Germanic war machine. In it, the experiences of the common soldier, Schweik, are depicted through a swirl of events that occur in an enormous number of places and over a lengthy stretch of time. Piscator used treadmills, projections, scenic fragments, film, giant caricature drawings, and many other devices to adapt the action to the stage and to comment on it. Piscator did not intend to be objective in his stage presentations; he wished to comment on society and to provoke his audiences to think and act.

Among Brecht's many plays, perhaps the best are *Man Is Man, The Three-Penny Opera, The Caucasian Chalk Circle, Mother Courage, Galileo,* and *The Good Woman of Setzuan.* The last of these has been chosen for extended discussion here as an example of epic theatre.

The Good Woman of Setzuan

The Good Woman of Setzuan, written between 1938 and 1940 and first produced in 1943, is a parable that has been historified by placing it in China, although the time is more or less contemporary.

In this play Brecht is concerned with the possibility of goodness. Shen Te, the heroine, wants and tries to be good, but as she points out:

When we extend our hand to a beggar, he tears it off for us
When we help the lost, we are lost ourselves
And so
Since not to eat is to die
Who can long refuse to be bad?

Two factors have created this situation: society and human nature. It is difficult to know which of these Brecht thinks most responsible. Much of his nonfictional writing suggests that society is the culprit and that a different economic system (presumably some form of socialism) would remove many of the incentives for immoral behavior that exist under capitalism. In *The Good Woman of Setzuan* the capitalist class is represented by Shu Fu, Mrs. Mi Tzu, and Shui Ta, who exploit the others. The methods of this class are most graphically illustrated through Shui Ta, the disguise Shen Te assumes to protect herself from her relatives.

But this is not the whole picture, for the capitalists are little worse than the proletariat. Shen Te's relatives are liars, thieves, and parasites. While they may have been forced into such behavior by social conditions, their vindictiveness and cruelty (for example, the enjoyment they get from seeing the Carpenter deprived of pay for honest work) make them as callous as the others. Ultimately Brecht shows human nature as consistent regardless of social class—all are ready to tear off the hand that is extended in help.

The exceptions are to be seen in Shen Te and Wong, and even with

Scene from Brecht's The Good Woman of Setzuan, *as presented at the University of Texas. Directed by Francis Hodge; setting by John Rothgeb; costumes by Paul Reinhardt.*

them goodness is more a matter of desire than accomplishment. Although Shen Te wants to be good, she is eventually driven to disguise herself as Shui Ta. When Shen Te sins, however, it is out of love for others and not out of self-love.

So much evil set against so little good gives the play a sense of hopelessness, and makes it difficult to believe in the possibility of change outside the theatre (as Brecht would desire). Herein lies one of the basic contradictions in Brecht's work as a whole. Brecht felt deeply man's inhumanity to man and deplored the failure to live in love and harmony. He longed for a better existence; at the same time, he implies that such ideals are hopeless because of man's essential selfishness.

Brecht is not entirely pessimistic. He always suggests that humans are partially responsible for their own fate and are not wholly at the mercy of hereditary and environmental forces. He insists that if an audience can be made to watch critically, it can reach conclusions about contemporary society and can take steps to alter what it does not like. Thus, the pessimism of the plays is modified by Brecht's optimism about the possibilities of action outside the theatre. Nevertheless, a sense of ambiguity always remains.

Plot and Structure. The "epic" nature of *The Good Woman of Setzuan* is established by the prologue, in which narration and dialogue are freely mingled and in which time and place are considerably telescoped. The irony that permeates the whole work is also established by the disparity between Wong's assurances to the Gods that everyone is waiting to receive them and the fact that they must accept lodgings with a prostitute.

The prologue also establishes the basic situation: the Gods find the good person for whom they have been searching and enjoin her to remain good. At the same time, they refuse to be concerned about how such a difficult assignment is to be carried out—they "never meddle with economics." Herein lies the basic conflict, for economic factors are the very ones that stand in the way of goodness. Thus, the Gods' demand that humans be good and their refusal to be concerned with the determinants of morality are clearly at odds. By this means Brecht implies that the solution to human problems is not to be sought in divine injunctions.

The Good Woman of Setzuan alternates short and long scenes. The short scenes serve two main purposes: to break up and to comment on the action. Both contribute to Brecht's aim of forcing the audience to think by giving it clues about the significance of what it has seen and time in which to reflect upon it.

The long scenes are devoted to the conflict between good and evil as seen in the two aspects of the "good woman." Her true self is shown in the person of Shen Te, while her evil self is embodied in Shui Ta, the disguise she assumes whenever her goodness has brought her to the edge of destruction. At first the impersonation is for brief periods, but, as the play progresses, she must become Shui Ta for longer periods. Brecht uses this device to show the progressive deterioration of morality. The play ends in a stalemate, for the Gods leave Shen Te with the same message as in the prologue, "Be Good." She is still no nearer to knowing how this is to be accomplished, and they are still unconcerned over such practical matters.

The long scenes have been broken up by the insertion of songs and speeches delivered directly to the audience. The songs are ostensibly about subject matter different from that of the scenes they accompany; some are parables in themselves. Nevertheless, all comment, directly or indirectly, on the action.

Brecht makes no attempt to create the illusion of real happenings. For example, when Wong says that he will find a place for the Gods to spend the night, he suggests the attempt, although the various houses are not represented onstage. The action, thus, is outlined, but many of the details are omitted.

This approach allows Brecht to telescope events and to eliminate transitions. For example, in the prologue the Gods are taken into Shen Te's house and the lowering of stage lights designates the passing of night. This device is analogous to the narrative technique in which a writer bridges a transition with "The next morning—." This technique can be seen more clearly in the scene in which Shen Te meets Yang Sun and falls in love with him. There has been no preparation for this turn of events, and again it is much as if a storyteller had said, "One day when Shen Te was walking in the park she saw a young man trying to hang himself." The need to motivate her presence or to show the connection of this scene with those that preceded it is ignored.

Again, however, Brecht's structural techniques are explained in part by his belief that scenes should be clearly separated as part of the alienation process. They are further explained by his insistence that the basic social content of each scene should be capable of expression in one simple sentence (for example, scene three of *The Good Woman of Setzuan* might be expressed by "Shen Te falls in love with a young aviator"), and that all parts of a scene should be clearly related to this simple statement. Brecht is not concerned with inner psychological truth but concentrates upon what he calls "social gestures"—or the embodiment of attitudes in social behavior. The clear depiction of a "gesture," then, is the aim of each scene.

Although Brecht desires simplicity and clarity, his techniques have puzzled many, for they deviate from traditional dramatic conventions. The introduction of songs, the failure to make clear connections between scenes, and other devices designed to achieve alienation frequently conflict with traditional conceptions of effective dramatic structure. For these reasons, Brecht's hoped-for clarity has become only obscurity for some unsophisticated spectators.

Given some understanding of Brecht's aims, however, the same devices that some find distracting become effective sources of contrast and vigor. The alternation of long and short scenes, of narration and dialogue, of song and speech, of direct appeal and oblique reference—all of these serve to increase interest and to embody those social gestures with which Brecht is concerned.

Characters and Acting. Brecht considerably oversimplifies characters, for he is principally concerned with social relationships. He is not interested in total personalities or the inner lives of his characters. Instead of names, the majority of speakers in *The Good Woman of Setzuan* have been given social designations such as Gods, Wife, Grandfather, and Policeman. All represent social relationships more than they do individuals. Their desires are also stated in terms of social action: Shen Te wishes to treat all persons honorably, to make it possible for Yang Sun to become a pilot, to provide proper food for the children, and so on. In each characterization, social and economic traits are the most important ones.

These social factors are modified by Brecht's belief that humans are basically selfish. In the social situations, therefore, the actions are in large part determined by each character's attempt to better his own situation at the expense of others. Brecht has not been accused of distorting human psychology as much as he might since his view of humanity is for the most part in keeping with modern psychological theories and with determinism. The modern world has accepted the idea that everyone is fundamentally selfish and that even good deeds fulfill some need within the individual. Thus, Brecht's picture of humanity has not offended as it would have had his exaggeration been in the direction of showing the goodness of humankind. Nevertheless, Brecht's characterizations are based on only a few traits and are confined principally to social factors and a limited number of psychological attitudes.

Brecht, however, did not intend to portray well-rounded individuals. He set out to present an interpretation of social reality, and his characters are important only insofar as they forward that presentation. The action does not exist to display character, but character to demonstrate social action.

The only character who rises to the level of moral decision is Shen Te. The plot progresses in large part through the series of choices which she makes: to accept the Gods' injunction to be good; to become Shui Ta in order to preserve her well-being; to help Yang Sun; and so on. These choices are necessary to demonstrate one of Brecht's basic concerns: the moral dilemma of man under the existing economic conditions.

Brecht's ideas on acting are in keeping with his general approach to the theatre: the actor should not impersonate a character so much as present the behavior of a person in a specific situation. Brecht wishes actors to avoid identifying with the characters or trying "to live the part." He suggests that the actor should analyze the basic social qualities of his role and concentrate upon "presenting" these to the audience in a kind of demonstration that comments upon the action and the characters. The actor, thus, aids the alienation effect and arouses a critical response in the audience.

The actor performing in Brecht's plays should be familiar with Brecht's ideas on acting, although it is doubtful that they can always be carried out. The members of Brecht's own acting troupe have stated that they did not approach the roles in his plays differently from those in other plays, and that Brecht himself did not insist that they accept his ideas. Nevertheless, his intentions are important to an understanding of his overall approach to the theatre.

Visual and Aural Elements. Brecht once characterized his use of visual elements as naïve and added, "The opposite of a naïve approach is naturalism." He strives for a childlike simplicity, a make-believe quality: "The natural must be made to look surprising."

The sweep of events and the rapid changes of time and place would in themselves prevent the full-stage representation of all the locales indicated in any of Brecht's plays. But Brecht desires neither historical accuracy nor the accumulation of naturalistic details in his settings; he wants only those elements that aid in the alienation effect. Scenery and costumes, therefore, remain only outlines or suggestions. Fragmentary settings, projections, and captions are his favorite devices. Costumes may use some historically accurate elements, but other elements of the same costumes may be modern or merely expressive of social factors rather than of a historical period.

The Good Woman of Setzuan is set in ten different places. Each of these, however, can be indicated by a few scenic pieces. For example, scene 4 is set in a square on which three shops open. Each shop may be suggested by a single flat and these may be carried onstage by the actors in full view of the audience. As Brecht wrote in one of his poems:

> . . . let the spectator
> Be aware of busy preparations, made for him
> Cunningly; he sees a tinfoil moon
> Float down; or a tiled roof
> Being carried in; do not show him too much,
> But show him something!

While little scenery is needed, what is used should be designed with great care so that it makes a definite contribution to the play's effect. In Brecht's theatre it is not enough to copy reality; reality must be clarified by transforming it and by making it strange. The right kind of scenery allows the spectator to view reality critically and to understand it—something that would not be possible were it presented in its everyday and familiar guise. With every aspect of drama, then, Brecht seeks to transform the old theatre into a new one in which the spectator can participate rather than merely observe passively.

All of Brecht's major works were written before the end of World War

II. Living in exile throughout the Nazi regime, Brecht was little known until after 1945. Since that time, however, his plays and theories have assumed increasing importance and have been among the most pervasive influences on contemporary dramatic and theatrical techniques.

The Living Newspaper

Setting for a Living Newspaper, One Third of a Nation *(1938), at the Federal Theatre, New York. Setting by Howard Bay. (From* Theatre Arts, *1938.)*

One of the forms most obviously related to Brecht's Epic Theatre is the *Living Newspaper* which grew out of the Federal Theatre project in America. During the economic depression of the 1930s, the United States government authorized a Federal Theatre as part of its Works Progress

Administration programs, designed to relieve unemployment. In operation between 1935 and 1939, the Federal Theatre had units in various parts of the country but was most active in New York, where unemployment in the theatre was most serious. While the New York branch of the Federal Theatre produced many kinds of plays, it is best remembered for its Living Newspaper productions. The Living Newspaper, as the title indicates, aimed at achieving in the theatre something similar to the printed newspaper, although in actuality it was more closely related to the documentary film. Each play treated a single problem. The most famous examples are *One Third of a Nation* (on slum housing), *Triple-A Plowed Under* (on the farm program), and *Power* (on public utilities and flood control). The plays alternate scenes illustrating social conditions with narrative sequences; statistical tables, still photographs, and motion pictures were projected on screens; offstage voices, music, and sound effects were used freely. The plays were written by many authors in collaboration and took a definite point of view (in favor of social reform and corrective legislation). This political and social bias eventually led to the discontinuance of the Federal Theatre, for in 1939 Congress refused to appropriate funds to support it. It was the United States government's first attempt at subsidizing the theatre.

The Living Newspaper used many of the same devices and upheld points of view similar to those advocated by Brecht and Piscator. But, this "epic" approach did not attract many imitators in the United States until the 1960s, and most plays dealing with social problems continued to be cast in the form popularized by Ibsen. The theatricality of epic staging, nevertheless, served, in conjunction with other movements, to turn staging away from illusionism.

By 1940 realism had been greatly weakened by the many artistic movements that had challenged it during the preceding quarter century. But still more than another decade would have to pass before its grip on theatrical production would be loosened.

12
Postwar Theatre and Drama

Theatre practice in the years following World War II can best be described as extremely diversified. It borrowed, combined, and modified elements from various modern movements, adapted staging devices from many earlier periods, and explored new techniques both in writing and staging. The diversity can best be illustrated by examining some of the most representative types of expression: modified realism, the musical, and absurdism.

Modified Realism

Until the 1950s realism continued to be the most common theatrical style, although by the late 1940s it had been modified considerably. Various modern movements had by that time conditioned audiences to accept simplification, suggestion, and distortion as basic techniques in art. In the theatre the result was greater emphasis on theatricality, less dependence on illusionism, and more willingness to recognize that art is different from reality. Stage settings, for example, came to rely on suggestion instead of detailed representation of period and place. Although locales were still indicated pictorially, many details were eliminated. Similarly, play structure became freer and less dependent on the techniques of the "well-made" play than it had been in the late nineteenth and early twentieth centuries. There also was a trend toward a larger number of scenes and away from the division into acts. Experimentation with dramatic techniques became common.

These modifications came about in part because of changes in man's view of himself and his world. In the late nineteenth century the discoveries of science were hailed as liberators from irrational explanations of social phenomena. But such advances as control over atomic energy (with all its potentialities for benefit and misuse) reemphasized the need for moral and spiritual values capable of guiding such power. With the realization that science cannot provide moral answers came a lessening of faith in the scientific method as the only source of truth. Furthermore, psychology had shown increasingly that many of man's most powerful motivations are subconscious and cannot be deduced from purely external signs. Reality, then, was no longer thought to be so simple as in the late nineteenth century, and the means for representing it in the theatre consequently became much more flexible. As realism gradually absorbed irrational elements from other movements, it also borrowed dramatic and theatrical techniques from them. Thus, postwar realism represented in part a fusion of elements made familiar and acceptable by earlier approaches.

Postwar American Dramatists

The fusion of elements drawn from many sources can most clearly be seen in the works of Tennessee Williams (1911–   ), who came to prominence in 1945 with *The Glass Menagerie* and who has contributed regu-

Tennessee Williams' Summer and Smoke. *Directed by David Schaal; scenery by Arnold Gillette.*

larly to the theatre since that time with such plays as *A Streetcar Named Desire, Summer and Smoke, The Rose Tattoo, Suddenly Last Summer, The Night of the Iguana, Slapstick Tragedy, Outcry,* and *This is [An Entertainment]*.

Williams uses many nonrealistic devices. Symbolism, of the type employed by Ibsen and Chekhov, is found in almost every play, and the titles of his works usually indicate some deeper symbolic meaning. Normally, Williams also demands fragmentary settings, although each fragment is usually realistic. Frequently his sets combine interiors and exteriors to allow fluidity without scene change. A good example is found in *Summer and Smoke,* which shows two interiors and a park simultaneously.

Time is also fluid in many of Williams' plays. *The Glass Menagerie* is especially noteworthy for its use of memory as the motivation for calling up scenes from the past. In its fluidity the play resembles some works by Strindberg.

But while Williams' plays may be extremely theatrical, the characters are usually lifelike. Williams is concerned principally with inner psychological realities that can best be projected through the manipulation (rather than the mere recording) of external elements. Complex Freudian motivations underlie most of the plays.

The conflicts in Williams' plays are frequently representative of larger human issues; spiritual and material drives are almost always at odds and the resolution of a dramatic action depends upon how well the characters can reconcile the demands of these two sides of human nature. Some of Williams' plays tend toward the abstract and allegorical, but in others the conflict is embodied in intensely powerful and lifelike portraits.

William Inge's Picnic *with the original (1953) cast: Arthur O'Connell, Eileen Heckart, Ralph Meeker, Janice Rule, Ruth McDevitt, Betty Lou Holland. Director, Joshua Logan. Setting Jo Mielziner. Produced by the Theatre Guild and Joshua Logan. (Photo – Alfredo Valente, courtesy Library and Museum of the Performing Arts, Lincoln Center.)*

Another aspect of Williams' realism is seen in his juxtaposition of comic and serious elements. Like Chekhov, Williams is able to depict multiple character traits and differing moods simultaneously. Amanda in *The Glass Menagerie,* for example, is admirable and pathetic, but she also is ridiculous; consequently the scenes in which she appears shift mood rapidly. Williams' portrayal of human limitations in conjunction with high aspirations produce both pathos and humor. His plays, therefore, are at once compassionate and bitter.

These characteristics show both the continuing power of realism and its modification by other approaches. In many ways, Williams' plays sum up twentieth-century movements prior to the 1950s.

The works of William Inge (1913–1973), such as *Picnic, Bus Stop, Come Back, Little Sheba,* and *The Dark at the Top of the Stairs,* show many of the same characteristics as those of Williams, although they are more limited in range and depth. Inge is concerned with internal anxieties—with facing "the dark at the top of the stairs." The resolutions of his plays are more optimistic than Williams', for Inge seems to indicate that to achieve happiness one need only face up to psychological realities. Since he is much less interested in the wider implications of psychological conflicts or with novel theatrical devices, Inge remains more clearly in the mainstream of realism than Williams.

The continuation of the Ibsenian tradition was best represented in the postwar period by Arthur Miller (1915–   ), who came to prominence with *All My Sons* (1947), and went on to write such plays as *The Crucible, A View from the Bridge, After the Fall, Incident at Vichy, The Price,* and *The Creation of the World and Other Business.* But it is *Death of a Salesman* (1949) that has insured Miller's position, for many consider it the finest American play of the postwar era. It will be examined here in detail as an example of modern American drama and of modified realism.

Death of a Salesman

Death of a Salesman dramatizes a primary conflict in the American consciousness, which tends to measure success in material terms even as it upholds love as a major value; as a result, it often mingles these goals so that approval is withheld from those who have not succeeded materially. Miller has embodied this conflict in Willy Loman's obsessive desire to succeed and his confusion of success with worthiness to be loved.

Willy wants to be recognized, liked, and admired and it is his perplexity over the gulf between his accomplishment and his ideal that precipitates the play's action. Success as Willy conceives it, however, is largely material, for to be well liked and to be materially successful are inextricably linked in his mind. Because to Willy material success seems so necessary, he believes that his sons cannot love him if he is not successful. Love becomes a commodity to be bought rather than a gift freely given. Willy has also conditioned his sons to believe that they do not deserve respect unless they are successful on his terms. It is only when Willy understands that Biff loves him, even though both are failures, that he achieves a degree of insight. It is too late to change the course of events, but he goes to his death more nearly at peace than he is at any time in the play.

The conflicts, then, arise from tensions between the passion for success and the need to be loved and understood. Miller has used two characters to represent the poles between which Willy is pulled. Uncle Ben, Willy's brother, epitomizes material success, while Linda, Willy's wife, gives love without question or conditions. Willy's dilemma grows out of his unconscious assumption that success is necessary before love is possible.

Many have seen in *Death of a Salesman* a condemnation of American business practices. Miller has stated that he did not have this aim in mind, and the play largely bears him out. Charley, a businessman, is one of the most admirable characters in the play and the one who has most nearly achieved success in both private and public life. Charley has never worried about being "a success," however, while Willy has thought of little else. Willy has condoned petty stealing, lying, and cheating so long as they lead toward his goals. His failure, therefore, does not result from being a salesman, but from the means he has used to get ahead. His failure in business is important only because it reflects his failure as a father, husband, and human being.

Plot and Structure. Miller has said that he originally conceived the action of *Death of a Salesman* within Willy's mind and that Willy's psychological state dictated the structure of the play. This concept is only partially evident in the script, however, since Willy does not participate in several scenes and could know nothing of them. But such scenes take place in the present; those scenes that go backward in time invariably grow out of Willy's stream of consciousness.

The present action occurs during a twenty-four-hour period (with the exception of the funeral), but the scenes from the past range over twenty years. Past and present flow together as Willy tries to find the answers to his questions: Why have I failed? Where did I go wrong? What is the secret of success?

It is interesting to compare Miller's play with works from earlier periods. Both *Death of a Salesman* and *Oedipus the King* involve a search into the past to find the roots of present evils. The scenes in *Oedipus the King*, however, are all drawn from the present and the past is revealed only through narration; *Death of a Salesman*, on the other hand, uses Willy's anxieties to transport the audience backward in time to witness scenes. As in *Faust*, there is a search for the meaning of life, but whereas Faust goes forward in time to find fulfillment, Willy goes backward in time to seek the causes of his failure. *Death of a Salesman* also recalls medieval drama in its use of a simultaneous setting and in the complete fluidity of time.

Jo Mielziner's sketched idea of the salesman, Willy Loman, and of the set for Arthur Miller's Death of a Salesman. *(Courtesy of Mr. Mielziner.)*

The only unusual structural feature of *Death of a Salesman* is the *flash-back*, for otherwise it is organized conventionally in terms of exposition, preparation, complications, climax, obligatory scene, and resolution. Each flashback is carefully introduced by wandering talk, off-stage voices, sound effects, music, or some similar cue. Most productions of the play have also used changes in lighting to lead the audience from the present to the past. The flashbacks are carefully engineered so that each reveals only a small part of the past. The outline gradually emerges but is incomplete until the climactic moment.

In *Death of a Salesman* psychological realism has replaced external realism and a greater freedom in dramatic structure has resulted. Although many of the scenes materialize out of Willy's mind and are treated only in fragmentary form, Miller's aim remains much the same as Ibsen's—to depict with fidelity a contemporary situation.

Characters and Acting. The major issues of the play are worked out between Biff and Willy. While Biff serves as a strong secondary interest, by far the most important character in *Death of a Salesman* is Willy Loman. Willy, now sixty-three years old, is on the verge of a physical and psychological breakdown. All his life, he has been trying to "sell" himself;

he has lied both to himself and to others out of a desire to believe that he is a success. Recent developments, however, have forced him to recognize that in actuality he is a failure. Yet he cannot see where he has taken the wrong path.

Willy is tired, puzzled, touchy, quick to anger, ready to hope; he cajoles his sons, offers advice when it is unwanted; he is always looking for the secret that will "open doors." Above all, he is dominated by the ideal of success, which he has tried to instill in his sons as well.

Uncle Ben personifies success, and in many ways is merely an extension of Willy. He represents the mystery of success, for he has gone into the jungle and come out rich; he has been to faraway and dangerous places and thus he gives a romantic aura to success. Ben also implies that success is bound up with the "law of the jungle," with shady deals and quick-wit-tedness.

Willy, however, wants to triumph on his own terms—as a salesman who is liked by everybody. Therefore, he can never completely accept Ben's advice just as he can never give up Ben's ideal. This division, at the root of his character, is seen even in Willy's death, a final attempt to achieve material gain and the gratitude of his family simultaneously. He is both a pathetic and powerful figure.

Biff is thirty-four years old but still adolescent in his attitudes. He is irresponsible, a wanderer, and incapable of happiness because of the sense of guilt aroused in him by Willy. From Willy he learned early that the way of success is to be found in lying, stealing, and powerful acquaint-ances. But the lure of success has been short-circuited in Biff by his disil-lusionment with Willy, dating from the discovery of his father's unfaith-fulness to his mother. Consequently, Biff rebels against success, flouts authority, and enjoys hurting his father.

Biff has his admirable side, nevertheless, for he tries to face the truth, and he has a sense of moral responsibility which his brother Happy is totally lacking. It is Biff who finally makes his father see the truth as they both come to understand that love is a gift freely bestowed rather than a bonus earned through material success. Miller gives no indication of what the future holds for Biff, but it will no doubt be more peaceful than the past.

Linda understands from the beginning what Willy and Biff learn during the play: love has no conditions. She knows Willy's shortcomings, but she loves him, accepts him, and fights fiercely for him, even against her own sons. Her sense of decency and rightness makes her put Willy above everyone, for to her it is not a question of whether Willy has earned love and respect—his right to them is unquestioned. Because she loves so unconditionally, Linda cannot understand why Willy commits suicide or why the boys have turned out as they have. Success holds no magic for Linda. She fears Ben and his lures. It is only because of Biff that Willy eventually begins to see the appeal of Linda's view.

Happy has inherited the worst of Willy's traits without the saving possibility of love. He is entirely selfish and unfeeling; lying and cheating are integral parts of his nature. He is a materialist and sensualist beyond redemption, but devoid of Ben's vision and strength.

Charley and Bernard have succeeded where Willy and Biff have failed; thus, their principal function in the play is to serve as contrasts. Charley maintains that he has succeeded because he has never been passionately dedicated to anything. Yet the play shows that Charley is dedicated to being morally upright, as opposed to being a success in Willy's terms. Although unaware of his dedication, Charley's unconscious commitment to *human* above *material* factors is the key to his happiness, just as the reverse is the key to Willy's failure.

Many have seen in Howard an indictment of the "businessman's morality." Miller has denied this and has said that Howard is a man of common sense and that he acts as he must. More importantly for the play, however, Howard spurs Willy on in his search for an answer. In real-life terms it might have been more humane for Howard to find a place for Willy in the home office, but in terms of dramatic action his decision is necessary to make Willy face his dilemma squarely.

In constructing his characters, Miller has concentrated upon sociological and psychological attitudes; other details have been cut away. Miller's success in creating convincing figures is indicated by the general tendency of audiences to see in the play a clear reflection of modern society.

Spectacle and Sound. Miller's ideas about staging *Death of a Salesman* are clearly indicated in the script, (although many of these ideas seem to have been contributed by Jo Mielziner, who designed the original production). The continuous presence of the house helps to establish the convention that the flashbacks are fragments of the past and to make clear the simultaneity of the past and the present in Willy's mind.

Miller has stated that the motion picture version of *Death of a Salesman* was not successful in large part because of the overly realistic depiction of the settings used for the flashback scenes. He believes that in this way the emphasis was shifted from the psychological conflict in Willy's mind to the physical background. The fragmentary and schematic setting specified by Miller eliminates many illusionistic details. It is entirely in keeping with the dramatic techniques used in the play.

Sound has also been used effectively. Music helps to set the mood and to mark transitions to flashback scenes. A special musical motif is played each time Ben appears; honky-tonk music accompanies Willy's scenes with the Other Woman; music helps to set the locale of the restaurant scene. And the method by which Willy commits suicide is made clear only through the offstage sound of a car driving away.

Although audiences have accepted as realistic the fragmentary setting and novel staging conventions and have never been puzzled by them, the realism of *Death of a Salesman* has been modified by cutting away the surface so that the inner reality may be seen more clearly. Miller's methods are representative of the way in which realism came to be practiced in the postwar theatre.

Postwar Production Style

Largely because of Miller and Williams, American drama seemed especially vital in the years following World War II. Their plays were also instrumental in establishing the major production style of the time, since the approach that dominated the American theatre from the 1940s until about 1960 was popularized by Elia Kazan (1909–   ) and Jo Mielziner (1901–1976) with productions of such plays as *A Streetcar Named Desire* (1947) and *Death of a Salesman* (1949). *A Streetcar Named Desire* also popularized a new style of acting with Marlon Brando's (1924–   ) characterization of the inarticulate, uneducated, and assertive Stanley Kowalski. The novelty of serious acting based upon substandard speech, untidy dress, and boorish behavior captured the public imagination and soon became associated with the Actors Studio, at which Brando had worked. The Actors Studio was founded in 1947 by Robert Lewis, Elia Kazan, and Cheryl Crawford, although the dominant figure in its operation was to be its artistic director, Lee Strasberg. Its founders conceived of it as an opportunity for selected actors to work and develop according to the Stanislavsky system. In the popular mind, however, it appeared to be a place

The final act of Williams' A Streetcar Named Desire. *This production, directed by Elia Kazan, designed by Jo Mielziner, and featuring Marlon Brando, did much to establish the dominant postwar style of the American theatre. (Courtesy Graphic House, Inc.)*

where actors were encouraged to explore their psyches without regard for the skills needed to project a characterization. This image was mistaken, although major emphasis in training was placed on discovering the "inner truth" of characters rather than on other technical skills. The Kazan–Mielziner–Brando style (earthy realism in acting and directing combined with simplified backgrounds) was not seriously challenged in America until the 1960s, when the turn away from psychological preoccupations made it seem too limited.

The Musical Play

During and after World War II, the musical play also steadily increased its following until it became (and perhaps remains) the most popular of all theatrical entertainments. The postwar musical was descended from many minor theatrical forms of the nineteenth century, most notably extravaganza, variety, burlesque, and vaudeville.

The *extravaganza* depended upon music, dance, and magical scenic transformations for its appeal; its subject matter was most frequently drawn from myths or fairy tales. It was a favorite form with nineteenth-century audiences. The *variety show,* as the name suggests, was composed of short acts of various types, but it emphasized singing, dancing, and comic routines. Although no attempt was made to link the parts through a connected story, the various kinds of entertainment were similar to those of later musical plays.

Burlesque has had a long and complex history. It was originally a term used for a parody of some well-known play, literary work, or social custom —for example, Buckingham's *The Rehearsal* (1671) and Sheridan's *The Critic* (1779) parodied the drama and theatrical conventions of their times. In the nineteenth century burlesque was converted into a travesty (or a farcical retelling) of well-known plays, theatrical conventions, or contemporary affairs. It was not until around 1870, however, that modern burlesque emerged. Taking its inspiration from an extravaganza, *The Black Crook* (1866), which became notorious because of its scantily clad dancers, burlesque had soon become a collection of monologues, comedy sketches, songs, and dances featuring a female chorus. The emphasis upon beautiful women and jokes with sexual implications rapidly made it an entertainment primarily for male audiences, but not until about 1929 did the strip tease become its main feature. Since that time it has led a precarious existence on the fringes of legality. Nevertheless, it is one of the forerunners of the musical because of its use of a chorus, comic acts, music, and dance.

Like burlesque, *vaudeville* has had a long and varied history. Originally vaudeville meant a satirical song; later it designated a play that contained songs set to well-known tunes. In the nineteenth century, *comédie-en-vaudeville* indicated a short comic play interspersed with incidental

The Grand Hall in the Palace of Haroun Al-Rashid, in the burlesque extravaganza The Magic Horn, *presented at the Lyceum Theatre in London in the 1840s. (Culver Pictures.)*

songs. Vaudeville in the modern sense developed in the late nineteenth century when Tony Pastor (1837–1908) and others altered the newly popular *Black Crook* form of burlesque into entertainment suitable to mixed audiences. Beginning around 1880, Pastor was successful in turning the emphasis away from sex and the off-color joke to a family entertainment with many characteristics of the variety show. The transition had been made successfully by the 1890s, and for many decades it remained the most popular form of entertainment. (In England, vaudeville was called "music hall.") The decline of vaudeville in the 1930s is usually attributed to the rise of the sound motion picture which could furnish entertainment at lower admission prices. Vaudeville and burlesque were training grounds for numerous great comedians of the twentieth century, among them Jack Benny, Jimmy Durante, George Burns, and Bert Lahr.

In the nineteenth century it was also usual to introduce songs and dances into plays, especially melodramas. Furthermore, singing and dancing were used as *entr'actes* in almost every theatre until the late nineteenth century, when the movement toward greater realism and the one-play bill gradually eliminated incidental entertainment in legitimate theatres. Perhaps because of this trend many elements from older forms were combined to create musical comedy around 1890.

The origin of musical comedy is usually traced to the work of George Edwardes at the Gaiety Theatre in London. In the 1890s, his productions, in which sketchy plots provided excuses for songs, dances, and chorus-ensemble numbers, proved so popular that a number of imitations soon appeared. Most of these early musical comedies were set in mythical places where barons and counts abounded. The stories, having little to do with everyday life, emphasized the romantic and exotic appeals of faraway places and unusual happenings.

Around World War I the vogue for ballroom dancing and ragtime music turned attention to more familiar characters and surroundings. The plots remained unimportant, however, and served principally as excuses for spectacular settings, songs, dances, and beautiful chorus girls. In the late 1920s another important change occurred when more concern began to be paid to plot and psychological motivations. The new stature of the musical was recognized when a Pulitzer Prize was awarded *Of Thee I Sing* in 1931. The new direction can also be seen in *Pal Joey* (1940) and *Lady in the Dark* (1941), psychological studies of characters. The new trend was completed in the works of Oscar Hammerstein II (1895–1960) and Richard Rodgers (1902–), especially with *Oklahoma!*, *Carousel*, and *South Pacific*, which fully integrated all the elements of production. Innumerable fine musicals were written after World War II. They include *Guys and Dolls, The Pajama Game, Damn Yankees, Candide, West Side Story, The Music Man, How to Succeed in Business Without Really Trying*, and *Mame*. One of the most successful writing teams was Alan Jay Lerner (1918–) and Frederick Loewe (1904–), with *Paint Your Wagon, My Fair Lady*, and *Camelot. My Fair Lady*, one

The original production of Rodgers and Hammerstein's Oklahoma! *in 1943. Setting Lemuel Ayers; costumes, Miles White; choreography, Agnes de Mille. (Photo – Vandamm Collection, courtesy Library and Museum of the Performing Arts, Lincoln Center.)*

Postwar Theatre and Drama

331

of the most popular musicals of the period, will be examined here as an example of the modern musical play. Since it is based on a well-known comedy, it also provides an opportunity to compare the script with its original source and to consider how an existing work is adapted to the demands of the musical stage.

My Fair Lady

My Fair Lady (1956) is adapted from George Bernard Shaw's *Pygmalion* (1912), "A Romance in Five Acts," which retells in modern terms the legend of Pygmalion, a sculptor, who falls in love with Galatea, one of his statues. After praying to the goddess of love to bring the statue to life, his wish is granted and he marries Galatea.

Shaw used this legend only as a point of departure, for his principal interest lay in showing that differences in dialect undergird the class structure of England. In a preface, he argued that if everyone were taught to speak English properly the mainstay of the class system would be destroyed. To make his point in the play, he showed how a flower girl can be passed off as a duchess by changing her speech. Other factors (how she dresses and walks, her topics of conversation) also change, but Shaw believed that these alterations would be useless unless her speech patterns were also changed.

Although Shaw's message may be pertinent, it has contributed little to the play's popularity. Most audience have seen in it only the romance that the title indicates—a Cinderella story. To *Pygmalion* Shaw eventually added a postscript in which he denied that Higgins marries Liza (Eliza in *My Fair Lady*). In spite of this denial, however, most audiences have interpreted the play more sentimentally, and Shaw's association of it with the Pygmalion legend invites such a view. A primary difference between *Pygmalion* and *My Fair Lady* is the more explicit love story of the musical. Nevertheless, the ending of *My Fair Lady* seems as much in keeping with the overall tone of the play as Shaw's postscript does.

Plot and Structure. Although *My Fair Lady* follows Shaw's play closely in basic outline, it makes many structural changes. *Pygmalion* is written in five acts, while *My Fair Lady* divides eighteen scenes into two acts. The musical breaks the acts into short scenes, dramatizes events only talked about in the play, and condenses Shaw's speeches to allow time for songs and dances.

The musical is much closer to the motion picture version than to the original play. For example, while the stage play does not show any of Eliza's voice lessons, both the movie and the musical use a series of short scenes to dramatize her training; likewise, unlike the play, both show the ball at which Eliza triumphs.

Well over half of the eighteen scenes of the musical have no direct counterpart in Shaw's play, although almost all are based on material in

the play. Many of the additions create variety and spectacle. For example, the slums from which Eliza comes are shown in the musical and offer opportunities for choral numbers. Some additions emphasize the love story: a new final scene has been added, and the role of Freddy, who falls in love with Eliza, is enlarged to show Eliza's desirability and to create a threat to Higgins.

Some scenes are also added to create suspense. For example, the break between the two acts follows a scene not shown in Shaw's play. At the ball, Karpathy, an expert on speech, repeatedly questions Eliza's identity and the authenticity of her title. He vows to find out the truth and as the curtain falls he is dancing with her. Thus, the act ends on a note of suspense that contrasts markedly with the exultation and triumph of the opening scene of Act II.

The division of *My Fair Lady* into two acts also marks a change in the plot. Act I is concerned with the decision to pass off a flower girl as a duchess. This purpose has been accomplished when Act II begins. The last half of the musical shows Eliza's refusal to be used and then abandoned.

Many departures from the original play have been dictated by conventions of the musical. In its original form the play requires almost as much playing time as the musical does. Changes had to be made, therefore, to allow the addition of music, song, and dance. Since when *My Fair Lady* was written a chorus was a standard feature of musicals, occasions for its use had to be created. In *Pygmalion* only Act I (outside the Covent Garden Theatre) readily accommodates a chorus. In *My Fair Lady,* slum and ballroom scenes are added. Furthermore, a racetrack is substituted for a drawing room. In Act III of Shaw's play Higgins takes Eliza to his mother's home for tea, at which only seven persons are present. In the musical the same purpose (to allow Eliza a trial appearance in the fashionable world) is served, and most of Shaw's dialogue preserved, by changing the setting to a racetrack to allow more scope for spectacle and the chorus. This change led to one of the most admired sequences in *My Fair Lady,* the Ascot Gavotte.

Although the differences between *Pygmalion* and *My Fair Lady* are numerous, the musical maintains the essence of Shaw's play while transforming it to meet the demands of the musical stage.

Characters and Acting. The writers of a musical face a dilemma, since excellence in both acting and singing are seldom found in one person. They are frequently forced, therefore, to subordinate one demand to another. In *My Fair Lady* the decision in most cases was made in favor of the actor. Only four of the major characters (Higgins, Eliza, Doolittle, and Freddy) are required to sing alone and only two of these (Eliza and Freddy) need to be trained singers.

The songs written for Higgins and Doolittle lie within so limited a range that almost anyone can sing them. On the other hand, those written for Eliza and Freddy demand considerable vocal ability. Since Freddy's acting is of secondary importance, only the role of Eliza demands outstanding ability in both acting and singing.

In terms of the action, *My Fair Lady* has only five principal roles: Higgins, Eliza, Pickering, Doolittle, and Freddy. Of these, Higgins and Eliza are of primary importance, Pickering, Doolittle, and Freddy of secondary importance.

Higgins has been made more polished and urbane in the musical than he is in Shaw's play, where he was inclined to be unfashionable in dress and unconventional in behavior. The Higgins of the musical is still an individualist, but the rough qualities are gone. Nevertheless, he is still self-confident, selfish, and unfeeling where others are concerned. Throughout the musical he is passionately devoted to his work and blind to the needs of others. Only at the end is Eliza able to make him recognize the power of love. His last line indicates, however, that he will not change very much, for instead of rising to embrace her he merely says, "Eliza? where the devil are my slippers?"

The greatest range in acting ability is required of Eliza. She must be able to give a convincing portrayal of a cockney flower girl and gradually transforms herself until the audience is willing to believe that she might pass as a duchess. Her emotions are varied: outrage, defiance, frustration, dejection, longing, triumph, love, and so on. Eliza's principal motivation is the desire to be loved and respected. This drives her in the beginning to accept Higgins' offer to transform her, and later to leave Higgins because he has merely used her for his own purposes instead of considering her feelings as a human being. Ultimately it is her personal integrity that forces Higgins to see himself more clearly and to recognize his need for Eliza. When he comes to respect and love her, both have reached a new basis for future action.

Although he is onstage during a large part of *My Fair Lady*, Pickering serves principally as a foil for Higgins. It is he who bets Higgins that he cannot pass Eliza off as a duchess; it is he who treats Eliza as a lady and points up Higgins' indifference to her as a human being. Pickering's principal characteristic is his gentlemanly behavior at all times. While he aids in advancing the plot, the events have no effect upon him personally, and he plays little part in the last act.

Doolittle is almost the opposite of Pickering. He is a wastrel, a near-drunkard, and an avoider of responsibility. He represents lower-class morality and attitudes, but eventually falls victim to respectability. His complete lack of conventionality and his frankness have made the character a favorite with audiences.

Freddy serves as another contrast to Higgins, for he sees Eliza almost completely from a sentimental point of view. He offers Eliza love and respect in large part because she has the strength he lacks. Higgins on the other hand has the strength that Eliza wants in a man, but is lacking in the love and consideration that Freddy offers. It is only when Higgins can make some compromise that the possibility of happiness for Eliza materializes.

The other characters have little effect on the outcome of the play and serve principally to supply the background of the action. Most are played by members of the singing or dancing choruses. Thus, while *My Fair Lady* has great variety and dramatic strength, it requires only a few outstanding actors. The lesser members of the cast are obviously still of importance, but need not be performers of the first rank.

The Ascot Gavotte from the racetrack scene of My Fair Lady. *The original production. (Photo by Friedman-Abeles, Inc.)*

Language and Music. Shaw has long been recognized as a master of the English language. The speeches in his plays are sharply outlined, clear, and graceful. Much of the dialogue in *My Fair Lady* is taken directly from *Pygmalion*; the rest has been written with Shaw's style in mind and successfully blended with the original.

Shaw was not afraid to make his characters express themselves clearly and at length. He believed that good speech is an essential part of the theatre, and had little patience with playwrights who make their characters inarticulate mumblers. Shaw's relish for the English language is carried over into *My Fair Lady*. Higgins, especially, is a sophisticated and urbane master of the well-turned phrase.

Nevertheless, much of Shaw's dialogue has been eliminated so that songs and dances may be included. The songs, therefore, must supply much that has been left out. For example, the first three solos (Higgins' "Why Can't the English Learn to Speak?"; Eliza's "Wouldn't It Be Loverly"; and Doolittle's "With a Little Bit of Luck") establish the basic traits of the characters who sing them.

Much time is saved in the musical by capitalizing on the audience's ready acceptance of forthright statements of feelings and intentions in song, for in a more realistic kind of drama the revelation of motivations must be carefully prepared for. Thus, the song is comparable to the soliloquy or aside in its ability to convey a great deal of information in a brief amount of time. When good use is made of songs, then, the time they take away from the spoken episodes is more than made up.

Music also makes the condensation of time more acceptable. For example, the lesson scenes in *My Fair Lady* are run together, with the entire sequence building to the song of triumph, "The Rain in Spain," based upon a phrase that has formed the motif of the lessons. Time may also be saved by the effective use of the reprise (the repetition of a song or musical phrase). Such repetitions associate events separated in time and establish connections without the need for lengthy or explicit statement.

Music also establishes moods and builds expectations. Even before the curtain opens the overture has given some idea of the general mood and the melodic qualities of the work to follow. Music also helps to establish the tone of individual scenes and to create audience expectation.

Music further aids in achieving variety. *My Fair Lady* contains musical numbers of widely contrasting types: songs of delight such as "The Rain in Spain" and "You Did It"; love songs such as "On the Street Where You Live," "I Could Have Danced All Night," and "I've Grown Accustomed to Her Face"; songs of rage and defiance such as "Just You Wait," "Show Me," and "Without You"; songs of boisterous enjoyment of life such as "With a Little Bit of Luck," and "Get Me to the Church on Time"; of longing such as "Wouldn't It Be Loverly"; descriptive musical numbers such as the "Ascot Gavotte," and the "Embassy Waltz."

Although effective, the music in *My Fair Lady* is relatively small in amount, for while many musicals include over thirty numbers, *My Fair Lady* has only twenty-one. Its superior effectiveness in underlining, adding to, and supplementing the drama is clearly attested by the play's great and continuing popularity.

Spectacle. The musical almost always offers great scope to designers. The mingling of song and dialogue usually places a production outside the restrictions of realism and indicates the need for an imaginative use of pictorial elements to match the musical and dramatic qualities of the script.

A listing of the settings needed for Act I of *My Fair Lady* indicates some of the demands made on the set designer: outside the opera house; the tenement section; Higgins' study; the tenement section; Higgins' study; near the race at Ascot; inside a tent at Ascot; outside Higgins' home; Higgins' study; promenade at the Embassy; the ballroom. Not only is a wide variety of places indicated, but the alternation and frequent repetition of some indicates that they must permit quick changes so that the flow of one scene into another will not be impeded. The designer's problem is simplified somewhat since some sets need accommodate only a few persons, while others are used by the entire cast. Some sets may be small, therefore, while others must occupy the entire stage.

The costumes are also numerous and equally a source of great visual variety and beauty. The time of *My Fair Lady* is 1912, a period noted for elegance. Cecil Beaton, who designed the costumes for the original production, made effective use of the period. Upper-class characters appear in the Ascot race scenes and at the Embassy Ball, while lower-class characters are seen in the flower market and tenement scenes. Not only did Beaton distinguish between the two classes but he also used great imagination in commenting upon the scenes. In the Ascot setting, for example, all characters were costumed in shades of black and white, thereby emphasizing the uniformity of the characters. On the other hand, for the flower market he took his inspiration from the paintings of Renoir, and through subtle gradations of pastel colors made the characters themselves resemble bouquets.

Since *My Fair Lady* covers a period of over six months, many costume changes are needed. The transformation of Eliza is indicated in what she wears as well as in how she sounds. Furthermore, the chorus changes its identity often and therefore needs a great variety of costumes: sometimes they represent slum dwellers, at others they are dancers at the Embassy Ball or loungers outside the opera house.

Dance adds to the visual effectiveness of the musical play. Like the music, it too comments upon the action and forwards the plot. It is not used extensively in *My Fair Lady*, but in other musicals it has played an extremely important part. Here, nevertheless, it is a source of considerable charm and visual beauty.

My Fair Lady combines an extremely effective story with interesting and unusual characters, memorable music, and charming and colorful spectacle. It is both a representative and a superior example of the post-war musical.

Motion Pictures and Television

In the late nineteenth century the theatre was probably still the major purveyor of mass entertainment, but since that time its appeal has steadily eroded as it competitors have multiplied. One of the most serious challenges has come from spectator sports—baseball, football, boxing, racing, and so on—which have been increasingly exploited during this century. More direct competition, however, has come from other dramatic media—films and television.

Motion pictures have grown steadily in popularity since penny arcades began to show miniature films soon after Thomas A. Edison demonstrated his kinetoscope in 1894. Only one person at a time could view a program, however, until George Eastman invented flexible film and Thomas Armat perfected the projector. The first motion picture theatre was opened in McKeesport, Pennsylvania, in 1905; by 1909 there were 8000 others. These early theatres seated only about 100 persons and showed only short films. But in 1914 the Strand Theatre in New York, with its 3300 seats, began the trend toward larger houses, and in 1915 D. W. Griffith's *The Birth of a Nation* popularized the full-length film. Two other events—the addition of sound to motion pictures in 1927 and the economic depression of 1929—gave the film such increased appeal that after 1930 the legitimate theatre rapidly declined in popularity.

The weakened theatre was dealt another serious blow after World War II with the introduction of television. In 1948 there were only 48 stations but by 1958 there were 512 stations and 50 million receivers. Television affected motion pictures almost as much as it did the theatre, for audiences were loath to pay for entertainment of the kind to be seen free in their own living rooms. Thus, television did much to make both film and theatrical producers reconsider the potentialities of their media. As a result, filmmakers became increasingly conscious of the motion picture as an art form, and theatrical producers sought to revitalize the theatre by offering plays that television, controlled by its advertisers, was reluctant or unable to broadcast. Some theatrical producers sought merely to offer entertainment sufficiently compelling that audiences would overcome their inertia. This became the typical approach of Broadway. Others sought to provide a more truthful, compelling or novel experience than could be gained from television. Consequently, much of the experimentation so prevalent since the 1950s has been motivated by the desire to make the theatre a penetrating, relevant, and exciting encounter with significant ideas, issues, and perceptions.

In New York, this challenge became a major stimulus to the Off-Broadway movement, which began in the late 1940s. Believing that financial conditions forced Broadway producers to cater almost exclusively to mass audiences, the new groups sought out-of-the-way buildings where rent was sufficiently low that they might offer short runs of classics or significant recent plays to appreciative though limited audiences. Furthermore, since many operated in buildings never intended for theatrical purposes, they almost inevitably had to experiment with such audience-actor spatial arrangements as arena and thrust stages. During the 1950s there were more than fifty Off-Broadway companies, of which the Circle in the Square and the Phoenix Theatre were the most influential. As a whole, they demonstrated that excellence does not depend on material resources. They also gave a number of actors and playwrights their first hearings in New York.

The Theatre of the Absurd

Though competition from other media aroused anxiety in the postwar era, most producers merely continued prewar practices without any extreme break with the past. Thus, for a time modified realism remained the major mode. But during the 1950s the absurdists posed a serious challenge both to established theatrical practices and to earlier views of man.

Absurdism is a term coined by Martin Esslin around 1960 to describe the work of several dramatists who had come to prominence during the preceding decade. It was never a conscious movement like many of those that had preceded it. Those writers considered to be its prime exponents —Beckett, Ionesco, and Genet—did share convictions, however, that permit grouping them into a common school. Their basic conception of the human condition can be summarized briefly.

Absurdism is a logical extension of the nineteenth-century scientific outlook. The naturalists argued that the only truths are those that can be apprehended through the five senses and verified by the scientific method. But thus far the only fields that have yielded readily to scientific treatment are the physical and biological sciences, only a small part of daily existence. Human beings' most difficult decisions normally involve moral questions (that is, the rightness or wrongness of possible courses of action) which are not subject to scientific verification. From a strictly naturalistic point of view, therefore, morality lies outside the realm of objective truth.

The naturalists never stated this view, for in spite of their attempts to restrict truth to scientific fact, they still believed for the most part in objective standards of morality. Nevertheless, the implication of a strictly scientific outlook is that, since it has no objective foundation, morality is based merely upon a set of conventions—on conformity to a code of behavior rather than verifiable premises.

The absurdists choose to see all aspects of human existence in this light, for to them all values, knowledge, and behavior are equally illogical. Adrift in a chaotic universe, human beings construct whatever fictions they can to help themselves survive. The absurdists assume that the world is entirely neutral, that fact and events do not have meanings, but that humans arbitrarily assign meanings to them. Thus if we regard an action as immoral, it does not necessarily mean that the act is immoral, only that we have chosen to label it such. The concept of morality itself is regarded as a human fabrication without logical foundation.

To the absurdist, ultimate truth consists of the chaos, contradictions, and inanities that make up everyday existence. Truth is the lack of logic, order, and certainty. Since there is no objective truth, each person may construct a set of values by which he lives, but he must be willing to recognize that ultimately his values are based on unverifiable premises.

Forerunners of Absurdism

While absurdism has gained prominence only since 1950, its roots go back to the late nineteenth century. It is now usual to label *Ubu Roi* (1896) by Alfred Jarry the first absurdist drama. While this play, with its grotesque and parodistic inversion of conventional values and its determinedly nonrealistic techniques, certainly anticipates many later works, it had no immediate successors. The first organized movement with an essentially absurdist outlook was dadaism (discussed in the preceding chapter). The absurdists also were to borrow many techniques from the surrealists. But neither dadaism nor surrealism produced a substantial body of drama.

The first major dramatist to express an essentially absurdist view was Luigi Pirandello (1867–1936). His plays, such as *Right You Are, If You Think You Are* (1918), *Six Characters in Search of an Author* (1921), *Henry IV* (1922), and *As You Desire Me* (1930), rest upon the premise that truth is a matter of one's point of view. Typically, in a play by Pirandello, although all of the principal characters have been involved in the same event or with the same person, each has a quite different version of what has happened and each is convinced that he is right. Pirandello does not settle these arguments, since to him there is no objective truth, only individual versions of truth. Out of such ideas Pirandello fashioned powerful plays that achieved worldwide renown. Although his dramas do not depart markedly from traditional structural patterns, Pirandello's view of reality is clearly similar to that of the absurdists.

The most significant forerunner of absurdism is existentialism. Many of the plays now labeled absurdist were originally called existentialist, and the beginnings of absurdist drama are clearly associated with existential philosophy.

Traditionally, philosophers have been concerned primarily with defining "essences"—the unchanging aspects of phenomena. But, existential

Jarry's Ubu Roi *as performed at the Théâtre Antoine, Paris, in 1908. (Sketch published in* Le Figaro, *Feb. 16, 1908.)*

philosophers argue that the first problem is to define "existence." In addition, they have been especially concerned about those aspects of existence that influence human freedom, choice, and action. Following World War II, existentialism attracted considerable attention because of the issues it raised about moral values in the civilization that had produced two world wars and an atomic bomb.

The best-known dramatists of this school are Jean-Paul Sartre (1905–) and Albert Camus (1913–1960), although Camus denied allegiance to any particular philosophical position. Sartre, a major spokesman for existentialism, has stated that all of his work is an attempt to draw logical conclusions from a consistent atheism. He argues that there are no universal and absolute moral laws or values, that humanity is adrift in a world devoid of purpose. Therefore, each person is free (since he is not bound to a god or to a set of verifiable principles governing behavior) and is responsible only to himself. Nevertheless, it is each person's duty to find his own values and to act in accordance with them. This viewpoint, set forth in a number of essays and philosophical treatises, forms the basis for such plays as *The Flies* (1943), *No Exit* (1944), *The Devil and the Good Lord* (1951), and *The Condemned of Altona* (1959).

Camus, the first theorist to use the term *absurd,* states that absurdity arises from the gulf between human beings' aspirations and the meaningless universe into which they have been thrust. The basic problem for humankind then, is to find their way in a world of chaos. Camus' plays, illustrating this position, include *Cross-Purposes* (1944), *Caligula* (1945), and *The Just Assassins* (1949).

Both Camus and Sartre, however, emphasize the necessity for each person to find a set of values capable of ordering an otherwise chaotic existence. Thus, they see a human being as determining his own course rather than being at the mercy of heredity and environment. Furthermore, both dramatists utilize traditional structural patterns in their plays.

Major Absurdist Dramatists

Camus and Sartre differ from the absurdists in two important respects: The later writers emphasize the absurdity of existence rather than the necessity of ordering absurdity; and they embody their chaotic subject matter in nontraditional dramatic form. It is these later dramatists, especially Beckett, Genet, and Ionesco, who are normally called the absurdists.

Absurdism first attracted wide attention with Samuel Beckett's (1906–) *Waiting for Godot* (1953), which soon was translated into more than twenty languages. Beckett, Irish by birth, has never acknowledged his allegiance to any school of philosophy, and certainly *Waiting for Godot* has as many religious as absurdist connotations. In it, two

One of the two tramps from Samuel Beckett's Waiting for Godot. *Directed by William Reardon.*

tramps improvise diversions while they wait for Godot, who never appears. Although it depicts waiting and hope, the play is also about the nonfulfillment of hope. Some critics find in it an argument that the hope of salvation gives meaning to life, while others see in it a comment upon the absurdity of hope.

Beckett's work as a whole suggests that it is impossible to be certain about anything, an attitude reflected in his subject matter and dramatic techniques. Beckett's works are rich in implications about the nature of human existence, but, as with symbolist drama, the essential mystery that lurks behind the action remains unexplained. Beckett leaves it to the audience to find its own meanings in the dramatic events. Among Beckett's later plays are *Endgame, Krapp's Last Tape, Happy Days, Not I,* and *That Time.*

Jean Genet (1910–   ), in *The Maids, Deathwatch, The Balcony, The Blacks,* and *The Screens,* depicts existence as an endless series of reflections in mirrors. Each image may for a moment be mistaken for reality, but upon examination it always proves an illusion. Truth (or the beginning of the set of reflections) can never be found. Genet's characters assume roles, but when the disguises are removed true identities are never revealed, for each appearance is only a new disguise. Genet, who has spent much of his life in prison, suggests that deviation is essential to society, for nothing has meaning without its opposite—law and crime, religion and sin, love and hate. Consequently, deviant behavior is as valuable as accepted virtue. He transforms life into a series of ceremonies and rituals that give order and an air of importance to what would otherwise be nonsensical behavior.

Eugene Ionesco's (1912–   ) first play, *The Bald Soprano,* was produced in Paris in 1950. To indicate his attempt to write something as unlike conventional drama as possible, Ionesco labelled it an *antiplay.* In it no action is developed, many of the characters are so alike that they may be interchanged, and the dialogue is made up almost entirely of clichés. The meaninglessness and repetitiousness of the subject matter is paralleled in the dramatic techniques, for the action does not progress to a resolution and the dialogue degenerates until the characters merely repeat letters of the alphabet.

Ionesco has continued to write regularly for the stage. Among the more important of his later works are *The Chairs, The Lesson, Victims of Duty, The Killer, Rhinoceros, Exit the King, Hunger and Thirst, Macbett,* and *The Man with the Suitcases.* Here *The New Tenant* (written 1953, first performed 1955) will be discussed as an example of Ionesco's work and of absurdist drama.

The New Tenant

Ionesco most often treats the absurdist vision in terms of middle-class life. Thus, his plays, especially the early ones, are frequently set in rather ordinary surroundings and usually begin relatively realistically. But as the action develops, the middle-class protagonist becomes for Ionesco a modern Everyman who epitomizes the human condition.

Ionesco, like the other absurdists, is convinced that there are no absolutes on which one can base behavior. On the other hand, he believes that all men share certain preoccupations and anxieties—"mysterious nostalgias," "nameless regrets," and, above all, a "true community of fear" about the "void at the center of things," of which for humankind the ultimate expression is death. But, though these are universals, they cannot be fully understood, explained, or resolved. Nevertheless, according to Ionesco, even a hint that the world is absurd terrifies the average person, who seeks to insulate himself against the void by filling it with concrete material objects, with comforting clichés of speech, and with rigid political, economic, or religious ideologies. Ionesco deplores this tendency toward conformity, especially in the theatre: "Committed theatre is dangerous—extremely dangerous. It leads directly to the concentration camp." By this he means that any commitment to a system—esthetic, philosophical, religious, or whatever—is the first step in denying the validity of any other way of thought, the ultimate outcome of which is to confine or kill those who disagree with us. So far as Ionesco is con-

cerned, the only true solutions lie in recognizing the need to resist conformity, in being willing to accept the right of others to find their own ways of coping with anxieties, and ultimately in going on despite the knowledge that at the center of existence there is a void into which we must all disappear after death. To do anything else is to capitulate to some system of thought, speech, or action that dehumanizes man (since, to the extent that he accepts any system, his responses are programmed). As Ionesco puts it: "It is the conformist . . . who is lost and dehumanized."

Themes and Structure. *The New Tenant* develops several themes typical of Ionesco's plays. First, it shows how language has been reduced to empty clichés. In the opening scenes, the Caretaker talks volubly and almost without pause, but what she says is a series of commonplaces. She does not seem to notice that she often contradicts herself, for to her language serves primarily as reassurance; rather than being a medium for ideas, it is a way of avoiding the need to think.

A second theme common to many of Ionesco's plays is the displacement of human beings by material objects. In *The New Tenant* this is not only the dominant motif, it is the principal action. It is also closely connected with a third theme—the dehumanization of man. At the beginning of *The New Tenant,* the Caretaker and the Gentleman meet in an empty room that creates no barriers to human contacts. Nevertheless, neither of them is really interested in the other. The Caretaker only views the Gentleman as a potential source of income, and he (in contrast with the concern he displays for his material possessions when they arrive shortly afterwards) all but ignores her. The Gentleman's preference for objects over people is further demonstrated when he has the movers block completely the room's only window, and when he permits them to place a radio by his chair only after they assure him that it does not work; when finally he is so walled in by his possessions that he can no longer move, he requests that the room's only light be turned off. Wholly shut off from human contacts, he seems entirely content in his tomblike room. In his world, things have completely replaced people.

The repercussions of this dehumanizing process extend far beyond the Gentleman's room, however, for the movers report that furniture now clogs the streets, subways, and even the river. Thus, Ionesco seems to suggest that what has happened in this room is also happening in the world at large as humans seek to deny the threat of a spiritual void by filling physical space to overflowing. As Ionesco has written: "Matter fills everything, takes up all space, annihilates all liberty under its weight; the horizon shrinks and the world becomes a stifling dungeon. . . . Words, obviously devoid of magic, are replaced by accessories, by objects."

It is this network of related themes that unifies *The New Tenant*. In contrast to its rather complex ideas, the play's story is very simple: a Gentleman arrives to claim his apartment, has a brief discussion with the Caretaker, and then supervises two movers who gradually fill the room with furniture and then leave him alone in it. There are no complications, crises, or resolutions in the traditional sense. Rather, themes are introduced and concretized. Nevertheless, there is beginning, middle, and end—a sense of completeness and wholeness—for everything one needs to know is contained within the play, and the ending is the logical outcome of what has gone before.

Characters and Acting. *The New Tenant* includes only four characters: the Caretaker, the Gentleman, and two furniture movers. As their designations suggest, they are not individuals so much as types.

The Caretaker epitomizes the qualities associated with that near-legendary French figure, the concierge, whose task it is to oversee the apartment-house domain placed under her charge. Her age is never specified, but the lines suggest that she is probably in late middle age. She is both obsequious (because she hopes to get something from the Gentleman) and tyrannical (because she is in a position to make life comfortable or miserable for those who live in her building); she is willing to say whatever she thinks the Gentleman wants to hear, even if it contradicts what she has just said; and, when crossed, she is equally ready to make the most outrageous accusations. Regardless of the tack she takes, she is always self-serving.

The Gentleman, in his turn, epitomizes bourgeois propriety. He is middle-aged, carries a brief case and gloves, and wears a bowler hat, patent leather shoes and dark, very sedate clothing. His manner is reserved and businesslike; at times he can be forceful, especially in rejecting human contacts and in protecting his possessions. In him, positive feeling is reserved for things, negative reactions for whatever threatens to establish a human relationship; most of the time his responses are studiedly neutral. He is as taciturn as the Caretaker is voluble. He speaks only when it is essential and says no more than is necessary.

No information is given about the age or appearance of the two furniture movers. It may be assumed that they are easily recognizable types and that they wear clothing that helps to identify their occupation. But though the script does not differentiate them, it is clear that in performance they must contrast sufficiently to be instantly distinguishable. Their primary function is to fill the stage with furniture, but during that process they are involved in quite varied stage business.

Visual Elements. In *The New Tenant,* spectacle is probably the most important element, for the play as a whole represents the visualization of a perception—how material objects fill space that should be occupied by people. The process of displacement both constitutes the physical action and sums up the play's themes. Dialogue is entirely secondary; even the characters are essentially visual objects. (Because the characters are typified through dress and the action is so explicit, the play would probably be entirely comprehensible even if the dialogue were omitted.) After a time, material objects assume a status equal to that of the human agents and even begin to move, seemingly under their own power. Thus, Ionesco follows his own advice: "The author [should] make actors of his props, bring objects to life, animate the scenery, and give symbols concrete form."

The style of production appropriate to the play is summed up in Ionesco's prefatory note to it (key portions of which have inexplicably been omitted in the English translation): "The action ought to be, in the beginning, very realistic, as should the setting and, later, the furniture that will be brought in. Then the rhythm, almost unnoticed, should imperceptibly impart to the play a certain ritualistic character. Realism should prevail, once more, in the final scene."

As this suggests, in the beginning everything seems completely natural. The Caretaker acts precisely as one might expect in real life, and even the routine of daily existence outside the room is suggested by various offstage sound effects. Only when the furniture begins to arrive does the sense of everyday reality alter. The first change is manifested in the movers' manner of handling objects: straining every muscle in carrying small vases, but moving heavy pieces of furniture with ease. At first the movers work as a team, but then they establish an alternating pattern as one goes out and the other returns; eventually they exit through one door only to return almost immediately, as if on a turntable, through another on the opposite side of the stage. Finally, the furniture begins to enter under its own power. About this accelerating rhythm and surrealistic effect, Ionesco has written: "That dreamlike state, the state of astonishment in the face of an increasingly disjunctive and dislocated reality . . . was something I managed to bring out . . . in *The New Tenant.*" Once the new situation —the dominance of matter—is fully established and accepted, the style becomes realistic again, for the Gentleman's world is now controlled by the logic of that system (which is just as matter-of-fact as that of the opening scene) to which he has capitulated in order to escape the threat of a metaphysical void.

The New Tenant has been produced less often than many others of Ionesco's plays, probably because of the enormous demands made by spectacle. To assemble objects of the type demanded by the script and in the quantity needed to fill the stage is difficult, even without considering the problems of making the furniture seem to move of its own volition or of handling it efficiently and stacking pieces on top of each other safely during a performance. Despite these difficulties, however, *The New Tenant* is an excellent example of absurdist vision and method.

Related Dramatists

The absurdist mode eventually was to affect the theatre of almost every country. It had a great vogue in West Germany, where French absurdist plays received their greatest number of productions. Nevertheless, few Germans wrote in this style. Perhaps the best known of those who did is Gunter Grass (1927–) with such plays as *Mister, Mister* (1956) and *The Wicked Cooks* (1957). In England, such early plays as *The Room* (1957) and *The Dumb Waiter* (1957) by Harold Pinter (1930–) are often called absurdist; and in America Edward Albee's

Scene from Mrozek's Tango. *Directed by Svone Sedlbauer; setting by William Evans. (Courtesy University of Kansas.)*

(1928–   ) *The Sandbox* (1959) and *The American Dream* (1960) and Arthur Kopit's (1938–   ) *Oh Dad, Poor Dad, Mama's Hung You in the Closet and I'm Feeling So Sad* (1960) have been placed in this category. In Eastern Europe, absurdism enjoyed great popularity after 1956, when Stalinism was denounced. Many of the plays from this area have strong political overtones. In Czechoslovakia, for example, Vaclav Havel (1936–   ) launched bitingly satirical attacks on bureaucracy in *The Garden Party* (1963) and *The Memorandum* (1965). In Poland, Slawomir Mrozek (1930–   ) followed a somewhat similar path with such plays as *The Police* (1958) and *Charlie* (1961). Mrozek is best known, however, for *Tango* (1965), a parable about the decline of values in Western society; he suggests that now only power remains and that those most willing to exercise it, ruthlessly and without regard for humanitarian principles, become the rulers of the world.

By the 1960s absurdism had been so widely disseminated that its techniques were being used by those who did not share its philosophical biases. Thus, after its initial strength waned, absurdism was partially assimilated into other movements.

Other Postwar Developments

In France, the most prestigious actor–director of the postwar period was Jean-Louis Barrault (1910–   ). A synthesizer of many prewar trends, he learned from the Cartel respect for a text and for precise workmanship, from Etienne Decroux the power of mime, and from Antonin Artaud the importance of subconscious impulses and nonverbal theatrical devices. Barrault has declared that the text of a play is like an iceberg, since only about one-eighth is visible; it is the director's task to complete the playwright's text by revealing the hidden portions through the imaginative use of all the theatre's resources. Since 1946, Barrault and his wife Madeleine Renaud have headed their own company (bearing their names), with which they have won high critical praise.

Artaud's influence was more pronounced on the work of Roger Blin (1907–   ), whose production of *Waiting for Godot* in 1953 brought absurdism its first wide recognition. Blin went on to direct other plays by Beckett and Genet. In part because of Blin's work, Artaud's reputation grew steadily throughout the 1950s.

A third major director of postwar France, Jean Vilar (1912–1971), remained true to the ideals of Copeau and the Cartel. As head of the Théâtre National Populaire from 1951 to 1963, he won a wide following for that company throughout France with productions simply but imaginatively mounted and powerfully acted.

After World War II, the French government became concerned about the restriction of theatrical activity to Paris, and set out to decentralize it. Therefore, in 1947 it began to subsidize "dramatic centers"—troupes based in large towns and serving the adjacent territory. There are now about ten of these centers scattered throughout France.

The war also provoked the British government to assist the theatre. Prior to 1940, England had never provided any subsidy for the arts. But German bombing so damaged the theatre (at one point only one theatre remained open in London) that funds were appropriated to send companies on tour as one means of building morale. At the end of the war, subsidization of the arts became a permanent policy, and support (both nationally and locally) has steadily increased since that time.

After the war the English theatre also gained considerably in international repute. Between the wars it had made little impact abroad, since it broke no important new ground. During the 1930s John Gielgud (1904–) and Tyrone Guthrie (1900–1971), through their outstanding directing had been most responsible for raising the level of production. After the war, the Old Vic, which Guthrie had headed between 1937 and 1944, was for a time the best of the English companies, especially from 1944 to 1949 under the direction of Laurence Olivier, Ralph Richardson, and John Burrell. From 1946 to 1952, the Old Vic also had an excellent acting school run by Michel Saint-Denis. By the 1950s the Old Vic had become perhaps the best known company in the English-speaking world. Then, it began to decline, although it continued to be an influential troupe until it was dissolved in 1963. As the Old Vic declined, the Shakespeare Festival Theatre in Stratford-on-Avon steadily grew in reputation as it began to attract major stars and offer improved working conditions. But its period of greatness would not come until after 1960.

English playwriting demonstrated little strength in the postwar period. Its greatest asset was poetic drama, especially such works as *The Lady's Not for Burning* (1949) and *Venus Observed* (1950) by Christopher Fry (1907–), and *The Cocktail Party* (1949) and *The Confidential Clerk* (1954) by T. S. Eliot (1888–1965), who before the war had already written *Murder in the Cathedral* (1935) and *The Family Reunion* (1939). Unfortunately, the appeal of such poetic dramas soon waned, and by the mid-1950s English playwriting seemed at a low ebb.

In Germany, all theatres were closed in 1944. Shortly after the hostilities ended, however, they began to reopen and soon subsidized companies throughout the country had been reestablished. Around 1950 new buildings began to replace the more than one hundred theatres that had been destroyed during the war. Consequently, Germany probably now has more up-to-date theatre buildings than any other country in the world.

Of the postwar German troupes, the best known is the Berliner Ensemble, founded in 1949 by Bertolt Brecht and his wife Helene Weigel. This troupe was the first to apply Brecht's theories of staging consistently and to make his plays the center of its repertory. Following the war, Brecht's reputation grew rapidly. By the time he died in 1956, he was recognized as one of the masters of modern drama, and epic theatre had become one of the major influences on postwar production techniques.

Jean Vilar, one of the major directors of postwar France as well as a fine actor, in Pirandello's Henry IV *as presented at the Théâtre de l' Atelier, Paris, in 1951. (Photo by Bernand.)*

But Germany was slow to produce significant new dramatists, perhaps because the Nazi era had destroyed so much potential talent. The major German-language dramatists were the Swiss authors, Max Frisch (1911–) and Friedrich Duerrenmatt (1921–). Frisch's reputation was built primarily with *The Chinese Wall* (1946), *Biedermann and the Firebugs* (1958), and *Andorra* (1961), all posing questions of guilt. In each, as the past is reviewed, the characters construct elaborate rationalizations to justify their cowardly actions. Duerrenmatt's fame came through such plays as *The Visit* (1956) and *The Physicists* (1962). Like Frisch, Duerrenmatt has been concerned with moral responsibility. He has stated that plays should frighten audiences and make them face up to the grotesque world in which they live; that such an experience should make men attempt to find some order. For Duerrenmatt, however, the possibilities of positive action are slight, since he once stated, "The universal for me is chaos." The most that men can hope for, therefore, is the courage to endure. Frisch and Duerrenmatt also established the direction that most German drama was to follow thereafter until the 1970s: the exploration of themes of guilt and responsibility. Thus, postwar German drama was quite unlike the French absurdist plays, which tended to be concerned with personal anxieties and the dehumanizing effects of a mechanistic and unfriendly world.

By the late 1950s, the theatre had almost fully recovered from the effects of World War II. At first, the postwar theatre had merely extended the modes inherited from the prewar years, but in the early 1950s absurdism introduced a new spirit of questioning and experimentation. By the end of the decade, the theatre was on the verge of one of its most innovative eras.

13

Contemporary Theatre and Drama

During the 1960s virtually all accepted theatrical practices and standards were called into question, and many new techniques and issues were introduced. As a result, it was one of the most expansive, exciting, and frustrating periods the theatre has known. During the 1970s such free-wheeling experimentation gradually gave way to reassessments of the preceding decade and attempts to assimilate its most effective elements into the mainstream of theatrical production. This process, still underway, has created a sense of uncertainty about the future direction of the theatre, although much of the vitality of the 1960s remains.

French Theatre and Drama Since 1960

During the 1950s French playwrights, especially the existentialists and absurdists, were pacesetters for the world. After 1960, however, France lost its place of preeminence because, though many older writers contin-

351

ued to be active, few new ones attracted an international following. Of those who did, the best known has been Fernando Arrabal (1932–   ), a native of Spain but a resident of France since 1955. Arrabal began to write plays in 1952 but did not become widely known until the 1960s.

Arrabal's early plays tend to emphasize a childish, thoughtless cruelty and to employ techniques popularized by the absurdists. *The Automobile Graveyard* (1958) is typical of these early works. Set in a junkyard run as though it were a luxury hotel, it is composed of several loosely connected stories; the most important concerns Emanou, a Christlike figure, who after being betrayed is bound to a bicycle as though to a cross. But unlike Christ's, Emanou's sacrifice has no meaning, for the world to which he has appeared is merely the rusty remains of a technological nightmare. As do most of Arrabal's plays, *The Automobile Graveyard* mingles the religious and the sacrilegious, the erotic and the sadistic, the innocent and the corrupt, the tender and the cruel.

Around 1962 Arrabal renounced his earlier approach and declared his concern for a théâtre panique, a "ceremony—partly sacrilegious, partly sacred, erotic and mystic, a putting to death and exaltation of life, part Don Quixote and part Alice in Wonderland." Among Arrabal's later works are *Solemn Communion* (1966), *The Architect and the Emperor of Assyria* (1967), *And They Handcuffed the Flowers* (1970) and *Young Barbarians Today* (1975). The second is perhaps the best known. In it two characters enact a series of ritualized situations: master and slave, mother and child, judge and criminal, male and female, and so on. Eventually one is killed and eaten by the other, but then a new figure appears and the process begins all over again. Through such plays Arrabal has called virtually all values and relationships into question and has ferreted out the hidden corners of the human psyche.

Although no other French playwright since 1960 has equaled Arrabal's impact, those who deserve recognition include René de Obaldia, Mar-

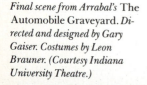
Final scene from Arrabal's The Automobile Graveyard. *Directed and designed by Gary Gaiser. Costumes by Leon Brauner. (Courtesy Indiana University Theatre.)*

guerite Duras, Jean-Claude Grumberg, André Benedetto, Pierre Bourgeade, Armand Gatti, and Jean-Paul Wenzel.

During the 1960s decentralization of the theatre continued to be a policy of the French government. Therefore, in addition to dramatic centers (or regional troupes serving specific areas of the country), it also promoted the concept of municipal cultural centers (*maisons de la culture*) and helped to finance buildings for them. Consequently, many of the larger cities of France now have up-to-date facilities for the performing arts.

In 1959 the government recognized the outstanding work of Barrault and Vilar. It installed Barrault's troupe in the Odéon, gave it a subsidy, and renamed it the Théâtre de France. Vilar's accomplishments were acknowledged by granting the Théâtre National Populaire a status equal to that of the Comédie Française and by a greatly increased subsidy. (Vilar resigned in 1963 and was replaced by Georges Wilson.) These two troupes were probably the most important in France during the 1960s because of their wide-ranging repertories and their openness to innovation.

In the late 1960s, France, like most countries, was subjected to widespread political and social upheaval. As one result, Barrault resigned his post in 1968, and, since the actors were under contract to him, the Odéon was left without a company. In 1970 the Odéon was assigned to the Comédie Française, which has since used it as a supplemental house and to host visiting companies. Since 1968 Barrault has staged a number of productions (*Rabelais* being the most successful), headed an annual international festival (the Théâtre des Nations) from 1971 to 1976, and directed his own company, housed in the Théâtre d'Orsay since 1974.

During the 1960s Barrault and Vilar came to be rivaled as directors by Roger Planchon (1931–), who in 1957 founded the Théâtre de la Cité in Villeurbanne, a suburb of Lyons, where he sought to attract a working-class audience with productions that drew heavily on cinematic and Brechtian techniques. His repertory included plays by Molière, Shakespeare, Racine, Brecht, and many other major writers, but which he interpreted from the proletarian point of view. Such productions made Planchon one of the most admired and controversial directors in France.

In the early 1970s the French government for the first time awarded a few companies outside of Paris the title "national" theatre. These include the Théâtre National de Strasbourg (a former dramatic center) and the Théâtre de l'Est Parisien (located in a suburb of Paris). More significant, Planchon's troupe in Villeurbanne was designated the Théâtre National Populaire (TNP), the title previously held by Vilar's troupe in Paris. The Parisian company was retitled the Théâtre National de Palais de Chaillot (for the building in which it performs).

Since 1972 Planchon has shared management of the TNP with Patrice Chereau (1944–), one of France's best young directors. (Chereau created a major controversy in 1976 with his interpretation of Wagner's

Ring cycle at Bayreuth for the one-hundredth anniversary of that festival.) The TNP is required to give two hundred performances each year in French towns other than Villeurbanne to ensure its national character. Today, it is probably France's finest company.

Another of France's major directors is Victor Garcia (1934–), who came to Paris in the early 1960s, and made a deep impression in 1966 with his staging of *The Automobile Graveyard,* which ran for two years. Since then he has been much in demand in France, Spain, England, and elsewhere. For one of his most spectacular productions (Genet's *The Balcony* in São Paulo, Brazil, in 1970), he completely gutted the interior of a theatre and built within it a sixty-foot-high tubular structure with balconies on which the audience sat and in the center of which the action progressed on transparent circular platforms that could be lowered and raised to different levels. It was one of the most radical restructurings of theatrical space attempted in modern times. Among his other major productions are Genet's *The Maids* and Valle-Inclán's *Divine Words.*

Like other countries, France has a large number of "alternative" theatres. Perhaps the best of these is the Grand Magic Circus, headed by Jerome Savary, who first attracted wide favorable attention in 1970 with *Zartan,* "the story of Tarzan's deprived brother," a work described by Savary as the "marvelous story of colonialism from the Middle Ages to the present." He has also produced *The Last Days of Solitude of Robinson Crusoe, Goodbye Mr. Freud, From Moses to Mao,* and *Adventures in Love.* Although Savary's productions comment on social issues, he does

The Last Days of Solitude of Robinson Crusoe *as performed by the Grand Magic Circus under the direction of Jerome Savary in 1972. (Photo by Bernand.)*

not consider this their primary function. Rather, he sees the theatre as a "life show"—an excuse for people to come together in joyful celebration. His troupe plays on beaches, in parks, hospitals, and elsewhere, and utilizes techniques associated with children's theatre, circus, and carnivals: there is considerable give and take between audience and performers (but all good-natured), and the productions are noted for their acrobatic feats, improvisations, and stunning visual effects.

In recent years the French theatre has been plagued by controversies over financial problems, the manner in which subsidies are distributed, and government attempts to shape artistic policies. Although it still is excellent in many respects. France's theatre today does not command the international respect it enjoyed in the 1950s.

Documentary Drama

Unlike France, Germany produced few dramatists of note in the immediate postwar period. But around 1960 a new generation of writers came to the fore. Whereas the French existentialists and absurdists had been concerned with philosophical problems and the anxieties of individuals, the German playwrights, perhaps haunted by memories of Nazi atrocities, emphasized questions relating to moral responsibility and guilt in the public sphere. The best known German plays of the 1960s—usually called documentary drama or "the theatre of fact"—coupled probing moral questions with subject matter taken from actual occurrences. Among the writers of this form, the best known were Hochhuth, Kipphardt, and Weiss.

Rolf Hochhuth (1931–) came to prominence in 1963 with *The Deputy,* a play that seeks to place part of the blame for the extermination of German Jews on Pope Pius XII because he did not take a decisive stand against German policies. This was followed by *The Soldiers* (1967), which suggests that Winston Churchill acquiesced in the death of General Sikorski, President of the Polish government in exile, so as not to endanger Anglo-Russian relationships. Heinar Kipphardt (1922–) is noted primarily for *In the Matter of J. Robert Oppenheimer* (1964), based on the United States government's hearings into the loyalty of the scientist after he resisted development of the hydrogen bomb. For the most part, the dialogue is based on documents relating to those hearings. Somewhat similarly, Peter Weiss (1916–) in *The Investigation* (1965) uses as dialogue excerpts from testimony given at the inquiry into the concentration camp at Auschwitz, where thousands of German Jews were exterminated by the Nazis during World War II. Weiss went on to write *The Song of the Lusitanian Bogey* (1967), which treats the suppression of African natives in Angola by the Portuguese, and in 1968 a play about Vietnam. But the best known of Weiss' plays is *The Persecution and Assassination of Jean-Paul Marat as Performed by the Inmates of the*

Asylum of Charenton under the Direction of the Marquis de Sade (usually called *Marat/Sade*, 1964). Although not as determinedly documentary as some of Weiss' later plays, *Marat/Sade* nevertheless is based on historical fact. More important, it set the tone for much subsequent drama of the 1960s.

Marat/Sade

Marat/Sade is a play within a play. The main action takes place in 1808 in the asylum of Charenton, where the Marquis de Sade is confined. Here he composes dramas that are performed by the patients for the amusement of a fashionable audience from nearby Paris. On this occasion, de Sade presents his play about the assassination by Charlotte Corday in 1793 of Jean-Paul Marat, a leader of the French Revolution. The inmates, attendants, director of the asylum and his family are on stage, while the audience supposedly is separated from them by bars.

Marat/Sade is grounded in historical fact: de Sade was confined at Charenton and he did write and present plays there; the material relating to the French Revolution is also based on fact, though some parts have been altered. Weiss uses this material much as Brecht might, for, though ostensibly writing about France in the years between 1790 and 1808, Weiss is ultimately concerned about our own times. Just as de Sade in his play looks back on events that have occurred fifteen or more years earlier, so Weiss is looking back on the bloodbaths, purges, and wars of the 1930s and 1940s, and he suggests that we are now reassuring ourselves that we have been freed from such barbarities. This idea is pointed up through exchanges between Coulmier, the director of the asylum, and the Herald. Coulmier objects several times to remarks in de Sade's play about social and political injustices, only to be reassured by the Herald that these "barbarous displays . . . could not happen nowadays. The men of that time . . . were primitive, we are more civilized."

Weiss' major concerns are summed up in the continuing argument between de Sade and Marat. The former argues that Nature is indifferent to humankind, that the strong always beat down the weak, that human beings are essentially selfish, and that it is useless to espouse idealistic schemes to better their lot. Marat argues that, rather than being paralyzed by Nature's indifference, we should invent meanings, act to right wrongs, and help humans overcome selfishness and live in harmony through mutual respect. Weiss' own conclusions seem to be voiced by Roux, the priest whose views are considered so dangerous that he is straitjacketed. It is Roux who advocates communal ownership of property, the conversion of churches into schools, and the end of all wars. And it is Roux who, at the end of the play after Marat is dead and the patients are out of hand, asks, "When will you learn to see? When will you learn to take sides?"

The structure of *Marat/Sade* owes much to Brecht. It is divided into

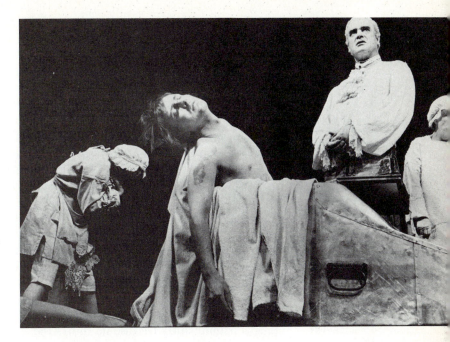

Scene from Weiss' Marat/Sade *as performed by the Royal Shakespeare Company. Directed by Peter Brook; Ian Richardson as Marat; Patrick Magee as de Sade. (Photo by Morris Newcombe. Courtesy Royal Shakespeare Company.)*

short scenes, each separately titled. Various devices are also used to alienate or distance the spectator from the action: historification; the asylum setting; the play within a play; the Herald who announces scenes; songs that comment on the action; and frequent interruptions and interpolations by Coulmier, the Herald, and various patients. Thus, incidents from the play about Marat are intermingled with others involving patients, and both with dialectical exchanges that transcend the context. The play is unified in part by the use of historical material and the asylum setting, but most of all by ideas and themes.

Characterization is at once simple and complex: simple because, except for de Sade and Marat, the personages are largely one-dimensional; complex because the play within the play is performed by patients and thus the actors playing those roles must present de Sade's characters without losing sight of the patients' aberrations. For example, Charlotte Corday is a naïve young girl but is played by a patient suffering from sleeping sickness, while her idealistic lover is played by an erotomaniac. Similarly, all of the main characters, with the exceptions of de Sade, Coulmier, and Roux, must perform on two levels simultaneously. Marat's role is especially difficult, for though in argumentation he is meant to be de Sade's equal, he is a patient whose malady is never specified and the lines he speaks supposedly have been written by de Sade. Both de Sade and Marat are intellectually complex, unlike Coulmier (who is always the self-serving bureaucrat) or Roux (whose only function is to voice uncompromisingly those solutions left vague by Marat).

Ultimately the play owes much of its success to spectacle and background action. The setting is a white and antiseptic room used for baths and massages. The patients not involved in de Sade's play create the appropriate atmosphere through such habitual movements as turning in circles or hopping and by muttering to themselves, wailing, screaming, and so on. The patients are kept in order by male nurses with the "appearance of butchers" and by nuns (played by athletic-looking men). Coulmier and his family (the representatives of normality) watch from a platform overlooking the room. The potential of these elements encourages the use of Artaudian techniques. (In large part because of the background activity, Peter Brook's production of *Marat/Sade* in London and New York was considered by most critics a major example of Artaud's "theatre of cruelty.")

Perhaps most important, the spectacle becomes a metaphor for the world about which de Sade and Marat argue. In de Sade's play one sees clearly the imperfections (the patients' maladies) behind the idealized stances (the roles), but the contrast also points up the need for transformation. The asylum represents in miniature the world at large, in which the representatives of the authorities in power keep an eye on any tendency of the people to become restless. At the end of the play, de Sade laughs triumphantly because he thinks the chaos around him verifies his arguments, but it is equally clear that the mob and Roux are capable of overpowering their keepers and de Sade.

Marat/Sade, with its blend of Brechtian and Artaudian modes, was to be one of the most successful plays of the decade. In turn, its success served to popularize Weiss' methods. Probably more than any other work, *Marat/Sade* established the approach that was to dominate the 1960s: moral, social, and political themes embedded in strongly theatricalized productions, making use of Artaudian devices.

Trends in Documentary Drama

By 1970 the vogue for documentary drama had begun to wane in Germany. Hochhuth, in *The Guerillas* (1970) and *The Midwife* (1972), turned to wholly fictional subjects, although he continued to be concerned with political and moral issues. Weiss used historical materials in *Trotsky in Exile* (1970) and *Hölderlin* (1971), but in these plays he is less concerned with fact than with universal truths. For example, in *Hölderlin* he uses the life of the nineteenth-century German poet to argue that society always destroys its visionaries. In this play he also returns to the approach he used so effectively in *Marat/Sade.*

If Germany most fully exploited the theatre of fact, it certainly did not have a monopoly on the type, for documentary drama made considerable impact in almost every country. As examples one might cite in France Jean Vilar's *The Oppenheimer Dossier* (1965), written out of unhappiness with Kipphardt's play on the same subject; in England, Peter

Brook's work on Vietnam, *US* (1967); and in America numerous plays dealing with such incidents as the massacre at My Lai and the *Pueblo* incident. Almost any actual event came to be considered potential material for stage treatment.

Dramatists of the theatre of fact raised a number of ethical issues, for while pretending to be factual, many writers brought public figures onto the stage and attributed to them immoral or criminal motives. But, critics asked, where does poetic license end and libel begin? Like the naturalists of the late nineteenth century, many documentary dramatists failed to draw a boundary between art and life, an important boundary because in placing characters onstage, playwrights automaticallly turn real human beings into fictional representatives. By pretending to present the truth, however, even as they invented motivations, some dramatists raised doubts about their own integrity. Although enthusiasm for documentary drama has waned, it has not wholly disappeared; under the impact of Watergate and related events, it seems in fact to have revived, especially in film and television.

Recent Trends in German Theatre

In the late 1960s a new group of German-language playwrights came to the fore, most of them seemingly weary of the preceding generation's preoccupation with guilt. The most admired of the new writers was Peter Handke (1942–   ), who was concerned above all with language and its relationship to reality and behavior. In such plays as *Kaspar* (1968), *The Ride Across Lake Constance* (1971), and *They Are Dying Out* (1974), Hanke is preoccupied with how human beings are dehumanized by conventions that reduce everything to conformity and are punished when they break out of mechanistic patterns. Other playwrights have turned for subjects to everyday patterns of existence, especially those that reflect indifference, callousness, and violence. Among the best known of these writers are Martin Sperr, Franz Xaver Kroetz, Wolfgang Bauer, Thomas Bernhard, and Ulrich Plenzdorf.

In the late 1960s the German theatre was faced by several crises. Perhaps the source of greatest conflict was the almost unlimited decision-making power of the government-appointed theatre managers. By 1969 dissatisfaction had become so great that actors in several cities demanded a voice in the theatre's affairs. This crisis was met in several ways. Some cities appointed a triumvirate of directors, others a six-member directorate; some adopted a scheme under which every member of a company had to be consulted on all major policy decisions, although the administrative work was left to a small group; in a few instances, communes were formed.

These controversies raised questions as to whether Germany needed all of its approximately two hundred subsidized stages. Inflationary prices created still other problems, especially since in West Germany government subsidies account for approximately eighty percent of all production costs. Threats of closures motivated several schemes for exchanging productions and personnel, sharing information and publicity, and exploring other forms of cooperation.

Of Germany's many theatres, the best now are probably those in Berlin, Stuttgart, Cologne, and Frankfurt. Peter Stein, with such productions as Gorky's *Summerfolk,* Kleist's *The Prince of Homburg,* and Stein's own tribute to Shakespeare and his age, *Shakespeare's Memory,* is considered to be Germany's finest director. Other major directors include Peter Zadek, Rudolf Noelte, and Claus Peymann.

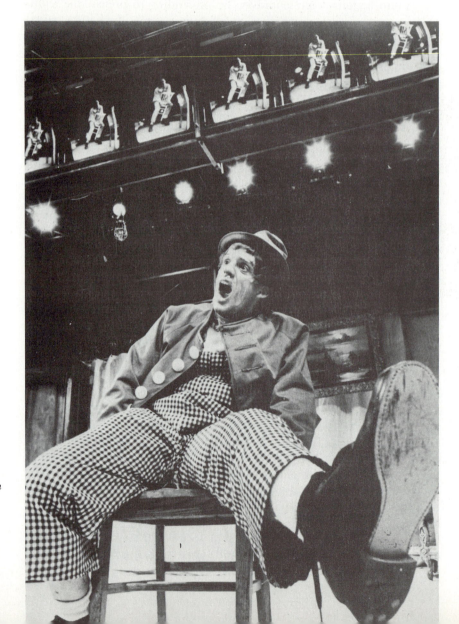

Christopher Lloyd in a scene from the Chelsea Theatre Center's electronic production of Peter Handke's Kaspar, *directed by Carl Weber. Note the closed-circuit television receivers at top.*

Overall, the German theatre in the late 1970s was still healthy, but there were signs of changes to come, perhaps most noticeably in the return to a more conservative repertory and a greater concern for entertaining rather than indoctrinating audiences.

The English Revival

In the mid-1950s, English drama seemed competent but unexciting. Then, in the late 1950s it underwent drastic change and since then has been outstanding. This new vitality evolved mainly through the leadership of the English Stage Company (often called the Royal Court after the theatre in which it performs) founded in 1956 by George Devine (1910–1966) with the intention of producing new English works and foreign plays not previously seen in England. But he soon discovered that there was no backlog of worthy unproduced English plays; it was in response to Devine's advertisement for new works that John Osborne (1929–) submitted *Look Back in Anger*; its production in 1956 is usually considered to mark the beginning of the English revival.

Osborne's play focuses on Jimmy Porter and his dissatisfactions with the class system, the intellectual inertia of all classes, and the widespread indifference to suffering. Although the play is essentially negative, it cap-

The original production of Osborne's Look Back in Anger *at the Royal Court Theatre, London in 1956. Directed by George Devine..(Photo by Houston Rogers.)*

tured the rebellious mood of its time so well that Jimmy Porter soon came to symbolize for the public all the "angry young men." Osborne has written regularly since 1956, but only a few of his later works—most notably *The Entertainer* (1957), *Luther* (1961), and *Inadmissible Evidence* (1965)—have achieved much success.

The English Stage Company has continued to be the principal champion in England of new playwrights. Those it has assisted are now numerous indeed, but perhaps the best known are Arden, Wesker, Bond, and Storey. John Arden (1930–) achieved his greatest success with *Sergeant Musgrave's Dance* (1959), in which a group of men set out to teach a town a lesson about the wastefulness of aggression by killing local residents in turn for those slaughtered abroad. Arnold Wesker (1932–), in such early plays as *Chicken Soup with Barley* (1958), *Roots* (1959), and *I'm Talking about Jerusalem* (1960), is concerned with the working classes, and argues that they have settled for too little and have erred because they have not taken collective action. From 1962 until 1971, Wesker was also head of Center 42, an organization designed to bring the best in the arts to working-class audiences throughout England. This group had little success, however, and eventually its program was confined to the Roundhouse, a converted railroad shop in north London. In the late 1960s Wesker moved away from social and political concerns, but such late plays as *The Friends* (1970) and *The Merchant* (1976) found little favor with critics. Thus, he is still honored primarily as England's most socially conscious playwright of the late 1950s and early 1960s.

Edward Bond (1935–) is probably the most controversial of England's contemporary playwrights. He achieved overnight notoriety in 1965 when the Royal Court gave a private performance of *Saved*, in which a baby is stoned to death in its carriage by its father and his companions. Equally shocking was *Early Morning* (1968), a surrealistic play about Victorian life in which virtually all the characters indulge in cannibalism. *Lear* (1971) uses many of Shakespeare's characters and situations but alters them to comment on inhumanity and brutality. Subsequent plays include *The Sea* (1973), *Bingo* (1973), and *The Fool* (1975). Bond has been denounced as sensational, decadent, and overly preoccupied with violence, but his works are concerned with a world in which the absence of love and compassion have bred a callousness so complete that horror is accepted as normality.

David Storey (1933–) has won international fame with such plays as *The Contractor* (1970), *Home* (1970), *The Changing Room* (1971) and *Life Class* (1974), all of which demonstrate enormous concern for realistic surface detail. For example, *The Changing Room* is set in the locker room of a rugby team, the members of which during the first act change into their uniforms and in the final act back into their street clothes. Every detail (down to total nudity) is recreated precisely. But beneath such surface realism can be glimpsed Storey's primary preoccupation: various kinds of alienation (class from class, person from person, man

Tom Stoppard's Travesties, *presented by the Royal Shakespeare Company, 1974. (Photo by Sophie Baker.)*

from himself, and so on). Because his intentions must be deduced from subtexts embedded within naturalistic frameworks, Storey's plays are often likened to Chekhov's.

In addition to the English Stage Company, the Theatre Workshop played a major role in the dramatic revival. Founded in 1945 by Joan Littlewood (1914–) to produce relevant plays for working class audiences, the Workshop settled in the east London suburb, Stratford, in 1953. Because of its work there and at the Théâtre des Nations in Paris, it was by the late 1950s considered one of the best companies in the world. In her attempt to make the theatre a place to which workers would go with the same enthusiasm as to fun palaces and penny arcades, Miss Littlewood drew on Brecht and Stanislavsky but above all on popular entertainments.

The Theatre Workshop contributed to the dramatic revival primarily through the work of two writers—Brendan Behan (1923–1964) with *The Quare Fellow* and *The Hostage,* and Shelagh Delaney (1939–), with *A Taste of Honey.* But the Workshop's greatest success was won with *Oh, What a Lovely War!* (1963), a bitingly satirical commentary on World War I done primarily through routines reminiscent of the music halls. Though the Workshop still exists, it ceased to be a vital force in English theatrical life after Miss Littlewood left it in the early 1960s.

But if the English Stage Company and the Theatre Workshop were most responsible for initiating a dramatic revival, they soon were joined by others. The result was a steady supply of outstanding new dramatists throughout the 1960s. Those deserving mention are too numerous to list here, but some of the most important are Peter Nichols (with *Joe Egg, The National Health, Forget-me-not Lane,* and *Privates on Parade*), Tom Stoppard (with *Rosencrantz and Guildenstern Are Dead, Jumpers,* and *Travesties*), and Joe Orton (with *Entertaining Mr. Sloane, Loot,* and *What the Butler Saw*).

Pinter

Of all contemporary English dramatists the most admired has been Harold Pinter (1930–   ), who began his playwriting career in 1957 with *The Room* and went on to produce such works as *The Dumb Waiter* (1957), *The Birthday Party* (1959), *The Caretaker* (1960), *The Home-coming* (1965), *Old Times* (1971), and *No Man's Land* (1975). Although there is much variety among these plays, they share a few characteristics: apparently realistic situations that gradually take on an air of menace or enigma; unexplained, unrevealed, or ambiguous motivations or background facts; and authentic, seemingly natural dialogue. Almost everything that happens in Pinter's plays could occur in real life; sometimes the situations and dialogue even suggest naturalism. Nevertheless, the overall impression is of ambiguity and mystery, primarily because the motivations of the characters are never fully revealed. Most of Pinter's

Scene from Pinter's The Birthday Party, *with McCann and Goldberg questioning Stanley. Directed and designed by William Kinzer; costumes by Barbara Alkofer. (Courtesy Indiana University Theatre.)*

Scene from Pinter's The Homecoming. *The actors are Vivian Merchant and Ian Holm. (Photo by David Sim. Courtesy Royal Shakespeare Company.)*

plays occur within the confined space of a single room, and there, out of quite ordinary events, crises arise that force the characters to face their anxieties or inner nature. But often the overall significance remains uncertain because so many questions are left unresolved. This uncertainty, however, is part of Pinter's vision, for he considers people to be "unreliable, elusive, evasive" in their relations with others. He has declared that most dramatists of the past have assumed that everything can be verified and made clear to audiences, whereas in actuality little can ever be known definitely.

Pinter's early works are often called "comedies of menace." Of these, *The Birthday Party* is typical. The central character, Stanley, lives in a boardinghouse, where he is mothered by his landlady. Then McCann and Goldberg arrive, presumably looking for rooms but actually for Stanley. They subject Stanley to intense cross-examination, during which they accuse him of a variety of contradictory acts, and organize a birthday party for him although he insists that it is not his birthday. The next morning they take him away. It is unclear what Stanley has done, who McCann and Goldberg are, who has sent them, or what they intend to do with Stanley. But it is this uncertainty that makes the play so disturbing. Critics have defined the basis of the threat variously as conformity, death, guilt, and retribution.

In Pinter's later works, menace gives way to enigma. Of these plays,

The Homecoming is usually considered the best. It is set in a house in north London inhabited by an all-male family: Max (the father), Sam (his chauffeur brother), Lenny (a pimp), and Joey (a would-be prize-fighter). Then the oldest son, Teddy (a philosophy professor in an American university), arrives with his wife, Ruth (who, though originally from London, has never met Teddy's family). Almost immediately the men make sexual overtures to Ruth, and eventually Lenny suggests that he set her up as a prostitute; after haggling over the arrangements, she agrees to remain, and Teddy calmly returns to America without her. Sam collapses after revealing that the boys' mother had used his cab for adulterous relations. At the end of the play, Max is kneeling before Ruth begging for her favors. The dialogue and action throughout *The Homecoming* seem wholly natural, but the play becomes enigmatic not because so little is revealed about the characters' pasts but because their unconventional interrelationships are treated so matter-of-factly. The resulting sense of ambiguity has led critics to offer numerous symbolic interpretations of the play: as a wish fulfillment of the Oedipus complex (with the sons taking possession of a surrogate mother); as Ruth's acceptance of the necessity that woman play many roles in the life of man; as an ironic variation on the prodigal son story; as an adaptation of the biblical story of Ruth; and as a conflict between mental, moral, and physical urges, with the last an easy winner. Such varying (though not necessarily contradictory) interpretations indicate the rich allusiveness of Pinter's plays.

As a dramatist, Pinter seems to fall somewhere between the absurdists and Chekhov. Like the former, he isolates his characters in an unverifiable universe; like Chekhov, he creates a realistic texture of background and dialogue in which both speech and deed are evasions or disguises of deeper conflicts and anxieties. But because the anxieties and their significance are never clearly defined, they are rich in connotations that vary somewhat with each member of the audience.

Major English Companies

In addition to its many fine playwrights, the vitality of England's theatre since 1960 has depended heavily on two groups—the Royal Shakespeare Company and the National Theatre. In 1961 the Memorial Theatre at Stratford was awarded a new charter and renamed the Royal Shakespeare Company (RSC). This new status owed much to Peter Hall (1930–   ), who had been named head of the company in 1960. Upon assuming his new post, Hall took a lease on the Aldwych Theatre in London and transformed the company into a year-round rather than a summer operation. Since then, the company has divided its energies between Stratford and London and has enlarged its repertory to include works by various authors from various periods and countries.

By 1962 the company's activities had become so extensive that the man-

The exterior of the new National Theatre in London. (Courtesy British Tourist Authority.)

agement was increased to include Peter Brook and Michel Saint-Denis. In 1963–1964, the RSC mounted an experimental "Theatre of Cruelty" season under the direction of Brook and Charles Marowitz. Brook drew heavily on this work in staging Weiss' *Marat/Sade,* one of the most influential productions of the decade. By 1965, the RSC had become London's most innovative troupe. In 1968, Hall, Brook, and Saint-Denis resigned, but their policies have been continued by Trevor Nunn, who succeeded them.

Since 1970 the RSC has been plagued by rampant inflation. Nevertheless, it has continued its extremely ambitious program of revivals and new plays both in its main theatres and in several other spaces. Without question, the RSC is one of the world's major companies.

Of the directors associated with the RSC, Peter Brook (1925–) has been the most influential. He began directing while still in his teens, and gradually built an outstanding reputation with productions of plays by such authors as Shakespeare, Fry, Anouilh, Duerrenmatt, and Genet. He is now known primarily for such productions as *King Lear* (1962), *Marat/Sade* (1964), *The Tempest* (1968), and *A Midsummer Night's Dream* (1970). Brook has been extremely eclectic, borrowing from many sources but always transforming his borrowings into his own form of expression. For example, in *A Midsummer Night's Dream* he drew on Meyerhold, commedia dell'arte, circus, and radical theatre groups of the 1960s, but the results were uniquely his own. In 1971 Brook became director of the International Center for Theatre Research, based in Paris and including participants from all over the world. Here Brook has experimented with acting and directing devices and techniques capable of transcending barriers created by language and culture. Some of the results have been incorporated into such productions as *Orghast* and *The Ik.*

The trial scene from Shakespeare's The Merchant of Venice *as performed at the National Theatre, London, in 1970. Joan Plowright is seen at left as Portia, and Laurence Olivier at right as Shylock. Directed by Jonathan Miller. (Photo by Anthony Crickmay.)*

In 1963 England, after decades of debate over the desirability of such action, inaugurated its National Theatre. At that time the Old Vic's company was dissolved and its building assigned to the new troupe, which was placed under the direction of Laurence Olivier. Through an extremely varied repertory of plays staged by the most eminent English and foreign directors and designers, the National Theatre rapidly built a reputation for excellence. In 1973 Peter Hall replaced Olivier as director of the National Theatre, and in 1976 the company moved into its new building, one of the most advanced theatre plants anywhere. It includes three performance spaces: the 890-seat Lyttleton proscenium theatre; the 1160-seat Olivier open-stage theatre; and the 400-seat Cottesloe laboratory theatre. Since the National Theatre receives more than twice the subsidy of any other theatre in Great Britain, much is expected of it.

Outside of London there are about fifty resident companies, many of them excellent and practically all subsidized by local governments. Within London there are a large number of "fringe" groups (comparable to American Off-Off-Broadway companies). These have come into existence largely since 1968, when the censorship that had been in existence since 1737 was abolished. The fringe companies perform in pubs, meeting halls, playgrounds, schools, or almost anywhere an audience can be assembled, and at lunchtime or late at night, as well as at the traditional times. Their great flexibility in their approach to production has done much to add variety to the English theatre. Among the most important of these groups are the Pip Simmons Group, the Joint Stock Theatre Group, the Welfare State, and Triple Action.

England now has a large number of young writers who promise to keep its stage vital. Among the best are Christopher Hampton with *The Philanthropist* (1970) and *Treats* (1976), David Hare with *Knuckle* (1974) and *Teeth 'n' Smiles* (1975), Trevor Griffiths with *The Party* (1972) and *Comedians* (1974), and Stephen Poliakoff with *City Sugar* (1976) and *Strawberry Fields* (1977).

Despite the seeming vigor of the English theatre, some critics have begun to declare that it has ceased to be innovative and that it has begun to falter under the stress of financial crises. If so, the decline has yet to become readily apparent.

Broadway

In the postwar period, American drama, primarily because of Williams and Miller, enjoyed considerable international prestige. But by the late 1950s, a decline was evident. This can be blamed partially on Broadway with its ever-increasing production costs and the consequent need to attract large audiences. As a result, emphasis came to be placed primarily on musicals, light comedy, or plays already proven elsewhere, either at one of the regional theatres or in England.

The musical remained the most vital form on Broadway. In the 1960s, *Hello, Dolly!* and *Fiddler on the Roof* set new records for longevity. In the 1970s some attempts were made to achieve greater unity by reducing concern for spectacle and making the chorus and principals the same, as in *Company* (1970) and *A Chorus Line* (1975). There were also several experiments with presentational techniques, most notably in the revised version of *Candide* (1973) and in *Pacific Overtures* (1976).

The most successful writer of comedy for the American stage has been Neil Simon (1927–) with such plays as *Barefoot in the Park* (1963), *The Odd Couple* (1965), *The Sunshine Boys* (1972), and *California Suite* (1976), all combining zany humor with eccentric characters.

The only new American author of serious plays to win and sustain a high critical reputation after 1960 was Edward Albee (1928–), whose first four short plays—*The Zoo Story, The Sandbox, The American Dream,* and *The Death of Bessie Smith*—were produced Off-Broadway in 1960–1961. These early works led many critics to consider Albee an absurdist. Then, in 1962 with *Who's Afraid of Virginia Woolf?*, his first

The phenomenal success of the 1970s, A Chorus Line, *was produced by Joseph Papp. Here Diana (Priscilla Lopez) describes her experience at the High School for the Performing Arts. (Photo by Martha Swope.)*

full-length and most successful play, Albee demonstrated his likeness to Strindberg and Williams with an essentially realistic work about characters who use psychological blackmail as their primary tool for dealing with others. In it, two college professors and their wives, during a night spent in drinking and playing cruel games, strip each other of illusions and demonstrate how people create hells for each other out of unwillingness to accept or admit weakness. Since 1962 Albee has written such plays as *Tiny Alice* (1964), *A Delicate Balance* (1966), *All Over* (1971), and *Seascape* (1975).

Broadway's shortcomings engendered many schemes for diversifying the American theatre. Among these was an attempt to establish permanent companies in New York like those found in virtually all major European cities. Consequently, around 1960 plans were launched for the Lincoln Center for the Performing Arts, with facilities for ballet, opera, concerts, and drama. In 1963 a repertory company was formed and in 1965 it moved into its newly completed house in Lincoln Center, the Vivian Beaumont Theatre. Unfortunately, this theatre, despite a number of changes in management, has seldom won high critical praise or strong audience support. Its potential has yet to be realized.

Although Broadway has declined considerably in importance as a producer of new plays, it remains the primary home of America's commercial theatre. In the early 1970s it underwent a considerable slump but since the season of 1974–1975 it has recorded the highest box office sales in its history.

Off-Broadway and Off-Off-Broadway

In the early 1960s many of the financial pressures that had plagued Broadway began to be felt Off-Broadway with the result that it became increasingly conservative. Out of the need to escape these strictures came a new solution—Off-Off-Broadway. The beginning of this trend is usually dated from 1958, when Joe Cino began to welcome various artistic activities into his Café Cino. By 1961 he was presenting plays regularly; other groups had also taken up his practice and were performing in all sorts of spaces and under all sorts of circumstances. Because of its ingenuity and adaptability, Off-Off-Broadway flourished. It has been estimated that between 1960 and 1965 about four hundred new plays by about two hundred new playwrights were produced by Off-Off-Broadway groups.

The most important of the Off-Off-Broadway groups has been the LaMama organization, founded by Ellen Stewart in 1961. By 1969–1970 LaMama was presenting more plays each season than all the Broadway theatres combined. In 1969 LaMama acquired its own building with two theatres. Beginning in 1964, Miss Stewart took some productions to Europe, where her freewheeling experiments attracted such favorable attention that she founded branches of LaMama in several countries.

LaMama's dedication to experimentation also extended to directorial techniques. The early results are best exemplified in the work of Tom O'Horgan, who after working at LaMama created a stir Off-Off-Broadway with *Futz* and *Tom Paine* and on Broadway with *Hair, Lenny, Jesus Christ, Superstar,* and others. O'Horgan tended to place primary emphasis on physical activity, tableaux, lighting effects, projections, amplified music, nonverbal sound, and anti-illusionistic devices of all sorts. His productions were usually colorful, frenetic, and uninhibited, but they also tended to obscure story and idea. Nevertheless, his "physicalization" of dramatic elements has become typical of much directing in recent years, in part because so much contemporary drama is verbally inarticulate.

In the 1970s LaMama has been concerned with developing ensemble companies, some of them ethnic (black, Puerto Rican, and Native American). The best known of LaMama's recent directors has been Andrei Serban, who has worked with mythic material, invented language, and ritualized action to create productions of great emotional impact in *Medea, The Trojan Women,* and *Electra.* Beginning in 1977, Serban worked with other companies and adapted his techniques to productions of such plays as *The Cherry Orchard, Agamemnon,* and *The Ghost Sonata.*

Since the late 1960s the differences between Off-Broadway and Off-Off-Broadway theatres have so eroded that the two are now often indistinguishable. Among the theatres that fit into these categories, the most important probably are the Circle in the Square, the American Place Theatre, the Chelsea Theatre Center, and the New York Shakespeare Festival and its Public Theatre. Other significant companies include the

A good example of Andrei Serban's use of ritualized action and of his unique directing techniques may be seen in this scene from the 1977 Lincoln Center production of The Cherry Orchard. *(Photo by George E. Joseph.)*

Circle Repertory Company, Manhattan Theatre Club, and The Brooklyn Academy of Music. The Circle in the Square, founded in 1951, has been a major Off-Broadway theatre since that time. After a slump in the 1960s, it made a comeback in the 1970s, opening a new theatre on Broadway and maintaining its original house Off-Broadway. The new theatre, where most of the organization's energies are now centered, is noted especially for productions of the classics, such as *Tartuffe* and *Saint Joan,* with major actors. The American Place Theatre, headed by Wynn Handman and largely attended by subscribers, seeks to encourage new writers of exceptional talent in its seasons of new plays. The Chelsea Theatre Center, headed by Robert Kalfin and located in Brooklyn, is noted for its adventurous program of foreign plays (such as Genet's *The Screens,* Bond's *Saved,* and Handke's *Kaspar*), classics, and new American plays.

But the most important of these groups is the New York Shakespeare Festival Theatre, headed by Joseph Papp (1921–   ). After a modest beginning in the 1950s, Papp was able to persuade municipal authorities

Scene from Hair; *Directed by Tom O'Horgan. (Photograph by Friedman-Abeles.)*

Scene from the Chelsea Theater
Center of Brooklyn's production of
Edward Bond's Saved. (Photo-
graph by Alan B. Tepper.)

to let him stage plays in Central Park. This program became so popular
that in 1962 the city built an amphitheatre there to house it, the Dela-
corte Theatre, seating 2236. In 1967 Papp acquired the former Astor
Library and transformed it into the Public Theatre, with five auditoriums. It opened with *Hair* (later restaged on Broadway by O'Horgan).
Since then Papp has presented an extremely varied repertory and many of
his productions have been moved to Broadway, among them Gordone's
No Place to Be Somebody, Rabe's *Sticks and Bones,* Miller's *That Cham-
pionship Season,* Shakespeare's *Much Ado about Nothing* and *Two Gentlemen of Verona,* Bennett's *A Chorus Line,* Shange's *For Colored Girls,*
and Swados' *Runaways.* From 1973 until 1977 Papp also headed the Lincoln Center Repertory Theatre. With his activities now centered at the
Public Theatre, he is probably the most influential force in New York's
theatre today.

   Off-Broadway and Off-Off-Broadway companies have probably exerted
their greatest influence on the theatre at large through their innovative
playwrights. As a group, these writers did much during the 1960s to alter

ideas about dramatic structure and to encourage disaffection from accepted mores and traditions. Most of their plays were organized around themes or motifs rather than causally related incidents; characterization has most usually reduced to broadly conceived types; ideas were typically presented through sharply contrasting (often oversimplified) positions; language was often downgraded in favor of aural and visual appeals, both of which were exploited extensively. Overall, the trend was away from realism toward a frank theatricality. Some of the most successful playwrights spawned Off-Broadway and Off-Off-Broadway have been: Sam Shepard with *Operation Sidewinder, The Tooth of Crime, Suicide in B-flat,* and *Curse of the Starving Class;* Rochelle Owens with *Futz* and *The Queen of Greece;* Paul Foster with *Tom Paine;* Terrence McNally with *Sweet Eros, Next,* and *Whiskey;* John Guare with *The House of Blue Leaves* and *Cop-out;* Lanford Wilson with *The Rimers of Eldritch, Hot L Baltimore,* and *The Mound Builders;* Ronald Ribman with *Ceremony of Innocence, The Poison Tree,* and *Cold Storage;* Israel Horovitz with *The Indian Wants the Bronx* and *The Primary English Class;* and Robert Patrick with *Kennedy's Children* and *Play by Play.*

Black Theatre

A development related to Off-Broadway was the appearance during the 1960s of a strong black theatre movement. It received its first significant impetus in 1964, when LeRoi Jones and others founded the Black Arts

Scene from LeRoi Jones' Home on the Range, *as performed at the Spirit House Movers. The growth in awareness and pride of black Americans has led to greatly increased theatrical activity among black playwrights, actors and producing groups. (Photo © 1968 by Fred W. McDarrah.)*

Repertoire Theatre School in New York. This organization soon came to an end because some of its productions offended officials, who cut off the government funds that had partially supported it. Nevertheless, this group served as an inspiration for others, and by the late 1960s there were more than forty black arts groups scattered throughout the country. Three of these—the Negro Ensemble Company, the New Lafayette Theatre, and the Spirit House—were of special importance. The Negro Ensemble Company (NEC), founded in New York in 1968 under the artistic direction of Douglas Turner Ward, has produced a wide range of plays that it considers meaningful to blacks. The New Lafayette Theatre, founded in 1967 by Robert Macbeth, served as a cultural center for Harlem until its demise in 1973 and aided other black groups throughout the country through an information bureau and *Black Theatre Magazine,* which it published. Neither of these groups was sufficiently separatist to suit LeRoi Jones (now known as Imamu Amiri Baraka), head of the Spirit House in Newark, New Jersey, where he sought to promote a wholly black culture.

This upsurge in theatrical activity brought a corresponding increase in the demand for black actors (among the best of whom were James Earl Jones, Ruby Dee, Diana Sands, Claudia McNeill, Ossie Davis, Roscoe Lee Brown, Moses Gunn, Robert Hooks, Ron O'Neal, and Cicely Tyson) and directors (among them Lloyd Richards, Robert Macbeth, Melvin van Peebles, and Michael Schultz).

The number of black dramatists also steadily grew. Among the first to win critical acclaim was Lorraine Hansberry (1930–1965) with *A Raisin in the Sun* (1959) and *The Sign in Sidney Brustein's Window* (1964). The first of these will be examined in detail as an example of black drama.

A Raisin in the Sun

A Raisin in the Sun was the first play by a black woman to be presented on Broadway, where it won the New York Drama Critics Circle Award. Its success did much to open the way for other black dramatists, and its themes foreshadowed those that would be developed extensively during the 1960s.

In many respects *A Raisin in the Sun* is traditional, since, like many American dramas, it focuses on the family unit and its dreams. In structure it is a well-made play of impeccable craftsmanship. Its straightforward story is developed through a clear cause-and-effect sequence of exposition, complications, climactic reversal, and denouement. It is divided into three acts, and its six scenes all take place in the same setting. Its overall style is realistic with a generous sprinkling of humor in a primarily serious plot.

Plot and Structure. *A Raisin in the Sun* tells the story of the Younger family: the matriarchal Lena, or Mama, a dignified woman in her sixties;

Beneatha, her twenty-year-old daughter who hopes to become a doctor; Walter, Lena's thirty-five-year-old son, a chauffeur; Ruth, Walter's wife, who does domestic work for white women; and Travis, the ten-year-old son of Walter and Ruth. All live together on the south side of Chicago in a cramped two-bedroom apartment (Walter and Ruth occupy one bedroom, Mama and Beneatha the other, and Travis sleeps on a couch in the combination living room–kitchen). There is only one small window for light and air, and the bathroom is shared by all the families on the floor. But, though the space is cramped and the furnishings worn, the apartment is clean and neat; thus, the setting reflects its occupants, who may be poor but are not without pride.

The opening scene of the play introduces the family as they anticipate the arrival of a check for $10,000, the life insurance of the deceased father. To the family the money represents a chance to realize its dreams, the most crucial of which are Beneatha's desire to attend medical school and Walter's to become a businessman. In the second scene, the money arrives, but by that time friction is beginning to tear the family apart. The opposition of Mama and Ruth to Walter's plan to invest in a liquor store alienates him so fully that Ruth, upon discovering that she is pregnant, makes an appointment to have an illegal abortion.

In Act Two, scene one, Mama, in an attempt to bring her family together, makes a down payment of $3500 on a house that can accommodate everyone comfortably. But it seems certain that trouble lies ahead because the house is located in an all-white neighborhood. Nevertheless, everyone except Walter is overjoyed, for the house will permit them to escape their present environment.

Not until a few weeks later (in Act Two, scene two), when the family is packing to move, does Mama come to understand Walter's deep need to be recognized as a man capable of making his own decisions. As a result, she designates him head of the family and gives him the remaining money with the stipulation that $3000 be put aside for Beneatha's medical education. As the scene closes, Walter, overjoyed, is envisioning his future as an executive.

Act Two, scene three, brings the play's major reversal. Karl Lindner, a white representative of the neighborhood into which the Youngers plan to move, arrives to tell the family of resentment against them and to offer them a sum substantially higher than they have paid for the house. They indignantly refuse. Then Walter learns that one of his prospective business partners has absconded with all the money Mama gave him, including that intended for Beneatha's education. The act ends in despair and recrimination.

At the opening of Act Three, one hour later, Beneatha is cynical and ready to abandon her dreams. The family is reconciled to remaining in the apartment. But Walter slips out and calls Lindner, intending to sell the new house and play the role of "polite darky" for a white-dominated world. When his plan is revealed, the family is horrified. Lindner arrives just as the moving van does (no one has canceled it), but Walter, forced by Mama to talk to Lindner with Travis present, cannot bring himself to go through with his plan. Recovering his pride, he tells Lindner that the family wants no trouble but insists on moving into its new home. As the play ends, the move is underway. In one of the play's final speeches, Mama says of Walter: "He finally came into his manhood today, didn't he?" Thus, although the family has realized few of its dreams, it has grown in understanding, dignity, and unity.

Themes and Ideas. Many features place *A Raisin in the Sun* firmly within the American tradition, but others set it apart. Perhaps most significantly, with one exception, all of the characters are black, and their experiences introduce almost every major theme that would be developed extensively by later black playwrights.

The play's title is taken from a work by Langston Hughes, *Montage of a Dream Deferred*: "What happens to a dream deferred? / Does it dry up / Like a raisin in the sun?" Almost everything that happens in the play is related to this concept of the "dream deferred." We learn that Mama and her husband were part of the "great migration" during the early twentieth century when blacks moved north in search of better conditions. She says: "In my time we was worried about not being lynched and getting to the North if we could and how to stay alive and still have a pinch of dignity too." But Walter and Beneatha are more concerned

A scene from the original production of A Raisin in the Sun *at the Ethel Barrymore Theatre in New York, with Sidney Poitier, and Diana Sands. Directed by Lloyd Richards; scenery and lighting by Ralph Alswang. (Courtesy Lincoln Center Library for the Performing Arts.)*

about what remains to be done than about what has been accomplished. Of the two, Walter is the more embittered, for as chauffeur to a rich white man he daily sees wealth that lies beyond his reach. Consequently, he all too eagerly leaps at the chance to acquire his own business as the first step toward riches, which he considers the key to happiness. Beneatha, on the other hand, wants to become a doctor so she can ease human suffering, although it is injustice that ultimately bothers her. In one sense, then, Walter represents the selfish and materialistic approach and Beneatha the altruistic and idealistic approach to realizing the dream deferred.

A closely related issue is integration versus separation of the races. This theme is dramatized in part through Beneatha's two suitors—the rich American student George Murchison and the Nigerian student Joseph Asagai. George is interested only with maintaining the security his family has achieved, and he is completely unconcerned about the injustices suffered by other members of his race. When Beneatha calls him an assimilationist (or integrationist), he tells Ruth that "it's just a college girl's way of calling people Uncle Tom," but Beneatha responds, "It means someone who is willing to give up his own culture and submerge himself completely in the dominant, and in this case, *oppressive* culture!" Joseph, on the other hand, arouses Beneatha's interest in her African heritage, questions the way she dresses (he calls her straightened hair "mutilated" and he brings her a Nigerian robe), and asks her to return to Africa with him. Above all, in the final act Joseph counters Beneatha's disillusionment by arguing the necessity of living one's dream despite suffering and disappointment.

The theme of integration and separation is also dramatized in the purchase of the house, but the response of whites makes it part of a still larger theme—the exploitation of blacks by whites who still deny blacks full civil rights. Walter's desperation stems in part from his awareness of how many more opportunities are open to white men of his age, and Mama's purchase of the house in a white neighborhood comes about only because "them houses they put up for colored in them areas way out all seem to cost twice as much as other houses." Although there is little direct denunciation of whites (even Lindner is treated objectively), a contrast is continuously implied between exploited blacks and exploiting (or uncomprehending) whites.

Another dominant theme concerns growth and maturity. It is reflected in part by Walter's sense of being denied his manhood both by his mother and by the jobs open to him. The theme is also developed through the repeatedly expressed longing for sunlight and garden space and most forcefully by Mama's spindly plant, which she nurtures in the feeble light of the window just as she has nurtured her family's spirit through all vicissitudes. This plant sums up Mama's faith and persistence, and as the play ends, after everyone has left the apartment, Mama returns for her plant. This final moment implies that neither the plant nor the family will "dry up like a raisin in the sun" but will thrive and grow. The deferred dream still has not been fully realized, but another step has been taken toward its fulfillment.

Although *A Raisin in the Sun* deals specifically with black life, it is universal in its appeal. Whatever one's race, one can sympathize with the dreams, disappointments, and triumphs of the Younger family. Without bitterness, the play makes clear the injustices done to blacks, and while it offers few solutions, it shows the human consequences of the problems.

Other Black Playwrights

The black writers who came after Hansberry were increasingly concerned with the injustices of a white-dominated society. Among the most important was LeRoi Jones (Imamu Amiri Baraka, 1934–), not only because he was one of the best dramatists of the 1960s but because he represents the trend away from concern with integration to a demand for complete separation. *The Toilet* (1964) is a good example of his early work. It shows a white boy being beaten unmercifully because he allegedly has been attracted to a black boy. Jones uses homosexuality to symbolize the kind of barriers society has erected to make it shameful for races to admit mutual love and respect. After 1965 Jones became increasingly separatist, and since then his plays have been designed either to induce hatred of whites or respect for blacks. One of the most powerful of the later plays is *Slave Ship* (1967), which traces the black experience from Africa to the present.

The Negro Ensemble Company has fostered the talents of several writers, among them Douglas Turner Ward, whose *Day of Absence* (1967) and *The Reckoning* (1969) use broad caricature to show blacks outwitting whites; Lonne Elder III, whose *Ceremonies in Dark Old Men*

Scene from the Chelsea Theatre Center's production of LeRoi Jones' Slaveship. *Photo by Bert Andrews.*

Scene from Ntozake Shange's "choreopoem" For Colored Girls Who Have Considered Suicide When the Rainbow Is Enuf. *Produced by Joseph Papp. (Photo by Martha Swope.)*

(1969) focuses on a family in Harlem and the illegal schemes they are talked into; and Joseph A. Walker, whose *The River Niger* (1972) symbolically traces the African stream flowing all the way to Harlem.

Joseph Papp produced Charles Gordone's *No Place to Be Somebody* (1969), a Pulitzer-Prize-winning drama about a black man's attempt to start his own version of the Mafia, and Ntozake Shange's *For Colored Girls Who Have Considered Suicide When the Rainbow Is Enuf* (1975), a "choreopoem" that explores black women's awareness.

One of the most important and seemingly the most prolific of black writers is Ed Bullins (1935–   ), for a time resident playwright at the New Lafayette Theatre and editor of *Black Theatre Magazine*. His work is varied in tone and subject but unified by its concern for what it means to be black. He is writing a lengthy cycle about life in the industrial North and West, of which *In the Wine Time* and *In New England Winter* are parts. Others of his plays include *Clara's Old Man* (1965), *The Pig Pen* (1970), and *The Taking of Miss Janie* (1975).

Other black playwrights who deserve mention include Richard Wesley,

Melvin van Peebles, Ron Milner, Ossie Davis, Adrienne Kennedy, Ben Caldwell, Vinette Carroll, and Leslie Lee. In recent years, black playwrights seem to have been moving away from defining black experience through negative pictures of whites and toward depicting blacks in relation to each other. Most encouraging, black theatre and drama seem for the first time in American history to be attracting wide audiences. Many of the plays and musicals seen on Broadway in recent seasons have been by black authors. The number of black companies throughout the country has also greatly increased and are now linked by membership in the Black Theatre Alliance.

Although it is the most extensively developed, black theatre is only one example of the effort to reflect the life of minorities in America. Others who are now developing their own drama include homosexuals, women, and various ethnic groups (such as Puerto Ricans, Native Americans, and Mexican Americans).

Resident Theatres

One of the most encouraging trends of the 1960s was a renascence of the resident company outside of New York. This type of organization that had thrived before 1875 but had virtually disappeared by 1900 was revitalized in the 1950s by a few groups, most notably the Arena Stage in Washington and the Actors' Workshop in San Francisco. It was given a major boost in 1959 when the Ford Foundation made large grants to several existing companies that had won considerable local support. It was further strengthened when Tyrone Guthrie decided to found a company in Minneapolis, for the example of a major director seeking a base outside established theatrical centers focused attention on the entire movement. The Tyrone Guthrie Theatre (home of the Minneapolis Theatre Company) was opened in 1963, and the favorable publicity surrounding its opening made other communities desirous of having resident troupes. By 1977 there were about fifty of these companies.

Most of the resident troupes present seasons of plays in which classics are mingled with recent works, each given a limited run. Thus, they resemble European subsidized companies more than Broadway theatres. But unlike their European counterparts, that can be certain of continuing government subsidies, most American resident theatres are dependent on box office receipts, gifts from private donors, or grants from government agencies or philanthropic foundations.

The first step toward government subsidization of the arts in the United States was taken in 1965 when federal legislation established the National Endowment for the Arts to make grants to projects showing outstanding potential. Money was also appropriated to encourage the formation of arts councils by individual states, most of which have now done so. Government appropriations for the arts have steadily increased and are

now larger than at any time in the past. Nevertheless, there still is no assurance of continued support, as there is in most European countries, and no company can depend on its grants being continued from one year to the next.

Resident theatres have become increasingly attractive to playwrights, since pressures there are considerably fewer than on Broadway. Resident companies usually are not concerned with long runs, nor do they expect to succeed or fail on the basis of a single production. Thus, they often are willing to take greater chances than Broadway producers are. Much the same can also be said of many Off-Broadway and Off-Off-Broadway theatres. It is probably for this reason that more and more plays are now presented on Broadway only after they have been proven elsewhere, either abroad or in the United States. Several resident theatres have become especially fruitful sources for Broadway, most notably the Arena Stage in Washington, the Long Wharf Theatre in New Haven, Connecticut, and the Mark Taper Forum in Los Angeles.

The Living Theatre

One of the greatest influences on the theatre of the 1960s, both in America and elsewhere, was the Living Theatre. Founded in New York in 1946 by Judith Malina (1926–   ) and Julian Beck (1925–   ), the Living Theatre was for many years devoted to poetic drama and innovative staging techniques, although these concerns gradually gave way to interest in Brecht, Artaud, and anarchism. In 1963 the Living Theatre was forcibly closed for failure to pay taxes and from 1964 to 1968 it performed in Europe, touring widely and building a large following, especially among the disaffected. Only two of its scripts during that time—Genet's *The Maids* and *Antigone*—originated outside the company. The group made

Contemporary Theatre and Drama

383

its greatest impact with *Frankenstein* (about a man–monster created by modern society and technology), *Mysteries and Smaller Pieces* (a series of short ritualized exercises championing anarchy), and *Paradise Now* (with which it won special notoriety, in part because the production coincided with and seemed to epitomize the political upheavals then under way in France, America, and elsewhere).

Paradise Now (1968) begins with actors circulating among the spectators and denouncing strictures on freedom. It then continues for four or five hours, depending on the receptivity of the audience. It is divided into eight sections, each subdivided into three parts: a rite, a vision, and a contemporary example. All this is further arranged in terms of growing awareness and passage of time, so that it moves ever nearer the present. With the final section, the play seeks to move the audience into the streets to continue the work toward revolution begun by the play. To achieve this goal, the actors had to override opposition, and consequently they

The Living Theatre's production of Frankenstein. *(Photo © 1968 by Fred W. McDarrah.)*

challenged all real or imagined resistance, often shouting accusations and obscenities at spectators. Thus, performances became a series of confrontations. Both audience and actors roamed the auditorium and stage indiscriminately, and often several scenes proceeded simultaneously in various parts of the theatre. *Paradise Now* is important in part because it sought to make the audience an integral part of the action. But because it also insisted on a predetermined response, the atmosphere during performances was often hostile, even violent. It was this aggressive behavior toward audiences, combined with its revolutionary stance, that won the Living Theatre its enormous notoriety.

By 1970 the Living Theatre had begun to disintegrate, and by the time the Becks returned to the United States in 1973, the Living Theatre's popularity had markedly declined. By 1976 it was once more seeking a permanent base in Europe. But, if its influence has subsided, the Living Theatre's importance in the late 1960s cannot be denied, for probably no group was better known or more widely emulated. Of its attitudes and practices, the most influential were: downgrading language in favor of Artaudian techniques; converting all texts into political arguments; insisting on confronting and overriding audiences; establishing an evangelical tone for all activities; and refusing to make any distinction between life style and theatrical style.

Radical and Guerilla Theatre

Many of the Living Theatre's concerns were reflected by several "radical" groups, who during the 1960s sought to use the theatre as a weapon for bringing about changes in society. Among the most important of these companies were the Bread and Puppet Theatre, the San Francisco Mime Theatre, and El Teatro Campesino. The Bread and Puppet Theatre, founded in New York in 1961 by Peter Schumann, uses puppets of various sizes (some as tall as twelve feet) in plays (based on fairy tales, legends, myths, the Bible, and other familiar sources) designed to demonstrate the superiority of love and humility over political, moral, and materialistic deceptions. It has performed about seventy works throughout America and Europe. The San Francisco Mime Theatre was founded in 1959 by R. G. Davis to do silent plays, but since silence seemed to dampen audience response, words were introduced. Originally its offerings were based on works from commedia dell'arte, Molière, Goldoni, and other sources, but in 1966 it embraced the radical cause and since then has performed plays about civil rights, women's liberation, and various other subjects. El Teatro Campesino was founded in 1965 by Luis Valdez to dramatize issues in the California grape pickers' strike, but it soon became a bilingual troupe devoted to creating pride in the heritage and accomplishments of Mexican-Americans. These three organizations have remained vital but the majority of the radical theatres have now disappeared.

In the 1960s, theatre also came to be used in ways analogous to guerilla warfare (thus the label "guerilla theatre"). Typically, those using this form seized the opportunity provided by some gathering, public place, or occasion to present unscheduled, brief, pithy skits designed to call attention to a specific issue. In recent years the diminished popularity of demonstrations and confrontations has made guerilla theatre almost a relic of the past.

Nudity and Obscenity

The numerous assaults made during the 1960s on accepted traditions and standards led to a gradual lessening of strictures on acceptable subject matter, behavior, dress, and speech for the stage. The changes are perhaps most graphically demonstrated by the introduction of nudity and obscenity.

The first notable use of nudity came in 1968 in the Broadway production of *Hair,* in which at the end of the first part the performers removed

Disrobing scene from Oh, Calcutta. *(Photo by Friedman-Abeles.)*

their clothes for one brief moment. Obscene language was also sprinkled liberally throughout the play. Both innovations created considerable controversy in America and elsewhere as productions of *Hair* were mounted in various other countries. Because it achieved such popularity and notoriety, *Hair* was also important for the innovations in the musical form it popularized.

Hair is held together not by its slight story but by a set of related themes (the war in Vietnam, the military draft, the conflict between generations) that are expressed primarily through music and song. Taken as a whole, it is a good-natured attempt to justify a life style and to promote peace and understanding. About it there is an air of improvisation; the emphasis on impersonation is minimal, for performers take on and discard roles (mostly types or caricatures) as the rapidly shifting action requires, but most of the time they seem merely to be themselves. The costumes, music, and dance reflect those in vogue outside the theatre; properties and scenic elements are brought on or improvised as needed. Many of these characteristics have now become relatively common.

Hair's use of nudity and obscenity was soon taken up and considerably extended by such productions as *Che!* and *Oh, Calcutta.* By the 1970s, though the limits of permissibility were still somewhat vague, almost any subject, behavior, or manner of speaking was potentially acceptable for theatrical use.

Grotowski

During the 1960s a number of people deplored the tendency of the theatre to borrow from other media and advocated the abandonment of every element not truly required by theatre *as theatre.* The outstanding exponent of this view was Jerzy Grotowski (1933–), director of the Polish Laboratory Theatre in Wroclaw (Breslau). Grotowski called his a "poor theatre" because he sought to eliminate the technological aids used by most groups and to concentrate on the two elements he considered indispensable: the actor and the audience. For his productions he used a space that could be rearranged to meet the specific needs of each production; he used no elaborate lighting effects; he forbade makeup and reduced costumes to the purely functional; he permitted no actor to change costume to indicate a change in role, status, or psychological condition; his properties were minimal and were chosen for their adaptability for many purposes; he used no scenery in the traditonal sense; his actors produced all music themselves, either by beating out rhythms, by vocal sound, or by playing musical instruments. Thus, the actor was thrown back on his own resources.

For this reason, Grotowski was especially involved in actor training, through which he sought to eliminate all blocks that prevented performers from giving themselves fully. Intensive physical training was coupled with other exercises designed to remove psychological barriers. The voice was developed as an instrument capable of exceeding the demands of speech. Ultimately, Grotowski wished to produce actors who could surpass so completely the spectators' capabilities that a sense of magic was aroused.

The other essential ingredient in Grotowski's theatre was the audience. In the beginning he tried to involve the audience directly in performances, but he came to believe that this only made spectators self-conscious, since they did not know what was expected of them. He then concentrated on creating the proper spatial relationship among spectators and actors so that they might interact appropriately and unself-consciously. For example, in his adaptation of Marlowe's *Doctor Faustus* the action supposedly occurs on the night the devil is to claim Faustus' soul; Faustus calls together his friends (represented by the audience) for a banquet at which he explains what has happened. Thus, the theatre became a banqueting hall and the audience, seated at long tables on which most of the action occurs, was asked merely to respond as people might on such an occasion. Similarly, in Grotowski's adaptation of *Kordian,* the action was set in an insane asylum and the audience, as though visitors, was scattered about among hospital beds, which served as the principal scenic elements.

Grotowski viewed the theatre as the modern equivalent of a tribal ceremony capable of uniting a community. Therefore, in preparing a script he searched in it for archetypal (or universal) patterns, actions, and images—things deeply embedded in the human psyche quite independent of religious faith or time and place. These were then accentuated and developed in ways calculated to make both actors and audience confront themselves and thereby undergo psychological catharsis. Thus, Grotowski's goals resembled those of Artaud, although his means differed markedly.

By 1970 Grotowski had come to believe that his group had reached the end of its search for technical mastery, and he decided to create no new productions. He then set out to eliminate the "idea of theatre," in the sense of an actor playing before an audience, and to find a way of incorporating spectators into the process. His main concern became how to lead participants back into the elemental connections between man and his body, his imagination, the natural world, and other human beings. The first major revelation of the new work came during the summer of 1975. Some of the activities involved groups going into the woods for twenty-four hours during which they were led through ritualized relivings of basic myths, archetypes, and symbols, including fire, air, earth, water, eating, dancing, playing, planting, and bathing. Through this process, participants were expected to rediscover the roots of theatre in pure ritualized experience, as well as to discover their own true being. Thus, it is clear that Grotowski's current approach differs markedly from the one he used in the 1960s. It is the subject of lively debate both in Poland and elsewhere.

The Open Theatre

Another "poor theatre," the Open Theatre, was founded in New York in 1963 by Joseph Chaikin and Peter Feldman, with a membership that included writers, actors, choreographers, musicians, and directors. More nearly a workshop than a producing organization, it showed its work publicly only at irregular intervals. The company was dissolved in 1974.

Like Grotowski, Chaikin and Feldman wanted to concentrate on those elements peculiar to the theatre. Thus, though they performed under a variety of conditions, they preferred a large open space that permitted a close relationship between actors and audience. Scenery was usually nonexistent and lighting minimal. The actors wore rehearsal or everyday garments throughout performances; they used no makeup and few properties. The emphasis was almost entirely on the actor and the action.

But if the Open Theatre shared many means with the Polish Laboratory Theatre it did not share its concern for ritual and purgation. Rather, most of the Open Theatre's work commented on contemporary political, moral, or social values. Furthermore, its work was grounded in contemporary psychological theories about role playing and in theatre games like those described by Viola Spolin in *Improvisation in the Theatre* (1963). Above all, it was concerned with "transformation"—that is, a constantly shifting reality in which the same performer took on and discarded identities as required by the context. The transformations might involve

Scene from Jean-Claude van Itallie's Motel, *a segment of* America, Hurrah! *as presented by the Open Theatre, New York. (Photo © 1968 by Fred W. McDarrah.)*

persons, animals or objects, situations, objectives, or time and place. The changes occurred rapidly with little transition; thus reality was treated not as fixed but as ever changing, and personality and role as states that constantly alter according to context. Since the actors in the Open Theatre did not use makeup or costume as aids in characterization, they had to convey these transformations entirely through improvisation and acting. For example, in Van Itallie's *The Serpent* (1969) the same actor passed rapidly from being a member in the crowd watching a parade, to an assassin, to part of a serpent or tree, to a suitor, to a child, to himself, and so on.

The Open Theatre's productions usually were based on scripts evolved in its workshop in close collaboration with its playwrights. Typically, a writer supplied an outline, situation, or idea; then, the actors, working through improvisation and other techniques, explored the possibilities, from among which the dramatist selected those that seemed to him most effective. Some of the company's most interesting productions came into being in this way.

Of the writers who worked with the Open Theatre, perhaps the best were Jean-Claude van Itallie (1936–) with *Interview, TV,* and *The Serpent,* and Megan Terry (1932–) with *Keep Tightly Closed in a Cool Dry Place* and *Viet Rock.* The last of these will be examined here as a play using transformational techniques and as a work motivated by social and political events of the 1960s.

Viet Rock

Viet Rock (1966) was written in the midst of the war in Vietnam, although prior to intense public controversy over it. Ultimately, it is not about any specific war but the folly of war in general. The issues in *Viet Rock* are simple: humanity, love, and life versus dehumanizing forces, hatred, and death. There is no doubt about which choice the play favors, for essentially it poses a question (Which do you favor, life or death?) that to most people can have only one answer. It does not inquire into the causes of the Vietnamese war, nor does it raise philosophical questions about whether there are ever injustices so great that war may be needed to right them. The play merely assumes that war (regardless of the reasons behind it) is an instrument that deprives men of what is most precious. Like many plays of the 1960s, *Viet Rock* tends to oversimplify issues. Nevertheless, its appeals are so basic and universal (the desire for peace, happiness, and love) that it remains powerful and moving despite its schematization.

The structure of *Viet Rock* is both simple and complex. On the level of story it is simple: men are inducted into the army, trained, sent to fight, and killed. Thus, there is a straightforward progression of events. This story is complicated, however, by interlarding it with other scenes that are

Megan Terry's Viet Rock *as presented at Yale University in 1966. (Courtesy Yale University School of Drama.)*

related to the war in various ways: demonstrations, Senate hearings, letters from soldiers and loved ones at home, off-duty pleasures, and so on. All of this is framed by opening and closing episodes that give meaning to the whole. The play opens with sounds and physical activity that evoke the beauty and simple pleasures of childhood and daily life; then at the end (after we have witnessed the men being removed from this happy environment, turned into fighting machines and killed) we see them resurrected and, now aware of how precious life is, go into the audience to share with the spectators the wonder and joy of merely being alive. But the play's principal source of complexity is its individual segments, which are composed of series of "transformations."

Transformations are intimately connected with characterization, acting, and other production elements. The number of roles in *Viet Rock* cannot be counted, for the actors are constantly shifting identities. Many characters are not even mentioned in the script, since all the performers are on-stage throughout and are involved in some way (often unspecified) in each scene; in some instances, each actor changes identity or functions several times within a single scene. The original production utilized about fifteen performers, but in a note the author declares: "As many actors should be employed as the director feels confident to work with." The performers wear simple clothing. According to the playwright, "the men should be dressed in blue work clothes and boots, and the women in free-flowing dresses or skirts and tights." They wear no makeup. There are no properties. The only scenery is two benches and four chairs. Thus, the actors must rely entirely on pantomime and other acting skills. Their task is simplified somewhat because they are not concerned with giving in-depth characterizations that are built up gradually and sustained throughout the play, but with getting across instantaneously the essence of a type or situation. They are not seeking to show what has happened

Postwar Theatre
and Drama

391

to specific individuals so much as to convey generalized impressions. Thus, they must project typifying behavior rather than idiosyncratic traits. But the actor's task is far from simple, since he must assume many different identities and undergo instantaneous transformations; furthermore, the audience must be able to recognize not only that a transformation has occurred but must easily grasp the nature of each new identity and its context.

The transformations in *Viet Rock* are of two basic types. The opening scene uses one typical of most scenes. The actors are first seen lying on the floor in a circle. "Their bodies, heads inward, form a giant flower or a small target." Then they begin to move as if a flower's petals are trembling in a breeze. After this, the performers, through vocal sound, evoke childlike delight in remembered games (including some involving war); after a time they rise and form a circle that moves with increasing tempo until it explodes and flings bodies about the stage, arousing in the participants increased joy and laughter. Then, the men instantly become babies, the women mothers; the mothers undress their babies and play with them until one male performer stands, immediately becomes a sergeant and calls the other men to attention; they fall in for a physical examination prior to induction into the army, and the women become the doctors who conduct the examination.

A second type of transformation is used in the Senate hearings, for, though the number of senators remains fixed, the actors who play them are constantly changing. Furthermore, the same actor may play different witnesses who have opposing views. The purpose behind this type of transformation is to focus attention on ideas rather than on those who voice them; in this instance, it is used to suggest that, regardless of who speaks, the same set of justifications, opposing views, platitudes, and irrelevancies are voiced.

Transformations also serve a philosophical purpose beyond their usefulness in characterization: they argue that reality is ever changing and capable of infinite alteration. Therefore, transformations suggest and the play demonstrates that life is made up of contradictions, potentialities, lost and retrieved chances. And, if reality is transformable, it can be shaped by us if we make the right choices and seize the opportunities offered us for improving life both for ourselves and others. Consequently, transformations are also a type of dialectic. But, the actors are not continuously involved in transformations; at the end, for example, there is no attempt at role playing: "Each chooses an audience member and touches his hand, head, face, hair. . . . They must communicate the wonder and gift of being actually alive together with the audience at that moment."

Like many plays of the 1960s, *Viet Rock* is grounded in the popular culture of its time. Its subtitle, "a folk-war movie," suggests this attempt, and the title itself indicates a desire to mingle topical issues with the most popular musical idiom of the day. Many of the play's important scenes are set to music, much of it parodying the popular songs of its time. The play's roots in popular culture are further indicated by slogans, instantly recognizable caricatures of well-known figures, obscenity and slang, go-go dances, and many other features. While these elements give the play a sense of immediacy and relevance to its time, this topicality is largely offset by the work's concern for human life and dignity—values that transcend time and place. Thus, *Viet Rock* remains a moving play, even though the events that motivated its composition are already beginning to fade into memory.

Multimedia Productions

Since 1960 approaches to theatrical spectacle have altered significantly. The causes are numerous, but one of the most important involves changing ideas about human perception. Marshall McLuhan, for example, argues that electronic media have now replaced the printed page as the primary means of human communication and that consequently contemporary audiences have become adept at assimilating multiple and concurrent stimuli. Thus, he declares, they no longer demand orderly sequence and a single primary focal point but can take in several things at once.

Many observers agree that the pace of life has accelerated significantly since 1950. In turn, this seems to have made audiences impatient with scenic devices that slow the tempo of performance. Furthermore, playwrights have gradually come to assume that time and place should be instantly transformable and infinitely variable. (This trend is in marked contrast with the prewar period when playwrights were urged to use as few settings as possible because it was usually assumed that each locale would be represented fully and three-dimensionally.) Another factor encouraging change has been the steady rise in production costs. The consequent need for more economical means of producing plays has been answered in part by war-time and space research that has perfected electronic equipment adaptable to theatrical uses. As a result of these and other causes, since 1960 spectacle has come to depend increasingly on light and sound, while three-dimensional elements have been restricted more and more to a few set pieces, furniture, and properties.

These changes contributed significantly to the development of multimedia (or mixed-media) productions involving some combination of live actors, projected still or motion pictures, stereophonic sound, light, dance, and music—in other words, elements drawn from several art forms. Nevertheless, to most observers the crucial element in multimedia production is the liberal use of slides or motion pictures.

The person most responsible for the development of multimedia production was the Czech artist Josef Svoboda (1920–   ), probably the best known of contemporary designers. Svoboda's contributions began in 1958, when in collaboration with the director Alfred Radok, he initiated two projects, Polyekran (multiple screen) and Laterna Magika. The first of

Multimedia production designed by Josef Svoboda, scene from Topol's Their Day *(1959) as presented at the National Theatre, Prague. (Photo copyright Jaromir Svoboda.)*

these is restricted to filmed images, but it seeks to overcome the "visual paralysis" of traditional productions by hanging several screens at various distances from the audience and by projecting a different image on each—to give the spectators a choice of things to watch. To this, Laterna Magika adds live performers. In 1959, Svoboda began to incorporate elements from these experiments into his stage work. Since then he has continued to seek means whereby the stage can be made completely flexible, so that its size, shape, and visual appearance can alter rapidly according to the changing dramatic context. In addition to projections, he has experimented with movable screens, variable platforms, and other elements. He has also worked in a great variety of visual styles and for virtually every major company in the world. Nevertheless, he is still best known for his work with multimedia.

Svoboda has not been alone in using multimedia. After 1960 several devices became increasingly common: rapidly changing projections of still pictures on multiple screens; filmed segments; stereophonic sound, the direction, volume, and quality of which could be fully controlled; infinitely varied lighting; and special effects of all sorts. The popularity of multimedia devices seems to have declined somewhat in recent years. Nevertheless, the potentials of electronic equipment will no doubt increase, and as they do, they will undoubtedly be adapted to theatrical uses. It seems likely, therefore, that multimedia will continue to evolve and remain important in theatrical production.

Happenings

Around 1960 a specialized type of multimedia event—the Happening —evolved from attempts to break down the barriers between the arts. The key figure in this movement was Allan Kaprow (1927–), a painter who out of his interest in "environments" (that is, in making the entire setting an extension of the art works on display) came to consider everyone who attended an exhibit a part of the total environment and gave them things to do. In 1959 he published a proposal for an event he called a "happening," and later that year gave the first public showing of the new form–*18 Happenings in 6 Parts*. For this work, a gallery was divided into three compartments and within each a number of elements progressed independently and simultaneously: various actions by participants, multiple projections, recordings, and so on. A number of other persons took up happenings, and soon the label was being used for any event in which chance or improvisation played a large part. Probably because such extensions made the concept almost meaningless, happenings declined sharply in popularity in the late 1960s.

Few happenings were specifically theatrical, but several innovations associated with them were carried over into the theatre. First, happenings tended to break down the barriers between the arts and to mingle elements borrowed from several; thus, they contributed to the development of multimedia events. Since they usually made little use of dialogue, they contributed to downgrading language and to increasing emphasis on visual and nonverbal elements. Second, happenings stressed participation

Allan Kaprow's Spring Happening, *1961. (Photo by Bob McElroy.)*

Luca Ronconi's production of Orlando Furioso. *This photograph shows a performance in Les Halles, the Paris food market, in 1970 as part of the Théâtre des Nations program. (Photo by Bernand.)*

in a creative process rather than arriving at a finished product. Third, instead of seeking to convey an artist's intention, happenings sought to sharpen the sensitivity of participants. Fourth, most happenings had no single, primary focus; rather, many events occurred simultaneously. Fifth, participants carried out tasks rather than impersonating characters; thus they helped to alter conceptions of acting. Sixth, happenings broke down the barriers between art and everyday life by removing art from the context of theatres, concert halls, and museums and taking it into parks, streets, and other commonly accessible places. Seventh, happenings did much to undermine interest in professionalism and disciplined technique, since anyone could participate and since there was no right or wrong way of doing things.

Environmental Theatre

The interest in environments that stimulated Kaprow to devise happenings motivated others in the 1960s to promote "environmental theatre"—a term popularized by Richard Schechner, then editor of *TDR* (*The Drama Review,* formerly *Tulane Drama Review*). According to Schechner, environmental theatre lies somewhere between happenings and traditional theatre. In it, audiences and actors occupy the same physical space, and the audience is a part of the total event, even if it thinks of itself merely as spectator. The event may take place in "found" space (that is, any kind of preexisting, unaltered, nontheatrical space) or it may occur in a location that has been converted to create an environment suited to what will occur there. Consequently, traditional theatre architecture is abandoned for places in which audience and actors can intermingle. The nature of the space and the audience–performer relationship means that focus is flexible and variable, and that more than one event may progress simultaneously.

In 1968 Schechner founded the Performance Group to carry out his ideas. The Group works in a converted garage where the space is completely flexible. There are no seats; a few platforms are scattered about on which the audience may sit or that may serve as performance areas. The Group aroused considerable interest and controversy with its first production, *Dionysus in 69* (a reworking of Euripides' *The Bacchae*). Since then it has presented *Makbeth,* based on Shakespeare's play; *Commune* (1970), a company-created montage exploring the American past and present; Sam Shepard's *The Tooth of Crime* (1973), which places rivalries in the popular music world within the context of gangsterism; Brecht's *Mother Courage*; and Seneca's *Oedipus.*

Although they were not always called "environmental," productions of the type described by Schechner became relatively common in the late 1960s. In 1969, Luca Ronconi achieved international success with *Orlando Furioso* (adapted from the sixteenth-century narrative poem by Lodovico Ariosto). Originally staged at the Festival of Two Worlds in Spoleto, Italy, it then played in Paris, New York, and elsewhere. This pro-

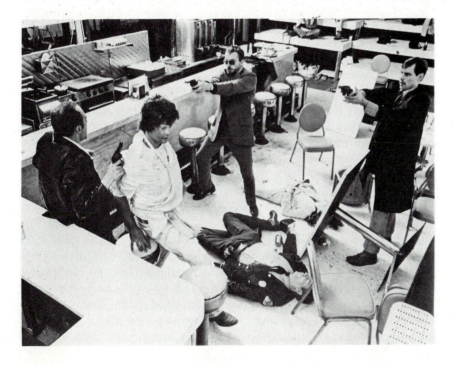

The entire theatre was carefully modeled after a Chicago all night diner to produce the environment for the Performance Group presentation of Cops, *written by Terry Curtis Fox and directed by Richard Schechner. (Photo by David Behl.)*

In this production of L'Age d'Or *(Age of Gold) at Théâtre du Soleil the audience was required to move from place to place with the actors. (Courtesy French Cultural Services.)*

duction utilized two stages that faced each other across a large open space, occupied by a standing audience and by tall movable platforms that were wheeled in and out at considerable speed. Different scenes were played simultaneously on each of the fixed stages and on one or more wagons in the central area. The audience moved about as it wished. Ronconi argued that the simultaneous playing of various plot strands approximates the same disordered effect created by the original story, which recounts several chivalric adventures featuring enchanted castles, sorcerers, captive maidens, and mythical creatures. The total effect was a combination of street pageant, parade, happening, and several playlets all progressing at once.

Another major example of environmental theatre was Jean-Louis Barrault's *Rabelais* (1968), given first in a sports arena in Paris and then in Brussels, London, Berlin, New York, and elsewhere. A three-hour-long adaptation of Rabelais' writings (some portions narrated and others acted out, sometimes several scenes at once), it was performed in a central ring and on ramps extending into the audience.

Still another significant environmental production was *1789,* a creation of the Théâtre du Soleil, a commune under the leadership of Ariane Mnouchkine. First performed in Milan in 1970, it was then moved to a disused munitions factory just outside Paris. It treated the early phases of the French Revolution and argued that the goals of the uprising were aborted out of a desire to protect property rights. For the production, platforms were set up around all four sides of the performance space; the audience, treated as the revolutionary mob, stood in the center. In 1975 the Théâtre de Soleil presented its *Age of Gold,* a complex variation on the theme of materialism that required the audience to move with the actors from one space to another. While such complex productions have not been numerous, they have served to enlarge conceptions of the theatre and to stimulate innovative production techniques.

Recent Trends

By the late 1970s the rather frenetic theatrical experimentation of the preceding decade had subsided considerably. In what remained, a few directions could be discerned. One involved the creation of works composed primarily of hallucinatory visual images. The groups most associated with this approach include the Ontological-Hysteric Theatre (directed by Richard Forman), the Mabou Mines (directed by Lee Breuer), and the Byrd Hoffman Foundation (directed by Robert Wilson). Probably the most distinctive work has been Wilson's in such productions as *Deafman Glance* (1970), *A Letter for Queen Victoria* (1974), and *Einstein on the Beach* (1976). Typically very long (most last around twelve hours but one required 168 hours), Wilson's productions are composed of a slow-moving sequence of images that shift almost imperceptibly (it often takes a character an hour to complete a single movement). Abstract, they are intended to induce contemplation rather than to tell a story. Through such means, Wilson has sought to alter perceptual awareness and place the audience and performers in touch with their own inner consciousness and obsessive fantasies.

Scene from Einstein on the Beach, *directed by Robert Wilson and Philip Lelan. Note the mimelike gestures, placing emphasis on the visual images, rather than interaction among the actors. (Photo ©1976 by Babette Mangolte.)*

Such essentially visual productions are related to happenings and multimedia events. They also continue the downgrading of spoken text as the primary ingredient in drama. Most companies involved in this kind of work have created their own pieces rather than interpreting already existing texts. Thus, their work promotes the concept of playwriting as a visual (rather than linguistic) art.

A related trend could be seen in the increased acceptance of the director as primary artist of the theatre, free to use existing texts however he wished in his own improvisations. In America the best known exponent of this approach is Andrei Serban; elsewhere the number of such directors is large indeed, especially in Germany and France. Thus, the conception of the director as an interpretive artist seeking to translate faithfully the playwright's text into theatrical terms has suffered a major decline.

On the other hand, many new playwrights demonstrated a renewed concern for language and nondidactic storytelling. Among the most prominent of these have been David Mamet with *American Buffalo* and *A Life in the Theatre*, Albert Innaurato with *The Transformation of Benno Blimpie* and *Ulysses in Traction*, Michael Cristofer with *The Shadow Box*, Preston Jones with *The Last Meeting of the White Knights of the Magnolia* and *The Oldest Living Graduate*, and Christopher Durang with *A History of the American Film*. These writers are sensitive to the rhythms and locutions of everyday speech and the mores and values of modern times. Many of the pictures they draw of American life are unflattering, but for the most part these writers avoid the derisory and superior tone often found in the 1960s. Overall, their work suggests that dramatists are returning to a more complex and more objective view of human behavior.

Among the best of the current playwrights is David Rabe, who has been especially concerned with American values. Here his *Streamers* will be examined in detail as an example of contemporary drama.

Streamers

Streamers is the third of Rabe's plays to use the Vietnam war as background. *The Basic Training of Pavlo Hummel* (1971) concerns the indoctrination and death of a common soldier, *Sticks and Bones* (1971) shows the aftermath of war as a blinded soldier returns home, and *Streamers* (1976) takes place just before the conflict in Vietnam escalated into a major war. But these plays are not essentially about war. Rather, Rabe uses the warrior mentality to explore significant contemporary attitudes. *Pavlo Hummel* shows how the unquestioned belief that soldiering is the ultimate test of manhood wastes human life; *Sticks and Bones* treats the tribalistic tendencies of the American family to view foreigners as less than human and to evade its responsibility for the destruction both of Vietnam culture and their own.

The two sergeants, Rooney and Cokes, reminisce in this scene from Streamers, *presented at Lincoln Center, New York. Directed by Mike Nichols. (Photo by Martha Swope.)*

Streamers also uses an American myth, a variation on that of *Pavlo Hummel*: Army life is the essence of masculinity. This explains Rabe's inclusion of the play's two most prominent (and for many viewers disturbing) features: homosexuality and violence. But, what greater threat to the myth of masculinity than homosexuality, and what more likely than violence from those trained for deadly combat? Although these elements give the play an explosive quality, neither is used sensationally or gratuitiously. Both are organic to Rabe's purposes.

The action of the play occurs at a time (1965) when, following a relatively uneventful period, army life is beginning to be dangerous once more. Vietnam is still so remote that it seems a fantasy world (it is referred to repeatedly as Disneyland), but because men on the base are receiving orders to go there, Vietnam brings to the surface anxieties that previously have been hidden. The opening scene sets the tone: Martin (a young soldier) slashes his wrist in his desperate desire to be sent home.

Streamers is compact and entirely realistic in style. Its language is the vernacular speech of the common soldier, replete with obscenity in almost every line. The story, told chronologically, occurs within the space of a few days. All the scenes are set in the cadre room of a barracks shared by three Specialists (Billy, Roger, and Richie), around whom the action centers. Billy and Roger accept the myth of the army, although with a measure of humor. Nevertheless, they voluntarily do pushups, compulsively clean the room, and spend their spare time in sports or on the town. Richie, on the other hand, declares: "There's no point to any of it." He makes playful sexual overtures to Billy, who at first ignores and then is outraged by them. Thus, Richie is the principal threat to the myth and becomes one of the prime elements in the explosive action.

All of these characters are complex. Billy acts the role of an ordinary, uneducated young man, but eventually he admits that he is a college graduate who has had problems because he "overcomplicates" everything; furthermore, his responses to Richie seem to reveal an uncertainty about his own sexual preferences. Roger, a black, has grown up in a ghetto and has been under psychiatric care for severe headaches. His primary goal has become to avoid all personal conflicts. When Richie was a child, his father abandoned the family, leaving his son to be brought up by a rich and indulgent mother. He has always followed his impulses. Thus, all three are evading self-knowledge. Strangely, it is Richie, completely unconcerned about the masculine myth, who has volunteered for army duty. Billy and Roger, who were drafted, nevertheless see the army as a male preserve and a proving ground for masculinity. Roger says to Richie: "I bet you never had a chance to really run with the boys before. I mean, regular normal guys like Billy and me." And about Vietnam, Billy declares: "Be a great place to come back from, man, you know? I keep thinkin' about that. To have gone there, to have been there, to have seen it and lived." Despite their anxieties, then, for Billy and Roger the trademark of the authentic hero is survival in combat.

Those who best represent the army (and who have been in combat and returned) are the two sergeants, Rooney and Cokes, parachutists in World War II and Korea. When the play opens, Rooney has just been ordered to Vietnam, and Cokes has just returned—sent back because he has leukemia. Both are rather pathetic men in their fifties, passing their time in childish games of hide-and-seek or in drinking and reminiscing about the past. Still, they consider themselves to be authentic heroes and real men, in contrast to Billy, Roger, and Richie who are not "regular army." While reminiscing, Cokes tells the story of how during the Korean War he threw a hand grenade into a bunker and sat on the lid while the North Korean soldier inside tried desperately to get out.

The sergeants also provide the title of the play, taken from the song they sing (set to the tune of "Beautiful Dreamer" and attributed to soldiers whose parachutes fail to open): "Beautiful streamer, / Open for me, / The sky is above me, / But no canopy." This title is appropriate since the play ultimately is concerned with questions about the nature of the canopy that suspends us and keeps us from crashing fatally. Most of the men in the play have chosen the army as a kind of parachute, for all are seeking that which sustains an illusion of happiness.

If the sergeants represent one extreme, Carlyle, a recent black draftee, represents another, opposite one. He is the most crucial character in the play—the catalyst who disrupts the relatively stable situation and turns it to violence. Carlyle has no interest whatever in the myth of masculinity. He is like a free animal who has been captured and placed in a zoo. This sense of being trapped and wanting out makes him alternately affable and

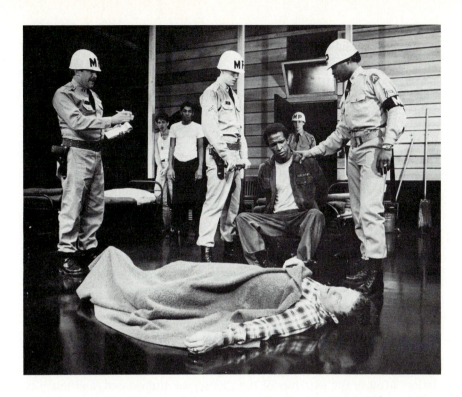

The final scene of Streamers. *(Photo by Martha Swope.)*

enraged. Like Richie he is an outsider, and Rabe uses this affinity to draw them together in a sexual liaison that leads to the violent and bloody climax. Billy, outraged and unheeding of Roger's frantic appeals for him to leave the room, tries to prevent Richie and Carlyle from going through with their sexual encounter; Carlyle draws a switchblade, cuts Billy across the palm of the hand, and then stabs him in the stomach. When the drunken Sergeant Rooney wanders in, Carlyle also kills him and insists that he has resigned from the army. After the bodies have been removed, Roger, typically and mechanically, mops up the blood and tidies up the room.

The play might have ended here, since the major action is over, but there follows a lengthy scene which gives shape and meaning to the play. Cokes, oblivious to all that has happened, comes looking for Rooney, with whom he has been playing hide-and-seek. His drunken monologue, in which he describes his day with Rooney, shows that his army life has been an eternal adolescence. But his awareness that he now has incurable leukemia makes him ponder his own existence and begin to see things in a new light. To comfort Richie, he says: "There's a lotta worse things in this world than bein' a queer. I seen a lot of 'em too." Haunting his consciousness is something as deadly as the leukemia in his blood—the memory of the North Korean soldier he killed with a hand grenade. "I'd let him out now, he was in there. Oh, how'm I ever gonna forget it?" And the play ends as he sings "Beautiful Streamer" in a makeshift language

Contemporary Theatre and Drama

403

imitating Korean. Streamers, then, do not concern only parachutists but all humanity. The awareness of human waste created by this final scene gives the play true tragic dimension.

Rabe is nondidactic in his handling of his subject. For this reason, many viewers have been conscious only of the sensational and violent elements and have been repelled by them. But *Streamers* is neither an antiwar play nor a defense of homosexuality. Rather, it is a perceptive observation of one human institution and the myths that have grown up around it. The meaning of the play is conveyed primarily through implications that raise fundamental questions: What does it mean to be "a man"? Is not the love of one man for another preferable to the killing described by Cokes? These questions are asked without bitterness. All the characters are treated compassionately; all have weaknesses, sometimes giving rise to humor, but none is ever ridiculed. They share in common their need for love and understanding—symbolized by the open parachute ("Just like a mother / Watching o'er me"), which prevents "streamers," the metaphor for desperation and destruction.

Postscript

Today the theatre seems to be in a period of reassessment and consolidation. Most of the extremes of the 1960s have disappeared, and much of what then was innovative has become standard practice. As are the other arts, the theatre today is attracting a larger audience than at almost any time in history. Its most pressing problems are not artistic but financial and organizational: How can theatre be supported, and how can it be made accessible in many more geographical locations?

What the future will bring can only be a subject for speculation, for accurate prediction would require the ability to foresee the course of events. Western drama has always reflected changing views about human beings and their world. Thus, as conceptions within the fields of psychology, morality, sociology, and politics have altered, so too have conceptions within the field of drama changed. Many recent innovations that now seem important will in the future no doubt fade into oblivion, whereas others, perhaps unnoted in this book, will in retrospect be recognized as forerunners of major changes. Only conceptions of human beings in the future—what sort of creature they will be; what kinds of appeals must be made to their senses; what kind of personal, moral, social, and political ideals they will be capable of understanding and sustaining—will determine the direction to be taken by theatre and drama. And these conceptions are yet to evolve.

Bibliography

1: General Works

Altman, George, *et al. Theater Pictorial: A History of World Theater as Recorded in Drawings, Paintings, Engravings, and Photographs.* Berkeley: University of California Press, 1953.

Berthold, Margot. *History of World Theatre.* New York: Frederick Ungar Publishing Co., Inc., 1972.

Bowman, Walter P., and Ball, Robert H. *Theatre Language: A Dictionary of Terms in English of the Drama and Stage from Medieval to Modern Times.* New York: Theatre Arts Books, 1961.

Brockett, Oscar G. *History of the Theatre.* 3d ed. Boston: Allyn and Bacon, Inc., 1977.

Cheney, Sheldon. *The Theatre: Three Thousand Years of Drama, Acting and Stagecraft.* Rev. ed. New York: Longmans, Green & Co., Inc., 1972.

Cheshire, David F. *Theatre: History, Criticism and Reference.* London: Bingley, 1967.

Clark, Barrett H., ed. *European Theories of the Drama.* Newly revised by Henry Popkin. New York: Crown Publishers, Inc., 1965.

Dukore, Bernard F., ed. *Dramatic Theory and Criticism: Greeks to Grotowski.* New York: Holt, Rinehart and Winston, 1974.

Duerr, Edwin. *The Length and Depth of Acting.* New York: Holt, Rinehart and Winston, 1962.

Freedley, George, and Reeves, John A. *A History of the Theatre.* 3d ed. New York: Crown Publishers, Inc., 1968.

Gascoigne, Bamber. *World Theatre: An Illustrated History.* Boston: Little, Brown and Company, 1968.

Gassner, John. *Masters of the Drama.* 3d ed. New York: Dover Publications, Inc., 1954.

————, and Allen, Ralph, eds. *Theatre and Drama in the Making.* 2 vols. Boston: Houghton Mifflin Company, 1964.

————, and Quinn, Edward, eds. *The Reader's Encyclopedia of World Drama.* New York: Thomas Y. Crowell Company, 1969.

Hartnoll, Phyllis, ed. *The Oxford Companion to the Theatre.* 3d ed. New York: Oxford University Press, 1967.

Izenour, George C. *Theatre Design.* New York: McGraw-Hill, Inc., 1977.

Laver, James. *Drama, Its Costume and Decor.* London: Studio Publications, 1951.

Leacroft, Richard. *The Development of the English Playhouse.* Ithaca, N.Y.: Cornell University Press, 1973.

Macgowan, Kenneth, and Melnitz, William. *The Living Stage.* Englewood Cliffs, N.J.: Prentice-Hall, Inc., 1955.

McGraw-Hill Encyclopedia of World Drama. 4 vols. New York: McGraw-Hill, Inc., 1972.

Molinari, Cesare. *Theatre Through the Ages.* London: Cassell & Co., Ltd., 1975.

Mullin, Daniel C. *The Development of the Playhouse: A Survey of Architecture from the Renaissance to the Present.* Berkeley: University of California Press, 1970.

Nagler, Alois M. *Sources of Theatrical History.* New York: Theatre Annual, Inc., 1952.

Nicoll, Allardyce. *The Development of the Theatre.* 5th ed. rev. London: George G. Harrap & Co., Ltd., 1966.

————. *World Drama from Aeschylus to Anouilh.* Rev. ed. London: George G. Harrap & Co., Ltd., 1976.

Oenslager, Donald. *Stage Design: Four Centuries of Scenic Invention.* New York: The Viking Press, Inc., 1975.

Roberts, Vera M. *On Stage: A History of the Theatre.* 2d ed. New York: Harper & Row, Publishers, 1974.

Southern, Richard. *The Seven Ages of the Theatre.* New York: Hill & Wang, Inc., 1961.

Stuart, Donald C. *The Development of Dramatic Art.* New York: Appleton-Century-Crofts, 1933.

Wimsatt, William K., and Brooks, Cleanth. *Literary Criticism: A Short History.* New York: Alfred A. Knopf, Inc., 1957.

2,3: Collections of Plays

Adams, Joseph Q. *Chief Pre-Shakespearean Dramas.* Boston: Houghton Mifflin Company, 1924.

Bates, Alfred, ed. *The Drama: Its History, Literature and Influence on Civilization.* 22 vols. London: The Athenian Society, 1903–1904.

Bentley, Eric. *The Classic Theatre*. 4 vols. Garden City, N.Y.: Doubleday & Company, Inc., 1958–1961. (Vol. I—*Six Italian Plays;* Vol. II—*Five German Plays;* Vol. III—*Six Spanish Plays;* Vol. IV—*Six French Plays*.)

———. *From the Modern Repertoire*. Series 1–3. Bloomington: Indiana University Press, 1949–1956.

———. *The Modern Theatre*. 6 vols. Garden City, N.Y.: Doubleday & Company, Inc., 1955–1960.

Block, Haskell M., and Shedd, Robert G., eds. *Masters of Modern Drama*. New York: Random House, Inc., 1962.

Brockett, Oscar G., and Brockett, Lenyth. *Plays for the Theatre: An Anthology of World Drama*. 3d ed. New York: Holt, Rinehart and Winston, 1979.

Clark, Barrett H. *World Drama . . . An Anthology*. 2 vols. New York: Appleton-Century-Crofts, 1933.

Corrigan, Robert. *The Modern Theatre*. New York: The Macmillan Company, 1964.

———, and Loney, Glenn M. *The Forms of Drama*. Boston: Houghton Mifflin Company, 1972.

Dickinson, Thomas H. *Chief Contemporary Dramatists*. Series 1–3. Boston: Houghton Mifflin Company, 1915–1930.

Duckworth, George E. *The Complete Roman Drama*. 2 vols. New York: Random House, Inc., 1942.

Gassner, John. *Best American Plays*. Series 1–4, and a supplementary volume. New York: Crown Publishers, Inc., 1939–1961.

———. *A Treasury of the Theatre;* Vol. I: *From Aeschylus to Ostrovsky*. 3d ed. New York: Holt, Rinehart and Winston, 1967.

———, and Dukore, Bernard. *A Treasury of the Theatre;* Vol. II: *From Henrik Ibsen to Robert Lowell*. 4th ed. New York: Holt, Rinehart and Winston, 1970.

Grene, David, and Lattimore, Richmond, eds. *The Complete Greek Tragedies*. 4 vols. Chicago: University of Chicago Press, 1960.

Macmillan, Dougald, and Jones, Howard M. *Plays of the Restoration and Eighteenth Century*. New York: Holt, Rinehart and Winston, 1954.

Matthews, Brander. *The Chief European Dramatists*. Boston: Houghton Mifflin Company, 1916.

Moody, Richard. *Dramas from the American Theatre, 1762–1909*. Boston: Houghton Mifflin Company, 1966.

Noyes, George R. *Masterpieces of the Russian Drama*. 2 vols. New York: Dover Publications, Inc., 1960.

Oates, Whitney J., and O'Neill, Eugene, Jr. *Complete Greek Drama*. 2 vols. New York: Random House, Inc., 1938.

Ottemiller, John H. *Index to Plays in Collections*. 6th ed. Metuchen, N.J. Scarecrow Press, Inc., 1976.

Parks, Edd W. and Beatty, R. C. *The English Drama: An Anthology of Plays, 900–1642*. New York: W. W. Norton & Company, Inc., 1935.

Quinn, Arthur H. *Representative American Plays, from 1767 to the Present Day*. 7th ed. New York: Appleton-Century-Crofts, 1957.

Rowell, George. *Nineteenth Century Plays*. New York: Oxford University Press, 1953.

Stanton, Stephen. *Camille and Other Plays*. New York: Hill & Wang, Inc., 1957.

Tucker, S. M., and Downer, A. S. *Twenty-Five Modern Plays*. 3d ed. New York: Harper & Row, 1953.

Ulanov, Barry. *Makers of the Modern Theatre*. New York: McGraw-Hill, Inc., 1961.

4: THEATRE AND DRAMA IN ANCIENT GREECE

Allen, James T. *Greek Acting in the Fifth Century*. Berkeley: University of California Press, 1916.

————. *The Greek Theatre of the Fifth Century before Christ*. Berkeley: University of California Press, 1920.

Arnott, Peter D. *Greek Scenic Conventions in the Fifth Century, B.C.* New York: Oxford University Press, 1962.

————. *The Ancient Greek and Roman Theatre*. New York: Random House, Inc., 1971.

Bieber, Margarete. *The History of the Greek and Roman Theater*. 2d ed. Princeton, N.J.: Princeton University Press, 1961.

Butler, James H. *The Theatre and Drama of Greece and Rome*. San Francisco: Chandler Publishing Company, 1972.

Cornford, Francis M. *The Origin of Attic Comedy*. London: Edward Arnold (Publishers) Ltd., 1914.

Else, Gerald F. *The Origin and Early Form of Greek Tragedy*. Cambridge, Mass.: Harvard University Press, 1965.

Flickinger, Roy C. *The Greek Theatre and Its Drama*. 4th ed. Chicago: University of Chicago Press, 1960.

Frankfort, Henri. *Ancient Egyptian Religion*. New York: Columbia University Press, 1948.

Gaster, Theodor. *Thespis: Ritual, Myth and Drama in the Ancient Near East*. New York: Abelard-Schuman Ltd., 1950.

Greene, William C. *Moira: Fate, Good, and Evil in Greek Thought*. Cambridge, Mass.: Harvard University Press, 1944.

Hamilton, Edith. *The Greek Way*. New York: W. W. Norton & Company, Inc., 1952.

Harsh, Philip W. *A Handbook of Classical Drama*. Stanford, Calif.: Stanford University Press, 1944.

Hunningher, Ben. *The Origin of the Theatre*. New York: Hill & Wang, Inc., 1961.

Jaeger, Werner. *Paideia: The Ideals of Greek Culture*. Trans. by Gilbert Highet. 3 vols. New York: Oxford University Press, 1939–1944.

Kitto, H. D. F. *Greek Tragedy*. 2d ed. London: Methuen & Co., Ltd., 1950.

Lawler, Lillian B. *The Dance of the Ancient Greek Theatre*. Iowa City: University of Iowa Press, 1964.

Lever, Katherine. *The Art of Greek Comedy*. London: Methuen & Co., Ltd., 1956.

Murray, Gilbert. *Euripides and His Age*. New York: Holt, Rinehart and Winston, Inc., 1913.

Pickard-Cambridge, A. W. *Dithyramb, Tragedy, and Comedy*. 2d ed. rev. by T. B. L. Webster. Oxford: Clarendon Press, 1962.

————. *The Dramatic Festivals of Athens*. 2d ed. rev. by John Gould and D. M. Lewis. Oxford: Clarendon Press, 1968.

————. *The Theatre of Dionysus in Athens*. Oxford: Clarendon Press, 1946.

Rees, Kelley. *The Rule of Three Actors in the Classical Greek Drama*. Chicago: University of Chicago Press, 1908.

Ridgeway, William. *The Dramas and Dramatic Dances of Non-European Races*. Cambridge: The University Press, 1915.

Sifakis, Gregory M. *Studies in the History of Hellenistic Drama*. London: Athlone, 1967.

Webster, T. B. L. *Greek Theatre Production*. 2d ed. London: Methuen & Co., Ltd., 1970.

5: ROMAN THEATRE AND DRAMA

Allen, James T. *Stage Antiquities of the Greeks and Romans and Their Influence*. New York: Longmans, Green & Co., Inc., 1927.

Arnott, Peter. *The Ancient Greek and Roman Theatre*. See under Chapter 4.

Beare, William. *The Roman Stage: A Short History of Latin Drama in the Time of the Republic*. 3d ed. London: Methuen & Co., Ltd., 1963.

Bieber, Margarete. *The History of the Greek and Roman Theatre*. See under Chapter 4.

Butler, James H. *The Theatre and Drama of Greece and Rome*. See under Chapter 4.

Duckworth, George E. *The Nature of Roman Comedy*. Princeton, N.J.: Princeton University Press, 1952.

Friedlander, Ludwig. *Roman Life and Manners Under the Early Empire*. 4 vols. 7th ed. New York: Barnes & Noble, Inc., 1965.

Hamilton, Edith. *The Roman Way*. New York: W. W. Norton & Company, Inc., 1932.

Hanson, J. A. *Roman Theater-Temples*. Princeton, N.J.: Princeton University Press, 1959.

Harsh, Philip W. *A Handbook of Classical Drama*. See under Chapter 4.

Lucas, Frank L. *Seneca and Elizabethan Tragedy*. Cambridge: The University Press, 1922.

Norwood, Gilbert. *Plautus and Terence*. New York: Longmans, Green & Co., Inc., 1932.

Segal, Erich W. *Roman Laughter: The Comedy of Plautus*. Cambridge, Mass.: Harvard University Press, 1968.

Vitruvius. *The Ten Books of Architecture*. Trans. by M. H. Morgan. Cambridge, Mass.: Harvard University Press, 1914.

6: THE MIDDLE AGES

Bevington, David. *From Mankind to Marlowe; Growth in Structure in the Popular Drama of Tudor England*. Cambridge, Mass.: Harvard University Press, 1962.

Chambers, E. K. *The Mediaeval Stage*. 2 vols. Oxford: Clarendon Press, 1903.

Collins, Fletcher. *The Production of Medieval Church Music-Drama*. Charlottesville: University of Virginia Press, 1971.

Craig, Hardin. *English Religious Drama of the Middle Ages*. New York: Oxford University Press, 1955.

Craik, Thomas W. *The Tudor Interlude: Stage, Costume, and Acting*. Leicester: The University Press, 1958.

Evans, Marshall B. *The Passion Play of Lucerne*. New York: Modern Language Association, 1943.

Farnham, Willard. *The Medieval Heritage of Elizabethan Tragedy*. Berkeley: University of California Press, 1936.

Frank, Grace. *The Medieval French Drama.* New York: Oxford University Press, 1954.

Gardiner, Harold C. *Mysteries' End: An Investigation of the Last Days of the Medieval Religious Stage.* New Haven, Conn.: Yale University Press, 1946.

Hardison, O. B. *Christian Rite and Christian Drama in the Middle Ages: Essays in the Origin and Early History of Modern Drama.* Baltimore: The Johns Hopkins Press, 1965.

Hunningher, Ben. *The Origin of the Theatre.* See under Chapter 4.

Kolve, V. A. *The Play Called Corpus Christi.* Stanford, Calif.: Stanford University Press, 1966.

Nagler, A. M. *The Medieval Religious Stage: Shapes and Phantoms.* New Haven, Conn.: Yale University Press, 1976.

Nelson, Alan H. *The Medieval English Stage: Corpus Christi, Pageants and Plays.* Chicago: University of Chicago Press, 1974.

Nicoll, Allardyce. *Masks, Mimes and Miracles.* New York: Harcourt Brace Jovanovich, Inc., 1931.

Potter, Robert. *The English Morality Play: Origins, History and Influence of a Dramatic Tradition.* London: Routledge & Kegan Paul, Ltd., 1975.

Salter, F. M. *Medieval Drama in Chester.* Toronto: University of Toronto Press, 1955.

Shoemaker, William H. *The Multiple Stage in Spain During the Fifteenth and Sixteenth Centuries.* Princeton, N.J.: Princeton University Press, 1935.

Southern, Richard. *The Medieval Theatre in the Round.* London: Faber & Faber, Ltd., 1957.

Stratman, Carl J. *Bibliography of Medieval Drama.* Berkeley: University of California Press, 1954.

Stuart, D. C. *Stage Decoration in France in the Middle Ages.* New York: Columbia University Press, 1910.

Weiner, Albert B. *Philippe de Mezieres' Description of the "Festum Praesentationis Beatae Mariae" Translated from the Latin and Introduced by an Essay on the Birth of Modern Acting.* New Haven, Conn.: Andrew Kner, 1958.

Wickham, Glynne. *Early English Stages, 1300–1660.* 2 vols. New York: Columbia University Press, 1959–1972.

Williams, Arnold. *The Drama of Medieval England.* East Lansing: Michigan State University Press, 1961.

Woolf, Rosemary. *The English Mystery Play.* Berkeley: University of California Press, 1972.

Young, Karl. *The Drama of the Medieval Church.* 2 vols. New York: Oxford University Press, 1933.

7: THE ITALIAN RENAISSANCE

Bjurstrom, Per. *Giacomo Torelli and Baroque Stage Design.* Stockholm: Almqvist and Wiksell, 1961.

Burckhardt, Jakob C. *The Civilization of the Renaissance in Italy.* 3d ed. New York: Phaidon Publishers, Inc., 1950.

Campbell, Lily Bess. *Scenes and Machines on the English Stage During the Renaissance.* Cambridge: The University Press, 1923 (Reprinted, New York: Barnes & Noble, Inc., 1960).

Duchartre, Pierre L. *The Italian Comedy: The Improvisation, Scenarios, Lives,*

Attributes, Portraits and Masks of the Illustrious Characters of the Commedia dell'Arte. Trans. by R. T. Weaver. London: George G. Harrap & Co., Ltd., 1929.

Hathaway, Baxter. *The Age of Criticism: The Late Renaissance in Italy.* Ithaca, N.Y.: Cornell University Press, 1962.

Herrick, Marvin. *Italian Comedy in the Renaissance.* Urbana: University of Illinois Press, 1960.

————. *Italian Tragedy in the Renaissance.* Urbana: University of Illinois Press, 1965.

————. *Tragicomedy: Its Origin and Development in Italy, France, and England.* Urbana: University of Illinois Press, 1955.

Hewitt, Barnard, ed. *The Renaissance Stage: Documents of Serlio, Sabbattini, and Furttenbach.* Coral Gables, Fla.: University of Miami Press, 1958.

Kennard, Joseph. *The Italian Theatre.* 2 vols. New York: W. E. Rudge, 1932.

Kernodle, George. *From Art to Theatre: Form and Convention in the Renaissance.* Chicago: University of Chicago Press, 1943.

Lea, Kathleen M. *Italian Popular Comedy: A Study of the Commedia dell'Arte, 1560–1620.* 2 vols. New York: Oxford University Press, 1934.

Nagler, Alois M. *Theatre Festivals of the Medici, 1539–1637.* New Haven, Conn.: Yale University Press, 1964.

Nicoll, Allardyce. *Masks, Mimes and Miracles.* See under Chapter 6.

————. *Stuart Masques and the Renaissance Stage.* London: George G. Harrap & Co., Ltd., 1937.

Schwartz, Isidore A. *The Commedia dell'Arte and Its Influence on French Comedy in the Seventeenth Century.* Paris: H. Samuel, 1933.

Smith, Winifred. *The Commedia dell'Arte.* New York: Columbia University Press, 1912.

Spingarn, Joel E. *A History of Literary Criticism in the Renaissance.* 2d ed. New York: Columbia University Press, 1908.

Strong, Roy. *Splendor at Court.* Boston: Houghton Mifflin Company, 1973.

Symonds, John A. *The Renaissance in Italy.* 7 vols. London: John Murray, Ltd., 1909–1937.

Vasari, Giorgio. *Vasari's Lives of the Artists.* New York: The Noonday Press, 1957.

Vitruvius. *The Ten Books of Architecture.* See under Chapter 5.

Weinberg, Bernard. *A History of Literary Criticism in the Italian Renaissance.* 2 vols. Chicago: University of Chicago Press, 1961.

White, John. *The Birth and Rebirth of Pictorial Space.* 2d ed. London: Faber & Faber, Ltd., 1967.

Worsthorne, S. T. *Venetian Opera in the 17th Century.* New York: Oxford University Press, 1954.

8: ELIZABETHAN ENGLAND AND SPAIN

Adams, John C. *The Globe Playhouse: Its Design and Equipment.* 2d ed. New York: Barnes & Noble, Inc., 1961.

Adams, Joseph Q. *Shakespearean Playhouses: A History of English Theatres from the Beginnings to the Restoration.* Boston: Houghton Mifflin Company, 1917.

Baldwin, T. W. *The Organization and Personnel of the Shakespearean Company.* Princeton, N.J.: Princeton University Press, 1927.

Barroll, J. L., et al. *Revels History of Drama in English.* Vol. 3: 1576–1613. New York: Barnes & Noble, Inc., 1975.

Beckerman, Bernard. *Shakespeare at the Globe, 1599–1609.* New York: The Macmillan Company, 1962.

Bentley, Gerald E. *The Jacobean and Caroline Stage.* 5 vols. New York: Oxford University Press, 1941–1956.

———. *The Profession of Dramatist in Shakespeare's Time, 1590–1642.* Princeton, N.J.: Princeton University Press, 1971.

———. *Shakespeare: A Biographical Handbook.* New Haven, Conn.: Yale University Press, 1961.

Boas, Frederick S. *An Introduction to Stuart Drama.* New York: Oxford University Press, 1946.

Brooke, C. F. T. *The Tudor Drama: A History of English National Drama to the Retirement of Shakespeare.* Boston: Houghton Mifflin Company, 1911.

Campbell, Lily Bess. *Scenes and Machines on the English Stage During the Renaissance.* See under Chapter 7.

Chambers, E. K. *The Elizabethan Stage.* 4 vols. London: Oxford University Press, 1923.

———. *A Short Life of Shakespeare.* Oxford: Clarendon Press, 1933.

Crawford, J. P. W. *Spanish Drama before Lope de Vega.* Rev. ed. Philadelphia: University of Pennsylvania Press, 1937.

Ebisch, Walther, and Schucking, L. L. *A Shakespeare Bibliography.* Oxford: Clarendon Press, 1931. Supplement, 1935.

Ellis-Fermor, Una. *The Jacobean Drama: An Interpretation.* 3d ed. London: Methuen & Co., Ltd., 1953.

Gildersleeve, Virginia. *Government Regulation of the Elizabethan Drama.* New York: Columbia University Press, 1908.

Harbage, Alfred. *Shakespeare's Audience.* New York: Columbia University Press, 1941.

Hodges, C. Walter. *The Globe Restored.* 2d ed. New York: Oxford University Press, 1968.

Hotson, Leslie. *Shakespeare's Wooden O.* New York: The Macmillan Company, 1960.

Joseph, Bertram. *Elizabethan Acting.* 2d ed. New York: Oxford University Press, 1964.

Lawrence, W. J. *The Elizabethan Playhouse and Other Studies.* 2 vols. Stratford-on-Avon: Shakespeare Head Press, 1912–1913.

———. *Pre-Restoration Stage Studies.* Cambridge, Mass.: Harvard University Press, 1927.

Nagler, A. M. *Shakespeare's Stage.* New Haven, Conn.: Yale University Press, 1958.

Nicoll, Allardyce. *Stuart Masques and the Renaissance Stage.* London: George G. Harrap & Co., Ltd., 1937.

Orgel, Stephen. *The Illusion of Power: Political Theatre in the English Renaissance.* Berkeley: University of California Press, 1975.

Parrott, Thomas M. *Shakespearean Comedy.* New York: Oxford University Press, 1949.

———, and Ball, Robert H. *A Short View of Elizabethan Drama.* New York: Charles Scribner's Sons, 1958.

Ralli, A. J. *A History of Shakespearean Criticism*. 2 vols. London: Oxford University Press, 1932.

Rennert, Hugo A. *The Life of Lope de Vega (1562–1635)*. Philadelphia: Campion and Co., 1904.

———. *The Spanish Stage in the Time of Lope de Vega*. New York: Hispanic Society of America, 1909.

Reynolds, George F. *The Staging of Elizabethan Plays at the Red Bull Theatre, 1605–1625*. New York: Modern Language Association, 1940.

Ribner, Irving. *Jacobean Tragedy*. New York: Barnes & Noble, Inc., 1962.

Rosen, William. *Shakespeare and the Craft of Tragedy*. Cambridge, Mass.: Harvard University Press, 1960.

Rossiter, A. P. *English Drama from Early Times to the Elizabethans: Its Background, Origins and Developments*. New York: Hutchinson's University Library, 1950. (Reprinted, New York: Barnes & Noble, Inc., 1959.)

"Shakespeare: An Annotated Bibliography," *Shakespeare Quarterly* (1924–present). [SQ was originally called *The Shakespeare Association Bulletin*.] Annual bibliography of writings about Shakespeare.

Shakespeare Survey: An Annual Review of Shakespearean Study and Production. New York: The Macmillan Company, 1948–present.

Shergold, N. D. *A History of the Spanish Stage from Medieval Times Until the End of the 17th Century*. New York: Oxford University Press, 1967.

Smith, Irwin. *Shakespeare's Blackfriars Playhouse: Its History and Its Design*. New York: New York University Press, 1964.

Southern, Richard. *The Staging of Plays Before Shakespeare*. New York: Theatre Arts Books, 1973.

Speaight, Robert. *Shakespeare on the Stage: An Illustrated History of Shakespearean Performance*. New York: William Collins Sons & Co., Ltd., 1972.

Sprague, A. C. *Shakespearean Players and Performances*. Cambridge, Mass.: Harvard University Press, 1953.

Welsford, Enid. *The Court Masque*. New York: Russell & Russell Publishers, 1962.

Wickham, Glynne. *Early English Stages, 1300–1660*. See under Chapter 6.

Wilson, Margaret. *Spanish Drama of the Golden Age*. Elmsford, N.Y.: Pergamon Press, Inc., 1969.

9: FRENCH CLASSICISM

Bjurstrom, Per. *Giacomo Torelli and Baroque Stage Design*. See under Chapter 7.

Hubert, Judd D. *Molière and the Comedy of Intellect*. Berkeley: University of California Press, 1962.

Jeffery, Brian. *French Renaissance Comedy, 1552–1630*. New York: Oxford University Press, 1969.

Lancaster, H. C. *A History of French Dramatic Literature in the Seventeenth Century*. 5 vols. in 9. Baltimore: The Johns Hopkins Press, 1929–1942.

Lawrenson, T. E. *The French Stage in the XVIIth Century: A Study in the Advent of the Italian Order*. Manchester: Manchester University Press, 1957.

Lockert, Lacy. *Studies in French Classical Tragedy*. Nashville, Tenn.: Vanderbilt University Press, 1958.

Lough, John. *Paris Theatre Audiences in the Seventeenth and Eighteenth Centuries*. New York: Oxford University Press, 1957.

Palmer, John. *Molière*. New York: Brewer and Warren, 1930.

Strong, Roy. *Splendor at Court*. See under Chapter 7.

Tilley, A. A. *Molière*. Cambridge: The University Press, 1936.

Turnell, Martin. *The Classical Moment: Studies in Corneille, Molière and Racine*. New York: New Directions Pub. Corp., 1948.

Vinaver, Eugene. *Racine and Poetic Tragedy*. Trans. by P. M. Jones. Manchester: Manchester University Press, 1955.

Wiley, W. L. *The Early Public Theatre in France*. Cambridge, Mass.: Harvard University Press, 1960.

Wright, C. H. C. *French Classicism*. Cambridge, Mass.: Harvard University Press, 1920.

10: THE EIGHTEENTH CENTURY

Baur-Heinhold, Margarete. *The Baroque Theatre*. New York: McGraw-Hill, Inc., 1967.

Beijer, Agne. *Court Theatres of Drottningholm and Gripsholm*. Trans. by G. L. Frolich. Malmo: J. Kroon, 1933.

Bernbaum, Ernest. *The Drama of Sensibility: A Sketch of the History of Sentimental Comedy and Domestic Tragedy, 1696–1780*. Cambridge, Mass.: Harvard University Press, 1915.

Boas, Frederick S. *An Introduction to Eighteenth Century Drama, 1700–1780*. New York: Oxford University Press, 1953.

Booth, Michael, et al. *Revels History of Drama in English*. Vol. 6: *1750–1880*. New York: Barnes & Noble, Inc., 1975.

Bredsdorff, Elias, et al. *An Introduction to Scandinavian Literature from the Earliest Time to Our Day*. Copenhagen: E. Munksgaard, 1951.

Bruford, Walter H. *Theatre, Drama, and Audience in Goethe's Germany*. London: Routledge & Kegan Paul, Ltd., 1957.

Burnim, Kalman. *David Garrick, Director*. Pittsburgh, Pa.: Pittsburgh University Press, 1961.

Campbell, Lily B. "A History of Costuming on the English Stage between 1660 and 1823," *University of Wisconsin Studies in Language and Literature*, II (1918), 187–223.

Cibber, Colley. *An Apology for the Life of Mr. Colley Cibber*. London: J. Watts, 1740. Reprinted many times.

Cook, John A. *Neo-Classic Drama in Spain: Theory and Practice*. Dallas: Southern Methodist University Press, 1959.

Dobrée, Bonamy. *Restoration Comedy, 1660–1720*. Oxford: Clarendon Press, 1924.

———. *Restoration Tragedy, 1660–1720*. Oxford: Clarendon Press, 1929.

Downer, Alan S. "Nature to Advantage Dressed: Eighteenth Century Acting," *PMLA* (1943), 1002–1037.

"English Literature, 1660–1800: A Current Bibliography," *Philological Quarterly* (1926–present). Annual list of publications.

Fitzgerald, Percy H. *The Sheridans*. 2 vols. London: R. Bentley, 1886.

Goldoni, Carlo. *Memoirs of Carlo Goldoni*. Trans. by John Black. New York: Alfred A. Knopf, Inc., 1926.

Gozzi, Carlo. *The Memoirs of Count Carlo Gozzi*. Trans. by J. A. Symonds. 2 vols. London: J. C. Nimmo, 1890.

Hawkins, Frederick. *The French Stage in the Eighteenth Century.* 2 vols. London: Chapman & Hall, Ltd., 1888.

Heitner, R. R. *German Tragedy in the Age of Enlightenment, 1724–1768.* Berkeley: University of California Press, 1963.

Highfill, Philip H., et al. *Biographical Dictionary of Actors, Actresses, Musicians, Dancers, Managers, and Other Stage Personnel in London, 1660–1800.* Carbondale: Southern Illinois University Press, 1973–. (In progress.)

Hotson, Leslie. *The Commonwealth and Restoration Stage.* Cambridge, Mass.: Harvard University Press, 1928.

Joseph, Bertram. *The Tragic Actor.* New York: Theatre Arts Books, 1959.

Jourdain, Eleanor. *Dramatic Theory and Practice in France, 1690–1808.* New York: Longmans, Green & Co., Inc., 1921.

Kennard, Joseph. *The Italian Theatre.* See under Chapter 7.

Krutch, Joseph W. *Comedy and Conscience after the Restoration.* New York: Columbia University Press, 1949.

Lancaster, H. C. *French Tragedy in the Time of Louis XV and Voltaire, 1715–1774.* Baltimore: The Johns Hopkins Press, 1950.

————. *Sunset: A History of Parisian Drama in the Last Years of Louis XIV, 1701–1715.* Baltimore: The Johns Hopkins Press, 1945.

Loftus, John, et al. *Revels History of Drama in English.* Vol. 4: *1660–1750.* New York: Barnes & Noble, Inc., 1976.

The London Stage, 1660–1800. 11 vols. Carbondale: Southern Illinois University Press, 1960–1968.

Lough, John. See under Chapter 9.

Lynch, James J. *Box, Pit and Gallery: Stage and Society in Johnson's London.* Berkeley: University of California Press, 1953.

Mayor, A. Hyatt. *The Bibiena Family.* New York: H. Bittner, 1945.

Melcher, Edith. *Stage Realism in France from Diderot to Antoine.* Bryn Mawr, Pa.: Bryn Mawr College, 1928.

Nicoll, Allardyce. *History of English Drama, 1660–1900.* 6 vols. London: Cambridge University Press, 1955–1959.

Odell, G. C. D. *Shakespeare from Betterton to Irving.* 2 vols. New York: Charles Scribner's Sons, 1920.

Palmer, J. L. *The Comedy of Manners.* London: Bell & Sons, Ltd., 1913.

Pascal, Roy. *The German Sturm und Drang.* Manchester: Manchester University Press, 1953.

Pedicord, Harry. *The Theatrical Public in the Time of Garrick.* New York: King's Crown Press, 1954.

Price, Cecil. *Theatre in the Age of Garrick.* Oxford: Basil Blackwell & Mott, Ltd., 1973.

Prudhoe, John. *The Theatre of Goethe and Schiller.* Oxford: Basil Blackwell & Mott, Ltd., 1973.

Rankin, Hugh F. *The Theatre in Colonial America.* Chapel Hill: University of North Carolina Press, 1965.

Richards, K. R., ed. *Essays on the Eighteenth Century English Stage.* London: Methuen & Co., Ltd., 1972.

Scholz, Janos. *Baroque and Romantic Stage Design.* New York: E. P. Dutton & Co., Inc., 1962.

Sherbo, Arthur. *English Sentimental Drama.* East Lansing: Michigan State University Press, 1957.

Slonim, Marc. *Russian Theatre from the Empire to the Soviets.* Cleveland: The World Publishing Company, 1961.

Southern, Richard. *The Georgian Playhouse.* London: Pleiades Books, 1948.

———. *Changeable Scenery: Its Origin and Development in the British Theatre.* London: Faber & Faber, Ltd., 1952.

Summers, Montague. *The Playhouse of Pepys.* London: Paul, Trench, Trubner & Co., 1935.

———. *The Restoration Theatre.* London: Paul, Trench, Trubner & Co., 1934.

Thaler, Alwin. *Shakespere to Sheridan.* Cambridge, Mass.: Harvard University Press, 1922.

Willoughby, Leonard A. *The Classical Age of German Literature, 1748–1805.* London: Oxford University Press, 1926.

11: THE NINETEENTH CENTURY

Abrams, M. H. *The Mirror and the Lamp: Romantic Theory and the Critical Tradition.* New York: Oxford University Press, 1953.

Appleton, William W. *Mme. Vestris and the London Stage.* New York: Columbia University Press, 1974.

Arvin, Neil S. *Eugène Scribe and the French Theatre, 1815–60.* Cambridge, Mass.: Harvard University Press, 1924.

Bernheim, A. L. *The Business of the Theatre.* New York: Actors Equity Association, 1932.

Birdoff, Harry. *The World's Greatest Hit: "Uncle Tom's Cabin."* New York: S. F. Vanni, 1947.

Bogard, Travis, et al. *Revels History of Drama in English.* Vol. 8: *American Drama.* New York: Barnes & Noble, Inc., 1977.

Booth, Michael, et al. *Revels History of Drama in English.* See under Chapter 10.

Booth, Michael R. *English Melodrama.* London: Herbert Jenkins, 1965.

Carlson, Marvin A. *The French Stage in the Nineteenth Century.* Metuchen, N.J.: Scarecrow Press, Inc., 1972.

———. *The German Stage in the Nineteenth Century.* Metuchen, N.J.: Scarecrow Press, Inc., 1972.

Clement, N. H. *Romanticism in France.* New York: Modern Language Association, 1939.

Coad, O. S., and Mims, Edwin, Jr. *The American Stage* (Vol. XIV of *The Pageant of America*). New Haven, Conn.: Yale University Press, 1929.

Cross, Gilbert. *Next Week East Lynne: Domestic Drama in Performance, 1820–1874.* Lewisburg, Pa.: Bucknell University Press, 1976.

Donohue, Joseph W. *Theatre in the Age of Kean.* Oxford: Basil Blackwell & Mott, Ltd., 1975.

———, ed. *The Theater Manager in England and America: Players of a Perilous Game.* Princeton, N.J.: Princeton University Press, 1971.

Downer, Alan S. "Players and the Painted Stage: Nineteenth Century Acting," *PMLA,* 61 (1946), 522–576.

Felheim, Marvin. *The Theater of Augustin Daly: An Account of the Late Nineteenth Century American Stage.* Cambridge, Mass.: Harvard University Press, 1956.

Fitzgerald, Percy H. *The World Behind the Scenes.* New York: Benjamin Blom, 1972.

Glasstone, Victor. *Victorian and Edwardian Theatres.* Cambridge, Mass.: Harvard University Press, 1975.

Grimsted, David. *Melodrama Unveiled: American Theatre and Culture, 1800–1850*. Chicago: University of Chicago Press, 1968.

Hewitt, Barnard. *Theatre USA, 1668–1957*. New York: McGraw-Hill, Inc., 1959.

Joseph, Bertram. *The Tragic Actor*. See under Chapter 10.

Kaufmann, F. W. *German Dramatists of the Nineteenth Century*. Los Angeles: Lymanhouse, 1940.

Lacey, Alexander. *Pixérécourt and the French Romantic Drama*. Toronto: University of Toronto Press, 1928.

Lucas, F. L. *The Decline and Fall of the Romantic Ideal*. New York: The Macmillan Company, 1936.

Mammen, Edward W. *The Old Stock Company School of Acting*. Boston: The Public Library, 1945.

Matthews, Brander. *French Dramatists of the Nineteenth Century*. 5th ed. New York: Charles Scribner's Sons, 1914.

——, and Hutton, Laurence. *Actors and Actresses of Great Britain and the United States, from the Days of David Garrick to the Present Time*. 5 vols. New York: Cassell, 1886.

Melcher, Edith. *Stage Realism in France from Diderot to Antoine*. See Chapter 10.

Moody, Richard. *America Takes the Stage: Romanticism in American Drama and Theatre, 1750–1900*. Bloomington: Indiana University Press, 1955.

Moses, Montrose J., and Brown, John M. *The American Theatre as Seen by Its Critics, 1752–1934*. New York: W. W. Norton & Company, Inc., 1934.

Moynet, Jean-Pierre. *French Theatrical Production in the Nineteenth Century*. Binghamton, N.Y.: Max Reinhardt Foundation, 1976.

Nicoll, Allardyce. *History of English Drama, 1660–1900*. See under Chapter 10.

Odell, G. C. D. *Annals of the New York Stage*. 15 vols. New York: Columbia University Press, 1927–1949.

——. *Shakespeare from Betterton to Irving*. See under Chapter 10.

Peacock, Ronald. *Goethe's Major Plays: An Essay*. New York: Hill & Wang, Inc., 1959.

Quinn, Arthur H. *A History of the American Drama from the Beginning to the Civil War*. 2d ed. New York: Appleton-Century-Crofts, 1943.

——. *A History of the American Drama from the Civil War to the Present Day*. 2d ed. New York: Appleton-Century-Crofts, 1949.

Rowell, George. *The Victorian Theatre*. New York: Oxford University Press, 1956.

Sachs, Edwin O., and Woodrow, E. A. E. *Modern Opera Houses and Theatres*. 3 vols. London: Batsford, 1897–1898.

Scholz, Janos. *Baroque and Romantic Stage Design*. See under Chapter 10.

Shattuck, Charles. *Shakespeare on the American Stage*. Washington: Folger Shakespeare Library, 1976.

Slonim, Marc. *Russian Theatre from the Empire to the Soviets*. See under Chapter 10.

Southern, Richard. *The Georgian Playhouse* and *Changeable Scenery: Its Origin and Development in the British Theatre*. See under Chapter 10.

Vardac, A. N. *Stage to Screen: Theatrical Method from Garrick to Griffith*. Cambridge, Mass.: Harvard University Press, 1949.

Walzel, Oskar F. *German Romanticism*. New York: G. P. Putnam's Sons, 1932.

Watson, Ernest B. *Sheridan to Robertson: A Study of the Nineteenth Century London Stage*. Cambridge, Mass.: Harvard University Press, 1926.

Wellek, René. *A History of Modern Literary Criticism*. 2 vols. New Haven: Yale University Press, 1955.

Willoughby, Leonard A. *The Romantic Movement in Germany*. New York: Oxford University Press, 1930.

Wilson, Garff. *A History of American Acting*. Bloomington: Indiana University Press, 1966.

———. *Three Hundred Years of American Drama and Theatre*. Englewood Cliffs, N.J.: Prentice-Hall, Inc., 1973.

Witkowski, Georg. *The German Drama of the Nineteenth Century*. 2d ed. New York: Benjamin Blom, 1968.

12: THE ORIENTAL THEATRE

Alley, Rewi. *Peking Opera*. Peking: New World Press, 1957.

Ambrose, Kay. *Classical Dances and Costumes of India*. London: A. & C. Black, Ltd., 1950.

Ando, Tsuruo. *Bunraku, the Puppet Theatre*. New York: Walker/Weatherill, 1970.

Arlington, Lewis C. *The Chinese Drama from the Earliest Times Until Today*. Shanghai: Kelly and Walsh, Ltd., 1930.

Bharata. *Natyasastra*. Trans. by Manmohan Ghose. Bengal: The Royal Asiatic Society, 1950.

Bowers, Faubion. *Japanese Theatre*. New York: Heritage House, 1952.

Brandon, James R. *The Theatre of Southeast Asia*. Cambridge, Mass.: Harvard University Press, 1967.

Chen, Jack. *The Chinese Theatre*. New York: Roy Publishers, Inc., 1948.

Ernst, Earle. *The Kabuki Theatre*. New York: Oxford University Press, 1956.

Gargi, Balwant. *Theatre in India*. New York: Theatre Arts Books, 1962.

Gupta, Chandra B. *The Indian Theatre*. Benares: Motilal Banarasidass, 1954.

Haar, Francis. *Japanese Theatre in Highlight: A Pictorial Commentary*. Tokyo: Charles E. Tuttle Co., 1952.

Hironaga, Shuzaburo. *Bunraku, Japan's Unique Puppet Theatre*. Tokyo: Tokyo News Service, 1964.

Iyer, K. Bharatha. *Kathakali: The Sacred Dance-Drama of Malabar*. London: Luzac, 1955.

Kawatake, Shigetoshi. *Kabuki: Japanese Drama*. Tokyo: Foreign Affairs Association of Japan, 1956.

Keene, Donald. *Bunraku: The Art of the Japanese Puppet Theatre*. Tokyo: Kodansha International, Ltd., 1965.

———. *Major Plays of Chikamatsu*. New York: Columbia University Press, 1961.

———. *No: The Classical Theatre of Japan*. Tokyo: Kodansha International, Ltd., 1966.

Keith, A. Berriedale. *The Sanskrit Drama*. London: Oxford University Press, 1924.

Kincaid, Zoe. *Kabuki, the Popular Stage of Japan*. London: Macmillan & Co., Ltd., 1925.

Liu, Wu-chi. *An Introduction to Chinese Literature*. Bloomington: Indiana University Press, 1966.

Mackerras, Colin. *The Chinese Theatre*. Amherst: University of Massachusetts Press, 1975.

———. *The Rise of Peking Opera, 1770–1870*. New York: Oxford University Press, 1972.

Mathur, Jagdesh. *Drama in Rural India*. New York: Asia Publishing House, 1964.

O'Neill, P. G. *A Guide to Nō*. Tokyo: Hinoki Shoten, 1953.

Pound, Ezra, and Fenolloso, Ernest. *The Classic Noh Theatre of Japan*. Reprint. Westport, Conn.: Greenwood Press, 1970 (originally published 1959).

Pronko, Leonard. *Theatre East and West: Perspectives Toward a Total Theatre*. Berkeley: University of California Press, 1967.

Sakanishi, Shio. *Kyogen*. Boston: Marshall Jones, 1938.

Scott, A. C. *The Classical Theatre of China*. New York: The Macmillan Company, 1957.

———. *The Kabuki Theatre of Japan*. London: George Allen & Unwin Ltd., 1955.

———. *Traditional Chinese Plays*. Madison: University of Wisconsin Press, 1967.

Shaver, Ruth M. *Kabuki Costume*. Tokyo: Charles E. Tuttle Co., 1966.

Shih, Chung-wen. *The Golden Age of Chinese Drama: Yuan Tsa-chu*. Princeton, N.J.: Princeton University Press, 1976.

Toita, Yasuji. *Kabuki, the Popular Theatre*. Elmsford, New York: Japan Publications, 1976.

Waley, Arthur. *The Nō Plays of Japan*. New York: Alfred A. Knopf, Inc., 1922.

Ze-ami. *Kadensho*. Trans. by Chûichi Sakurai, Shûseki Hagashi, Rokurô Satoi, Bin Miyai. Kyoto: Sumiya-Shinobe Publishing Institute, 1971.

Zucker, Adolf E. *The Chinese Theatre*. Boston: Little, Brown and Company, 1925.

13: THE BEGINNINGS OF THE MODERN THEATRE, 1875–1915

Antoine, André. *Memories of the Théâtre Libre*. Trans. by Marvin Carlson. Coral Gables, Fla.: University of Miami Press, 1964.

Appia, Adolphe. *The Work of Living Art and Man Is the Measure of All Things*. Coral Gables, Fla.: University of Miami Press, 1960.

Bablet, Denis. *Edward Gordon Craig*. New York: Theatre Arts Books, 1967.

Becker, George J. *Documents of Modern Literary Realism*. Princeton, N.J.: Princeton University Press, 1963.

Bentley, Eric. *The Playwright as Thinker: A Study of Drama in Modern Times*. New York: Reynal & Company, Inc., 1946.

Bradbrook, M. C. *Ibsen, the Norwegian*. London: Chatto & Windus, Ltd., 1946.

Brockett, Oscar G., and Findlay, Robert R. *Century of Innovation: A History of European and American Theatre and Drama Since 1870*. Englewood Cliffs, N.J.: Prentice-Hall, Inc., 1973.

Brustein, Robert. *The Theatre of Revolt: An Approach to Modern Drama*. Boston: Little, Brown and Company, 1964.

Carter, Huntly. *The Theatre of Max Reinhardt*. New York: Benjamin Blom, 1964.

Carter, Lawson A. *Zola and the Theatre*. New Haven, Conn.: Yale University Press, 1963.

Chiari, Joseph. *Symbolism from Poe to Mallarmé*. 2d ed. New York: Gordian, 1970.

Cornell, Kenneth. *The Symbolist Movement*. New Haven, Conn.: Yale University Press, 1951.

Craig, Edward Gordon. *On the Art of the Theatre*. 2d ed. Boston: Small, Maynard, 1924.

Fowlie, Wallace. *Age of Surrealism.* Bloomington: Indiana University Press, 1960.

Garten, H. F. *Modern German Drama.* New York: Essential Books, 1959.

Gassner, John. *Form and Idea in the Modern Theatre.* New York: Holt, Rinehart and Winston, 1956.

———. *The Theatre in Our Times: A Survey of the Men, Materials and Movements in the Modern Theatre.* New York: Crown Publishers, Inc., 1954.

Gorchakov, Nikolai A. *The Theater in Soviet Russia.* Trans. by Edgar Lehman. New York: Columbia University Press, 1957.

Gorelik, Mordecai. *New Theatres for Old.* New York: Samuel French, 1940.

Jasper, Gertrude. *Adventure in the Theatre: Lugné-Poë and the Théâtre de l'Oeuvre to 1899.* Brunswick, N.J.: Rutgers University Press, 1947.

Kochno, Boris. *Diaghilev and the Ballets Russes.* New York: Harper & Row, Publishers, 1970.

Lehmann, Andrew G. *The Symbolist Aesthetic in France, 1885–1895.* Oxford: Basil Blackwell & Mott, Ltd., 1950.

Lumley, Frederick. *Trends in Twentieth Century Drama: A Survey Since Ibsen and Shaw.* 2d ed. London: Barrie and Rockliff, 1960.

MacCarthy, Desmond. *The Court Theatre, 1904–1907.* Coral Gables, Fla.: University of Miami Press, 1966.

Matlaw, Myron. *Modern World Drama: An Encyclopedia.* New York: E. P. Dutton & Co., Inc., 1972.

Melchinger, Siegfried. *The Concise Encyclopedia of Modern Drama.* New York: Horizon Press, 1964.

Miller, Anna Irene. *The Independent Theatre in Europe, 1887 to the Present.* New York: Ray Long and Richard R. Smith, 1931.

Northam, John. *Ibsen's Dramatic Method: A Study of the Prose Dramas.* London: Faber & Faber, Ltd., 1953.

Rischbeiter, Henning. *Art and the Stage in the 20th Century.* Greenwich, Conn.: New York Graphic Society, 1968.

Roose-Evans, James. *Experimental Theatre: From Stanislavsky to Today.* Rev. ed. New York: Universe, 1973.

Sayler, Oliver M., ed. *Max Reinhardt and His Theatre.* New York: Brentano's, 1926.

Seltzer, Daniel, ed. *The Modern Theatre: Readings and Documents.* Boston: Little, Brown and Company, 1967.

Shattuck, Roger. *The Banquet Years: The Arts in France, 1885–1918.* New York: Random House, Inc., 1968.

Slonim, Marc. *Russian Theatre from the Empire to the Soviets.* Cleveland: The World Publishing Company, 1961.

Stein, Jack M. *Richard Wagner and the Synthesis of the Arts.* Detroit: Wayne State University Press, 1960.

Stone, Edward. *What Was Naturalism? Materials for an Answer.* New York: Appleton-Century-Crofts, 1959.

Valency, Maurice. *The Flower and the Castle: An Introduction to Modern Drama.* New York: Grosset & Dunlap, Inc., 1963.

Volbach, Walther. *Adolphe Appia, Prophet of the Modern Theatre.* Middletown, Conn.: Wesleyan University Press, 1968.

Wagner, Richard. *Opera and Drama.* Trans. by Edwin Evans. London: W. Reeves, 1913.

Waxman, S. M. *Antoine and the Théâtre Libre*. Cambridge, Mass.: Harvard University Press, 1926.

Wellek, René. *A History of Modern Criticism*. Vols. 3–4. New Haven, Conn.: Yale University Press, 1965.

Williams, Raymond. *Drama from Ibsen to Eliot*. London: Chatto & Windus, Ltd., 1952.

14: THE THEATRE FROM 1915 TO 1940

Artaud, Antonin. *The Theatre and Its Double*. Trans. by Mary C. Richards. New York: Grove Press, Inc., 1958.

Balakian, Anna E. *Surrealism*. New York: Farrar, Straus & Giroux, Inc., 1959.

Bentley, Eric. *The Playwright as Thinker: A Study of Drama in Modern Times*. See under Chapter 13.

Bradshaw, Martha. *Soviet Theatres, 1917–1941*. New York: Research Program on the USSR, 1954.

Braun, Edward. *Meyerhold on Theatre*. New York: Hill & Wang, Inc., 1969.

Brecht, Bertolt. *Brecht on Theatre*. Trans. by John Willett. New York: Hill & Wang, Inc., 1965.

Breton, André. *What Is Surrealism?* London: Faber & Faber, Ltd., 1936.

Brockett, Oscar G., and Findlay, Robert R. *Century of Innovation: A History of European and American Theatre and Drama Since 1870*. See under Chapter 13.

Brustein, Robert. *The Theatre of Revolt: An Approach to Modern Drama*. See under Chapter 13.

Clurman, Harold. *The Fervent Years: The Story of the Group Theatre in the Thirties*. New York: Hill & Wang, Inc., 1957.

Dahlstrom, C. E. W. L. *Strindberg's Dramatic Expressionism*. Vol. VII of *University of Michigan Publications, Language and Literature*. Ann Arbor: University of Michigan Press, 1930.

Davis, Hallie Flanagan. *Arena*. New York: Duell, Sloane & Pearce-Meredith Press, 1940.

Downer, Alan S. *Fifty Years of American Drama, 1900–1950*. Chicago: Henry Regnery Co., 1951.

Esslin, Martin. *Brecht: The Man and His Work*. Garden City, N.Y.: Doubleday & Company, Inc., 1960.

Fuerst, Walter R., and Hume, Samuel J. *Twentieth Century Stage Decoration*. 2 vols. New York: Alfred A. Knopf, Inc., 1928.

Garten, H. F. *Modern German Drama*. See under Chapter 13.

Gassner, John. *Form and Idea in the Modern Theatre*.

———. *The Theatre in Our Times*. See under Chapter 13.

Gorchakov, Nikolai A. *The Theater in Soviet Russia*. See under Chapter 13.

Gorelik, Mordecai. *New Theatres for Old*. See under Chapter 13.

Greene, Naomi. *Antonin Artaud: Poet Without Words*. New York: Simon & Schuster, Inc., 1970.

Hainaux, René, ed. *Stage Design throughout the World since 1935*. New York: Theatre Arts Books, 1956.

Hoover, Marjorie. *Meyerhold: The Art of Conscious Theatre*. Amherst: University of Massachusetts Press, 1974.

Houghton, Norris. *Moscow Rehearsals: An Account of Methods of Production in the Soviet Theatre*. New York: Harcourt Brace Jovanovich, Inc., 1936.

Innes, C. D. *Erwin Piscator's Political Theatre*. New York: Cambridge University Press, 1972.

Kirby, Michael. *Futurist Performance*. New York: E. P. Dutton & Co., Inc., 1971.

Knowles, Dorothy. *French Drama of the Inter-war Years, 1918–39*. New York: Barnes & Noble, Inc., 1967.

Krutch, Joseph W. *The American Drama Since 1918*. Rev. ed. New York: George Braziller, Inc., 1957.

Ley-Piscator, Maria. *The Piscator Experiment: The Political Theatre*. New York: James H. Heineman, Inc., 1967.

Lumley, Frederick. *Trends in Twentieth Century Drama: A Survey Since Ibsen and Shaw*. See under Chapter 13.

Macgowan, Kenneth, and Jones, Robert E. *Continental Stagecraft*. New York: Harcourt Brace Jovanovich, Inc., 1922.

Marshall, Norman. *The Other Theatre*. London: J. Lehmann, 1947.

Matlaw, Myron. *Modern World Drama: An Encyclopedia*. See under Chapter 13.

Melchinger, Siegfried. *The Concise Encyclopedia of Modern Drama*. See under Chapter 13.

Moderwell, Hiram K. *The Theatre of To-day*. New York: Dodd, Mead & Company, Inc., 1925.

Moussinac, Leon. *The New Movement in the Theatre: A Survey of Recent Developments in Europe and America*. London: Batsford, 1931.

Richter, Hans. *Dada: Art and Anti-Art*. London: Thames and Hudson, 1965.

Rischbieter, Henning. *Art and the Stage in the 20th Century*. See under Chapter 13.

Roose-Evans, James. *Experimental Theatre: From Stanislavsky to Today*. See under Chapter 13.

Saint-Denis, Michel. *Theatre, the Rediscovery of Style*. New York: Theatre Arts Books, 1960.

Samuel, Richard, and Thomas, R. H. *Expressionism in German Life, Literature and the Theatre (1910–1924)*. Cambridge: W. Heffer & Sons, Ltd., 1939.

Seltzer, Daniel. *The Modern Theatre: Readings and Documents*. See under Chapter 13.

Simonov, Reuben. *Stanislavsky's Protégé: Eugene Vakhtangov*. New York: DBS Publications, Inc., 1969.

Slonim, Marc. *Russian Theatre from the Empire to the Soviets*. See under Chapter 13.

Sokel, Walter H. *The Writer in Extremis: Expressionism in Twentieth-Century German Literature*. Stanford, Calif.: Stanford University Press, 1959.

Symons, James M. *Meyerhold's Theatre of the Grotesque: The Post-Revolutionary Productions, 1920–32*. Coral Gables, Fla.: University of Miami Press, 1971.

Tairov, Alexander. *Notes of a Director*. Trans. by William Kuhlke. Coral Gables, Fla.: University of Miami Press, 1969.

Willett, John. *Expressionism*. New York: McGraw-Hill, Inc., 1970.

———. *The Theatre of Bertolt Brecht*. New York: New Directions Pub. Corp., 1959.

Williams, Raymond. *Drama from Ibsen to Eliot*. See under Chapter 13.

15: POSTWAR THEATRE AND DRAMA

Allsop, Kenneth. *The Angry Decade*. London: P. Owen, 1958.

Bentley, Eric. *In Search of Theatre*. New York: Alfred A. Knopf, Inc., 1953.

Bowers, Faubion. *Broadway, USSR: Theatre, Ballet and Entertainment in Russia Today*. New York: Thomas Nelson & Sons, 1959.

Brockett, Oscar G., and Findlay, Robert R. *Century of Innovation*. See under Chapter 13.

Browne, Terry. *Playwrights' Theatre: The English Stage Company at the Royal Court*. New York: Pitman Publishing Corp., 1975.

Brustein, Robert. *The Theatre of Revolt*. See under Chapter 13.

Chiari, Joseph. *The Contemporary French Theatre: The Flight from Naturalism*. London: Barrie and Rockliff, 1958.

Donoghue, Denis. *The Third Voice: Modern British and American Verse Drama*. Princeton, N.J.: Princeton University Press, 1959.

Engel, Lehman. *American Musical Theatre*. Rev. ed. New York: The Macmillan Company, 1975.

Esslin, Martin. *The Theatre of the Absurd*. Rev. ed. Garden City, N.Y.: Doubleday & Company, Inc., 1969.

Fowlie, Wallace. *Dionysus in Paris: A Guide to Contemporary French Theater*. New York: Meridian Books, Inc., 1960.

Garten, H. F. *Modern German Drama*. See under Chapter 13.

Gassner, John. *Theatre at the Crossroads: Plays and Playwrights of the Mid-Century American Stage*. New York: Holt, Rinehart and Winston, Inc., 1960.
———. *Form and Idea in the Modern Theatre*.
———. *The Theatre in Our Times*. See under Chapter 13.

Gorchakov, Nikolai A. *The Theatre in Soviet Russia*. See under Chapter 13.

Grossvogel, David I. *The Self-Conscious Stage in Modern French Drama*. New York: Columbia University Press, 1958.

Guicharnaud, Jacques. *Modern French Theatre from Giraudoux to Beckett*. New Haven, Conn.: Yale University Press, 1961.

Hainaux, René, ed. *Stage Design throughout the World Since 1950*. New York: Theatre Arts Books, 1964.

Hinchliffe, Arnold. *British Theatre, 1950–1970*. Oxford: Basil Blackwell & Mott, Ltd., 1974.

Houghton, Norris. *Return Engagement: A Postscript to "Moscow Rehearsals."* New York: Holt, Rinehart and Winston, 1962.

Kienzle, Siegfried. *Modern World Theatre: A Guide to Productions in Europe and the United States Since 1945*. New York: Frederick Ungar Publishing Co., Inc., 1970.

Krutch, Joseph W. *The American Drama Since 1918*. See under Chapter 14.

Lee, Vera. *Quest for a Public: French Popular Theatre Today*. Cambridge, Mass.: Schenkman Publishing Co., 1970.

Lumley, Frederick. *Trends in Twentieth Century Drama*. See under Chapter 13.

Matlaw, Myron. *Modern World Drama*. See under Chapter 13.

Melchinger, Siegfried. *The Concise Encyclopedia of Modern Drama*. See under Chapter 13.

Price, Julia. *The Off-Broadway Theatre*. Metuchen, N.J.: Scarecrow Press, Inc., 1962.

Richman, Robert, ed. *The Arts at Mid-Century*. New York: Horizon Press, 1954. Contains separate chapters on the theatre in each of the following countries: France, Italy, Germany, England, and U.S.

Rischbeiter, Henning. *Art and the Stage in the 20th Century*. See under Chapter 13.

Roose-Evans, James. *Experimental Theatre*. See under Chapter 13.

Seltzer, Daniel. *The Modern Theatre*. See under Chapter 13.

Slonim, Marc. *Russian Theatre from the Empire to the Soviets*. See under Chapter 14.

Smith, Cecil. *Musical Comedy in America*. New York: Theatre Arts Books, 1950.

Strasberg, Lee. *Strasberg at the Actors Studio*. New York: The Viking Press, Inc., 1965.

Styan, J. L. *The Dark Comedy: The Development of Modern Comic Tragedy*. Cambridge: The University Press, 1962.

Weales, Gerald. *American Drama Since World War II*. New York: Harcourt Brace Jovanovich, Inc., 1962.

16: CONTEMPORARY THEATRE AND DRAMA

Abramson, Doris E. *Negro Playwrights in the American Theatre*. New York: Columbia University Press, 1969.

Addenbrooke, David. *The Royal Shakespeare Company: The Peter Hall Years*. London: William Kimber, 1974.

Ansorge, Peter. *Disrupting the Spectacle: Five Years of Experimental and Fringe Theatre in Britain*. New York: Pitman Publishing Corp., 1975.

Bentley, Eric. *What Is Theatre? Incorporating the Dramatic Event and Other Reviews, 1944–1967*. New York: Atheneum Publishers, 1968.

Biner, Pierre. *The Living Theatre*. 2d ed. New York: Horizon Press, 1972.

Brockett, Oscar G. *Perspectives on Contemporary Theatre*. Baton Rouge: Louisiana State University Press, 1971.

————, and Findlay, Robert R. *Century of Innovation*. See under Chapter 13.

Brook, Peter. *The Empty Space*. New York: Atheneum Publishers, 1968.

Brustein, Robert. *Revolution as Theatre: Notes on the New Radical Style*. New York: Liveright, 1971.

Burian, Jarka. *The Scenography of Josef Svoboda*. Middletown, Conn.: Wesleyan University Press, 1971.

Chaikin, Joseph. *The Presence of the Actor*. New York: Atheneum Publishers, 1974.

Clark, Brian. *Group Theatre*. New York: Theatre Arts Books, 1971.

Cook, Judith. *The National Theatre*. London: Harrap, 1976.

Croyden, Margaret. *Lunatics, Lovers and Poets: The Contemporary Experimental Theatre*. New York: McGraw-Hill, Inc., 1974.

Engel, Lehman. *American Musical Theatre*. See under Chapter 15.

Esslin, Martin. *The Peopled Wound: The Work of Harold Pinter*. Garden City, N.Y.: Doubleday & Company, Inc., 1970.

————. *The Theatre of the Absurd*. See under Chapter 15.

Grotowski, Jerzy. *Towards a Poor Theatre*. New York: Simon & Schuster, Inc., 1968.

Hainaux, René, ed. *Stage Design Throughout the World, 1960–1970*. New York: Theatre Arts Books, 1972.

————. *Stage Design Throughout the World, 1970–1975*. New York: Theatre Arts Books, 1976.

Hinchliffe, Arnold. *British Theatre*. See under Chapter 15.

Kienzle, Siegfried. *Modern World Theatre: A Guide to Productions in Europe and the United States Since 1945*. See under Chapter 15.

Kirby, Michael. *Happenings*. New York: E. P. Dutton & Co., Inc., 1965.

Kostelanetz, Richard. *The Theatre of Mixed Means.* New York: The Dial Press, Inc., 1968.

Lee, Vera. *Quest for a Public: French Popular Theatre Today.* See under Chapter 15.

Lesnick, Henry. *Guerilla Street Theatre.* New York. Avon Books, 1973.

Little, Stuart. *Enter Joseph Papp: In Search of a New American Theatre.* New York: Coward, McCann & Geoghegan, Inc., 1974.

Marowitz, Charles, and Trussler, Simon. *Theatre at Work: Playwrights and Productions in the Modern British Theatre.* New York: Hill & Wang, Inc., 1967.

Matlaw, Myron. *Modern World Drama.* See under Chapter 13.

Mitchell, Loften. *Black Drama.* New York: Hawthorn Books, Inc., 1967.

Neff, Renfreu. *The Living Theatre USA.* Indianapolis: The Bobbs-Merrill Company, Inc., 1970.

Novick, Julius. *Beyond Broadway.* New York: Hill & Wang, Inc., 1968.

O'Connor, Garry. *French Theatre Today.* New York: Pitman Publishing Corp., 1975.

Pasolli, Robert. *A Book on the Open Theatre.* Indianapolis: The Bobbs-Merrill Company, Inc., 1970.

Patterson, Michael. *German Theatre Today.* New York: Pitman Publishing Corp., 1976.

Poggi, Jack. *Theatre in America: The Impact of Economic Forces, 1870–1967.* Ithaca, N.Y.: Cornell University Press, 1968.

Rischbeiter, Henning. *Art and the Stage in the 20th Century.* See under Chapter 13.

Roose-Evans, James. *Experimental Theatre.* See under Chapter 13.

Sainer, Arthur. *The Radical Theatre Notebook.* New York: Avon Books, 1975.

Schechner, Richard. *Environmental Theatre.* New York: Hawthorn Books, Inc., 1973.

———. *Public Domain: Essays on the Theater.* Indianapolis: The Bobbs-Merrill Company, Inc., 1969.

Schevill, James. *Breakout! In Search of New Theatrical Environments.* Chicago: University of Chicago Press, 1972.

Taylor, John R. *The Angry Theatre.* Rev. ed. New York: Hill & Wang, Inc., 1969.

———. *Second Wave: British Dramatists for the Seventies.* New York: Hill & Wang, Inc., 1971.

Taylor, Karen M. *People's Street Theatre in Amerika.* New York: DBS Publications, Inc., 1973.

Temkine, Raymond. *Grotowski.* New York: Avon Books, 1972.

Trewin, J. C. *Peter Brook.* London: Macdonald and Co., 1971.

Vinson, James, ed. *Contemporary Dramatists.* 2d ed. New York: St. Martin's Press, Inc., 1977.

Weales, Gerald. *The Jumping Off Place: American Drama in the 1960s.* New York: The Macmillan Company, 1969.

Ziegler, Joseph. *Regional Theatre: The Revolutionary Stage.* New York: Da Capo Press, 1973.

Index

427

428

429

Futurism, 301
Futz, 372, 375

Gaiety Theatre (London), 331
Gale, Mrs. Lyman W., 305
Galileo, 312
Galleries, 83, 88, 97, 100, 123, 149
Galliari family, 175
Galsworthy, John, 265, 266
Game of Love and Chance, The, 169
Gamester, The, 160
Gammer Gurton's Needle, 94
Garcia, Victor, 354
Gardener's Dog, The, 120
Garrick, David, 115, 150, 154, 155
Gas I, 294
Gas II, 294
Gas lighting, 215
Gatti, Armand, 353
Gauguin, Paul, 291
Gaultier-Garguille, 123, 124
Gay, John, 160, 161, 172
Gedatsu, 248
Gelosi Troupe, 90
General Lien Pʻu, 235
Gênet, Jean, 339, 342–43, 348, 354
Germany
    beginnings of theatre, 180–81
    18th-century, 181–84
    epic theatre, 310–18
    expressionism, 291–300
    19th-century, 185–95, 196–97, 200, 212, 219
    since 1945, 347, 349–50, 355–58, 359–61, 374
Ghosts, 260, 273, 274
Ghost Sonata, The, 293
Giboyer's Son, 259
Gidayn Takemoto, 246
Gielgud, John, 349
Gigaku, 240
Glass Menagerie, The, 321–23
Globe Theatre, The (London), 96, 106
Glories, 87
Goethe, Johann Wolfgang von, 183, 189–95
Gogol, Nikolai, 267
Golden Boy, 307
Goldsmith, Oliver, 162
Goodbye Mr. Freud, 354
Good-Natured Man, The, 162
Good Soldier Schweik, The, 312
Good Woman of Setzuan, The, 312–18
Gorboduc, 94
Gordone, Charles, 374, 381
Gorky, Maxim, 271, 360
Gottsched, Johann Christoph, 181
Götz von Berlichingen, 189
Gozzi, Carlo, 176
Grand Magic Circus, 354
Grass, Gunter, 347
Great God Brown, The, 300
Great World Theatre, The, 120
Greece
    actors and acting, 6, 7, 8, 9–10, 14–15, 16, 25–27, 27–28, 32, 35
    admission prices, 10
    audience, 10, 28, 31–32
    beginnings of drama, 4–6
    chorus, 4, 6, 8, 9, 16–17, 25–26, 27, 34
    comedy, 10, 27–33, 40
    compared with Elizabethan England, 101
    compared with medieval era, 76
    contests and prizes, 9, 27, 29
    costumes, 15–16, 26, 27–28, 34
    dance, 4, 15, 17, 25–26, 33
    directing, 9–10, 33–34

dithyrambs, 4, 10, 27
drama and religion, 4
dramatists, 6–8, 28, 33
festivals, 4, 9–10, 27, 35
Hellenistic period, 33–35
machinery, 13, 26, 33
masks, 4, 6, 15, 26, 28, 34
music, 15, 17, 25, 27, 33, 35
playwrights' working conditions, 9–10, 33–35
process of producing plays, 9–10, 27–29, 33–35
raised stage, 13, 34–35
relationship to Roman theatre, 35, 36, 40–41, 48–49
satyr play, 6, 7, 8–9, 27
scenery, 13, 33, 34–35
theatre architecture, 10–13, 33, 34–35
tragedy, 4, 6–8, 14–15, 18–26, 27, 33
value placed on drama, 9–10, 33–35
Green, Paul, 306
Grein, J. T., 274
Griffith, D. W., 338
Griffiths, Trevor, 369
Groove shifting, 86, 149
Gros-Guillaume, 123, 124
Grotowski, Jerzy, 387–88
Grouch, The, 33
Ground rows, 150
Group theatre, 307
Grumberg, Jean-Claude, 353
Guare, John, 375
Guarini, Giambattista, 76
Guerilla theatre, 385–86
Guerillas, The, 358
Guilds, 60–61
Gunn, Moses, 376
Guthrie, Tyrone, 21, 349, 382
Guys and Dolls, 331

Haase, Friedrich, 219
Hair, 372, 373, 374, 386–87
Hairy Ape, The, 300, 306
Hall, Peter, 366, 368
Hallam, Lewis, 178
Hamburg Dramaturgy, 182
Hamlet, 107, 152, 154, 215, 219, 287
Hammerstein, Oscar II, 331
Hampton, Christopher, 369
Hanamichi, 251
Handel, George Frederick, 161
Handke, Peter, 359, 360
Hansberry, Lorraine, 376–80
Hanswurst, 181, 183
Happenings, 395–96
Happy Days, 342
Hardy, Alexandre, 123, 124
Hare, David, 369
Harlequin, 89, 161, 181
Harrison, Rex, 332
Harsha, King, 225
Hartley, Mrs., 156
Hashigakari, 244–45
Hauptman, Gerhart, 271, 274
Havel, Vaclav, 348
Haymarket Theatre, 147
Heartbreak House, 267
Hebbel, Friedrich, 196
Heckart, Eileen, 322
Hedda Gabler, 260
Hell mouth, 56
Hello Dolly, 331, 369
Henri III and His Court, 198
Henry IV (Pirandello), 340, 349

Henry IV (Shakespeare), 106, 212
Henry V, 106
Henry VI, 106
Henry VIII, 106
Henslowe, Philip, 99
Hernani, 197–98
Heroic tragedy, 156–57
Heywood, John, 69
Heywood, Thomas, 117
Hindu dance, 227–28
Hippolytus, 7, 133
Historical accuracy in costuming and scenery, 194–95
Historical Register of 1736, The, 161
Historification, 311
History of the American Film, A, 400
History of the American Theatre, 180
History play, 105, 106
Histriones, 50
Hochhuth, Rolf, 355, 358
Hodges, C. Walter, 98
Holberg, Ludwig, 178
Hölderlin, 358
Holland, Betty Lou, 322
Holm, Ian, 364
Holmes, Sherlock, 359
Home, 362
Homecoming, The, 364, 365, 366
Home on the Range, 375
Hooks, Robert, 376
Hope, The, 96
Hôpital de la Trinité, 122
Hopkins, Arthur, 306
Horace, 74
Horace (Corneille), 131
Horowitz, Israel, 375
Hostage, The, 363
Hôtel de Bourgogne, 122, 123, 124, 125, 126, 138, 144, 145, 173
Hot L Baltimore, 375
House of Blue Leaves, The, 375
Householders, 103
How to Succeed in Business Without Even Trying, 331
Howard, Sidney, 306
Hsiung, S. I., 240
Hugo, Jean, 302
Hugo, Victor, 197, 212
Humours, 116
Hunchback, The, 188
Hunger and Thirst, 343
Hurry, Leslie, 108
Hutt, William, 139

Ibsen, Henrik, 259–65, 266, 267, 268, 273, 290, 322, 323
Ik, The, 367
Ikhernofret, 3
Iliad, The, 312
Illegitimate Son, The, 170
Illusionism, 213–15
Imaginary Invalid, The, 139
Imitation, 1
Impressionism, 291
Improvisation, 88, 89, 389–90
Improvisation in the Theatre, 389
I'm Talking About Jerusalem, 362
In New England Winter, 381
In the Matter of J. Robert Oppenheimer, 355
In the Wine Time, 381
Inadmissible Evidence, 362
Incident at Vichy, 323
Independent Theatre (London), 274
Independent theatre movement, 273–74

435

437